# The Law Commission

(LAW COM No 231)

# MENTAL INCAPACITY

## Item 9 of the Fourth Programme of Law Reform: Mentally Incapacitated Adults

*Laid before Parliament by the Lord High Chancellor pursuant to section 3(2) of the Law Commissions Act 1965*

*Ordered by* The House of Commons *to be printed* 28 February 1995

*LONDON:* HMSO

£21.85 net

189

The Law Commission was set up by section 1 of the Law Commissions Act 1965 for the purpose of promoting the reform of the law.

The Commissioners are:

> The Honourable Mr Justice Brooke, *Chairman*
> Professor Andrew Burrows
> Miss Diana Faber
> Mr Charles Harpum
> Mr Stephen Silber QC

The Secretary of the Law Commission is Mr Michael Sayers and its offices are at Conquest House, 37-38 John Street, Theobalds Road, London, WC1N 2BQ.

# LAW COMMISSION
# MENTAL INCAPACITY

## CONTENTS

## PART IV: GENERAL AUTHORITY TO ACT REASONABLY

## PART V: ADVANCE STATEMENTS ABOUT HEALTH CARE

## PART VI: INDEPENDENT SUPERVISION OF MEDICAL AND RESEARCH PROCEDURES

## PART VII: CONTINUING POWERS OF ATTORNEY

v

# PART VIII: DECISION-MAKING BY THE COURT

vi

# PART IX: PUBLIC LAW PROTECTION FOR VULNERABLE PEOPLE AT RISK

# LAW COMMISSION

**Item 9 of the Fourth Programme of Law Reform: Mentally Incapacitated Adults**

# MENTAL INCAPACITY

*To the Right Honourable the Lord Mackay of Clashfern, Lord High Chancellor of Great Britain*

# PART I
# INTRODUCTION

### Scope of this report

1.1 This report is concerned with the ways in which decisions may lawfully be made on behalf of those who are unable to make decisions for themselves. It covers issues of both substantive law and of procedure, and the decisions under consideration may relate to personal, financial or medical affairs. The Commission undertook this study as Item 9 of its Fourth Programme of Law Reform. This programme item prescribed an investigation into the adequacy of the legal and other procedures for the making of decisions on behalf of mentally incapacitated adults.[1] It is widely recognised that, in this area, the law as it now stands is unsystematic and full of glaring gaps. It does not rest on clear or modern foundations of principle. It has failed to keep up with social and demographic changes. It has also failed to keep up with developments in our understanding of the rights and needs of those with mental disability.

1.2 In the report we also discuss the extent of the powers which should be available to public authorities to intervene and protect adults who are at risk of abuse or neglect. The existing law in this area is patchy and out of date. Such powers as are available are little used, and as a result vulnerable people may not be getting all the help and protection they need and deserve. Because this part of the law is not at present tied to concepts of mental incapacity we have been obliged, in making coherent recommendations for reform, to address ourselves to a slightly wider client group. We refer to the people in this wider group as "vulnerable" adults.

1.3 In Part II of this report we describe in some detail the legal and social context within which our present proposals are set. We draw attention to the continuing increase in the proportion of very old people in our population;[2] we mention the way in which many who used to be placed in large mental hospitals are now living in the community;[3] and we describe how advances in medical science now enable people to survive, often with their mental capacity impaired, who would formerly

---

[1] Fourth Programme of Law Reform (1989) Law Com No 185 Cm 800.

[2] See para 2.35 below.

[3] See para 2.32 below.

have died.[4] At the same time we show how it is only in very recent years that the common law has taken cognizance of the fact that there is now nobody who can lawfully take decisions on behalf of adults who lack the capacity to take decisions for themselves, and we refer to the makeshift remedies by way of High Court declarations which are now temporarily in place pending the introduction of a coherent new statutory scheme.[5]

**History of this project**

1.4     Our decision to investigate the law relating to mental incapacity was made after a number of outside bodies drew problems and deficiencies in the present law to our attention. The Law Society in particular provided much of the stimulus for the review by publishing a discussion document in January 1989[6] and by holding a conference in May of that year. Coincidentally the important case which is generally referred to as *Re F*[7] was heard in the Court of Appeal in January 1989, with the final speeches in the House of Lords also being delivered in May of that year. This case drew public attention to the fact that English law now possesses no procedure whereby any other person or a court can take a medical decision on behalf of an adult patient without capacity to take that decision. The programme item we published in September 1989 referred to suggestions that "existing legal mechanisms are complicated, inflexible and piecemeal" and stated that the decision in *Re F* could not provide a comprehensive solution.[8] In April 1991 we published our first consultation paper,[9] its aim being to provide an overview of this large and complex area which would enable us to assess the necessity for law reform and explore the best ways forward.[10]

1.5     Nobody who responded to our overview paper thought that the present law was entirely satisfactory. The great majority of respondents took the view that reform of the law was a pressing priority and encouraged us to take the project forward. The main message we derived from this initial round of consultation was one of great concern, particularly among carers and service providers, about gaps and uncertainties in the present law. The most obvious deficiencies in private law were the lack of any effective procedures for resolving disputes between individuals about the care of people without capacity, or generally for legitimating and regulating the

---

[4]   See para 2.37 below.

[5]   See paras 2.24 - 2.26 below.

[6]   The Law Society's Mental Health Sub-Committee, *Decision Making and Mental Incapacity: A Discussion Document* (1989).

[7]   *Re F (Mental Patient: Sterilisation)* [1990] 2 AC 1.

[8]   Fourth Programme of Law Reform (1989) Law Com No 185, Item 9; Cm 800.

[9]   Mentally Incapacitated Adults and Decision-Making: An Overview, Consultation Paper No 119.

[10]  *Ibid*, para 1.17.

substitute decision-making which in practice regularly takes place. Concern about the public law concentrated on the absence of acceptable powers for protecting incapacitated or vulnerable people from abuse and neglect. We found a lot of support for an overall rather than a piecemeal approach to reform, although some respondents feared that this would take too long to construct and implement. There was a general view that any new procedures must be quick, cheap, flexible, accessible and easy to use, whilst providing effective safeguards for the people concerned. It was against this background that we embarked on a second round of consultation. Between February and May 1993 we published three further consultation papers. Each of these papers examined a discrete area of law and made provisional proposals for reform.

1.6 Our consultation paper on A New Jurisdiction[11] included proposals for the reform of the private law by clarifying the legal rights of carers and other informal decision-makers; by extending the scope of Enduring Powers of Attorney to cover personal welfare decisions; and by the creation of a jurisdiction giving a judicial forum power to make a range of orders or directions relating to the personal welfare of an incapacitated adult or the management of his or her finances.

1.7 Our consultation paper on Medical Treatment and Research[12] proposed the extension of this new jurisdiction so that substitute decisions about medical treatment might be authorised, and determinations made about the scope and validity of any "advance directive" or "living will" made before the onset of incapacity. We also proposed that Enduring Powers of Attorney should be able to encompass health care decisions. Our work in the area of medical treatment overlapped in some respects with the enquiry of the House of Lords Select Committee on Medical Ethics appointed in February 1993.[13] We submitted written evidence to this Committee and kept it informed of the progress of our work towards the end of 1993. A number of the Committee's recommendations are considered later in this report.[14] In view of the overlap between the Committee's

---

[11] Mentally Incapacitated Adults and Decision-Making: A New Jurisdiction, Consultation Paper No 128, published on 26 February 1993.

[12] Mentally Incapacitated Adults and Decision-Making: Medical Treatment and Research, Consultation Paper No 129, published on 28 April 1993.

[13] The Select Committee, under the chairmanship of Lord Walton of Detchant, was appointed to consider the ethical, legal and clinical implications of a person's right to withhold consent to life-prolonging treatment, and the position of persons who are no longer able to give or withhold consent; and to consider whether and in what circumstances actions that have as their intention or a likely consequence the shortening of another person's life may be justified on the grounds that they accord with that person's wishes or with that person's best interests; and in all the foregoing considerations to pay regard to the likely effects of changes in the law or medical practice on society as a whole (Report of the Select Committee on Medical Ethics (1993-94) HL 21-I p 7). The Report was published in February 1994 and debated in the House of Lords in May 1994: see *Hansard* (HL) 9 May 1994, vol 554, col 1344.

[14] See paras 2.48, 5.4 - 5.5, 6.18, 7.7, 10.6 and 10.26 below.

remit and some of our own work, the Government has postponed its final response to some of the Committee's observations until publication of the present report.[15]

1.8 Our final consultation paper in the series, on Public Law Protection,[16] proposed the reform of the present emergency intervention powers by giving local authorities a duty to investigate allegations that a vulnerable adult was at risk of harm. We also proposed a new set of short term powers to help local authorities protect such adults from abuse, neglect or other forms of harm. Some limited reforms to the guardianship scheme in the Mental Health Act 1983 were also suggested.

1.9 It had always been our hope to produce a single coherent set of recommendations across all three areas covered in the 1993 consultation papers, and the provisional proposals made in those papers were designed to fit into a single internally consistent framework. Although some respondents confined themselves to comments on only one or two of the consultation papers, a great many of them commented on all three and on the comprehensive scheme which emerged from them all. The provisional proposals were given very wide support by those we consulted. The principles upon which we had based our proposals, and our general approach to reform, commanded widespread acceptance, with discussion concentrating on points of detail. In that context, this report can bring back into one place the three arms of the project which were considered separately in the 1993 papers.

**Structure of this report**

1.10 Our four consultation papers dwelt in considerable detail on the defects of the present law and on the need for reform. In view of the strong and broadly-based agreement generated by our provisional proposals, it would be superfluous to rehearse in this report matters which are analysed at length in the four earlier papers. The various options for reform were canvassed in those papers and we need only mention them in the course of this report as and when they arise.

1.11 In Part II we summarise and review the legal and social context in which the need for reform has arisen, and we describe the broad approach to reform which we have decided to adopt. In later parts we go on to provide a step-by-step guide to the new legislative scheme which we recommend. For the most part our analysis will proceed in the same order as the provisions of the draft Mental Incapacity Bill at Appendix A. Part III deals with two concepts which are fundamental to our scheme. The first of these is the meaning of "incapacity" and the second is the meaning of "best interests", when applied to substitute decision-making for persons without capacity. In Part IV we discuss actions which can be undertaken, without formal or judicial

---

[15] Government Response to the Report of the Select Committee on Medical Ethics (1994) Cm 2553 pp 1, 3, 4, 5 and 6.

[16] Mentally Incapacitated and Other Vulnerable Adults: Public Law Protection, Consultation Paper No 130, published on 14 May 1993.

authority, by anyone responsible for the particular decision in question. Part V deals with advance statements about health care, particularly the sort of statement often described as an "advance directive" or "living will". Part VI discusses serious medical treatments and procedures which should always be subjected to independent supervision. Part VII deals with powers of attorney which are intended to continue in force after capacity has been lost ("continuing powers of attorney"). Part VIII describes a new court-based jurisdiction to make formal decisions or appoint a substitute decision-maker where necessary. New powers enabling public authorities to protect vulnerable adults from risk are considered in Part IX. Finally, in Part X, we set out our suggestions for an appropriate judicial forum to administer the various substantive legal remedies described in earlier parts of this report.[17] A summary of our recommendations can be found in Part XI, while at Appendix A we attach the draft Bill which would give legislative effect to our recommendations.

**Acknowledgements**

1.12 Publication of our programme item[18] led to the organisation of a major one-day conference by the University of Southampton and the King's Fund Centre in March 1990. Many helpful views were expressed by conference participants with experience in the provision and design of services for those who lack mental capacity. Throughout the subsequent consultation process we were greatly helped by views expressed in the many meetings we had with representatives of government departments, the Law Society, the British Medical Association, other professional bodies, voluntary organisations, academics and other interested individuals. Both the provisional proposals in the consultation papers and the final recommendations in this report were developed in the light of comments made at these meetings and also by the many respondents to our consultation papers. We are very grateful to everyone who took part in the meetings and to everyone who responded to one or more of our papers. The names of those who assisted us, whether orally or in writing, are set out at Appendices B and C.

1.13 This project was initiated by Professor Brenda Hoggett during her term of office as a Commissioner. The consultation process, the analysis of responses and all the essential work on the formation of policy were completed before she left the Commission for the High Court Bench at the end of December 1993. We are very grateful to her for continuing to act as an honorary consultant to the project, despite the demands of her new role. The final shape of this report bears the marks of her special expertise in the law relating to mental health and her long experience as a member of the Commission.

---

[17] Throughout this report we refer to the judicial forum which will administer the proposed new jurisdiction as "the court".

[18] See para 1.1 above.

# PART II
# THE CONTEXT AND THE BASIC
# APPROACH TO REFORM

## (1) The Legal Context

2.1    This report seeks to provide a new set of coherent answers to a single question. The question, put simply, is "who decides?". Although it may be asked in a variety of situations and for a variety of reasons, it arises whenever a person lacks the mental ability to make a legally effective decision for himself or herself. There are various supplementary questions which must then be put. "On what basis?" and "with what formalities?" are examples of these. The types of decision which may be called for can be divided into three broad categories: "personal welfare" decisions, "health care" decisions and "financial" decisions. These categories prove useful in the brief review of the present law conducted below, since there is a sharp contrast between the legal context of problems about the financial affairs of a person without capacity, and that of problems about personal or medical matters. There is a substantial body of statute law in relation to financial decisions for people who lack capacity, while the regulation of personal and health care decisions is left to some rather uncertain provisions of the common law.

*The Mental Health Act 1983*

2.2    We made it clear in our original overview paper that discussion about the provisions for compulsory admission to hospital and compulsory treatment for psychiatric disorder which are contained in the Mental Health Act 1983 ("the 1983 Act") would form no part of the present project.[1] It may be helpful if we restate our approach here, in order to dispel any remaining suspicion that the main legal context for this project can be found in that Act. The central provision of the 1983 Act governs the procedure for admitting to hospital any person suffering from specified mental disorder "of a nature or degree which makes it appropriate for him to receive medical treatment in a hospital".[2] A later provision establishes that "the consent of a patient shall not be required for any medical treatment given to him for the mental disorder from which he is suffering".[3] Although many patients detained in hospital under the Act may lack decision-making capacity, at least temporarily and in relation to some matters, the doctors and social workers who arrange their admission are not concerned with this question of capacity. The Act asks instead whether it is "necessary for the health or safety of the patient or for the protection of other persons" that he should receive treatment.[4] The distinction

---

[1]    Consultation Paper No 119, para 1.17.

[2]    Mental Health Act 1983, s 3(2)(a).

[3]    *Ibid*, s 63. Special safeguards apply to treatments listed in ss 57 and 58.

[4]    *Ibid*, s 3(2)(c).

between the general law about decision-making capacity and the policy of the 1983 Act was made crystal clear in a recent case involving a patient detained under section 3 of the Act.[5] It was held by Thorpe J that the patient did have capacity to refuse the treatment being offered to her and was refusing it, but that she could nevertheless lawfully be given it by virtue of section 63 of the Act because it was "for" her mental disorder within the meaning of that section. Our present report does not re-open the policy decisions embodied in the treatment provisions of the 1983 Act. Although many people who lack mental capacity will have some form of mental disorder, few of them will require compulsory treatment in hospital for that disorder. Instead, we are addressing in this report the legal problems which result from the fact that mental disorder may affect people's decision-making capacity in relation to a much wider range of issues. The law relating to mental incapacity and decision-making must address quite different legal issues and social purposes from the law relating to detention and treatment for mental disorder.

2.3     The "guardianship" scheme set out in section 7 of the 1983 Act can be applied to mentally disordered people who are living outside hospital and it does address matters other than treatment for mental disorder. Again, however, questions of mental capacity have little relevance to these provisions. Guardianship enables a social worker (or, much more rarely, a family member) to acquire three essential powers. It cannot, however, be applied to the majority of people with a mental disability, since the criteria require that where mental impairment is in question it must be "associated with abnormally aggressive or seriously irresponsible conduct".[6] Nor do the three powers available to a guardian necessarily cover the range of likely problems.[7]

2.4     A limited review of the 1983 Act was carried out by the Department of Health during 1993, in response to several widely publicised incidents which involved formerly detained patients living in the community. The review examined whether the legal powers which are available under the Act are sufficient to ensure that mentally ill people *in the community* receive the care they need, and whether new powers are needed.[8] At the same time the House of Commons Health Committee

---

[5]     *B v Croydon District Health Authority*, 20 July 1994, Family Division, unreported judgment of Thorpe J. This decision was upheld in the Court of Appeal (*The Times* 1 December 1994).

[6]     Mental Health Act 1983, s 7(2) and s 1(2).

[7]     These are limited to (1) power to require the patient to reside at a place specified, (2) power to require the patient to attend at places for medical treatment, occupation, education or training and (3) power to require access to the patient to be given (Mental Health Act 1983, s 8(1)). See paras 9.46 - 9.52 below for further discussion of the 1983 Act's guardianship scheme.

[8]     Written Answer, *Hansard* (HC) 13 January 1993, vol 216, col 731.

was considering many of the same issues, and its report was published in July 1993.[9] The Department of Health's own report was published the following month,[10] its main recommendation being that there should be a new "supervised discharge" arrangement for mentally ill people who need continuing support on being discharged from hospital.[11] The mischief the new power is intended to address is the fact that "failure of the care of a mentally ill person may well mean catastrophe for that person and others affected".[12] Legislation to provide for "supervised discharge" will be brought forward in the current session of Parliament.[13] In that context, the Government has reviewed the guardianship scheme in the 1983 Act and formed the preliminary view that no immediate amendments should be made.[14]

2.5 Neither the existing guardianship scheme nor the proposed supervised discharge scheme revolve around the concept of legal incapacity. As the Department of Health review team said, the guardianship provisions of the 1983 Act already embody "the principle of supervised care in the community", with which the proposed new power is consistent.[15] This principle of "supervised care" addresses the need to *control* the decisions which some people might make. This is entirely different from providing for what should happen when people are *unable* to make their own legally effective decisions. Neither guardianship nor supervised discharge addresses the need for substitute decision-making which is the focus of our project.

2.6 Part VII of the 1983 Act constitutes a self-contained statutory scheme for the management of the "property and affairs" of patients by the Court of Protection. This scheme is in fact concerned with substitute decision-making for people without capacity, and we discuss it further below.[16]

2.7 The 1983 Act also contains some short term protective powers which we will consider later in this report, in connection with other existing powers of emergency

---

[9] Fifth Report of the Health Committee, Community Supervision Orders, (1992-93) HC 667-I.

[10] Department of Health, Report of the Internal Review, *Legal Powers on the Care of Mentally Ill People in the Community* (August 1993).

[11] *Ibid*, para 8.15.

[12] *Ibid*, para 11.10.

[13] The Queen's Speech, *Hansard* (HL) 16 November 1994, vol 559, col 3.

[14] Letter from Department of Health (Administration), dated 21 October 1994, with annex, "Mental Health Act Guardianship: A Discussion Paper". Comments invited before 31 January 1995.

[15] Report of the Internal Review, *op cit*, para 11.8.

[16] See paras 2.9 - 2.13 and also paras 8.31 - 8.40 below.

intervention.[17] We will be recommending a new, properly integrated set of emergency powers which would make the powers now contained in sections 115 and 135(1) of the Mental Health Act 1983 redundant.

2.8    It follows that a few of the provisions of the 1983 Act do, more by accident than by design, form part of the legal context within which this project is set. It can easily be seen, however, that the Act in no sense provides a general decision-making jurisdiction to govern the many issues which can arise when a person lacks legal decision-making capacity.

*The Court of Protection*

2.9    The Court of Protection is not a court, but an office of the Supreme Court with a long and venerable pedigree.[18] The "lunacy" jurisdiction originally exercised by the Court of Protection and its predecessors in title was part statutory and part inherent, derived from the Royal Prerogative. The prerogative powers extended to the body as well as the estate of a patient. Over time, however, the jurisdiction of the Court of Protection became wholly statutory.[19] It also became restricted to questions of "property and affairs".[20] This very significant limitation has recently come to appear problematic.[21]

2.10   The statutory jurisdiction is couched in very wide terms. It can be invoked when the judge is satisfied after considering medical evidence that a person is incapable by reason of mental disorder of managing and administering his property and affairs.[22] The judge may then "with respect to the property and affairs of a patient, do or secure the doing of all such things as appear necessary or expedient (a) for the maintenance or other benefit of the patient, (b) for the maintenance or other benefit of the patient's family, (c) for making provision for other persons or purposes for whom or which the patient might be expected to provide if he were not mentally disordered, or (d) otherwise for administering the patient's affairs".[23] There is a

---

[17]  See Part IX below.

[18]  The title "Court of Protection" dates only to 1947, before which point the office was known as the "Management and Administration Department" (*Heywood and Massey, Court of Protection Practice* (8th ed 1961) p 8). A useful brief history is offered at pp 5 - 9 of this edition of the standard practice text.

[19]  It is now set out in Part VII of the Mental Health Act 1983.

[20]  It was authoritatively established in *Re F (Mental Patient: Sterilisation)* [1990] 2 AC 1 that the word "affairs" in the phrase "property and affairs" includes "only business matters, legal transactions and other dealings of a similar kind"; *per* Lord Brandon of Oakbrook at 59.

[21]  See paras 2.18 - 2.23 below on personal welfare and health care decisions.

[22]  Mental Health Act 1983, s 94(2). The Act refers to such a person as a "patient".

[23]  *Ibid*, s 95.

specific power to appoint a "receiver" with particular powers conferred by the judge.[24]

2.11  It has been noted that this widely-stated jurisdiction cannot encompass decisions other than those of a financial or business nature. It is also a matter of concern that the jurisdiction is premised on an assumption that capacity is an all-or-nothing status. No provision is made for a partial intervention in a person's affairs, limited in scope or in duration because the person concerned has partial or fluctuating capacity.[25] It can be difficult for a patient to obtain a discharge, the test being "Is the patient now capable of managing and administering his property and affairs?".[26] Nor does the Court permit a patient to execute an enduring power of attorney over any of his or her property, since this would conflict with the global approach it takes to each case. It traditionally requires full disclosure of all the patient's assets and almost invariably requires control of any capital assets to rest with the Public Trust Office. Those to whom receivership powers are delegated must usually give security and submit detailed yearly accounts. The costs of this highly protective system of state supervision are charged to the patients.[27] The affairs of some 30,400 patients are currently managed in this way.[28]

2.12  We were repeatedly told on consultation that many carers and disabled people are most anxious to avoid any involvement with the Court of Protection; they are afraid of its costs and they do not understand its procedures, particularly the complex relationship between the Court and the Public Trust Office. Many complained that the Court has a single location in central London, whereas they wanted a local and "user-friendly" venue.

2.13  The present jurisdiction of the Court of Protection is arguably too limited, in that it can only address financial and business issues, and yet too wide, in that it does not cater for partial and limited interventions. The present procedures do not appeal to many who might benefit from the exercise of the jurisdiction, and the status of the Court as an office of the Supreme Court is confusing and anomalous. Before discussing our basic approach to solving these problems, we turn to consider the

---

[24]  *Ibid*, s 99.

[25]  There is authority to the effect that once under the jurisdiction of the Court of Protection a patient cannot be bound by any act of his or her own done in relation to his or her property, even if the act was in fact done when the patient had capacity to do it, *Re Walker* [1905] 1 Ch 160 and *Re Marshall* [1920] 1 Ch 284.

[26]  *Heywood and Massey, Court of Protection Practice* (12th ed 1991) p 61.

[27]  The National Audit Office has recently reported on the performance of the Public Trust Office and identified a number of areas where improvements could be made (National Audit Office, *Looking after the Financial Affairs of People with Mental Incapacity* (1994)).

[28]  National Audit Office, *op cit*, para 1.4 and figure 1. Figures as at 31 March 1992.

other mechanisms available where financial decisions need to be made.

*Enduring powers of attorney ("EPAs")*

2.14 Since the coming into force of the Enduring Powers of Attorney Act 1985 ("the 1985 Act"), a person with capacity may appoint an "attorney" to manage his or her finances even after the person who has made the appointment loses mental capacity.[29] In such cases there may be no need for an order of the Court of Protection. The system of state supervision, and its concomitant costs, can largely be avoided. Some safeguards for donors, mostly administrative in nature, are carried out by the Public Trust Office on behalf of the Court of Protection. This new statutory scheme has proved popular, with the number of registered Enduring Powers of Attorney steadily rising since their introduction in 1986. 15,000 have already been registered,[30] and many more will have been executed by now.

2.15 The present EPA scheme, like the jurisdiction of the Court of Protection, is limited to property and business matters. While there is no reason why a person could not give an attorney the power to take decisions about non-financial matters, such as medical or residence decisions, the 1985 Act scheme for *enduring* powers of attorney only extends to "property and affairs".[31] Enduring powers of attorney are particularly attractive to older people or to those with a progressive illness who wish to organise their affairs in advance by involving a trusted adviser or family member rather than a judicial forum or administrative agency. At present, these wishes may be fulfilled so far as money matters are concerned. Effective long-term arrangements about health care matters or, for example, where to live are, however, ruled out. It is also a matter of concern that the 1985 Act, like Part VII of the Mental Health Act 1983,[32] adopts an all-or-nothing attitude to capacity.[33] In addition, there are cogent arguments in favour of rationalising and simplifying the statutory safeguards which were imposed when the scheme was created nearly ten years ago.[34] A number of our respondents also regretted the fact that the decision-making scheme in Part VII of

---

[29] The common law rule is that the supervening incapacity of the principal terminates the authority of any agent, *Yonge v Toynbee* [1910] 1 KB 215.

[30] National Audit Office, *op cit*, para 2.20.

[31] It therefore follows from the decision in *Re F* on the meaning of the phrase "property and affairs" that personal and medical matters are excluded. See para 2.9 and n 20 above.

[32] See para 2.11 above.

[33] Although a donor of an EPA does retain power to do most things which he or she has capacity to do, the 1985 Act specifies that once an enduring power of attorney has been registered with the Court of Protection the donor may not revoke it without "confirmation" of the Court, nor alter its scope in any way (Enduring Powers of Attorney Act 1985, s 7(1)(a) and (c)). This bar operates regardless of the donor's actual capacity to revoke or amend the power, although confirmation cannot be refused if the revocation is (apart from the confirmation) valid (s 8(3)).

[34] See Consultation Paper No 128, paras 7.4 - 7.23.

the 1983 Act and the EPA scheme in the 1985 Act operate, quite unnecessarily, as mutually exclusive procedures. There was support for flexibility, or what we called in our consultation paper "switching jurisdictions",[35] as between a court-based scheme and one allowing for the appointment of an attorney with enduring powers.

*Social Security appointees*

2.16    The present law offers a further solution in relation to money deriving from state benefits. If a person who is in receipt of or entitled to such benefits is "unable to act" then the Secretary of State for Social Security may appoint another person to act on that person's behalf.[36] That other person may then collect the benefits and use them for the benefit of the claimant. Concern has been expressed about the nature of the enquiries conducted before such appointments are made, and about the absence of regular supervision or monitoring of the performance of appointees.[37]

*Access to funds*

2.17    A number of statutory schemes provide for money accruing due to a person without capacity to be paid instead to a suitable person.[38] Some privately managed pension schemes or insurance policies may make provision in the contract between the customer and the company for payments to be made to someone other than the customer, in the event of the customer lacking mental capacity when payments fall due. Some of the larger building societies make similar provision in their contractual arrangements with customers. Such arrangements are far from universal and in our opinion there is scope for a standard statutory scheme offering institutions protection from liability if funds are released to enable a customer to be cared for.[39]

*Personal welfare and health care decisions*

2.18    We have now described the various procedures whereby the financial affairs of a person without capacity can be resolved within the law as it stands at present. There is no statutory scheme for the making of a non-financial decision on behalf of a person who cannot decide for himself or herself, or for the appointment of a substitute decision-maker with continuing powers. Nearly 25 years ago the United Nations *Declaration on the Rights of Mentally Retarded Persons* proclaimed that "the mentally retarded person has a right to a qualified guardian when this is required

---

[35]   *Ibid*, para 5.34.

[36]   Social Security (Claims and Payments) Regulations 1987 (SI 1987 No 1968), reg 33.

[37]   See the analysis by R Lavery and L Lundy, "The Social Security Appointee System" [1994] J Soc Wel & Fam L 313.

[38]   See for example Mental Health Act 1983, s 142; Local Government Act 1972, s 118; Clergy Pensions Measure 1961, s 36; Parliamentary and other Pensions Act 1987 (and regulations thereunder); Industrial and Provident Societies Act 1965, s 26 and National Savings Bank Regulations 1972 (SI 1972 No 764), reg 7(4).

[39]   See paras 4.12 - 4.21 below.

to protect his personal well-being and interests",[40] thereby identifying the right to a guardian as one of a number of rights which disabled people should possess. The word "guardian" refers to a person who is granted legal powers to take decisions on behalf of a person whose disability affects his or her legal competence. We have seen that the Court of Protection has jurisdiction to make all necessary provision regarding the financial "interests" of a person without capacity, especially by appointing a "receiver" to deal with matters for the patient. In contrast, the only form of guardianship to protect "personal well-being" which is currently available in England and Wales is guardianship under the Mental Health Act 1983. Statistics indicate a negligible recourse to these provisions, although the number of annual applications is steadily increasing. There were only 228 new cases of reception into guardianship in the year 1992-3.[41] We have suggested above that the guardianship scheme contained in the Mental Health Act was not principally designed to provide a disabled person with a proxy decision-maker but to enable a mentally ill person to live safely in the community.[42] Since it is apparent that the present state of English law offends against the spirit, if not the letter, of the United Nations Declaration,[43] it is important to understand how this situation has come about.

2.19 Under ancient prerogative powers of the Crown, delegated to the Lord Chancellor by the issue of a Royal Warrant under the Sign Manual, it used to be possible to appoint both a "committee of the person" and a "committee of the estate" for anyone found to be "of unsound mind and incapable of managing *himself and* his affairs".[44] In 1957 a Royal Commission (the "Percy Commission") reported that 19 patients had committees of the person.[45] A much more significant number, some 2,800, were subject to "guardianship" under the Mental Deficiency Acts.[46] These Acts gave a guardian all the powers of a parent over a child under fourteen years of age.

2.20 The Percy Commission's approach to non-financial guardianship was to treat it exclusively as an aspect of "compulsory control". The intrusive nature of plenary legal guardianship is still often stressed. One commentator has called it "the most

[40] 1971 UN General Assembly 26th Session, Resolution 2856, para 5.

[41] Department of Health statistics, "Guardianship under the Mental Health Acts 1959 and 1983" (1993) Table 3.

[42] See para 2.4 above.

[43] See further M J Gunn, "Mental Health Act Guardianship: Where Now?" [1986] J Soc Wel L 144, 151.

[44] Lunacy Act 1890, s 90(1) (emphasis added).

[45] Report of the Royal Commission on the Law relating to Mental Illness and Mental Deficiency (1957) Cmnd 169 para 255 n 15.

[46] *Ibid*, p 314, table 5a.

extensive form of legal control of the person outside institutional commitment".[47] The other side of the guardianship coin, however, is "guardianship as protective advocacy",[48] a civil right of those in need, as depicted in the UN Declaration. This benign, rights-based type of guardianship does not feature at all in the Percy Commission recommendations which led to the Mental Health Act 1959. That Commission commented that "compulsory control over patients receiving community care should not often be necessary".[49] The philosophy of the 1959 Act was that compulsory measures should only be put into operation where necessary, which was taken to refer to situations where actual coercion was required. To that end, any "guardian" under the Mental Health Act 1959 had all the powers of a father over a child under 14. When the Mental Health Act 1959 came into force, the Royal Warrant under the Sign Manual was revoked.

2.21 In the governmental review of the operation of the 1959 Act which preceded the enactment of new mental health legislation in the early 1980s, it was noted that the numbers of those with a guardian had steadily declined.[50] In the new legislation, guardianship was again approached as a subset of the compulsory powers which were being updated and improved. The powers of a guardian were severely cut back and the categories of people who could be received into guardianship were radically restricted. Guardianship cannot now be used for clients who suffer from any form of arrested or incomplete development of mind unless it is associated with "abnormally aggressive or seriously irresponsible conduct".[51] Unless the meaning of these words is distorted, the vast majority of those with a learning disability (mental handicap) will be excluded from guardianship. The benign side of the guardianship coin was nowhere in evidence in the new legislation. The present state of the statute book therefore reflects a single-minded view of personal guardianship as a method of restricting civil rights and liberties rather than as a method of enhancing them.

2.22 A guardian under the Mental Health Act 1983 now has power "to require" the patient to do two particular things: to reside at a specified place and to attend at specified places for medical treatment, occupation, education or training. In addition, the guardian has power "to require" access to the patient to be given to

[47] Robin Creyke, "Guardianship: Protection and Autonomy - Has the Right Balance Been Achieved?" in J Eekelaar and D Pearl (eds) *An Ageing World: Dilemmas and Challenges for Law and Social Policy* (1989) p 545.

[48] M Fisher, "Guardianship under the Mental Health Act Legislation: A Review" [1988] J Soc Wel L 316, 325.

[49] *Op cit*, para 832.

[50] Review of the Mental Health Act 1959 (1978) Cmnd 7320 para 4.7. Only 133 people were subject to guardianship in 1978 (S Millington, *Guardianship and the Mental Health Act 1983* (1989) p 4).

[51] Mental Health Act 1983, s 7(2)(a) and s 1(2).

doctors, social workers or other specified persons.[52] It is important to note that this form of guardianship is not structured to allow the "patient's" family to intervene. The assumption is - wrongly - that they are already in charge; thus Mental Health Act guardianship is there to allow *others* to take over from them. In conformity with the philosophy behind this part of the legislation, there is also no assumption that the patient is unable to take any of these decisions for himself or herself, but rather that, left alone, the decision made would be inconsistent with his or her own "welfare" or the protection of other persons.[53]

2.23    Although English law acknowledges that legal difficulties may arise where a person is incapable of making decisions about his or her financial affairs, such statutory provision as we now possess in relation to personal or medical matters is restricted to the quite different difficulties which are caused where a person has a psychiatric disorder leading to self-destructive or dangerous personal decision-making. What happens when a person is simply incapable of taking any decision about where might be the best place to live, or about whether consent to a particular medical procedure should be given? The consequences of the whittling away of any comprehensive protective guardianship scheme for non-financial decisions became all too clear in the leading case of *Re F*.[54]

*The declaratory jurisdiction*

2.24    The High Court has both an inherent and a statutory jurisdiction to make a declaration as to whether an act is lawful or not.[55] In *Re F* it was held in the House of Lords that since English law has no procedure whereby a substitute or proxy can be appointed to take medical decisions for an incompetent patient, the declaratory jurisdiction should be used to fill the gap.[56] A High Court declaration to the effect that it would not be unlawful to perform a sterilisation operation on an adult who lacked the mental capacity to consent to its being performed was upheld in both the Court of Appeal and the House of Lords.

2.25    A declaration by the High Court does not answer the question "who decides?". Nor does it answer the question "what will be best?" It has been said that "the essence

---

[52]  *Ibid*, s 8(1).

[53]  *Ibid*, s 7(2)(b).

[54]  *Re F (Mental Patient: Sterilisation)* [1990] 2 AC 1.

[55]  The statutory version is governed by Ord 15 r 16 of the Rules of the Supreme Court. The House of Lords, however, has held that reference to the statutory provision is not necessary (*Re F (Mental Patient: Sterilisation)* [1990] 2 AC 1, 66).

[56]  *Re F (Mental Patient: Sterilisation)* [1990] 2 AC 1, 65, *per* Lord Brandon of Oakbrook. All three members of the Court of Appeal had expressed the view that the declaration procedure was not satisfactory and that a new Rule should be drafted, enabling the High Court to approve or disapprove a proposed medical procedure. See especially the speech of Lord Donaldson of Lymington MR, pp 20-21.

of the jurisdiction is that the court is like a camera photographing the relevant legal terrain. It registers what exists, and declares what it finds".[57] In spite of the fact that the declaration cannot change anything, the court has expressed the view that certain serious procedures should always be referred to it for a declaration in advance.[58] It has also expressed a willingness to respond to new and difficult dilemmas, such as those which may arise when a patient who has now lost capacity appears to have refused consent to a particular procedure being performed.[59] The declaration procedure has now been used in several reported cases about the cessation of artificial sustenance for a patient in a persistent vegetative state.[60] It has been used to clarify the effect of purported refusals of treatment.[61] It has also been invoked where the parents of a disabled woman who was alleged to lack capacity to decide for herself were in dispute as to whether she was being prevented from having contact with her mother. Although that case never came to a full hearing, Eastham J accepted that there was jurisdiction in the High Court to make a declaration about such a matter.[62] In yet another recent case declarations were sought as to whether a stroke victim should remain within the jurisdiction to receive treatment and care at his home in England.[63]

2.26 Conversely, the court has displayed some anxiety to restrict the availability of declarations and it has told applicants that no declaration is needed in a number of cases.[64] This is perhaps the best illustration of the severe limitations on the usefulness or desirability of the declaratory jurisdiction, except in so far as it is a necessary stop gap while more permanent measures are devised. If a person proposes to do something and doubts whether it would be lawful then a declaration may be granted confirming that it would be lawful. Alternatively, a declaration may

---

[57] F Bennion, "Consent to Surgery on a Mentally Handicapped Adult" (1989) 133 SJ 245, 246.

[58] Namely, sterilisation for contraceptive purposes (*Re F (Mental Patient: Sterilisation)* [1990] 2 AC 1) and the withdrawal of artificial feeding from a patient in a persistent vegetative state (*Airedale NHS Trust v Bland* [1993] AC 789). The Official Solicitor has stated that 20 applications for a declaration in connection with a proposed sterilisation operation were made between 1989 and 1993 (House of Lords Select Committee on Medical Ethics (1993-94) HL 21-II p 191).

[59] *Re T (Adult: Refusal of Treatment)* [1993] Fam 95, 115.

[60] *Airedale NHS Trust v Bland* [1993] AC 789; *Frenchay NHS Trust v S* [1994] 1 WLR 601 and *Swindon and Marlborough NHS Trust v S, The Guardian* 10 December 1994.

[61] *Re T (Adult: Refusal of Treatment)* [1993] Fam 95; *Re S (Adult: Refusal of Treatment)* [1993] Fam 123; *Re C (Adult: Refusal of Treatment)* [1994] 1 WLR 290; *Secretary of State for the Home Department v Robb, The Times* 21 October 1994.

[62] *Re C (Mental Patient: Contact)* [1993] 1 FLR 940.

[63] *Re S*, 26 September 1994, Family Division, unreported judgment of Hale J.

[64] Those involving adults are *Re SG (Adult Mental Patient: Abortion)* [1991] 2 FLR 329 and *Re GF (Medical Treatment)* [1992] 1 FLR 293 (proposed hysterectomy).

be refused on the basis that no such declaration is needed. In either case, the court is quite unable either to decide what steps should be taken or to give the applicant or anybody else the authority to take decisions in the future. This result is a far cry from what the UN Declaration identifies as "the right to a qualified guardian".

*Protective powers*

2.27 The UN Declaration states that "the mentally retarded person has a right to protection from exploitation, abuse and degrading treatment".[65] Careful regard to this principle of protection permeates all the recommendations for the reform of the public law we will be making in Part IX below. We have also borne it in mind, however, when considering the present state of our private law for substitute decision-making on behalf of an incapacitated person. As we pointed out in our overview paper, this obligation of protection is often described as being inherently at odds with the equally important right to maximum freedom and autonomy.[66]

2.28 Statutory provisions already exist to give public officials powers to take protective measures in order to help vulnerable people. However, we have no confidence at all that these powers strike the appropriate balance between the protection principle and the autonomy principle. Two of the powers are to be found in the Mental Health Act 1983: a power to enter and inspect premises in which a mentally disordered person is living[67] and a power to apply for a warrant to enter premises and remove a patient to a place of safety.[68] There is also an ageing power to apply for a "removal order" in the National Assistance Act 1948,[69] linked to an ex parte version of the same power in the National Assistance (Amendment) Act 1951. This power arises in relation to people who are suffering from grave chronic disease or people who are aged, infirm or physically incapacitated, and are living in insanitary conditions. In either event it must also be shown that they are unable to devote proper care and attention to themselves, and are not receiving it from others. There is no need to show that they are lacking in capacity, or even that they are mentally disordered. The power may therefore be invoked against those who choose, in the exercise of their own free will, to live in situations which others find "insanitary" or to enjoy care and attention which others find less than "proper". This is objectionable. So, too, is the fact that the power may *not* apply to some vulnerable persons who are at risk of harm but do not fall within the wording of the section. If, for example, a mentally disabled person is in a sanitary home and is not suffering

---

[65] *Declaration on the Rights of Mentally Retarded Persons*, 1971 UN General Assembly 26th Session, Resolution 2856, para 6.

[66] Consultation Paper No 119, para 1.12.

[67] Section 115.

[68] Section 135(1).

[69] Section 47.

from grave chronic disease then nothing can be done, however vulnerable he or she may be to abuse or exploitation. We believe that a new set of modern and acceptable emergency protective powers should be introduced. The exercise of these powers would serve where necessary as a preliminary to invoking the new decision-making jurisdiction, if it should transpire that the person who appears to be in need of protection in fact lacks decision-making capacity.

*Other countries*

2.29 Over the past twenty years or so it has been recognised in many other countries that there is a need to create a legal framework within which decisions concerning the welfare of incapacitated adults can be taken. We described several of these schemes in our overview paper[70] and new legislation has been introduced in a number of different jurisdictions since that time.[71] Many of these schemes have resulted from law reform projects similar to our own and we have found it instructive to examine the range of statutory provisions adopted elsewhere in the world.

2.30 In September 1991 the Scottish Law Commission published a Discussion Paper[72] which examined existing Scots law in relation to decisions about the personal welfare and financial affairs of mentally disabled adults who lack legal capacity.[73] In August 1993 that Commission published a second Discussion Paper[74] in which it sought comments on "public law protection" proposals broadly comparable to those in our Consultation Paper No 130. We have worked closely with the Scottish Law Commission and we both aim to produce recommendations which are founded on mutually consistent principles, while taking into account differences in law and procedure on each side of the border. In particular, the history of the law of "personal guardianship" has been different in Scotland. Guardianship under the mental health legislation in Scotland is not structured so as to rule out the majority of those with mental handicap (learning disability).[75] Nor were the ancient common law powers of the courts to appoint "tutors" or "curators" (the Scots equivalents to

---

[70] Consultation Paper No 119, Part V.

[71] See for example Ontario's Substitute Decisions Act 1992, British Columbia's Adult Guardianship Act 1993 and South Australia's Guardianship and Administration Act 1993. In March 1994 the former Chief Judge of the Family Court of Japan visited us to discuss the need for new legal provision for Japanese citizens who lack mental capacity, in accordance with Japan's international obligations under the UN Declarations on the Rights of Mentally Retarded Persons and on the Rights of Disabled Persons.

[72] Discussion Paper No 94, Mentally Disabled Adults: Legal Arrangements for Managing their Welfare and Finances.

[73] *Ibid*, para 1.1.

[74] Discussion Paper No 96, Mentally Disordered and Vulnerable Adults: Public Authority Powers.

[75] See Mental Health (Scotland) Act 1984, ss 36 and 1(2). The effect of these provisions is that anyone with mental illness or mental handicap might be a candidate for guardianship.

committees of the person or estate) ever superseded by statute in such a way that they could not be resurrected when the need for them recently reappeared.[76] Even the provisions for enduring powers of attorney are different: in Scotland it is already possible to create a power of attorney over non-financial matters which can outlast the donor's incapacity.[77] The result is that although we are satisfied that we are at one with our Scottish counterparts on matters of principle, the details of the legislative schemes we will be recommending will display significant differences.

## (2) The Social Context

2.31    We will now turn to consider some of the social background to the existing law about mental incapacity and decision-making. This will show how a number of different changes and developments have highlighted the gaps and deficiencies in this area of law, and have exposed the pressing need for reform which was identified by respondents to our overview paper.

### Community care

2.32    Two distinct social policies are often brought under the single heading of "community care". The first, and by far the older, is the policy of discharging mentally disordered and mentally handicapped people from large, isolated hospitals. This has already resulted in extensive change to the ways in which mentally ill and mentally disabled people are cared for.[78] In the days when most people with mental disabilities or illnesses lived in highly-regimented institutions issues about decision-making or the need for a substitute decision-maker were not likely to arise. Living in the community offers greatly increased opportunities for decision-making. Many people with mental disabilities or mental health problems are quite able to take many of the decisions which crop up in everyday life by themselves, or with support, guidance and training where these are needed. People with disabilities living in the community may, however, sometimes be called upon to perform acts of legal significance which highlight a problem about legal capacity. A lengthy tenancy agreement may have to be signed, the local doctor may be worried about the patient's capacity to consent to treatment, the bank manager may be doubtful about a prospective customer's capacity to enter into a contract for banking services. Moreover, the existence of choices inevitably means the possibility of disagreement about which choice is best. In the course of our consultation, we were repeatedly told that disputes and disagreements arise about the most appropriate living

---

[76]   See Adrian D Ward,"Tutors to Adults: Developments" (1992) 33 SLT 325.

[77]   See Law Reform (Miscellaneous Provisions)(Scotland) Act 1990, s 71(1). This statutory provision was intended, however, to be an interim measure pending review of the law by the Scottish Law Commission. See further Discussion Paper No 94, *op cit*, para 5.5.

[78]   In 1981 there were on average 48,000 NHS beds available each day for those with learning disability; in 1990-91, 23,000. The numbers of those being discharged from mental illness and learning disability hospitals and units after stays of five or more years continue to rise. *Social Trends 23* (1993), tables 7.27 and 7.32 respectively.

situation for a person with a disability. Options might be a hospital, a group home, supported independent living or sharing with one of a number of relatives. Such disputes may arise between relatives, or between a relative and the local social services authority.

2.33 The second policy which the rubric "community care" now embraces involves rather wider questions about the way in which social care needs should be determined and provided for. It has been summarised as a policy of "providing the right level of intervention and support to enable people to achieve maximum independence and control over their own lives".[79] Fundamental legislative change was effected by the National Health Service and Community Care Act 1990. Most of the provisions of this Act were implemented in April 1993, towards the end of our consultation process. Government guidance issued to accompany the legislation states that the new approach "seeks to recognise the individuality of need by challenging practitioners to identify the unique characteristics of each individual's needs".[80] Against this modern thinking, most of the older legislative provisions we have reviewed above are shown to be sorely wanting.

2.34 The now discredited practice of committing people to institutional care was also a way of discharging the obligation to protect those who cannot protect themselves. Community living may expose people to new or at least different dangers of abuse. Some of our respondents expressed concern about what has been called the "abusive normalisation" of disabled people. This means that they are being exposed to risks which they are ill-equipped to guard against because of an ideology of non-intervention on the part of service providers or advisers, who place the autonomy principle above everything else. Community care in fact requires the difficult balance between autonomy and protection to be struck at an entirely new point.

*Demographics*

2.35 In common with many developed countries the United Kingdom has an ageing population. Of particular significance for this project is the startling rise in the proportion of the population aged 80 and over (2.3% of the population in 1971, 3.7% in 1991), a rise which is predicted to continue at a sharp angle (to 4.7% in 2011 and 6.9% in 2031).[81] All studies agree that both the prevalence and the incidence rates of dementia increase exponentially with age.[82] The implications of

---

[79]  *Caring for People: Community Care in the Next Decade and Beyond* (1989) Cm 849 para 2.2.

[80]  Department of Health Social Services Inspectorate and Scottish Office Social Work Services Group, *Care Management and Assessment: Summary of Practice Guidance* (1991) p 11.

[81]  *Social Trends 24* (1994), table 1.4.

[82]  D W K Kay, "The epidemiology of dementia: a review of recent work" (1991) 1 Reviews in Clinical Gerontology 55, 63.

this population trend for many areas of social provision are already under scrutiny.[83] Elderly people with dementia suffer a progressive loss of mental capacity, so that an increasing number of decisions about their personal care, health care and finances inevitably fall to be made by others.

2.36   By the end of the 1980s the policy of care in the community was being explicitly applied to the provision of services for elderly people, with legislative endorsement in the National Health Service and Community Care Act 1990.[84] This development has implications for the ways in which the care of elderly people is funded. While it is a principle of our national insurance system that *health service* provision should be mainly free at the point of use, no such principle applies to *social care* provision. Local authorities can charge elderly people for all the most important services supplied to them, and they have a duty to charge for the provision of residential care.[85] It should not be assumed that most elderly people will lack the means to pay for services. The average real net income of pensioners grew by nearly a third between 1979 and 1987, with income from occupational pensions and savings growing particularly rapidly.[86] It has also been estimated that by the year 2001 nearly two-thirds of those over 65 will be owner-occupiers,[87] many owning most if not all of the equity in the house where they live. The value of a home is taken into account when a person's means to pay for residential care are assessed.[88] It seems inevitable that complex decisions about the management and disbursement of the funds of elderly people who lack mental capacity will in future be necessary in many more cases. Moreover, financial decisions will increasingly have to be taken in explicit association with decisions about residential or other services, something which cannot be achieved under the present arrangements for decision-making by the Court of Protection.

---

[83]   See for example F McGlone and N Cronin, *A Crisis in Care? The Future of the Family and State Care for Older People in the European Union* (1994) Family Policy Studies Centre and Centre for Policy on Ageing, suggesting that the German policy of compulsory long-term insurance merits consideration.

[84]   A Tinker, C McCreadie, F Wright and A V Salvage, *The Care of Frail Elderly People in the United Kingdom* (1994) p 11.

[85]   National Assistance Act 1948, ss 22 and 26. If a resident cannot pay the standard charge then the local authority must assess ability to pay under a statutory means test (National Assistance (Assessment of Resources) Regulations 1992 (SI 1992 No 2977)).

[86]   F McGlone, *Disability and Dependence in Old Age: A demographic and social audit*, Family Policy Studies Centre Occasional Paper 14 (1992) p 31.

[87]   *Ibid*, p 36.

[88]   There is provision for the value of any premises occupied by a third party (for example, a spouse/partner or incapacitated or elderly relative) to be disregarded where the local authority considers it reasonable to do so (National Assistance (Assessment of Resources) Regulations 1992 reg 21(2) and Sched 4 para 18). There is also provision to take into account the value of any asset alienated by the resident in order to decrease any liability to pay charges (reg 25(1)).

*Medical advances*

2.37    The third significant change which has exposed a need for reform of the law is the onward march of medical science. The lives of many people who would in earlier times have died from trauma or disease can now be saved. Some, however, will survive with impaired mental capacity or even in a "persistent vegetative state" where they can express no decision about what should happen to them in future. The sad litigation about Tony Bland[89] came to an end shortly before the publication of our consultation paper on medical treatment and it highlighted the fact that statute does not explain how decisions may be lawfully made in such situations. In the House of Lords, Lord Browne-Wilkinson expressed grave concern about the legal problems cast up by "modern technological developments" and said that it seemed to him "imperative that the moral, social and legal issues raised by this case should be considered by Parliament".[90] The case generated much comment from our consultees and we have no doubt that there is a clear need for a decision-making procedure for those who are unconscious or quite unable to express any decision, although they may not suffer from any condition which would be thought of as mental illness or handicap.

2.38    The achievements of medical science have also created difficult dilemmas about the appropriate measure of medical care which should be given at the end of life, particularly where unconscious or incapacitated people have, in advance, indicated an unwillingness to be kept alive once their health has deteriorated. The House of Lords Select Committee to which we have already referred[91] carried out a wide-ranging examination of a number of the "medico-legal" issues which the present state of medical science has thrown up. We have also been impressed by the great public interest in "living wills" and have taken note of international moves towards the acceptance and regulation of such documents.

2.39    A further aspect of the march of medical science is evidenced by the fact that certain procedures are now possible and are in fact being performed by medical personnel in spite of the fact that, as the law now stands, they are probably unlawful. It seems wholly unsatisfactory that respected doctors and scientists should carry out procedures of dubious legality with the approval of ethics committees and with funding from responsible professional bodies, all of them believing the procedures to be both ethical and reasonable. The prime example of this problem is the carrying out of research on a person who is incapable of consenting to what is done, where the research is not intended to benefit the individual participant but rather to ensure better treatment or care for other people in the future. Another example is the mechanical ventilation of an unconscious and dying person, where this is done

---

[89]    *Airedale NHS Trust v Bland* [1993] AC 789.

[90]    *Ibid*, pp 878-880.

[91]    See para 1.7 and n 13 above.

in order that donated organs can be maintained in a usable state.[92] Yet another is the performing of tests for genetic disorders on someone who is unable to consent to what is proposed, and where the tests are performed to benefit another family member or a wider segment of the population. The present law allows a doctor to effect any treatment which is in the best interests of a person who cannot consent, but it is most unlikely that there is any legal justification for the performance of procedures such as those described above, since they do not purport to promote the best interests of the particular patient. We believe that this unhappy state of affairs must be resolved by a clear statement of what the law does and does not permit.

*The "rights" agenda*

2.40 Another social change has further exposed the defects of our existing law. We have mentioned the UN Declaration of 1971 on the Rights of Mentally Retarded Persons.[93] This takes its place within a considerable body of international opinion which identifies unacceptable discrimination in the ways in which those who have mental disabilities (and especially mental illness) have been dealt with in the past by medical practitioners, the law and society as a whole. "Civil rights" arguments were cogently deployed in order to achieve the legislative change which is now embodied in the Mental Health Act 1983.[94] More topically, the "rights" agenda is the driving force behind the Government's introduction of a Citizen's Charter, which emphasises that users of public services are entitled to certain standards of information and service. Many local and voluntary organisations are also adopting "charters" which stress the obligations of providers to consumers of services.[95] The National Health Service and Community Care Act 1990 and the Government's policy guidance on that Act both make it clear that those who are charged with arranging community care services must consult with those who will use or benefit from them.[96]

---

[92] Often referred to as "interventional" or "elective" ventilation. In October 1994 the Department of Health issued a guidance note referring to "some instances" of this practice being carried out and advising that "in cases where the clinician's intention in referring the patient to intensive care is not for the patient's own benefit but is to ensure his or her organs can be retrieved for transplantation the practice would be unlawful"; NHS Executive HSG(94)41. See further paras 6.23 - 6.24 and 6.26 below.

[93] See para 2.18 above. In 1975 the UN made a further Declaration on the Rights of Disabled Persons, while in 1991 the General Assembly adopted *Principles for the protection of persons with mental illness and the improvement of mental health care* (Resolution 46/119 of 17 December 1991).

[94] See the account given by L Gostin, "Contemporary Social Historical Perspectives on Mental Health Legislation" (1983) 10 J Law & Soc 47.

[95] For a useful discussion see A Wertheimer, *Speaking Out: Citizen Advocacy and Older People* (1993) ch 2.

[96] 1990 Act, s 46(2). *Community Care in the Next Decade and Beyond*, Policy Guidance (1990) paras 2.7 - 2.10.

2.41 It has been said that "the idea that patients have rights sits ill with the general shape of English health care law".[97] However, the House of Lords Select Committee on Medical Ethics, which did not confine itself to strictly legal matters, reported that the principle of patient autonomy "has become important in relation to medical treatment, as the relationship between doctor and patient has changed to one of partnership".[98] A new awareness that patients have rights in relation to their medical treatment underlies the increasing interest in "living wills" and other advance directives for health care.

*Abuse of vulnerable people*

2.42 The "rights" agenda can also be seen at work in growing concern about the abuse and neglect of older people. The phrase "elder abuse" has gained considerable currency over the course of the four years since we published our first consultation paper in connection with this project. With hindsight, it seems clear that the start of our work coincided with the emergence of elder abuse as a significant item on the social policy agenda.[99] In September 1993 the Parliamentary Under-Secretary of State for Health was present at the launch of a new national forum, "Action on Elder Abuse". The first national conference of this new organisation was held in March 1994 and focused on "Elder Abuse and the Law": one session of the conference was devoted to our provisional proposals for law reform. In her closing address Professor Olive Stevenson expressed the view that the proposals set out in our consultation papers reflected the best that can be done to balance the principles of autonomy and protection in this area, and that the case for urgent law reform on the basis we had proposed was fully made out.[100]

2.43 Revelations and concerns about abuse have not been limited to older victims. A series of scandals and court cases has suggested that many younger people with learning disabilities are abused by those who care for them in institutional as well as family settings. The National Association for the Protection from Sexual Abuse of Adults and Children with Learning Disabilities (NAPSAC) was launched in April 1992. The results of a major survey of the sexual abuse of adults with learning disabilities were published in 1993,[101] with the authors concluding that there is a

---

[97] J Montgomery, "Power over death: the final sting" in R Lee and D Morgan (eds) *Death Rites: Law and ethics at the end of life* (1994) p 37.

[98] Report of the Select Committee on Medical Ethics (1993-94) HL 21-I para 40.

[99] See further Consultation Paper No 130, paras 1.8 - 1.12.

[100] The conference papers (*Working Paper No 2: Elder Abuse and the Law*) will be published by Action on Elder Abuse in early 1995.

[101] V Turk and H Brown, "The Sexual Abuse of Adults with Learning Disabilities: Results of a Two Year Incidence Survey" (1993) 6 Mental Handicap Research 193.

need to provide support for victims and also develop preventative strategies.[102] Publication of this research was followed by an inter-agency conference convened by the Social Services Inspectorate of the Department of Health in March 1994. The Parliamentary Under-Secretary of State for Health was once again the keynote speaker, and he stressed the need for a multi-agency approach to prevent abuse of adults with learning disabilities.[103]

*Citizen advocacy*

2.44 The anti-discrimination and "rights" agenda also lies behind the citizen advocacy movement. In this form of advocacy "an ordinary citizen develops a relationship with another person who risks social exclusion or other unfair treatment because of a handicap. As the relationship develops, the advocate chooses ways to understand, respond to, and represent the other person's interests as if they were the advocate's own."[104] One recent commentator has linked the development of the citizen advocacy movement to "the concept of citizenship - namely the empowerment of individuals to say how they wish to live their lives and which public services they need to help them do so".[105] Some of our consultees were disappointed to see so few references to citizen advocacy in the provisional proposals we developed in our three 1993 consultation papers. However, we believe it should be clear from what we have said above that citizen advocacy addresses problems which are quite distinct from those which our law reform proposals must tackle. A citizen advocate is not a substitute decision-maker.[106] There are many people with disabilities who will benefit from an advocacy relationship (or from training in self-advocacy) and who may, with the emotional support and factual information provided by the advocate, never need a substitute decision-maker. There is thus no conflict between the advocacy movement and the need for substantive law reform. They address different issues. The advocacy movement cannot deal with the legal difficulty which arises when a legally effective decision is needed and the person concerned does not have the capacity to make that decision. An advocate might sometimes be the best person to gain the legal status which would enable him or her to take the substitute decision, but he or she would then have the choice of two distinct hats to wear as and when the need should arise.

---

[102] *Ibid*, p 213.

[103] Social Services Inspectorate, "It Could *Never* Happen Here, Report on an Inter-Agency Study Day" (1994) p 1.

[104] This definition was drafted by John O'Brien and is repeated in B Sang and J O'Brien, *Advocacy: the UK and American experiences* (1984) p 27, King's Fund Project Paper No 51.

[105] A Wertheimer, *Speaking Out: Citizen Advocacy and Older People* (1993) p v.

[106] "Advocates do not dominate or control their friends, or dictate what is best", B Sang and J O'Brien, *op cit*, p 28.

### The Basic Approach to Reform

2.45　The legal context to this project is one of incoherence, inconsistency and historical accident. The social context now makes the reform of the unsatisfactory state of the law an urgent necessity. Those who responded to our first consultation paper almost four years ago recognised that the need for reform would become increasingly pressing in the face of community care policies, demographic changes, medical advances and an increasing awareness of the rights agenda. Developments over the past three years, in particular the perceived need for a decision-making jurisdiction which is being illuminated by case-law, the growth in interest in "living wills" and the increasing concern about abuse of the elderly and disabled, have only strengthened the case for rationalisation and reform.

2.46　Our overview paper suggested that the aims of policy for this project should be:

(i) that people are enabled and encouraged to take for themselves those decisions which they are able to take;

(ii) that where it is necessary in their own interests or for the protection of others that someone else should take decisions on their behalf, the intervention should be as limited as possible and should be concerned to achieve what the person himself would have wanted; and

(iii) that proper safeguards should be provided against exploitation and neglect, and against physical, sexual or psychological abuse.[107]

These policy aims have received very broad support throughout the consultation process. We should, however, now stress that there is no place in the scheme we recommend in this report for the making of decisions which would protect other persons but would not be in the best interests of the person without capacity. We have already argued that the protection of others is the proper preserve of the controlling jurisdiction of the Mental Health Act 1983, whether by way of compulsory detention in hospital or compulsory reception into guardianship.[108] Subject to this proviso, however, our original policy aims still govern our present recommendations.

2.47　In our first consultation paper we invited views on the most desirable broad approach to reform. We were particularly struck by a description of the existing law offered to us by the Master of the Court of Protection; "a string bag, which can stretch further and hold more than a basket but which is essentially a group of holes and whose use is therefore more limited." The string bag may indeed have proved

---

[107] Consultation Paper No 119, para 4.27.

[108] See paras 2.2 - 2.8 above.

to be flexible and capacious enough to contain particular difficulties brought to it in recent years.[109] We have little doubt, however, that many people lack the confidence, money or expertise to test the boundaries of the common law in order to find out whether it might help them too. Nor would the system be able to cope if they did. It is highly unsatisfactory that the law should fail to provide a clearly defined structure within which families and professionals can work together within the law to arrive at the best solution for an individual who cannot make all his or her own decisions. The provision of a court-based remedy is only one function of the law. Another is the delineation of clear principles and procedures which allow for the satisfactory settlement of disputes or difficulties without the need to resort to a court-based remedy in relation to every new set of facts. We are now firmly of the view that an *overall* approach is the only one which offers an adequate response to the variety of law reform problems with which this project is concerned. Before we expound our preferred approach we will say briefly why we have rejected possible less comprehensive solutions.

*Royal prerogative powers*

2.48 We have always doubted whether it would be desirable to seek to solve the perceived gap in the law as regards authority over the "person" of a person without capacity by reviving the ancient all-encompassing prerogative powers of the Crown.[110] There are complex technical arguments which lead us to doubt whether this could in fact be done.[111] In any event the ancient powers depended on a finding of lunacy and probably resulted in every aspect of the person's civil status being transferred to the High Court or to an appointed "committee of the person". Such a procedure is quite out of step with our policy aims, which stress that intervention must be as limited as possible and that a person must be allowed to make every decision which he or she has capacity to make. Many of our consultees were also extremely anxious that decisions should be available locally and with as little formality as possible. To re-adopt a solution which gave exclusive jurisdiction to the Chancery Division of the High Court would not meet their understandable concerns. Many decisions which do need to be taken can be resolved with a single hearing and order, at a much less exalted level of the court hierarchy, and at much lower cost. Although the House of Lords Select Committee observed that there had been some calls for revival of the *parens patriae* jurisdiction,[112] these calls did not find favour with them. Instead the Committee supported our own provisional

---

[109] See the discussion of the development of the High Court declaratory jurisdiction at paras 2.24 - 2.26 above.

[110] Consultation Paper No 119, paras 3.35 - 3.36.

[111] B Hoggett, "The Royal Prerogative in relation to the Mentally Disordered: Resurrection, Resuscitation or Rejection?" in M D A Freeman (ed) *Medicine, Ethics and the Law* (1988) p 85.

[112] Report of the Select Committee on Medical Ethics (1993-94) HL 21-I paras 169 - 171.

proposals that there should be a new jurisdiction in which (inter alia) the commencement, withdrawal or withholding of specific medical treatment could be given legal authority.[113] We are in no doubt that, even if it could be done, the revival of the ancient prerogative jurisdiction would not meet any of the policy aims of law reform in this field and would merely give rise to procedural complexity, waste and expense.

### An incremental approach

2.49 There is a statutory scheme for financial decision-making under Part VII of the Mental Health Act 1983. The 1985 Act provides a statutory scheme for enduring powers of attorney in relation to financial matters. There is a very circumscribed statutory scheme of personal guardianship under the Mental Health Act 1983. There is the High Court declaratory jurisdiction in relation to serious medical decisions, contact between parents and adult children and the validity of advance directives about medical treatment. There are emergency powers in the National Assistance Acts and the Mental Health Act. Although the result is piecemeal and incoherent we are still bound to ask ourselves whether reform could not be satisfactorily achieved by specific reform of some or all of these particular measures.

2.50 We believe it must already be clear from what we have said in this Part of our report that *all* these procedures would require substantial reform to bring them into line with modern policy aims and to make them conform to any consistent principles. They have all emerged in response to particular problems and they all bear the marks of particular inheritances. They do not add up to an effective or practical body of law, and we are convinced that any attempt to make them do so by deletions, insertions and amendments would prove much more daunting and complicated than a single comprehensive solution. If we take as an example Part VII of the 1983 Act, that Act could not simply be amended to give the judge power to make orders about personal welfare and health care matters. The provisions are premised on an "all or nothing" idea of capacity which is incompatible with modern thinking. Equally, there is nothing to indicate the principles upon which the court should act in making or declining to make any particular order. The provisions are also premised on the anomalous nature of the Court of Protection, with decisions of a judicial nature being made by personnel who fall outside the normal judicial hierarchy, and with a single office in central London. Similar root-and-branch objections exist to all the other statutory provisions we have mentioned. In any event, the fact that any solutions which may now be available are scattered throughout the statute-book and the law reports makes for over-elaborate and costly procedures which are often then rationed by price. What is needed is a usable scheme without exorbitant costs, in which the courts take their appropriate place as a decision-making forum of last resort.

---

[113] *Ibid*, paras 245 - 249.

*A unified approach*

2.51 We propose that the "group of holes" within which people who lack mental capacity must now exist should be replaced with a carefully designed and well-constructed legal basket. The existence of a well-woven basket of procedures will ease the burden of many disabled people, carers and professional workers who now live in a state of doubt and uncertainty about what the law allows or requires them to do. Our unified approach will involve the repeal of Part VII of the Mental Health Act 1983 and the repeal of the Enduring Powers of Attorney Act 1985 in its entirety. The draft Bill which we have prepared creates a coherent statutory scheme to which recourse can be had when any decision (whether personal, medical or financial in nature) needs to be made for a person aged 16 or over who lacks capacity. The essential provisions of our draft Bill:

- define lack of capacity

- establish a single criterion for the taking of decisions on behalf of people who lack capacity

- clarify the law where action is taken without formal procedures or judicial intervention

- extend and improve the law for powers of attorney which outlast incapacity

- provide for a decision to be made, or a decision-maker appointed by, a court.

As far as the public law is concerned, our draft legislation creates a new scheme for emergency protective action to be taken where a vulnerable person is at risk of harm; this would replace the emergency powers in sections 115 and 135(1) of the Mental Health Act 1983, and those in section 47 of the National Assistance Act 1947 and the National Assistance (Amendment) Act 1951, which should be repealed.

> **We recommend the introduction of a single piece of legislation to make new provision for people who lack mental capacity; and to confer new functions on local authorities in relation to people in need of care or protection.**

*Age*

2.52 Although the focus of our project has always been *adults* who lack decision-making capacity, we provisionally proposed in our 1993 consultation papers that any new jurisdiction should apply to those aged 16 and over.[114] We explained that a number of the statutory provisions in the Children Act 1989 do not apply to those in the 16-18 age group, or only apply in "exceptional" circumstances.[115] For some purposes in the health care field, patients aged 16 and 17 are treated as if they were of full age.[116] On a practical level, respondents confirmed that both statutory and voluntary sector service agencies tend to have special arrangements for those aged 16 and over, with an emphasis on preparations for independent adult life, making suitable long-term provision if necessary. It is often not at all appropriate simply to continue to offer services designed to support younger children within their families. If continuing substitute decision-making arrangements are needed by someone aged 16 or 17 it may well be because that young person lacks mental capacity and not because he or she is under the age of legal majority. In cases where legal proceedings are required, so that disputes can be resolved or legally effective arrangements made, it would be wasteful to require two sets of legal proceedings to be conducted within a short time period where it is obvious that the problem which has to be resolved will not disappear when the person concerned reaches 18. Respondents, including those who specialise in work with young adults with mental disabilities, supported our proposal to bring those aged 16 and over who lack mental capacity within the new statutory scheme. Most agreed that the resultant overlap with the Children Act 1989 and the inherent jurisdiction of the High Court would pose no great problems in practice.

*We recommend* **that the provisions of the legislation should in general apply to those aged 16 and over.** (Draft Bill, clauses 1(2) and 36(2).)[117]

*Codes of practice*

2.53 A considerable number of our expert respondents expressed the view that any new legislation in this field would have to be accompanied by explanatory guidance. We were impressed by the fact that the Mental Health Act Commission, a body which has direct experience of supervising a statutory scheme supplemented by an authoritative Code of Practice, was strongly of the view that "[g]iven the difficulties of dealing explicitly with the multitudinous issues which are involved in this area" a Code of Practice would be required. Others who favoured a Code of Practice pointed out that it should become available as soon as the legislation is implemented, instead of tagging along years later as happened with the Mental

---

[114] Consultation Paper No 128, paras 3.4 - 3.6; Consultation Paper No 129, paras 2.22 - 2.23; Consultation Paper No 130, para 2.30.

[115] Consultation Paper No 128, para 3.4.

[116] See further Consulation Paper No 129, para 2.22 and n 65.

[117] See paras 5.18, 7.20 and 8.32 below for exceptions to the general rule in special cases.

Health Act Code.[118] In relation to the new public law powers we will be recommending,[119] the existing law already addresses the need for guidance, in providing that local authorities shall act under the general guidance of the Secretary of State.[120] In relation to our private law recommendations, however, the range of the draft legislation is such that a single document might not be the best way of guidance being given. Our respondents pointed to a clear need for guidance about a number of discrete topics and we mention these topics as they arise later in this report.[121] In addition, however, the Secretary of State should have a general power to issue such guidance as he or she may think fit about any matters concerned with the legislation.[122] We hope that the relevant guidance will be available to accompany the new legislation upon its implementation.[123]

> **We recommend** that the Secretary of State should prepare and from time to time revise a code or codes of practice to give guidance in connection with the legislation. There should be consultation before any code is prepared or revised, and preparation of any part of any code may be delegated. (Draft Bill, clause 31(1) and (2).)

---

[118] Most of the Mental Health Act 1983 came into force on 30 September 1983. The Code of Practice prepared in pursuance of s 118 of the Act was not laid before Parliament until December 1989. See further P Fennell, "The Mental Health Act Code of Practice" (1990) 53 MLR 499.

[119] See Part IX below.

[120] Local Authority Social Services Act 1970, s 7.

[121] See paras 3.22, 4.37, 5.39 and 8.54 below and draft Bill, clause 31(1)(a) - (c).

[122] Draft Bill, clause 31(1)(d).

[123] In the cases of the Children Act 1989 and the National Health Service and Community Care Act 1990 comprehensive guidance was prepared and issued so as to be available upon implementation of the main provisions of the two Acts.

# PART III
# TWO FUNDAMENTAL CONCEPTS: LACK OF CAPACITY AND BEST INTERESTS

### Introduction

3.1 In this Part we introduce the two concepts which underlie the legislative scheme we are recommending in this report. The essence of our recommendations is that new legislation should provide a unified and comprehensive scheme within which people can make decisions on behalf of, and in the best interests of, people who lack capacity to make decisions for themselves. We must therefore explain what we will mean by the expressions "capacity" and "best interests".

## (1) Capacity and Lack of Capacity

*Presumption of capacity and standard of proof*

3.2 It is presumed at common law that an adult has full legal capacity unless it is shown that he or she does not. If a question of capacity comes before a court the burden of proof will be on the person seeking to establish incapacity, and the matter will be decided according to the usual civil standard, the balance of probabilities. We proposed in Consultation Paper No 128[1] that the usual civil standard should continue to apply and the vast majority of our respondents agreed with this proposal. A number, however, argued that it would be helpful if the new statutory provisions were expressly to include and restate both the presumption of capacity and the relevant standard of proof.

> *We recommend* that there should be a presumption against lack of capacity and that any question whether a person lacks capacity should be decided on the balance of probabilities. (Draft Bill, clause 2(6).)

*The functional approach*

3.3 In our overview paper we described the variety of tests of capacity which already exist in our law, and we also discussed some medical and psychological tests of capacity.[2] There are three broad approaches: the "status", "outcome" and "functional" approaches. A "status" test excludes all persons under eighteen from voting and used to exclude all married women from legal ownership of property. Under the present law, the status of being a "patient" of the Court of Protection[3]

---

[1] Paragraph 3.42.

[2] Consultation Paper No 119, paras 2.9 - 2.42.

[3] That is, a person "incapable, by reason of mental disorder, of managing and administering his property and affairs", Mental Health Act 1983, s 94(2).

is used in a variety of enactments to trigger other legal consequences.[4] Case-law also suggests that the status of being a "patient" has the extremely significant effect of depriving the patient of all contractual capacity, whether or not as a matter of fact the patient actually had such capacity.[5] The status approach is quite out of tune with the policy aim of enabling and encouraging people to take for themselves any decision which they have capacity to take.

3.4 An assessor of capacity using the "outcome" method focuses on the final content of an individual's decision. Any decision which is inconsistent with conventional values, or with which the assessor disagrees, may be classified as incompetent. This penalises individuality and demands conformity at the expense of personal autonomy. A number of our respondents argued that an "outcome" approach is applied by many doctors; if the outcome of the patient's deliberations is to agree with the doctor's recommendations then he or she is taken to have capacity, while if the outcome is to reject a course which the doctor has advised then capacity is found to be absent.

3.5 We explained in Consultation Paper No 128[6] that most respondents to our overview paper strongly supported the "functional" approach. This also has the merit of being the approach adopted by most of the established tests in English law.[7] In this approach, the assessor asks whether an individual is able, at the time when a particular decision has to be made, to understand its nature and effects. Importantly, both partial and fluctuating capacity can be recognised. Most people, unless in a coma, are able to make at least some decisions for themselves, and many have levels of capacity which vary from week to week or even from hour to hour.

3.6 In view of the ringing endorsement of the "functional" approach given by respondents to the overview paper, we formulated a provisional "functional" test of capacity and set this out in all three of our 1993 consultation papers.[8] This test focused on inability to understand or, in the alternative, inability to choose. We also

---

[4] For example, a "patient" is ineligible to serve on a jury (Juries Act 1974, s 1 Sched 1) and any Public Service Vehicle operator's licence automatically terminates when an individual becomes a "patient" (Public Passenger Vehicles Act 1981, s 57).

[5] See para 2.11 and n 25 above. Heywood & Massey state that this principle will apply while proceedings subsist in the Court of Protection (although not applying to contracts under seal), *Court of Protection Practice* (12th ed 1991) p 227.

[6] Paragraph 3.2.

[7] A party has capacity to marry if able to understand the nature of the contract being entered into, *Hunter v Edney* (1885) 10 PD 93. A person with capacity to marry might, on the same day, lack capacity to make a complex will, *In the Estate of Park, Park v Park* [1954] P 112.

[8] See Consultation Paper No 128, paras 3.7 - 3.43; Consultation Paper No 129, paras 2.3 - 2.24; Consultation Paper No 130, paras 2.18 - 2.20.

made specific provision for those unable to communicate a decision they might in fact have made. We were encouraged to find that many respondents approved our draft test, and we have been able to build on it while taking into account suggestions made on consultation. Although one respondent argued that the whole idea of a test of capacity was ill-conceived and unhelpful,[9] many said that it was vital to have a clear test, and one which catered explicitly for partial and fluctuating capacity. Professor Michael Gunn has referred to "the virtue of certainty" and written that our proposals for a statutory test of capacity will be welcomed, "if for no other reason than introducing certainty and clarity".[10]

3.7 The present law offers a number of tests of capacity depending on the type of decision in issue.[11] Case-law has offered answers to some problems put to it; individual statutes include occasional definitions; the Mental Health Act Code of Practice deals in some detail with capacity to make medical treatment decisions; and Part VII of the 1983 Act addresses capacity in relation to the management of "property and affairs". For the purposes of our new legislative scheme, a single statutory definition should be adopted. We turn now to consider the terms of such a definition.

*A diagnostic threshold*

3.8 In the consultation papers we suggested that a person (other than someone unable to communicate) should not be found to lack capacity unless he or she is first found to be suffering from "mental disorder" as defined in the Mental Health Act 1983. The arguments for and against such a diagnostic hurdle are very finely balanced and they are set out in full in Consultation Paper No 128.[12] In the event, most respondents agreed with our preliminary view that a diagnostic hurdle did have a role to play in any definition of incapacity, in particular in ensuring that the test is stringent enough *not* to catch large numbers of people who make unusual or unwise decisions. There may also be a small number of cases where a finding of incapacity could lead to action which could amount to "detention" as defined in the European Convention of Human Rights. The case-law of the European Court of Human Rights requires that any such detention should be pursuant to a finding of unsoundness of mind based on "objective medical expertise".[13] Although we gave very careful consideration to the arguments against the inclusion of any diagnostic

---

[9] D Carson, "Disabling Progress: The Law Commission's Proposals on Mentally Incapacitated Adults' Decision-Making" [1993] J Soc Wel & Fam L 304, 317.

[10] M Gunn, "The Meaning of Incapacity" (1994) 2 Med L Rev 8, 13.

[11] These are set out in Consultation Paper No 119, paras 2.14 - 2.35.

[12] Paragraphs 3.10 - 3.14.

[13] *Ibid.*

threshold,[14] we have concluded that such a threshold would provide a significant protection and would in no sense prejudice or stigmatise those who are in need of help with decision-making.

3.9     That said, a significant number of respondents, including many who favoured a diagnostic threshold of some sort, expressed misgivings about the new legislation "coat-tailing" on the statutory shorthand of "mental disorder" and the definition set out in the Mental Health Act 1983. The full definition in the 1983 Act is that "'mental disorder' means mental illness, arrested or incomplete development of mind, psychopathic disorder *and any other disorder or disability of mind*".[15] Although this definition is extremely broad and may well cover all the conditions which a diagnostic threshold should cover we no longer favour its incorporation into the new legislation. We learned at first hand in working party meetings how "mental disorder" is equated in many minds, both lay and professional, with the much narrower phenomenon of psychiatric illness or with the criteria for compulsory detention under the Mental Health Act 1983.

3.10    Many respondents raised these issues of "mind-set" about the phrase "mental disorder". Medical professionals advised us that doctors who are not professionally involved with the treatment of psychiatric illnesses (surgeons, gynaecologists, obstetricians or intensive care specialists, for example) have no familiarity with the provisions or definitions of the Mental Health Act and assume that it is irrelevant to their own work. Those who work with people with learning disabilities argued that it would be rare for their clients to have any involvement with the psychiatric specialism. They suggested that the shorthand "mental disorder" is not appropriate and that its adoption could discourage the use of the new scheme for this group of people, for whom it is in fact most specifically designed. A similar point was made in relation to people with brain damage, autism and sensory deficit.

3.11    There may, moreover, be an issue of substance here as well as one of "mind-set". Many respondents to our medical treatment consultation paper were concerned to ensure that all the conditions which can result in incapacity to take medical decisions should be included in the new definition. Some of these will have very little in common with psychiatric illnesses or congenital impairments of the kind addressed by the provisions of the 1983 Act. It was argued that some relevant conditions might not qualify as disorders or disabilities "of mind" at all. Temporary toxic confusional states (whether resulting from prescription or illicit drugs, alcohol or other toxins) and neurological disorders were given as examples. Some doctors would argue that these are properly labelled disorders of *brain* rather than mind.

---

[14]   The arguments are perhaps most trenchantly put by D Carson in "Disabling Progress: The Law Commission's Proposals on Mentally Incapacitated Adults' Decision-Making" [1993] J Soc Wel & Fam L 304, 311- 314.

[15]   1983 Act, s 1(2), emphasis added.

One respondent pointed out that women can lack capacity to take obstetric decisions after prolonged labour, and queried whether the effects of pain and exhaustion were a disability "of mind". We are persuaded that there are many good reasons for departing from the 1983 Act definition.

3.12 We take the view that (except in cases where the person is unable to communicate[16]) a new test of capacity should require that a person's inability to arrive at a decision should be linked to the existence of a "mental disability". The adoption of the phrase "mental disability" will distinguish this requirement from the language of the Mental Health Act 1983 and will stress the importance of a mental condition which has a *disabling effect* on the person's capacity.

> ***We recommend*** **that the expression "mental disability" in the new legislation should mean any disability or disorder of the mind or brain, whether permanent or temporary, which results in an impairment or disturbance of mental functioning.** (Draft Bill, clause 2(2).)

3.13 We took the provisional view in the consultation papers that those who cannot communicate decisions should be included within the scope of the new jurisdiction.[17] We had in mind particularly those who are unconscious. In some rare conditions a conscious patient may be known to retain a level of cognitive functioning but the brain may be completely unable to communicate with the body or with the outside world.[18] In other cases, particularly after a stroke, it may not be possible to say whether or not there is cognitive dysfunction. It can, however, be said that the patient cannot communicate any decision he or she may make. In either case, decisions may have to be made on behalf of such people, and only two respondents expressed the purist view that they should be excluded from our new jurisdiction because they do not suffer from true "mental incapacity". It appears to us appropriate that they should be brought within the scope of our new legislation rather than being left to fend for themselves within the uncertain and inadequate principles of the common law.

*The definition of incapacity*

3.14 The functional approach[19] means that the new definition of incapacity should emphasise its decision-specific nature. A diagnostic threshold of "mental disability" should be included, except in cases of inability to communicate.

---

[16] See paras 3.20 - 3.21 below.

[17] Consultation Paper No 128, paras 3.39 - 3.41; Consultation Paper No 129, para 2.21.

[18] Guillain-Barre or "locked-in" syndrome. See *Auckland Area Health Board v Attorney General* [1993] 1 NZLR 235.

[19] See para 3.5 above.

**We recommend** that legislation should provide that a person is without capacity if at the material time he or she is:

**(1) unable by reason of mental disability to make a decision on the matter in question, or**

**(2) unable to communicate a decision on that matter because he or she is unconscious or for any other reason.** (Draft Bill, clause 2(1).)

*(1) Inability to make a decision*

3.15    It would defeat our aim of offering clarity and certainty were no further guidance given as to the meaning of the phrase "unable to make a decision". In the consultation papers we identified two broad sub-sets within this category, one based on inability to understand relevant information and the other based on inability to make a "true choice". Although many respondents expressed disquiet about the elusiveness of the concept of "true choice", there was broad agreement that incapacity cannot in every case be ascribed to an inability to understand information. It may arise from an inability to use or negotiate information which has been understood. In most cases an assessor of capacity will have to consider both the ability to understand information and the ability to use it in exercising choice, so that the two "sub-sets" should not be seen as mutually exclusive. This was emphasised by Thorpe J in the very important High Court case of *Re C (Adult: Refusal of Treatment)*,[20] perhaps the first reported case to give any clear guidance on questions of capacity in relation to medical treatment decisions.[21] Thorpe J had to make a preliminary finding as to whether the patient concerned had capacity to refuse consent to amputation of his leg. He found it helpful to analyse decision-making capacity in three stages: first, comprehending and retaining information, second, believing it and, third, "weighing it in the balance to arrive at choice." He mentioned that we had proposed a similar approach in our consultation paper.[22] Thorpe J adopted the same approach to the question of capacity in the later case of *B v Croydon District Health Authority*,[23] while upholding a wide view of the scope of section 63 of the Mental Health Act 1983, which authorises treatment for mental disorder regardless of capacity and consent.

---

[20]    [1994] 1 WLR 290.

[21]    Although there is discussion of capacity in *Re T (Adult: Refusal of Treatment)* [1993] Fam 95, and although the ultimate decision was unanimous, each of the four judges involved decided the question of the patient's capacity differently.

[22]    *Re C (Adult: Refusal of Treatment)* [1994] 1 WLR 290, 295.

[23]    20 July 1994, Family Division, unreported judgment of Thorpe J. See para 2.2 and n 5 above.

*(a) Understanding or retaining information*

3.16 Respondents favoured our suggestion that it was more realistic to test whether a person can understand information, than to test whether he or she can understand "the nature of" an action or decision.[24] It was, however, suggested that an ability to "appreciate" information about the likely consequences of a decision might be conceptually different from an ability to understand such information.[25] We prefer to approach this question in a slightly different way, on the basis that information about consequences is one of the sorts of information which a person with capacity understands. Respondents supported the express mention of foreseeable consequences in our draft test, and we still see advantage in drawing attention to the special nature of information about likely consequences, as information which will in every case be relevant to the decision.

> **We recommend that a person should be regarded as unable to make a decision by reason of mental disability if the disability is such that, at the time when the decision needs to be made, he or she is unable to understand or retain the information relevant to the decision, including information about the reasonably foreseeable consequences of deciding one way or another or failing to make the decision. (Draft Bill, clause 2(2)(a).)**

*(b) Using information*

3.17 There are cases where the person concerned can understand information but where the effects of a mental disability prevent him or her from using that information in the decision-making process. We explained in Consultation Paper No 128[26] that certain compulsive conditions cause people who are quite able to absorb information to arrive, inevitably, at decisions which are unconnected to the information or their understanding of it. An example is the anorexic who always decides not to eat. There are also some people who, because of a mental disability, are unable to exert their will against some stronger person who wishes to influence their decisions or against some *force majeure* of circumstances. As Thorpe J said in *Re C*,[27] some people can understand information but are prevented by their disability from being able to believe it. We originally suggested that such cases could be described as cases where incapacity resulted from inability to make a "true choice". Common to all these cases is the fact that the person's eventual decision is divorced from his or her ability to understand the relevant information. Emphasising that the person must be able to use the information which he or she has successfully understood in

---

[24] Consultation Paper No 128, para 3.22.

[25] M Gunn, "The Meaning of Incapacity" (1994) 2 Med L Rev 8, 18 - 20.

[26] Paragraphs 3.31 - 3.35.

[27] *Re C (Adult: Refusal of Treatment)* [1994] 1 WLR 290.

the decision-making process deflects the complications of asking whether a person needs to "appreciate" information as well as understand it. A decision based on a compulsion, the overpowering will of a third party or any other inability to act on relevant information as a result of mental disability is not a decision made by a person with decision-making capacity.

> **We recommend that a person should be regarded as unable to make a decision by reason of mental disability if the disability is such that, at the time when the decision needs to be made, he or she is unable to make a decision based on the information relevant to the decision, including information about the reasonably foreseeable consequences of deciding one way or another or failing to make the decision.** (Draft Bill, clause 2(2)(b).)

*Broad terms and simple language*

3.18 In the draft test of incapacity which appeared in the consultation papers we suggested that a person should be found to lack capacity if he or she was unable to understand an explanation of the relevant information *in broad terms and simple language*. Many respondents supported this attempt to ensure that persons should not be found to lack capacity unless and until someone has gone to the trouble to put forward a suitable explanation of the relevant information. This focus requires an assessor to approach any apparent inability as something which may be dynamic and changeable. As one commentator on our original draft test has written, we chose "to import the patient's right to information by implication into the test of capacity".[28] Further guidance on the way the new statutory language may impinge on the methods of assessing capacity in day to day practice should be given in a code of practice accompanying the legislation.[29]

> **We recommend that a person should not be regarded as unable to understand the information relevant to a decision if he or she is able to understand an explanation of that information in broad terms and simple language.** (Draft Bill, clause 2(3).)

*Excluding imprudence*

3.19 In the consultation papers we invited views on the need for a proviso stipulating that a person should not be regarded as lacking capacity because the decision made would not have been made by a person of ordinary prudence. We provisionally doubted the need for any such proviso.[30] Those we consulted, however,

---

[28] P Fennell, "Statutory Authority to Treat, Relatives and Treatment Proxies" (1994) 2 Med L Rev 30, 39.

[29] See para 3.22 below.

[30] Consultation Paper No 128, para 3.25; Consultation Paper No 129, para 2.16.

overwhelmingly urged upon us the importance of making such an express stipulation. This would emphasise the fact that the "outcome" approach to capacity has been rejected, while recognising that it is almost certainly in daily use.

> **We recommend that a person should not be regarded as unable to make a decision by reason of mental disability merely because he or she makes a decision which would not be made by a person of ordinary prudence.** (Draft Bill, clause 2(4).)

*(2) Inability to communicate a decision*

3.20  As most of our respondents appreciated, we intend the category of people unable to communicate a decision to be very much a residual category. This test will have no relevance if the person is known to be incapable of deciding (even if *also* unable to communicate) but will be available if the assessor does not know, one way or the other, whether the person is capable of deciding or not. Contrary to the views of one expert commentator, "inability to communicate a decision" cannot be paraphrased as "inability to express a view", nor should it be taken to apply to persons with the more severe forms of mental disability.[31] This second category is a fall-back where the assessor cannot say whether any decision has been validly made or made at all but nonetheless can say that the person concerned cannot communicate any decision.

3.21  In relation to persons who are not simply unconscious, many respondents made the point that strenuous steps must be taken to assist and facilitate communication before any finding of incapacity is made.[32] Specialists with appropriate skills in verbal and non-verbal communication should be brought in where necessary.

> **We recommend that a person should not be regarded as unable to communicate his or her decision unless all practicable steps to enable him or her to do so have been taken without success.** (Draft Bill, clause 2(5).)

*The assessment of incapacity: a code of practice*

3.22  Many respondents who commented on our provisional tests of incapacity and were content with the broad outlines of the proposed test addressed themselves to technical questions about the methods of assessment and testing which should be applied. Some were insistent that outdated and discredited psychometric testing

---

[31]  P Fennell, *op cit*, p 37. The writer assumes that the plaintiff in the leading case of *Re F* could have been taken to be unable to communicate a decision about the proposed sterilisation operation. It appears quite clear from the report, however, that she was unable to make a decision about the proposal at all.

[32]  The reference to "reasonable attempts" in the consultation papers was too weak (Consultation Paper No 128, para 3.41; Consultation Paper No 129, para 2.21).

should not be used. There was grave concern about the concept of "mental age". We found the arguments against the use of any such concept extremely compelling. It is unhelpful to discuss, for example, the merits of sterilisation as opposed to barrier contraception for a mature woman with a learning disability on the basis that she is somehow "equivalent" to a child of three.[33] Particular professional bodies, for example the College of Speech and Language Therapists and the British Psychological Society, asserted that their members had the relevant skills to assess mental capacity. Others reminded us that cultural, ethnic and religious values should always be respected by any assessor of capacity. These are all very important matters, albeit not apt subjects for primary legislation. One of the matters which should certainly be covered by a code of practice is the way in which any assessment of capacity should be carried out.

> *We recommend* **that the Secretary of State should prepare and from time to time revise a code of practice for the guidance of persons assessing whether a person is or is not without capacity to make a decision or decisions on any matters.** (Draft Bill, clause 31(1)(a).)

*Existing tests of capacity*

3.23 The new test of incapacity in our draft Bill is expressed to apply "for the purposes of [Part I of] this Act."[34] Schedule 8 to our draft Bill makes consequential amendments to existing statutes, inserting the new definition of what it means to be "without capacity" into any provisions which currently depend on the test in Part VII of the Mental Health Act 1983.[35] We did not consult on the need to replace any existing definitions of capacity *at common law* with the new statutory definition, and our draft Bill makes no attempt to do this. After implementation of the new statutory definition, it is likely that common law judges would consider it and then adopt it if they saw fit. The new definition expands upon, rather than contradicting, the terms of the existing common law tests. The only point of difference is the provision requiring an explanation of the relevant information to have been made, if a finding of incapacity is to have prospective effect.

---

[33] The concept of "mental age" appears in many of the reported cases involving people with learning disabilities. The plaintiff in *Re F* was said to have "the fertility of any other 35-year-old woman" but "the verbal capacity of a two-year-old and the general mental capacity of around a four-or-five-year-old" ([1990] 2 AC 1, 10 and 8). The fact that one can apparently have two mental ages well illustrates the unhelpfulness of the concept. In the recent case of *Cambridgeshire County Council v R and others* evidence was submitted to the effect that the 21-year-old woman concerned had "an overall IQ of 76 with a poor vocabulary indicating that she had a mental age of 13 years" ([1994] 2 FCR 973, 977). This was not accepted as evidence of her incapacity to make the decisions in question.

[34] Draft Bill, clause 2(1).

[35] We recommend the repeal of Part VII in its entirety.

**(2) "Best Interests"**

3.24  We will set out in later Parts of this report a graduated scheme for decision-making, designed to ensure that any substitute decision is taken at the lowest level of formality which is consistent with the protection of the person without capacity, both from the improper usurpation of his or her autonomy and from inadequate or even abusive decision-making. Although decisions are to be taken by a variety of people with varying degrees of formality, a single criterion to govern any substitute decision can be established. Whatever the answer to the question "who decides?", there should only be one answer to the subsequent question "on what basis?".

3.25  We explained in our overview paper that two criteria for making substitute decisions for another adult have been developed in the literature in this field: "best interests" on the one hand and "substituted judgment" on the other.[36] In Consultation Paper No 128 we argued that the two were not in fact mutually exclusive and we provisionally favoured a "best interests" criterion which would contain a strong element of "substituted judgment".[37] It had been widely accepted by respondents to the overview paper that, where a person has never had capacity, there is no viable alternative to the "best interests" criterion.[38] We were pleased to find that our arguments in favour of a "best interests" criterion found favour with almost all our respondents, with the Law Society emphasising that the criterion as defined in the consultation papers was in fact "an excellent compromise" between the best interests and substituted judgment approaches.

> ***We recommend*** **that anything done for, and any decision made on behalf of, a person without capacity should be done or made in the best interests of that person.** (Draft Bill, clause 3(1).)[39]

*The meaning of "best interests"*

3.26  Our recommendation that a "best interests" criterion should apply throughout our scheme cannot be divorced from a recommendation that statute should provide some guidance to every decision-maker about what the criterion requires. No statutory guidance could offer an exhaustive account of what is in a person's best interests, the intention being that the individual person and his or her individual circumstances should always determine the result. In our 1993 consultation papers, however, we suggested that certain principles of general application would always

---

[36]  Consultation Paper No 119, paras 4.22 - 4.23.

[37]  Paragraph 2.14.

[38]  Substituted judgment is provided for in our recommendations about advance health care statements and continuing powers of attorney made by people with capacity who choose to engage in anticipatory decision-making (see Parts V and VII below respectively).

[39]  See paras 6.16 - 6.39 below for special cases where it is justifiable to depart from this general criterion.

be relevant. At least insofar as substitute health-care decisions are concerned, the principles we suggested probably involve a significant departure from the present state of the law. This, as set out in *Re F*, appears to provide that a doctor who acts in accordance with an accepted body of medical opinion is both (1) not negligent and (2) acting in the best interests of a patient without capacity.[40] This apparent conflation of the criterion for assessing complaints about professional negligence with the criterion for treating persons unable to consent has been the butt of vehement criticism.[41] No medical professional or body responding to Consultation Paper No 129 argued in favour of retaining such a definition of "best interests". Many were extremely anxious to see some clear and principled guidance given as to what "best interests" might involve. The British Medical Association, for its part, supported our provisional proposals for statutory guidance "without reservation".

3.27   It should be made clear beyond any shadow of a doubt that acting in a person's best interests amounts to something more than not treating that person in a negligent manner. Decisions taken on behalf of a person lacking capacity require a careful, focused consideration of that person *as an individual*. Judgments as to whether a professional has acted negligently, on the other hand, require a careful, focused consideration of how that particular professional acted as compared with the way in which other reasonably competent professionals would have acted. Lord Mustill, who was both a member of the appellate committee of the House of Lords which decided the case of *Airedale NHS Trust v Bland*[42] and a member of the House of Lords Select Committee on Medical Ethics, said during oral evidence to the latter committee that "[o]ne of the things that is not very good is that the phrase "best interest" has been put into play without any description of what it means. This, I think, actually increases the difficulties for the doctors rather than helps to solve them. What is at the back of my mind is whether perhaps Parliament could give some more specific definition of...what are the relevant factors...".[43]

*A checklist of factors*

3.28   In putting forward a "best interests" criterion in our 1993 consultation papers, we

---

[40]   *Re F (Mental Patient: Sterilisation)* [1990] 2 AC 1, 78, *per* Lord Goff of Chieveley; also at p 69, *per* Lord Griffiths. It may be that all they were saying was that a doctor must *both* (1) meet the standard of care required to avoid liability in negligence and (2) act in an incapacitated patient's best interests. However, since they gave no indication of how those "best interests" were to be identified, some commentators have concluded that the two requirements were in fact one. The speeches of the law lords in *Airedale NHS Trust v Bland* [1993] AC 789 cannot be said to have resolved this important point, and Lord Goff again referred to the professional negligence standard when discussing what was in the patient's best interests (pp 870 - 871). See the discussion in Consultation Paper No 129, paras 3.46 - 3.50.

[41]   See further Consultation Paper No 119, paras 2.22 - 2.24 and notes.

[42]   [1993] AC 789.

[43]   Select Committee on Medical Ethics (1993-94) HL 21-II, Oral Evidence p 21 para 41.

linked it to a checklist of factors which should be taken into account by a substitute decision-maker. Respondents were very supportive of the factors we provisionally identified and largely confined themselves to suggesting refinements of detail. In Consultation Papers Nos 128 and 130 we provisionally proposed three factors; broadly, the person's past and present wishes and feelings, the need to encourage the person to participate and the principle of least restrictive option.[44] In Consultation Paper No 129 three slightly different factors were suggested; broadly, the person's past and present wishes and feelings, any more conservative treatment option and the factors the person concerned would have considered.[45] In that paper we also included a specific and separate duty to consult a "nearest relative" in relation to treatment options.[46] In considering the various fields of decision-making together, we have now developed a single checklist which includes all the elements originally identified as important and commended by consultees. We take this opportunity to repeat some of the general comments made in our report on Guardianship and Custody when we recommended a checklist of factors relevant to the welfare of children. First, that a checklist must not unduly burden any decision-maker or encourage unnecessary intervention; secondly, that it must not be applied too rigidly and should leave room for all considerations relevant in a particular case;[47] thirdly, that it should be confined to major points, so that it can adapt to changing views and attitudes.[48] All these considerations are equally applicable to this project and we have borne them in mind in deciding upon the final content of the checklist we now recommend.

> **We recommend** that in deciding what is in a person's best interests regard should be had to:-
>
> **(1) the ascertainable past and present wishes and feelings of the person concerned, and the factors that person would consider if able to do so;**
>
> **(2) the need to permit and encourage the person to participate, or to improve his or her ability to participate, as fully as possible**

[44] Consultation Paper No 128, para 2.15 (and throughout); Consultation Paper No 130, paras 5.13 - 5.14.

[45] Paragraph 3.56.

[46] Paragraphs 3.62 - 3.67.

[47] Some respondents to our consultation papers expressed concern that a phrase such as "have regard to" was a weak formulation which would not give the decision-maker a strong enough push in the desired direction. Any more forceful form of words could, however, become over-prescriptive and detract from "best interests" as the pre-eminent consideration.

[48] Family Law: Review of Child Law; Guardianship and Custody (1988) Law Com No 172, para 3.19.

**in anything done for and any decision affecting him or her;**

**(3) the views of other people[49] whom it is appropriate and practicable to consult about the person's wishes and feelings and what would be in his or her best interests;**

**(4) whether the purpose for which any action or decision is required can be as effectively achieved in a manner less restrictive of the person's freedom of action. (Draft Bill, clause 3(2).)**

*(1) Wishes, feelings and putative factors*

3.29    This first element in the checklist establishes the importance of individual views. Realistically, the former views of a person who is without capacity cannot in every case be determinative of the decision which is now to be made.[50] Past wishes and feelings may in any event conflict with feelings the person is still able to express in spite of incapacity. People who cannot make decisions can still experience pleasure and distress. *Present* wishes and feelings must therefore be taken into account, where necessary balanced with past wishes and feelings. One of the failings of a pure "substituted judgment" model is the unhelpful idea that a person who cannot make a decision should be treated as if his or her capacity were perfect and unimpaired, and as if present emotions need not also be considered.

3.30    We have included reference to the factors the person "would have considered" if able to do so. Case law in relation to the powers of the Court of Protection to make a "statutory will" has already stressed the importance of considering such matters, whether or not the person concerned has ever had capacity in relation to the act in question. It was said that a judge is to consider the antipathies and affections of the particular person concerned.[51] If that person has never had capacity and "the record of her individual preferences and personality is a blank on which nothing has been written" then the court will assume that she would have been "a normal decent person, acting in accordance with contemporary standards of morality".[52]

3.31    It is worth pointing out that the factors the person concerned "would consider"

---

[49]    Such people would be (1) any person named in advance by the person who is without capacity, (2) a person (for example a spouse, relative or friend) engaged in caring for the person or who is interested in the person's welfare, (3) any attorney whose powers continue after the person has lost capacity and (4) any manager appointed by the court (draft Bill, clause 3(2)(c)(i) - (iv)). See Part VII on attorneys and Part VIII on court-appointed managers.

[50]    See Part V below for a detailed discussion about advance decisions on health care matters.

[51]    *Re D(J)* [1982] Ch 237.

[52]    *Re C (A Patient)* [1991] 3 All ER 866, 870.

might include altruistic sentiments and concern for others. Some organisations representing unpaid family carers disputed the applicability of a "best interests" criterion to situations where one family member is voluntarily caring for another. They argued that such carers should not be expected to consider the best interests of the cared-for person to the exclusion of the interests of anyone else, or of the family as a whole. A number of other respondents argued that people who know they are losing capacity can be anxious to ensure that their deeply felt unselfish desires not to burden their loved ones are still respected in the future. Although we do not accept the argument that the best interests criterion itself is inapplicable in family care-giving situations, we do stress that the inclusion of a specific reference to the factors the person without capacity would have considered if able to do so addresses these very points.

### (2) Maximum participation

3.32    Respondents agreed that even where a person does not have capacity to make an effective decision, he or she may have an important contribution to make to any decision-making process. Those who work with young adults with learning disabilities were particularly anxious that any lack of capacity should be seen as a situation which could and should be altered. In response to comments from such respondents, this factor now includes reference to encouraging the development of decision-making skills.

### (3) Consultation

3.33    A small number of respondents to both Consultation Paper No 128 and Consultation Paper No 129 regretted the fact that we had provisionally rejected the grant of decision-making authority as an automatic consequence of a family relationship.[53] We have described how a small number of respondents also challenged the idea that an unpaid family carer should have to act in the best interests of a person lacking capacity, when the carer's life and interests are intimately bound up with the other person's.[54] While the vast majority of respondents agreed with our approach on both these points, we see the force of the argument that family members should be made visible in the new statutory scheme. This is particularly true for the parents of children born with mental disability, those who live with sufferers from psychotic illnesses and the carers of elderly dementia sufferers. Such family members take on onerous and often distressing responsibilities thereby relieving society as a whole of a heavy burden of care. It has recently been reported that "[t]he vast majority of disabled and older people live in private households, and the majority of these are supported and assisted by their family,

---

[53]    Consultation Paper No 128, para 2.9; Consultation Paper No 129, para 3.70.

[54]    See para 3.31 above.

friends and neighbours".[55]

3.34 A number of respondents highlighted problems with the definition of "nearest relative" in the Mental Health Act 1983. This led them to have reservations about the duty to consult the "nearest relative" which we provisionally proposed in Consultation Paper No 129.[56] It was said that "[t]he one person who has no say in defining who the nearest relative should be under the Mental Health Act is the patient"; the same commentator welcomed our provisional proposal that the patient should be able to name someone who would displace the nearest relative.[57] Others, however, doubted whether it was right in principle that a person should have to execute a document in order to displace a statutory right granted against his or her will to a little-liked relative. There was quite widespread concern that the person conducting the consultation should be able, or indeed obliged, to use discretion in identifying appropriate consultees in each individual case. As Robert Francis QC put it, consultation "in a world of divided families" is necessarily a delicate process. The many helpful comments made on consultation have led us to a less formulaic approach which will still achieve what we and most respondents sought to establish. We can still provide for the person concerned naming in advance a person who is to be consulted. It is also appropriate to mention any person who is engaged in caring for that person. So as to ensure maximum flexibility we have also included reference to any person who is interested in the welfare of the person without capacity. If the person has appointed an attorney who is to retain authority once the donor loses capacity then it is likely that the attorney will be an appropriate consultee, even in relation to matters falling outside the scope of the authority granted by the power of attorney. The same considerations apply where the court has appointed a manager.[58] It is inevitable, on this approach, that the consultee must be a person whom it is "practicable" and "appropriate" to consult. This is not to give absolute discretion to the decision-maker. If challenged, decision-makers will have to be prepared to explain why a consultation which they declined to carry out was either impracticable or inappropriate.

---

[55] G Parker and D Lawton, *Different Types of Care, Different Types of Carer: Evidence from the General Household Survey* (1994) p 3, citing G Parker, *With Due Care and Attention: A Review of Research on Informal Care* (2nd ed 1990). Our own recent report on personal injury compensation referred to evidence highlighting the extent to which close family members of those who have received compensation for injuries have to take on responsibility for their care (Personal Injury Compensation: How Much is Enough? (1994) Law Com No 225, para 3.8).

[56] Paragraphs 3.62 - 3.67.

[57] P Fennell, "Statutory Authority to Treat, Relatives and Treatment Proxies" (1994) 2 Med L Rev 30, 44 and 45.

[58] If the decision in question is within the scope of the decision-making authority of the attorney or manager then the attorney or manager will of course be making the decision himself or herself.

3.35    The process of consultation should be tied to two matters which already concern the prospective decision-maker. First, a relative, carer or person who is closely involved with the person's life as attorney or manager is very likely to have information about the wishes and feelings of the person concerned which might not otherwise filter through to the decision-maker. If the person who now lacks capacity has taken the trouble to nominate someone whom he or she would like to see consulted, then it is even more likely that this nominee has such information. Someone who is in close contact with the person may also have the ability to interpret non-verbal or idiosyncratic signs which give an indication of the person's present wishes and feelings.

3.36    Secondly, a person who is in close contact with the person concerned may have a valid and important view as to what action or decision would be in that person's best interests. Thus, in addition to assisting in ascertaining *information* about the person's wishes the consultee should be invited to express a *view* on the question of "best interests".

*(4) The least restrictive option*

3.37    This factor addresses the "least restrictive alternative" principle which has been developed over many years by experts in this field and is now widely recognised and accepted.

# PART IV
# GENERAL AUTHORITY TO
# ACT REASONABLY

## Introduction

4.1 There can be no doubt at all that action is already taken daily and hourly on behalf of people without capacity, without recourse to the circumscribed statutory schemes outlined in Part II above. In all three of the broad areas we have identified — personal, medical and financial — there is and should remain scope for some informal decision-making without certifications, documentation or judicial determinations. The present law governing such action is far from clear, but a passage in the speech of Lord Goff in *Re F* is a most helpful general statement of the relevant legal principles. In the context of medical treatment, Lord Goff said that "the principle of necessity" governed treatment without consent where:

> "not only (1) must there be a necessity to act when it is not practicable to communicate with the assisted person, but also (2) the action taken must be such as a reasonable person would in all the circumstances take, acting in the best interests of the assisted person."[1]

If this "principle of necessity" applies, actions which would otherwise amount to civil wrongs will be lawful.[2] A similar common law "defence of necessity" may be available to defendants in criminal proceedings.[3]

4.2 We suggested in our consultation papers that there was a strong case for clarifying in statute the circumstances in which decisions can be taken for people who lack capacity, but without anyone having to apply for formal authorisation.[4] We did not envisage this conferring any new power on anyone, but rather as a clarification of the uncertain "necessity" principle. Respondents gave an enthusiastic welcome to our provisional proposals. There was very broad agreement that a statutory provision would be invaluable in dispelling doubt and confusion and setting firm and appropriate limits to informal action.

4.3 Lord Goff referred to the assisted person being unable to communicate. We have already dealt in Part III with our recommendation for a more strenuous requirement that the person concerned must *lack capacity* to make his or her own decision. Lack

---

[1] *Re F (Mental Patient: Sterilisation)* [1990] 2 AC 1, 75.

[2] *Ibid*, 76.

[3] We recently reported that this defence is "of uncertain scope" (Legislating the Criminal Code: Offences Against the Person and General Principles (1993) Law Com No 218 Cm 2370 para 27.4 and notes).

[4] Consultation Paper No 128, para 2.10; Consultation Paper No 129, para 3.40.

of capacity is decision-specific and the authority of another person to act will be limited to those matters where the person lacks capacity.[5] Equally, we have discussed our recommendation for a statutory version of the "best interests" criterion, together with a new checklist of factors to elucidate it.[6] It remains for us to address that part of the law comprised in Lord Goff's statement that any "action taken must be such as a reasonable person would in all the circumstances take."

4.4 In the consultation papers we provisionally proposed a new statutory authority whereby "carers"[7] and "treatment providers"[8] might act reasonably to safeguard and promote the welfare and best interests of a person without capacity. Our original formulation provoked some misunderstanding on consultation, with respondents fearing that disagreements and disputes would arise as to the identity of "the carer" or "the treatment provider" in possession of the authority. In fact, reasonable action at the informal level can be taken by a variety of different people. On any one day it might be reasonable for the primary carer to dress the person concerned in suitable clothes, for the district nurse to give a regular injection and nursing care, for a worker from a voluntary organisation to take the person out on a trip and for another family member to bring round the evening meal and help the person to eat it. Just as the common law affords each person whose actions fall within the principle of necessity a defence to a suit for trespass, so a statutory "general authority" should make the qualifying actions of any such person lawful. It is not, therefore, helpful to suggest that any one person can be defined and identified as the holder of the authority. We consider it preferable to refer to actions which are reasonable for the person doing them to do. This underlines the fact that a number of people may have power to act on any one day. It also serves as a reminder that independent restrictions on who should be taking action are not superseded. Such restrictions might be imposed by employment contracts, by professional rules of conduct or by the law of negligence. In the example given, it would not be reasonable for the district nurse to administer treatment which requires prior authorisation from a registered medical practitioner; nor for the voluntary organisation worker to take actions expressly prohibited by the terms and conditions of his or her employment.

> *We recommend* that it should be lawful to do anything for the personal welfare or health care of a person who is, or is reasonably believed to be, without capacity in relation to the matter in question if it is in all the circumstances reasonable for

---

[5] See para 3.14 above and draft Bill, clause 2(1).

[6] See paras 3.24 - 3.37 above and draft Bill, clause 3.

[7] Consultation Paper No 128, paras 2.10 - 2.13.

[8] Consultation Paper No 129, para 3.40.

**it to be done by the person who does it.** (Draft Bill, clause 4(1).)

The obligation to act in the best interests of the person without capacity, having regard to the statutory factors, will immediately apply to anyone purporting to exercise this "general authority".[9]

4.5   It would be out of step with our aims of policy, and with the views of the vast majority of the respondents to our overview paper, to have any general system of certifying people as "incapacitated" and then identifying a substitute decision-maker for them, regardless of whether there is any real need for one.[10] In the absence of certifications or authorisations, persons acting informally can only be expected to have reasonable grounds to believe that (1) the other person lacks capacity in relation to the matter in hand and (2) they are acting in the best interests of that person.[11]

**Financial matters**

4.6   In the consultation paper we raised the possibility that financial dealings on behalf of a person without capacity might be conducted under statutory authority, and proposed a specific statutory permission to sell a person's chattels for up to £100.[12] The many helpful comments of respondents have enabled us to integrate informal financial decision-making into the "general authority" we have just described. While our respondents confirmed that those who live with and care for persons without capacity often have to spend money on their behalf, many had misgivings about granting a person a new legal right to dispose of another person's property, however low the financial limit might be. Some argued that the existing law in relation to "necessaries" already plays an important role which could be built upon.

4.7   We are not here concerned with ways in which a person may gain access to another person's income or assets. Where assets are held by a bank or other institution, specific authority will certainly be required before they can be transferred to anyone other than the legal owner. We are concerned, rather, with the situation where a carer arranges for something which will cost money to be done for a person without capacity. Family members often arrange for milk to be delivered, or for a hairdresser, gardener or chiropodist to call. More costly arrangements might be for roof repairs, or for an excursion or holiday. In many cases it may be reasonable for

---

[9]   Draft Bill, clause 3.

[10]   See the discussion in Consultation Paper No 128, paras 2.6 - 2.9 and Consultation Paper No 129, paras 3.68 - 3.70.

[11]   Draft Bill, clause 4(1) and clause 3(3). There is no need for any such qualification if these matters are being put before a court for a judicial determination. See para 8.14 and n 28 below.

[12]   Consultation Paper No 128, paras 5.19 - 5.23.

a family member to arrange such matters, if it is done in the best interests of the person without capacity. Such actions could therefore fall within the confines of the general authority to provide for the person's welfare and care recommended above. Who, however, is to pay the provider of the goods or services supplied?

4.8    The law already deals with the enforceability of contracts "with" a person who lacks capacity. If a person lacks capacity to form a particular contract at a particular time, it will be voidable at his or her option *but only if* the other party knew (or ought to have known) of the incapacity.[13] A further common law rule provides that where goods or services which are "necessaries" are supplied to a person with a disability then even if the supplier knew or ought to have known of the disability (and therefore cannot enforce the contract itself) that supplier has a right to recover a reasonable price.[14] This rule has been given a statutory form but only in relation to goods.[15] The statutory definition of "necessaries" in this context requires that they are both suitable to the condition in life of the recipient and suitable to his or her actual requirements at the time of the sale and delivery.[16] It has been suggested that the terms of the statutory provision, with its reference to goods being "sold and delivered to" the person, are not appropriate to people who are so severely disabled that they have been passive participants in the transaction, and that in such cases the doctrine of "agency of necessity" will give the supplier of goods or services a remedy of reasonable remuneration.[17]

4.9    Where there is a question as to who is to pay a supplier in a case where some third party has arranged for something to be supplied to a person without capacity, two distinct problems need to be addressed. The first is whether the supplier should be paid at all, and the answer is already provided by the "necessaries" rules. Insofar as these rules apply to people who lack mental capacity, a single statutory provision applying to both goods and services is required. This should take its place in the new legislation about mental incapacity.

**We *recommend* that where necessary goods are supplied to, or necessary services are provided for, a person without capacity to**

---

[13]    If a person's property is under the control of the Court of Protection, however, the contract will not bind the patient (even if the other party had no knowledge, actual or constructive, of any disability). See para 2.11 and n 26 above.

[14]    If the supply was of money on loan, the lender can recover so much of the loan as was spent on necessaries, *Re Beavan* [1912] 1 Ch 196.

[15]    Sale of Goods Act 1979, s 3(2): "Where necessaries are sold and delivered to a minor or to a person who by reason of mental incapacity or drunkenness is incompetent to contract, he must pay a reasonable price for them."

[16]    Sale of Goods Act 1979, s 3(3).

[17]    G H Treitel, *The Law of Contract* (8th ed 1991) pp 502-503.

**contract, he or she must pay a reasonable price for them.** (Draft Bill, clause 34(1).)[18]

4.10 Since the supplier is to be paid, a second problem arises. Whose money is to be used for this purpose? The "necessaries" rule, even in the new form we recommend, simply establishes that the person without capacity must pay. Where that person lacks the capacity to arrange for such payment to be made, the person who has arranged for the goods or services may also have to arrange settlement of the bill. The legal position of someone in this position is at present extremely obscure. We wish to make it clear that the person who has reasonably arranged for goods or services in the best interests of a person without capacity may also settle the bill for such goods or services in one of three ways. First, if neither the person without capacity (P) nor the person who has arranged for the goods or services (A) can produce the necessary funds, then A may promise that P will pay. Secondly, if P is in possession of money, then A may use that money to pay the supplier. Thirdly, A may choose to pay the supplier with his or her own money and acquire a right to be indemnified out of P's money.[19] In the first and third cases, the problem may simply be that more formal steps for the management of P's property have been put into motion but have not yet resulted in anyone having access to P's funds.

> *We recommend* **that where reasonable actions for the personal welfare or health care of the person lacking capacity involve expenditure, it shall be lawful for the person who is taking the action (1) to pledge the other's credit for that purpose or (2) to apply money in the possession of the person concerned for meeting the expenditure; and if the person taking the action bears the expenditure then he or she is entitled to be reimbursed or otherwise indemnified from the money of the person concerned.** (Draft Bill, clause 4(2).)

4.11 Some people may already be in lawful control of money belonging to the person who is without capacity. They may have been appointed under the Social Security regulations,[20] they may have signing privileges on the other's bank account or they

---

[18] We see no need for any substantive change to the definition of "necessaries" (draft Bill, clause 34(2)). The words "mental incapacity or" in the Sale of Goods Act 1979, s 3(2) should be repealed, with the provisions of the 1979 Act remaining in place in relation to contracts by minors or drunken people (draft Bill, Sched 9).

[19] It has been regretted that English law has no general doctrine of necessitous intervention, whereas it is sound legal policy to recognise a restitutionary claim in such circumstances (Goff and Jones, *The Law of Restitution* (4th ed 1993) p 384). The effect of our recommendation will be to give a restitutionary remedy of reimbursement to those who intervene in the particular circumstances we have outlined, building on the approach advocated by commentators on the law of restitution.

[20] See para 2.16 above.

may simply have been given the money to "look after". The law already imposes obligations in such circumstances and the new statutory provision is not intended to interfere with the general law of bailment, agency or trusts.[21]

### A release of payments scheme

4.12 We explained in Consultation Paper No 128 that a few scattered statutory provisions allow for funds to be released even where their legal owner has lost capacity.[22] We invited views on the merits of creating a single statutory scheme in broad terms, to apply (subject to the person or the institution opting out) to funds held by banks, building societies, insurance companies or other institutions.[23] It was agreed by the great majority of our consultees that there was a pressing need for a simple and inexpensive scheme allowing small sums of money to be realised without the disproportionate expense and formality of a judicial process. Support came from representatives of both sides of the question; from the banking, insurance and building societies' associations and from individuals and organisations who work with informal carers. We were told of many instances where access to a small sum of money which could be put to very good use cannot be gained without undue delay and legal costs. Some of the larger building societies already release funds to carers on a contractual basis, and they confirmed that such arrangements can work well for all concerned. We have refined our provisional proposals in the light of helpful comments on points of detail. We are persuaded that a general statutory scheme can provide adequate safeguards for the interests of the person who lacks capacity without sacrificing the aims of simplicity and low cost. The purpose of the new statutory scheme is to enable a person without capacity to be better cared for by making funds available which can be spent on his or her care and welfare.

> *We recommend* **that there should be a statutory scheme enabling certain payments which would otherwise be made to a person without capacity to be made instead to a person acting on his or her behalf.** (Draft Bill, clause 4(4) and Schedule 1.)

4.13 The scheme we propose is permissive only. It will simply provide that if an institution releases payments in accordance with the terms of the scheme then that institution will be protected from liability for having done so. No fund-holding institution will be obliged to operate the scheme. Those who prefer to look to existing statutory or to contractual authority may do so. Those who prefer to require a judicial order may continue to do so. Those who decline to adopt the scheme in relation to particular sorts of account or product may do so. Equally, a customer who wishes to ensure that the institution with which he or she is depositing money

---

[21] Draft Bill, clause 4(3).

[22] Paragraph 5.6.

[23] Paragraphs 5.11 - 5.13.

should never apply the scheme to his or her funds will be able to opt out.

4.14    In the consultation paper we invited views on the sorts of payment which should be covered by the scheme.[24] Respondents referred us to an extremely wide range of possible payments. We have therefore provided that the new scheme should apply to payments by banks to their customers, by building societies to their members or depositors, by insurance companies to their policyholders, by companies (of dividends or interest on shares or securities) to their shareholders and by trade unions to their members.[25] There should also be provision for the Secretary of State to specify further types of payments.[26]

4.15    The scheme will require the paying institution to enter into an agreement with the proposed recipient of the payments. If the statutory requirements are complied with, the agreement will protect the institution from liability to its now incapacitated customer. The protection will not be available where the customer has opted out, by instructing the institution not to enter into such an agreement. Nor will it be available where the original customer, at any time when the agreement is in force, informs the institution that a payment is not to be made. Nor should the institution benefit from the protection from liability if it has reasonable cause to believe that the recipient is likely to misapply the money received.[27]

4.16    There should be two preconditions to the institution entering into the agreement with the recipient. First, the recipient must furnish a certificate that the original customer is without capacity to manage his or her financial affairs. Respondents to our consultation paper were mostly of the view that such a certificate should be signed by a registered medical practitioner, though many also said that doctors themselves need better guidance on the meaning of incapacity. Secondly, the proposed recipient must state in writing that he or she:

> (1) understands the obligation to apply any money received in the best interests of the original customer, and

> (2) is aware that civil or criminal liability may be incurred if the money is misapplied, and

---

[24]    Consultation Paper No 128, para 5.12.

[25]    Draft Bill, Sched 1 para 1(a) - (e). Payments to *employees* of these institutions will not be covered. The provisions about public service pay and pensions in the Mental Health Act 1983, s 142 are re-enacted with consequential amendments in Sched 1 paras 8 - 10 to the draft Bill. See also draft Bill, Sched 8 para 15.

[26]    Draft Bill, Sched 1 para 1(f).

[27]    *Ibid*, para 2.

(3) is not aware of any other person who has authority to receive the money.[28]

This final stipulation is consistent with the purpose of the scheme, which is to circumvent any need for more formal steps. If the customer has appointed an attorney or if a court has made an order facilitating access to the funds in question then there will be no need for the less formal scheme to be used. In rare cases, an attorney or court-appointed manager may deem it appropriate to consent to another recipient gaining access to the payments. If so, written consent from the attorney or manager should be furnished to the institution.

4.17 In the consultation paper[29] we asked whether the scheme should be subject to a financial limit. Those we consulted in the banking industry took the view that an informal scheme might be appropriate where what was needed was the release of small sums to settle the cost of a person's maintenance and provide a modest income. They were, however, extremely anxious that the scheme should not be used to circumvent the need for a proper and authoritative judicial enquiry where control over a person's capital, or even over large sums of income, was to be ceded to someone else. A number of other respondents were keen to set some limit to the scheme, while acknowledging the considerable difficulties of doing so. Any figure chosen might be a high proportion of one person's life savings but only cover a few week's maintenance for another person in an exclusive private nursing home.

4.18 We are convinced by the results of our consultation that the scheme must be made subject to a financial limit.[30] The agreement between institution and recipient must, in any event, detail the payments to which the agreement applies and the agreed maximum amounts which may be realised by the recipient.[31] The statutory maximum will simply set an upper limit to the figures which may be set in any individual agreement. In some cases much lower figures will be agreed as appropriate. It is our view that the statutory limit should be £2,000 per annum.[32] In the case of one-off payments (such as the proceeds of insurance policies) this will operate as a capital limit. Where the agreement provides for periodic payments this would represent almost £39 per week. There should be power for the Secretary of

---

[28]  Draft Bill, Sched 1 para 3.

[29]  Consultation Paper No 128, para 5.12.

[30]  We have benefited from discussions with our counterparts in the Scottish Law Commission who are also inclined to set a defined maximum in any comparable scheme they may recommend.

[31]  Draft Bill, Sched 1 para 4(1).

[32]  *Ibid*, para 4(3).

State to increase this financial limit from time to time.[33]

4.19    A number of our respondents also raised the question of a maximum time limit for these arrangements. In some of our other provisional proposals in the consultation paper we had indicated disquiet about indefinite arrangements being made for people without capacity.[34] We are now persuaded that agreements made under the new release of funds scheme should be subject to a statutory maximum time limit of two years. This will cause no difficulty in relation to agreements designed to facilitate the release of a small capital sum, such as the proceeds of an insurance policy. Where the agreement is for periodic payments then it will expire after a maximum period of two years but the recipient may of course furnish new documentation at the end of that period, with a new agreement then being made.[35]

4.20    Direct payments to those providing services to the person without capacity raise less difficult questions about the protection of that person; a number of our respondents suggested that such payments should be covered by any new scheme. It was said that payments could be made by standing order or direct debit to a landlord or residential care home owner, and to the utility companies. The details will be for the institution and recipient to cover in the terms of their agreement. We have provided that the fund-holding institution may make payments direct to persons or bodies providing accommodation, goods or services to the person who is without capacity (in addition to the maximum annual payment of £2,000 to a recipient).[36]

4.21    We have sought to allow individual institutions flexibility in adapting the statutory scheme to their particular requirements. The documentary requirements and the statutory limits will, however, give the necessary protection to customers who have lost capacity to deal with their financial affairs. An institution will have no protection against liability for any loss to the estate of the person without capacity if the statutory maxima have been breached.

### Appointees under the Social Security Regulations

4.22    For many people lacking capacity who have little capital and receive income only from state benefits, the necessary financial arrangements can be made under the Social Security Regulations.[37] Regulation 33 provides that the Secretary of State may

---

[33]    *Ibid*, para 6.

[34]    Consultation Paper No 128, para 5.8 on Social Security appointees and para 5.28 on receivership appointments by the Court of Protection.

[35]    Draft Bill, Sched 1 para 4(2). Paragraph 6 provides that the Secretary of State should have power to alter this maximum time limit.

[36]    Draft Bill, Sched 1 para 5.

[37]    The Social Security (Claims and Payments) Regulations 1987 (SI 1987 No 1968).

appoint someone to act for a claimant who is "unable to act". It appears that this administrative scheme is very widely used, though the Department of Social Security was unable to provide us with any statistics as to the numbers of Regulation 33 appointees.

4.23 In the consultation paper we invited views on the need for tighter regulation of those acting as appointees under Regulation 33.[38] Many respondents called for improvements to the scheme, with concern focusing on the sketchy nature of the initial enquiry as to whether a person is "unable to act", and on the lack of supervision once an appointment is made. In view of the fact that the Social Security Regulations are the responsibility of the Secretary of State (now exercising the power in section 5 of the Social Security Administration Act 1992) we express the results of our consultation on these matters as suggestions for the reform of the secondary legislation. We have not prepared any new draft regulations.

4.24 Our respondents were almost unanimous in agreeing with our provisional view[39] that the test to be applied before making a Regulation 33 appointment should be a test of the claimant's capacity. *We suggest* that the question should be whether the claimant has capacity to exercise his or her rights under the Social Security Administration Act 1992 and to receive or deal with sums payable, and that the new definition of incapacity set out in our draft Bill should be adopted in the regulations.

4.25 We provisionally proposed that an appointee should agree to submit an account if required to do so, and that appointments should be time-limited to six or twelve months.[40] Although respondents were concerned about the possibility of abuse when appointments are unsupervised and open-ended, they also acknowledged that many appointees are family members struggling to fulfil onerous caring obligations. It was said that it is sometimes extremely difficult for the Department of Social Security to find anyone who is prepared to act as appointee at all. It was also said that the short time limits we had suggested were unrealistic in the light of the Department's available resources and when many claimants suffer from a long-term incapacitating condition. In the light of comments by consultees, *we suggest* that consideration should be given to the sending out of an annual enquiry form to be completed by all appointees, giving at least a broad indication of the items on which money has been spent. *We also suggest* that a lengthy maximum time limit, of perhaps three to five years, should be imposed on appointments, with a requirement that appointees apply for re-appointment after that time. While allowing appointees to operate for a reasonable period of time without repeated form-filling, such a time-limit would impose a measure of control and periodic supervision.

---

[38]   Consultation Paper No 128, paras 5.7 - 5.8.

[39]   *Ibid*, para 5.7.

[40]   *Ibid*, para 5.8.

4.26 Many of our consultees were very concerned about the apparently not uncommon practice of a nursing or residential home manager acting as a Regulation 33 appointee for one or more residents. We suggested in Consultation Paper No 128[41] that in some circumstances there may be no better candidate to act as appointee. We went on to ask whether any further guidance was needed when a hospital or home manager is acting as an appointee.[42]

4.27 The Department of Social Security confirmed to us that its policy is always to seek a friend or relative to act as appointee, and to appoint a home manager only as a last resort. The Government's guidance, as embodied in the code of practice for residential care, is that "[p]roprietors and staff should not become involved in the handling and management of residents' monies".[43] Many of our respondents wholeheartedly supported this principle but said that it is not adhered to in practice. Some suggested that local authority staff or voluntary sector workers should be brought in if no relative or friend will act, so that home managers and proprietors are never appointed to handle residents' monies. Much of the concern they expressed related to issues of practice and procedure which apply equally where hospital patients or home residents do possess capacity to deal with their own finances. *We suggest* that the concerns of our respondents should be given due consideration by those responsible for these matters in the Departments of Health and Social Security. We also suggest that departmental guidance should always cater expressly for the specific problems which arise in relation to persons who lack decision-making capacity.

4.28 The existing law in Scotland differs significantly from ours in providing that hospital managers may take over the management of a patient's affairs where the responsible medical officer states that the patient is incapable of managing and administering them.[44] We understand that the Scottish Law Commission will recommend that a similar scheme with improved procedures should be extended to residents of residential and nursing homes who are certified to lack capacity. We have explained that our respondents were opposed in principle to the managers of institutions running the finances of incapacitated residents. We therefore make no recommendations which would bring our law into line with Scots law in this regard.

---

[41] Paragraphs 5.9 - 5.10.

[42] Paragraphs 5.14 - 5.18.

[43] Centre for Policy on Ageing, *Home Life: a code of practice for residential care* (1984) p 65 para 56. The Secretaries of State for Social Services and Wales ask local authorities to regard this document "in the same light as the general guidance that we issue from time to time under our powers in section 7 of the Local Authority Social Services Act 1970" (*ibid*, p 7).

[44] Mental Health (Scotland) Act 1984, s 94(1).

### Restrictions on the general authority

4.29 One benefit of setting out a clear general authority in statute is that the statute can then specify which matters fall outside the scope of that general authority. The general law already provides that certain acts can only be effected by a person acting for himself or herself. Examples would be entering into marriage or casting a vote in a public election. For the avoidance of doubt, our draft Bill lists certain matters which must be done by a person acting for him or herself.

> *We recommend* **that no person should be able to make decisions about the following matters on behalf of a person without capacity:**
>
> **(1) consent to marriage, (2) consent to have sexual relations, (3) consent to a divorce petition on the basis of two years separation, (4) agreement to adoption or consent to freeing a child for adoption, (5) voting at an election for any public office or (6) discharging parental responsibilities except in relation to a child's property. (Draft Bill, clause 30.)**

In many areas, however, it is at present quite unclear whether action may lawfully be taken on behalf of a person without capacity. If no-one is sure what can lawfully be done, then no-one can be sure what cannot and must not be done. We will now consider a number of actions which should never be lawful simply on the basis of the broad general authority to act reasonably in another's best interests.

*(1) Coercion and confinement*

4.30 We suggested in our consultation papers[45] that a person without capacity should not be forced to comply with a proposed action to which he or she objects without the authorisation of a judicial body. In the light of concern about restraint techniques which are adopted to prevent disruptive or risk-taking behaviour by disabled people, we also suggested that there should be a general prohibition against the confinement of a person without capacity.[46] In each case, we suggested a proviso where the coercive or confining action was essential to prevent an immediate risk of serious harm to the person concerned or to others. As we explain below, we are now persuaded that no reference to harm to *others* is called for in any new provision, since this contingency is adequately covered in the existing law.

4.31 Our respondents confirmed that a line has to be found between justifiable protection and persuasion of people who have impaired decision-making capacity on the one

---

[45] Consultation Paper No 128, para 2.18; Consultation Paper No 129, para 3.45.

[46] Consultation Paper No 128, para 2.17 and n 21, where the effect of the European Convention on Human Rights was discussed.

hand and unjustified restraint or coercion, including mental coercion, on the other. The general law already draws certain lines. Most acts of confinement or coercion will amount to criminal offences and/or civil wrongs. The criminal law allows various defences where the act of coercion or confinement is justified by "duress of circumstances", self-defence or the prevention of crime.[47] The defence of consent will, however, often be more relevant if the reality is that the coercive or confining action was intended to protect the "victim" himself or herself. Where, in the cases we are considering, the person against whom the coercive or confining action is directed lacks the capacity to consent, then the law may bite against a well-meaning carer in an unduly harsh way. The uncertain defence of necessity[48] may be all that the carer can hope to rely on.[49] Conversely, however, the uncertain defence of necessity might, in some circumstances, give an unduly broad latitude to those who decide to confine or coerce those under their care. Some of our consultees confidently asserted that locking a door on a demented resident is illegal, but we doubt the accuracy of this claim. Others expressed concern about the lawfulness of "time out" techniques, which can involve both confinement and coercion, used in some behavioural therapies. Taking into account that *Re F*[50] established that a major abdominal operation with irreversible effects was lawful according to the principle of necessity, it is highly likely that in appropriate circumstances acts of confinement or coercion could equally be found lawful if performed "in the best interests of" the person concerned. In any event, it is clear and hardly surprising that many people with day-to-day care of other people who lack capacity have no idea what actions they may or may not take within the law. Our consultees confirmed that there is a pressing need for this lack of clarity to be resolved.

4.32    We saw some force in the arguments put forward by some of our expert legal respondents, to the effect that any stipulation about confinement and coercion would be redundant, since the proposed general authority is already constrained by the notions of both reasonableness and best interests. We also took careful note of the views of those professional and family carers who argued that enactment of the "high principle" that confinement and coercion are unlawful would mean many homes and hospitals grinding to a standstill. We reject, however, the suggestion made by a small number of respondents, that no "objection" by a person without capacity need be given any credence. There is an important distinction between a person passively acquiescing in something and a person who raises positive objections, whether in words or by actions, and therefore has to be subjected to

---

[47]   See our report on Legislating the Criminal Code: Offences against the Person and General Principles (1993) Law Com No 218 Cm 2370 paras 35.1 - 40.4.

[48]   See para 4.1 and n 3 above.

[49]   See the discussion of the interaction of the defence of "duress of circumstances" and the defence of "necessity" in Law Com No 218, *op cit*, paras 35.4 - 35.7.

[50]   *Re F (Mental patient: Sterilisation)* [1990] 2 AC 1.

physical force to secure compliance.

4.33 We have concluded that two important messages can be conveyed by a new statutory provision about confinement and coercion. First, the fact that the civil liberties of people without capacity are regularly infringed by coercive and restraining treatment can be challenged by the introduction of a statutory prohibition against such treatment expressed in clear terms. On the other hand, however, the difficult realities of the caring situation can be addressed by a clear statement of the circumstances in which coercive or confining behaviour will in fact be justified. This will provide reassurance to people who can at present only rely on common law defences whose scope and very existence are known only to a select band of legal experts.

> *We recommend* that the general authority to provide care to a person without capacity should not authorise the use or threat of force to enforce the doing of anything to which that person objects; nor should it authorise the detention or confinement of that person, whether or not he or she objects. This provision is not to preclude the taking of steps which are necessary to avert a substantial risk of serious harm to the person concerned. (Draft Bill, clause 5.)

We are concerned here with informal acts and decision-making. If the court or a court-appointed manager has taken a decision after due consideration and due process then that decision should of course be capable of being enforced in the usual way.[51]

*(2) The superior authority of an attorney or manager*

4.34 Informal action is only justifiable where it is not in conflict with a judicial decision, or a decision by a person with formal legal powers. The general authority should not validate an action which conflicts with a decision made by an attorney acting under a valid power of attorney[52] or by a manager appointed by the court.[53] Situations may, however, arise where a person without formal authority seeks to challenge some decision by that attorney or manager, on the basis that it is not in the best interests of the person without capacity. In most circumstances, the formal decision-maker's authority will stand until the court removes it, whether by revoking a power of attorney or varying or discharging an order appointing a manager. Special provision needs to be made for those unusual situations where the decision of the person with formal authority would lead to the death of the person without capacity

---

[51] See para 8.11 below.

[52] See Part VII below on enduring and continuing powers of attorney.

[53] See Part VIII below.

before the court can issue any determination. In those circumstances, the person without formal authority should be entitled to take minimal steps to maintain the other person's life.

> **We recommend** that the general authority should not authorise the doing of anything which is contrary to the directions of, or inconsistent with a decision made by, an attorney or manager acting within the scope of his or her authority. However, this restriction will not apply to actions necessary to prevent the death of, or a serious deterioration in the condition of, the person concerned while an order is being sought from the court.
> (Draft Bill, clause 6.)

*(3) The superior authority of an advance refusal of treatment*

4.35 The topic of "advance directives" for health care was considered in detail in Consultation Paper No 129[54] and we discuss our recommendations in Part V below. It should be noted here that, in relation to health care decisions, an effective anticipatory refusal of treatment will restrict the scope of the general authority to treat.[55]

*(4) Independent supervision in health care matters*

4.36 There was unanimous agreement from our consultees that certain serious and controversial health care procedures should always be subject to independent supervision.[56] Special provisions, which we will discuss in Part VI below, will therefore restrict the scope of the informal general authority in particular cases.[57]

**Acting reasonably: a code of practice**

4.37 A number of our consultees qualified their enthusiasm for a general authority for people to act at the informal level by urging that a code of practice giving guidance as to what might be "reasonable" in particular circumstances should be prepared and issued. We agree that further guidance about the necessarily broad terms of the statute should be given, and see this as one of the matters which should be addressed by a code of practice.

> **We recommend** that the Secretary of State should prepare and from time to time revise a code of practice for the guidance of persons acting in pursuance of the general authority to act and

---

[54] Paragraphs 3.1 - 3.36.

[55] See para 5.20 below and draft Bill, clause 9(2).

[56] Our provisional proposals were made in Consultation Paper No 129, Part VI.

[57] These cases are described in clauses 7 and 8 of the draft Bill.

the statutory restrictions which apply to it. (Draft Bill, clause 31(1)(b).)

### An offence of ill-treatment

4.38   In Consultation Paper No 128[58] we provisionally proposed that the existing offence of ill-treating a "mentally disordered patient"[59] should be extended to protect anyone without capacity. Many respondents supported the creation of a new offence, and also expressed concern about the efficacy of the criminal justice system in protecting people with mental disabilities. The points they raised about the attitude of the police and prosecuting authorities, and about the inflexibility of procedural rules which mean that witnesses with disabilities do not get the help they deserve, are outside the scope of this project.[60] We do, however, see a need for a specific offence of ill-treatment, independent of the existing offence in the Mental Health Act. The new offence should address the fact that the draft Bill creates a number of ways in which a person can acquire powers over another person who lacks some decision-making capacity. It is right that a person with such powers should be subject to criminal sanction for ill-treating or wilfully neglecting the other person concerned.

*We recommend* **that it should be an offence for anyone to ill-treat or wilfully neglect a person in relation to whom he or she has powers by virtue of the new legislation. (Draft Bill, clause 32(1).)**[61]

---

[58]   Paragraph 2.22.

[59]   Mental Health Act 1983, s 127(2).

[60]   As recommended by the Royal Commission on Criminal Justice ((1993) Cm 2263 p 125) the Home Secretary has asked the Commission to consider the law of England and Wales relating to hearsay evidence and evidence of previous misconduct in criminal proceedings; and to make appropriate recommendations, including, if they appear to be necessary in consequence of changes proposed to the law of evidence, changes to the trial process, Written Answer, *Hansard* (HC) 28 April 1994, vol 242, col 245. These terms of reference may be relevant to the difficulties faced by witnesses with disabilities.

[61]   The offence can be committed by anyone acting informally (as described in this Part), a donee of a Continuing Power of Attorney (see Part VII below) or a manager appointed by the court (see Part VIII below) (draft Bill, clause 32(2)). It should be punishable on indictment by a fine or a maximum of two years imprisonment (draft Bill, clause 32(3)).

# PART V
# ADVANCE STATEMENTS ABOUT HEALTH CARE

### Introduction

5.1 In Consultation Paper No 129[1] we made provisional proposals for legislation to govern "anticipatory decisions" about health care. Our aim was to clarify the legal status of health care decisions which are intended to have effect even if a patient loses the capacity to make such a decision at some future time. Anticipatory decisions of this kind are often discussed under the rubric of "advance directives". Some commentators also use the term "living will".[2] A disadvantage of both these terms is that they concentrate attention on the existence and terms of a piece of paper. The fundamental question which has to be considered is the nature and legal effect of the views which have been expressed by the person concerned. Our approach to this topic will emphasise that there is a clear distinction to be drawn between the legal effect of an advance *expression of views and preferences* on the one hand, and an advance *decision* on the other. If the patient has in fact made an advance decision then a further important distinction is to be drawn between the legal effect of a decision *in favour of* a particular (or all) treatment and a decision *against* such treatment. In this Part, we will first explain how the recommendations we have already made in Part IV make satisfactory legal provision to accommodate many of the views which are commonly expressed in "advance directives" and "living wills". We will go on to recommend specific statutory provision for those cases where the patient has *decided* in advance to *refuse* some particular form of treatment.

5.2 1993 saw the common law in relation to anticipatory health care decisions receiving unwonted attention. We discussed the comments made by Lord Keith and Lord Goff in the case of *Airedale NHS Trust v Bland*[3] in our consultation paper.[4] In October 1993 judgment was given in the High Court in the case of *Re C*.[5] Thorpe J held in that case that a patient with capacity to make a decision about a particular proposed treatment (amputation of a gangrenous leg) was entitled to an injunction

---

[1]  Paragraphs 3.1 - 3.36.

[2]  In the course of the House of Lords debate on the Report of the Select Committee on Medical Ethics Lord Allen of Abbeydale suggested that the description "living will" reflected an American gift for "phrases which defy intellectual analysis" (*Hansard* (HL) 9 May 1994, vol 554, col 1363). Lord McColl of Dulwich suggested that "declaration" should be used instead of "directive", which, meaning "an order, an issue of command", is "technically incorrect" (*ibid*, col 1372).

[3]  [1993] AC 789.

[4]  Consultation Paper No 129, para 3.2.

[5]  *Re C (Adult: Refusal of Treatment)* [1994] 1 WLR 290.

to prevent him ever being subjected to that treatment without his express written consent, even if he should in future lose his decision-making capacity. This case-law, the publication of our consultation paper and the inquiry conducted by the House of Lords Select Committee on Medical Ethics all generated considerable public and scholarly debate about the legal, ethical, clinical and practical issues involved in anticipatory decisions about health care.[6]

5.3    A clear majority of those who responded to our consultation paper supported our provisional proposal that legislation should be introduced to govern the topic of anticipatory decisions.[7] On the other hand, a number of respondents, which then included the British Medical Association ("BMA"), argued that legislation would be unnecessary and unhelpful, and that the common law could be relied on to provide adequate guidance. In January 1994, however, the Council of the BMA decided to alter its policy and to approve in principle the concept of limited legislation which would place the law in this area on a clear statutory basis.[8] Although some of our other respondents expressed the view that advance directives should not be "legally binding" it became clear, on closer examination, that they were applying this argument only to directives which had not anticipated the particular problem or had not taken into account developments in medical science. A smaller group, defined by firm Christian and specifically Roman Catholic views, opposed the introduction of legislation because they did not wish to see anticipatory decisions by patients becoming binding on doctors in all circumstances. One respondent who shared the view that advance decisions should not always be binding on doctors argued that legislation was in fact required to establish this (by reversing the effect of the common law).[9] Our consultation revealed many genuine concerns which any new law must address. On the other hand, it reflected an almost unanimous view that patients should be enabled and encouraged to exercise genuine choice about treatments and procedures.

5.4    Many "advance directives" seek to govern treatment which might be given at the end of life. The topic therefore came within the terms of reference of the House of

---

[6]    See for example, R Gordon and C Barlow, "Competence and the right to die" (1993) 143 NLJ 1719; A Holt and S Viinikka, "Living wills" Legal Action, April 1994; S Meredith, "A Testament of Intent" (1994) 91/15 Law Soc Gaz 26; D Morgan, "Odysseus and the Binding Directive: Only a Cautionary Tale?" (1994) 14 Legal Studies 411; K Stern, "Advance Directives" (1994) 2 Med L Rev 57; E Roberts, "Re C and the Boundaries of Autonomy" (1994) 10 PN 98.

[7]    Consultation Paper No 129, para 3.11.

[8]    BMA Statement on Advance Directives, revised January 1994. The Annual General Meeting of the BMA has not yet reconsidered the question of advance directives. The BMA and Royal College of Nursing are currently co-ordinating a steering group to prepare a code of good practice about advance statements. See para 5.39 below.

[9]    The Linacre Centre for Health Care Ethics.

Lords Select Committee chaired by Lord Walton of Detchant.[10] That committee received a considerable body of evidence on the subject of advance directives, much of it overlapping with the responses we received to our consultation paper.[11] In its report, the committee commended the development of advance directives,[12] and recommended that the colleges and faculties of the health-care professions should develop a code of practice to guide their members about the issue.[13] It saw no necessity for "legislation for advance directives generally", fearing in particular that "it could well be impossible to give advance directives in general greater legal force without depriving patients of the benefit of the doctor's professional expertise and of new treatments and procedures which may have become available since the advance directive was signed".[14] This conclusion effectively challenges the notion that an advance directive is always a unilateral boon to all patients. We accept that there is a need to address the danger that a patient who has made an advance directive could unwittingly be depriving himself or herself of professional medical expertise or of beneficial advances in treatment.

5.5    Two of our respondents specifically told us that, although they did not favour free-standing legislation about advance directives, they accepted the need for it in the context of a new legislative scheme to regulate decision-making of all types on behalf of those lacking capacity. It is not, in our view, open to us to omit all reference to the increasingly visible issue of health care advance directives from the scope of the integrated legislative scheme we set out in this report. We have, however, benefitted greatly from the inquiry and conclusions of the Select Committee and, in formulating our recommendations, we have sought to address the reservations it expressed about legislative reform.

**Requests for illegal, futile or inappropriate treatment**

5.6    One of the matters which has always concerned doctors is the notion that an "advance directive" could somehow require a doctor to carry out a positive act which is either illegal or contrary to his or her clinical judgment.[15] Since no contemporaneous or oral statement by a patient can have any such effect, this may be another example of excessive influence being attributed to the fact that "advance directives" are often written down and signed. It is quite clear that the law will not

---

[10]    See para 1.7 and n 13 above for the Select Committee's terms of reference.

[11]    The evidence is summarised in the Report of the Select Committee on Medical Ethics (1993-94) HL 21-I paras 181 - 215. The oral and written evidence appears in two companion volumes, (1993-94) HL 21-II and (1993-94) HL 21-III respectively.

[12]    Paragraph 263.

[13]    Paragraph 265.

[14]    Paragraph 264.

[15]    See the discussion in Consultation Paper No 129, para 3.12.

"second-guess"[16] a doctor who has formed a reasonable and responsible clinical judgment that a particular form of treatment is not called for because it would be futile or inappropriate. No document signed by a patient in advance can override such a judgment.

**Acting reasonably in a patient's best interests**

5.7 The recommendations we have made in Part IV above at once clarify and modify the ability of a treatment provider lawfully to treat a patient who lacks capacity to consent to a proposed treatment. Anything done in relation to the health care of a person who lacks capacity to make his or her own decision about that matter must be (1) reasonable and (2) in the best interests of that person.[17] In deciding what is in his or her best interests regard must be had to four listed matters, namely:

(1) the ascertainable past and present wishes and feelings of the person, and the factors he or she would consider,

(2) the need to permit and encourage the person to participate,

(3) the views of other appropriate people, and

(4) the availability of an effective less restrictive option.[18]

As far as health care is concerned, these new rules mean that treatment will not be lawful unless it is both reasonable and in the best interests of the particular patient. It will not be in the best interests of the patient unless the doctor has taken into account the ascertainable past and present wishes and feelings of the patient and the factors which he or she would have considered. If the treatment given is not lawful then the doctor is liable to an action in damages for battery if, as is likely, he or she has touched the patient.

5.8 These new substantive rules of law will provide a wholly appropriate framework within which many of the statements made in "advance directives" or "living wills" may be considered and assessed. The starting-point is the rule that the treatment provider must act in the patient's best interests. This answers the Select Committee's fear that patients might be deprived of the benefit of "the doctor's professional expertise".[19] The reference to factors the patient "would have considered" means that the treatment-provider should relate the patient's advance

[16] I Kennedy and A Grubb, *Medical Law: Text with Materials* (2nd ed 1994) p 1278.

[17] See para 4.4 above and draft Bill, clauses 4(1) and 3(1).

[18] See paras 3.28 and 3.37 above and draft Bill, clause 3(2).

[19] See para 5.4 above.

statements to any new treatments or procedures which have since been developed, another matter which concerned the Select Committee and many of our respondents.

5.9 We can illustrate the effect of the proposed new rules of law by considering two provisions from "advance directives" submitted to us by consultees. "I wish to be kept alive for as long as reasonably possible using whatever forms of medical treatment are available."[20] Although the health care provider will still be required to make a clinical judgment about what forms of medical treatment to make available,[21] this wording gives a clear indication that the patient wishes to receive all life-prolonging treatments deemed appropriate. Alternatively, a patient may have stated, "I wish it to be understood that I fear degeneration and indignity far more than I fear death. I ask my medical attendants to bear this statement in mind when considering what my intentions would be in any uncertain situation."[22] A doctor might form the view that it was in the best interests of the first patient, but not of the second, to give an invasive treatment in circumstances where the likelihood was that the patient would survive to regain mental capacity but would become completely and permanently dependent on a ventilator.

**Anticipatory decisions by patients**

5.10 We suggested in the consultation paper that there is a distinction between an "anticipatory decision" about whether to accept or reject medical treatment in the future and "views" or "wishes and feelings" about medical treatment expressed prior to incapacity.[23] Few of our respondents appreciated this distinction, and most of them concentrated instead on the different question of whether an "advance directive" is in existence or not. Many of the difficulties which are laid to the door of "advance directives" are in fact difficulties which apply only to anticipatory *decisions*. We have already shown that some model advance directives contain statements which are more properly described as statements of wishes than as "anticipatory decisions". The general rules of law we are recommending adequately cater for such statements. If we now consider whether this is equally true where the patient has made an anticipatory decision, whether to consent to a particular treatment or refuse it, we will find that any special difficulties are limited to cases where the patient has made an anticipatory decision to *refuse* treatment.

**Advance consents to treatment**

5.11 Many model "advance directives" comprise anticipatory decisions to consent to

---

[20] The Terrence Higgins Trust and King's College London, Living Will (2nd ed 1994), quoted with kind permission.

[21] See para 5.6 above.

[22] Voluntary Euthanasia Society, Advance Directive, quoted with kind permission.

[23] Consultation Paper No 129, para 3.21.

particular forms of treatment. "I consent to being fed orally and to any treatment that may...relieve pain and suffering."[24] "[My consent] includes the administration of non-blood volume expanders such as saline, dextran, Haemaccel, hetastarch and Ringer's solution."[25] "My directions are...that any distressing symptoms...are to be fully controlled by appropriate analgesic or other treatment...I consent to anything proposed to be done...in compliance with the directions expressed above."[26]

5.12    It is no accident that such case-law on the validity of anticipatory medical decisions as now exists concentrates on advance refusals of consent. Under the present law, a doctor who is considering how to treat a patient without capacity must always exercise clinical judgment about the treatment which might be appropriate,[27] and will then decide what is necessary in the patient's best interests.[28] If the patient has made no anticipatory decision then the treatment proposed by the doctor will be carried out. If the patient has consented in advance to what the doctor proposes to do then the result will be the same. Our proposed statutory rules, that a doctor should act reasonably in the best interests of a patient without capacity, will merely reinforce the result which is achieved under the present law wherever a patient has made an advance consent.

5.13    The extent to which a patient with capacity can lawfully consent, whether contemporaneously or in advance, to something which is not in fact in his or her best interests has been a matter of debate.[29] So far as criminal liability is concerned, a victim's consent to an act involving "actual bodily harm" will not be effective to prevent the person inflicting the harm from being convicted of assault;[30] in the health care context, however, "reasonable surgical interference" constitutes an exception to this rule.[31] We have now recommended that reasonable treatment which is in a person's best interests will be lawful. Advance consent to *other* sorts of treatment would not, however, have the effect of rendering them lawful.

---

[24]    D Lush, Living Will (1993), quoted with kind permission.

[25]    Watch Tower: Bible and Tract Society of Pennsylvania, Advance Medical Directive/Release (1995), quoted with kind permission.

[26]    Voluntary Euthanasia Society, Advance Directive.

[27]    See *Re J (A Minor) (Wardship: Medical Treatment)* [1991] Fam 33, 41.

[28]    See *Re F (Mental Patient: Sterilisation)* [1990] 2 AC 1.

[29]    See P D G Skegg, *Law, Ethics and Medicine* (1984) p 36. See our recent Consultation Paper No 134, Consent and Offences Against the Person (1994).

[30]    *A-G's Reference (No 6 of 1980)* [1981] QB 715 and *R v Brown* [1994] 1 AC 212.

[31]    *A-G's Reference (No 6 of 1980)* [1981] QB 715, 719 *per* Lord Lane CJ.

**Advance refusals of treatment**

5.14 When the case of *Re C*[32] came before him in October 1993, Thorpe J was able to say that the legal principles applicable to the case were "readily ascertained" from certain propositions set out by the Court of Appeal in *Re T*.[33] The first of these is that an adult patient has the right and capacity to decide whether or not to accept medical treatment (although the presumption of capacity is rebuttable). Where, however, "an adult patient did not have the capacity to decide at the time of the purported refusal and still does not have that capacity, it is the duty of the doctors to treat him in whatever way they consider, in the exercise of clinical judgment, to be in his best interests". It was also common ground that a refusal of treatment can take the form of a declaration of intention never to consent to that treatment in the future, or never to consent in some future circumstances.[34] Under the present law, therefore, the rule that a patient may make an anticipatory refusal of treatment operates independently of the rule which governs the treatment of a patient without capacity. An advance refusal made with capacity simply survives any supervening incapacity.

5.15 The law does not and should not require doctors always to tailor their own views of a patient's best interests to the patient's own decisions. In *Re C*[35] itself, the vascular surgeon who had charge of C and his infected leg believed that C's only hope of regaining mobility was to agree to amputation. However, he gave evidence that people frequently did not want amputation and that he believed "in the sanctity of the individual's choice, even if it be wrong".[36] This surgeon did not withhold the treatment because he believed that it was in C's best interests for him to do so, but because C had chosen to refuse it. This analysis, which applies to patients like C who still retain decision-making capacity, also applies to those who have lost the decision-making capacity which they once had.

5.16 To maintain the effect of the present law is consistent with our policy aim of enabling people to make such decisions as they are able to make for themselves. In order to give full effect to this aim, special provision is now required for cases where a person makes an anticipatory refusal of treatment which is intended to remain in effect even when the maker no longer has capacity to review the decision made.

> *We recommend* that an "advance refusal of treatment" should be defined as a refusal made by a person aged eighteen or over with

---

[32] *Re C (Adult: Refusal of Treatment)* [1994] 1 WLR 290.

[33] *Ibid*, p 294 and *Re T (Adult: Refusal of Treatment)* [1993] Fam 95, 115 - 116.

[34] *Re C (Adult: Refusal of Treatment)* [1994] 1 WLR 290, 294.

[35] *Re C (Adult: Refusal of Treatment)* [1994] 1 WLR 290.

[36] *Ibid*, p 293.

**the necessary capacity of any medical, surgical or dental treatment or other procedure and intended to have effect at any subsequent time when he or she may be without capacity to give or refuse consent.** (Draft Bill, clause 9(1).)

*Capacity to make an advance refusal*

5.17 "The right to decide one's own fate presupposes a capacity to do so."[37] It should therefore be an essential characteristic of an advance refusal that it was made at a time when the maker had capacity to make it.[38] The new statutory definition of incapacity will be applied in any case where a doubt about capacity needs to be resolved.[39]

*Age*

5.18 There would be little point in our recommending that an anticipatory refusal of treatment can be made by persons under the age of eighteen since it is now settled if controversial law that the court in the exercise of its statutory and/or inherent jurisdiction (and possibly also any person who has parental responsibility) may overrule the refusal of a minor, competent or not, to accept medical treatment.[40]

*Terminal conditions*

5.19 None of our respondents disagreed with our preliminary view[41] that it would be wrong to stipulate that advance decisions can only apply when a patient is in a "terminal condition". Such stipulations were common in early statutes in the United States which laid down strict formalities for the making of "living wills",[42] but they would be out of place in a scheme which seeks to build upon and clarify the fundamental legal principle that patients with capacity can refuse *any* treatment.[43]

5.20 If an "advance refusal" has been made then a treatment provider cannot rely on the authority which would otherwise be available to enable a patient without capacity

---

[37] *Re T (Adult: Refusal of Treatment)* [1993] Fam 95, 112, *per* Lord Donaldson of Lymington MR.

[38] This is not necessarily coterminous with capacity to make a contemporaneous refusal, *Re C (Adult: Refusal of Treatment)* [1994] 1 WLR 290, 295 obiter.

[39] See para 3.14 above and draft Bill clause 2(1).

[40] *Re W (A Minor) (Medical Treatment: Court's Jurisdiction)* [1993] Fam 64, and see also *Re R (A Minor) (Wardship: Consent to Treatment)* [1992] Fam 11.

[41] Consultation Paper No 129, para 3.22.

[42] T Klosterman, *Analysis of Health Care Directive Legislation in the United States* (1992). Legislation introduced in Denmark in October 1992 similarly specifies that the patient must be inevitably dying.

[43] See para 5.34 below in relation to "basic care" of patients without capacity.

to be treated reasonably and in his or her best interests.[44] Obviously, the treatment provider will not be liable for proceeding with treatment unless he or she knows or has reasonable grounds for believing that there is an advance refusal.[45]

**We recommend that the general authority should not authorise any treatment or procedure if an advance refusal of treatment by the person concerned applies to that treatment or procedure in the circumstances of the case.** (Draft Bill, clause 9(2).)

*Validity and applicability*

5.21 The recommendation made in paragraph 5.20 above will effectively take the place of the proposition in *Re T* that an advance refusal of treatment must be "clearly established" and "applicable in the circumstances".[46] As was made clear in *Re T*, "doctors will need to consider what is *the true scope and basis* of the decision".[47] They must ask whether the patient has refused consent to the treatment or procedure which it is now desired to carry out, in the circumstances in which it would now be carried out. Inevitably, problems of evidence will sometimes arise. Equally, however, it can be seen from certain model forms that patients are already able to make the terms of their refusals absolutely clear. A Jehovah's Witness might have stated that "my express refusal of blood is absolute and is not to be overridden in ANY circumstances".[48] Someone else might have provided that "if I become permanently unconscious with no likelihood of regaining consciousness... I wish medical treatment to be limited to keeping me comfortable and free from pain, and I REFUSE all other medical treatment".[49]

5.22 Statutory provisions cannot resolve the problems and questions which may arise in relation to the validity and applicability of advance refusals. The development of a code of practice[50] and of model forms which direct patients towards making the terms of any refusal clear will help to address the most likely problems. In the words of Lord Donaldson, "what really matters" is "the declaration by the patient of his decision with a full appreciation of the possible consequences, the latter being

---

[44] As provided for in the draft Bill, clauses 4 and 3.

[45] See para 5.27 below and draft Bill, clause 9(4)(b).

[46] See Consultation Paper No 129, paras 3.4 - 3.5 and *Re T (Adult: Refusal of Treatment)* [1993] Fam 95, 114.

[47] *Ibid*, p 116 (emphasis added).

[48] Watch Tower: Bible and Tract Society of Pennsylvania, Advance Medical Directive/Release (1995).

[49] Terrence Higgins Trust and King's College London, Living Will (2nd ed 1994).

[50] See para 5.39 below.

expressed in the simplest possible terms".[51] It may be that the most effective format will be one which uses succinct and non-technical language, and avoids detailed provisions about particular ailments or conditions or particular treatments or procedures.[52] As a matter of evidence, a document which refers to particular circumstances, but not to those which have arisen, may be found not to apply to the present circumstances. Similarly, a document which does not mention, expressly or impliedly, the particular treatment which is now proposed would not be an effective refusal of that treatment. The technique (adopted by the THT/King's College model form) of referring to treatments with particular purposes rather than any particular treatments may be one way of avoiding some of the difficulties. We do not believe that primary legislation can elucidate the many questions which can arise about the "applicability" of a particular advance refusal. Our respondents consistently raised with us two matters in particular in relation to questions about applicability and we would expect to see these points addressed in any code of practice. First, many respondents were anxious to ensure that treatment which has become available since the time the refusal was made should not be withheld unless it was very clear that the patient intended to refuse this treatment as well. Secondly, it was said that a statement about health care matters which was made independently of any discussion with a health care professional might often be based on erroneous ideas and information. This is not to suggest that any refusal made without such a discussion would always be "inapplicable"; a Jehovah's Witness would be unlikely to be swayed by any such discussion. These are, however, two of the many matters which will be relevant to the determination of whether any advance refusal "applies to" the treatment or procedure now proposed "in the circumstances of the case".[53]

*Life-sustaining treatment*

5.23  A number of north American cases indicate the great reluctance of both doctors and courts to approve the withholding of treatment which is imperative to prevent death, unless any refusal of such treatment expressly contemplates the possibility of such an avoidable death.[54] This was also an issue in the leading English case of *Re T*. The public interest in preserving the life and health of citizens does not prevent an adult patient from refusing life-sustaining treatment, although any doubt will be resolved

---

[51]  *Re T (Adult: Refusal of Treatment)* [1993] Fam 95, pp 114 - 115.

[52]  In contrast, some recent model forms submitted to us attempt to cover every possible medical condition and every possible treatment option, requiring patients to plot their choices on a complex graph.

[53]  See draft Bill, clause 9(2).

[54]  *In re Estate of Dorone* (1987) 534 A 2d 452, *Werth v Taylor* (1991) 475 NW 2d 426, *In the Matter of Alice Hughes* (1992) 611 A 2d 1148.

in favour of the preservation of life.[55] Patients should therefore be aware that they should address their minds to the possibility of dying if they wish any refusal of treatment to apply notwithstanding this possibility. Some model forms already make express reference to the danger of death.[56]

*Pregnant women*

5.24 The case of *Re S*[57] involved a refusal by a pregnant woman to consent to a Caesarian section. The woman's refusal was effectively overruled by the High Court, which declared (after a brief hearing arranged at very short notice) that it would be lawful to perform the operation in the circumstances. Either this decision is in conflict with the later decision in *Re C*[58] or its ratio is limited to cases where the life of an unborn viable foetus is in danger. It has been heavily criticised[59] and a number of our respondents urged us to address the problem of principle it appears to pose, namely that a pregnant woman may lawfully be subjected to what would otherwise be an unlawful battery.

5.25 The majority of the US states with living will legislation set statutory limits to the effectiveness of any declarations during the maker's pregnancy.[60] Similarly, it has been suggested here that "[i]f a living will comes into operation in relation to a woman who is pregnant, any instructions to forego life-sustaining treatment should be regarded as invalid during the course of the pregnancy".[61] We do not, however, accept that a woman's right to determine the sorts of bodily interference which she will tolerate somehow evaporates as soon as she becomes pregnant. There can, on the other hand, be no objection to acknowledging that many women do in fact alter their views as to the interventions they find acceptable as a direct result of the fact that they are carrying a child. By analogy with cases where life might be needlessly shortened or lost, it appears that a refusal which did not mention the possibility that the life of a foetus might be endangered would be likely to be found not to apply in

---

[55] *Re T (Adult: Refusal of Treatment)* [1993] Fam 95, 112 *per* Lord Donaldson of Lymington MR.

[56] "[My] refusal remains in force even though I may be unconscious...and the doctor(s) treating me consider that such refusal may be life-threatening," Watch Tower: Bible and Tract Society of Pennsylvania, Advance Medical Directive/Release (1995).

[57] *Re S (Adult: Refusal of Treatment)* [1993] Fam 123.

[58] *Re C (Adult: Refusal of Treatment)* [1994] 1 WLR 290.

[59] M Thomson, "After *Re S*" (1994) 2 Med L Rev 127, 128 contends that "*Re S* was not only based on unsound authority, it also runs counter to accepted principles of law". See also J Bridgeman, "Medical Treatment: The Mother's Rights" [1993] Fam Law 534 and I Kennedy and A Grubb, *Medical Law: Text with Materials* (2nd ed 1994) p 359.

[60] T Klosterman, *Analysis of Health Care Directive Legislation in the United States* (1992) p 12.

[61] "The Living Will: Consent to Treatment at the End of Life" (1988) Age Concern Institute of Gerontology and Centre of Medical Law and Ethics, King's College London, p 60.

circumstances where a treatment intended to save the life of the foetus was proposed. Women of child-bearing age should therefore be aware that they should address their minds to this possibility if they wish to make advance refusals of treatment.

*A presumption of non-applicability*

5.26 There are likely to be particular problems in relation to questions of applicability where life-sustaining treatment or treatment which would save the life of a foetus are at issue. The best way of balancing the continuing right of the patient to refuse such treatment with the public interest in preserving life is to create a statutory presumption in favour of the preservation of life.

> ***We recommend*** **that in the absence of any indication to the contrary it shall be presumed that an advance refusal of treatment does not apply in circumstances where those having the care of the person who made it consider that the refusal (a) endangers that person's life or (b) if that person is a woman who is pregnant, the life of the foetus. (Draft Bill, clause 9(3).)**

*Liability of health care providers*

5.27 The maker of an advance refusal should be on notice that the treatment provider who withholds treatment as a result of the refusal will not be liable for the consequences. Equally, the treatment provider is entitled to reassurance that he or she will be relieved of liability (in the tort of negligence) for failing to provide treatment. This does not change the present law but it appears to us that the importance of the rule is such that it should be set out in the statute. Conversely, however, a doctor should not be liable for providing treatment which has in fact been refused if the doctor did not know or have any reason to believe that there was a relevant advance refusal. It is the responsibility of a patient making an advance refusal to ensure that the existence of the refusal comes to the notice of any treatment provider.

> ***We recommend*** **that no person should incur liability (1) for the consequences of withholding any treatment or procedure if he or she has reasonable grounds for believing that an advance refusal of treatment applies; or (2) for carrying out any treatment or procedure to which an advance refusal applies unless he or she knows or has reasonable grounds for believing that an advance refusal applies. (Draft Bill, clause 9(4).)**

*Conscientious objections*

5.28 We have experienced some difficulty with the notion, put forward by a very small number of our respondents, that special provisions should cater for the fact that doctors may have a "conscientious objection" to withholding treatment which a

76

patient has refused. The law, clearly stated in *Re T*, is that treating a patient despite a refusal of consent "will constitute the civil wrong of trespass to the person and may constitute a crime".[62] The majority of our respondents were keen to see statutory force given to this clear principle and we ourselves fail to see the significance of the fact that some doctors may disagree with a patient's motives in making a refusal or advance refusal of treatment.[63] If the principle of self-determination means anything, the patient's refusal must be respected. There is therefore no need for any specific statutory provision. We note the clear view of the BMA that it is unethical for a doctor to flout a competent refusal of treatment, including one made in advance; and that a doctor placed in difficulties by such an advance directive "should relinquish the patient's management to colleagues".[64]

*Formalities*

5.29 In the consultation paper[65] we discussed the possible merits of a prescribed form for anticipatory decisions. We suggested that the importance of flexibility was such that there should simply be a presumption that a written, signed and witnessed decision was "clearly established".[66] Our respondents generally favoured maximum flexibility, although a number of them told us that a model form would often be very helpful to patients.[67] Some model forms are already widely available and more seem always to be being produced. Both the BMA and the Law Society expressed misgivings about any rules which would invalidate a patient's genuine choices simply because those choices were made in ways which fell short of formalities laid down in statute. To disregard valid decisions on that account would be contrary to our aims of policy. Matters of form and execution are essentially questions of evidence in any particular case. We have said that the present common law position is that the issue is the "true scope and basis" of the decision, rather than the way it has been recorded.[68] The existence of a formal document is no guarantee of either validity or applicability, nor is the absence of such a document any guarantee that a valid and

---

[62] *Re T (Adult: Refusal of Treatment)* [1993] Fam 95, 102.

[63] See the discussion at paras 5.14 and 5.15 above on the interaction between the doctor's duty to act in a patient's best interests and the patient's right to refuse. Those who argue in favour of special conscientious objection provisions believe that the doctor's view of the patient's best interests should always determine the end result.

[64] BMA Statement on Advance Directives (revised January 1994) para 6.

[65] Consultation Paper No 129, paras 3.14 - 3.21.

[66] *Ibid*, para 3.19.

[67] Some respondents referred us to developments in the US where it is now quite common for people to make tape recordings or video recordings of their "living wills".

[68] See para 5.21 above.

applicable advance refusal has not been made.[69] Although we gave careful consideration to the introduction of statutory requirements prescribing the form and contents of any advance refusal, we concluded that these would benefit no-one.

5.30 We do, however, see merit in at least encouraging patients to express any advance refusals of treatment in writing, to sign the document and to have their signature witnessed. Such a step would be likely to furnish some definite proof that the refusal was made by the patient and intended to have effect in the future. We take the view that a rebuttable presumption is the best way to balance the need for flexibility and the desirability of formal writing.[70] It would not, of course, answer the questions the doctor must ask as to whether (1) the patient had capacity to make the refusal and whether (2) the refusal applies to the treatment now proposed and in the circumstances which now exist.

> *We recommend* **that in the absence of any indication to the contrary it should be presumed that an advance refusal was validly made if it is in writing, signed and witnessed.** (Draft Bill, clause 9(5).)

We would certainly expect any code of practice to recommend the making of any refusal in writing.

### Withdrawing or altering an advance refusal

5.31 The consultation paper suggested that it should be possible to revoke an anticipatory decision at any time when the maker has capacity to do so.[71] Consultees favoured a flexible approach to "revocation", although some concern was expressed about the possibility of claims being made that a carefully considered refusal had been revoked in the privacy of a doctor's consulting room. This, again, is inevitably a question of fact and evidence in any particular case. It would seem entirely wrong to stipulate that an advance refusal must stand until, for example, paper and pencil and an independent witness can be found.

5.32 Some respondents pointed out that disputes could arise as to whether a "revocation" was intended to be permanent, or only to apply to a particular

---

[69] In *Re T* itself, the patient had signed a standard form refusing a blood transfusion. Lord Donaldson MR was "dismayed" at the layout of the form and stressed that such forms would be ineffective (in relieving treatment providers from liability) if the patient did not have capacity to understand, or did not understand, what he was signing, *Re T (Adult: Refusal of Treatment)* [1993] Fam 95, 114. There is no indication in *Re C (Adult: Refusal of Treatment)* [1994] 1 WLR 290 that the patient had made a formal or written "advance directive" or "living will".

[70] Compare the presumption of non-applicability recommended at para 5.26 above (and draft Bill, clause 9(3)).

[71] Consultation Paper No 129, paras 3.32 - 3.34.

proposed procedure. This led us to conclude that "revocation" was an unhelpful term in the context of a policy favouring maximum flexibility. The essential point is that the maker should retain power, commensurate with his or her capacity, to depart from the terms of an advance refusal.

> **We recommend** that an advance refusal of treatment may at any time be withdrawn or altered by the person who made it, if he or she has capacity to do so. (Draft Bill, clause 9(6).)

5.33 Respondents generally agreed with our provisional view[72] that automatic revocation after a period of time would be unduly restrictive. We would expect any code of practice to give guidance to patients on updating any refusal on a regular basis, so as to reduce the risk of it being found not to apply to circumstances which arise many years later.

*Exclusion of "basic care"*

5.34 In the consultation paper we proposed that an advance directive should never be effective in refusing either pain relief or basic care.[73] On consultation, there was general agreement to the proposition that a patient's right to self-determination could properly be limited by considerations based on public policy. A number of respondents highlighted the effect on staff and other patients if patients were to have power to refuse in advance even the most basic steps to ensure comfort and cleanliness. One respondent argued that since a patient with capacity can refuse all types of treatment the same rule should apply to those making anticipatory refusals, but this minority view did not appeal to us.[74] We were grateful for the assistance of the BMA on the details of the proposed exclusion clause. We accept that patients with capacity regularly refuse certain types or levels of pain relief because they prefer to maintain alertness, and we prefer now to refer only to the alleviation of severe pain. We have also replaced reference to "spoon-feeding" with reference to direct oral feeding, to cater for the administration of nutrition and hydration by syringe or cup. Our proposed definition of "basic care" reflects a level of care which it would be contrary to public policy to withhold from a patient without capacity.

> **We recommend** that an advance refusal of treatment should not preclude the provision of "basic care", namely care to maintain bodily cleanliness and to alleviate severe pain, as well as the provision of direct oral nutrition and hydration. (Draft Bill, clause

---

[72] *Ibid*, para 3.34.

[73] *Ibid*, para 3.26. Our provisional proposal included both nursing care and spoon-feeding in the concept of "basic care".

[74] In the consultation paper we alluded to the argument that a capable patient may in fact be bound by similar questions of public policy (*ibid*, para 3.25 n 77).

9(7)(a) and (8).)

*Accident and emergency situations*

5.35 One of our respondents suggested that any provision restricting the power or duty to treat should not be applicable in accident and emergency situations. The House of Lords Select Committee stated that "there should be no expectation that treatment in an emergency should be delayed while enquiry is made about a possible advance directive."[75] The broad scheme of a general authority based on reasonable treatment in a patient's best interests appears to us quite flexible enough to cover any distinction there might be between emergency situations and others.[76] There is no need for any special provision exempting accident and emergency personnel from the broad terms of that scheme.

**The role of the court**

5.36 Most respondents agreed with our provisional proposal that the court should not have power to override a valid and applicable anticipatory decision in the exercise of its "best interests" jurisdiction.[77] Although some respondents appeared to favour such a power, it was apparent on close reading that they were concerned about out-of-date refusals (where new treatments had become available), or those made in a state of depression or mental frailty. These issues go to applicability and validity respectively and do not necessitate any power to "override". Resort to the court will only be available and necessary where a decision is required about the validity of the refusal (including any issue as to whether it has been withdrawn or altered) or its applicability.[78] Where there is any doubt about such matters and an application to the court is made, treatment providers should have authority to take minimum steps to prevent the patient's death or deterioration in the interim.

> *We recommend* that an advance refusal should not preclude the taking of any action necessary to prevent the death of the maker or a serious deterioration in his or her condition pending a decision of the court on the validity or applicability of an advance refusal or on the question whether it has been

---

[75] Report of the Select Committee on Medical Ethics (1993-94) HL 21-I para 265.

[76] The strictly-defined terms of most early US "living will" legislation often did not apply to emergency treatment by para-medical and ambulance staff. There is now perceived to be a need to modify the legislation, so as to ensure that refusals (of resuscitation especially) take effect even if the treatment is by an emergency team. E Wood, L A Stiegel, C P Sabatino, S Edelstein, "Overview of 1992 State Law Changes in Guardianship, Durable Powers of Attorney, Health-Care Decisions, and Home Equity Mortgages" Clearinghouse Review (1993) 1277, 1285.

[77] Consultation Paper No 129, para 3.29.

[78] See para 8.8 below and draft Bill clause 23, for the jurisdiction of the court to make a declaration on such questions.

**withdrawn or altered.** (Draft Bill, clause 9(7)(b).)

### Independent supervision

5.37    Certain types of health-care decision should require independent sanction from a court or a second-opinion doctor.[79] Where, however, the patient has already refused the procedure in a valid and applicable advance refusal then there can be no question of it being carried out. No reference to the court or a second-opinion doctor will change that.[80]

### An offence of concealing or destroying a document

5.38    In the consultation paper we proposed the creation of new offences of falsifying, forging, concealing, altering or destroying an "advance directive"[81] and many respondents agreed that criminal sanctions were appropriate in such circumstances. Some expert respondents, however, believed that the existing law would cover such behaviour, and we accept that no new offence is required in relation to forging or falsifying.[82] It is not, however, clear that the existing criminal law would cover the concealment or destruction of a document containing an advance refusal with intent to deceive the treatment provider.[83]

> *We recommend* **that it should be an offence punishable with a maximum of two years imprisonment to conceal or destroy a written advance refusal of treatment with intent to deceive.** (Draft Bill, clause 33.)

### Advance statements: a code of practice

5.39    It will already be clear from our discussion of the whole topic of advance statements about health care that this is an area where further guidance in the form of a code of practice would be very valuable. We agree with the House of Lords Select

---

[79]    See Part VI below.

[80]    Draft Bill, clauses 10(5) and 11(6).

[81]    Consultation Paper No 129, para 3.36.

[82]    Such actions would fall foul of the Forgery and Counterfeiting Act 1981, s 1 and s 9(2) respectively. These offences are reproduced without substantive amendment in the draft Criminal Code Bill (clauses 167 and 165) appended to our report Criminal Law: A Criminal Code for England and Wales, Law Com No 177 (1989) Vol 1.

[83]    The offence in the Theft Act 1968, s 20(1) concerns the destruction, defacing or concealment of any "valuable security, any will or other testamentary document or any original document of or belonging to, or filed in or deposited in, any court of justice or any government department" (see also draft Criminal Code Bill clause 162). An advance refusal of treatment would not fall within these categories of documents. The offence in the Law of Property Act 1925, s 183 is limited to fraudulent concealment of documents in the context of the disposal of property. At an appropriate time it may be desirable to bring all these similar types of dishonesty offence into a single place on the statute book, but this is beyond the compass of the present project.

Committee that a code of practice on "advance directives" to guide health care professionals should be prepared.[84] This will be able to address the many points of detail and practice that our primary legislation cannot hope to cover. The British Medical Association and Royal College of Nursing are already co-ordinating a steering group to produce a code of practice in accordance with the recommendation made by the House of Lords Select Committee. If such a code were adopted by all the Royal Colleges then the Secretary of State might wish to consider whether any further guidance was in fact necessary. The recommendations which we have already made provide that the Secretary of State should give guidance to people acting in pursuance of the provisions of Chapter II of Part I of the draft Bill;[85] this covers people acting in pursuance of the general authority as limited by the provisions about advance refusals of treatment. We have also provided a general power to give guidance about such other matters as the Secretary of State thinks fit.[86]

[84]   See para 5.4 above.

[85]   See para 4.37 above and draft Bill, clause 31(1)(b).

[86]   See para 2.53 above and draft Bill, clause 31(1)(d).

# PART VI
# INDEPENDENT SUPERVISION OF
# MEDICAL AND RESEARCH PROCEDURES

## Introduction

6.1 In Part IV of this report we recommended a new "general authority" to care for a person without capacity. Where certain serious medical interventions are proposed, however, there should always be an independent check on whether the procedure would be in the best interests of the person concerned. In some unusual circumstances, provision must also be made for action to be taken on a basis other than the best interests of the person concerned. A number of respondents to our consultation paper (including the BMA, MIND and the Law Society) saw a role for a rather less laborious form of independent supervision than that involved in an application to the court. In this Part, we make recommendations which distinguish between treatments which must be considered on every occasion by the court; those which should always be the subject of an independent second opinion; those which should be subject to *either* a court decision or a second opinion; and those (relating to certain types of research) which require another special kind of supervisory mechanism.

6.2 A number of our respondents doubted that any form of "independent supervision" was required if the person concerned had made arrangements in advance. There may be a valid and applicable advance refusal of the treatment or procedure now proposed.[1] Alternatively, the person might have given an attorney a continuing authority to take a decision about the matter.[2] As will be seen in Part VIII below, the court itself may have made the necessary arrangements by making an order or granting a court-appointed "manager" authority to take decisions in such a situation. The recommendations we make below integrate these various possibilities into the new provisions for independent supervision which we are proposing.

## Treatments requiring court approval

6.3 Respondents to the consultation paper[3] were unanimous in agreeing that some medical decisions should always require prior judicial approval. A clear consensus emerged in relation to certain treatments. In cases involving such treatments an application will have to be made to the court for specific authorisation unless the court has already considered the matter and made a specific order, or granted a manager authority to take the decision in question.[4] The court need not be involved

---

[1] See Part V above.

[2] We deal with "continuing powers of attorney" in Part VII below.

[3] Provisional proposals were made in Consultation Paper No 129, Part VI.

[4] See para 8.26 below.

if the patient has appointed an attorney[5] to take the relevant decision on his or her behalf in the event of incapacity.

> **We recommend** that the general authority should not authorise certain listed treatments or procedures, which will require authorisation by the court or the consent of an attorney or manager. (Draft Bill, clause 7(1).)

*(1) Sterilisation*

6.4    We suggested in the consultation paper that sterilisation operations could be divided into three sub-sets: those intended to treat a disease of the reproductive organs; those intended for "menstrual management"; and those intended for contraceptive purposes.[6] None of our respondents suggested that statutory supervision should be applied to those in the first category, which can properly be carried out under the general authority, with access to the court if there is a dispute or difficulty. A number of respondents confirmed, however, that the need for "menstrual management" can too easily be invoked to avoid the judicial supervision which should currently apply to any operation intended to sterilise the patient as a method of contraception.[7] We were greatly assisted by discussions with those in the Official Solicitor's Department who have experience of representing patients in actions involving proposed sterilisations. We are persuaded that there is a valid distinction to be drawn between an operation which is intended to address an existing harmful condition associated with menstruation and one intended to guard against any future distress which might arise from an unintended pregnancy. The phrase "menstrual management" may obfuscate this crucial distinction instead of emphasising it. We take the view that sterilisation operations designed to relieve the immediate and genuine harmful effects of menstruation can be distinguished from those intended to prevent conception and need not attract supervision by the court. In view of the concern expressed by respondents, however, we suggest a different form of independent supervision for such cases.[8]

> **We recommend** that any treatment or procedure intended or reasonably likely to render the person permanently infertile should require court authorisation unless it is to treat a disease of the reproductive organs or relieve existing detrimental effects of menstruation. (Draft Bill, clause 7(2)(a).)

---

[5]    Any such attorney would have to be the donee of a new-style "continuing power of attorney" described in Part VII, and would have to have specific authority to take such decisions (see para 7.18 below).

[6]    Consultation Paper No 129, paras 6.4 - 6.8.

[7]    The court's involvement is not necessary if an operation will only have the incidental effect of sterilising the patient, *Re GF (Medical Treatment)* [1992] 1 FLR 293.

[8]    See para 6.9 below.

*(2) Donation of tissue or bone marrow*

6.5   Respondents supported our suggestion[9] that an operation to facilitate the donation of non-regenerative tissue or bone marrow by a person without capacity should automatically be referred to the court. The need for any such decision will not stem from any existing distressing condition of the person without capacity, but from the illness of some other person. Organ donation will only rarely, if ever, be in the best interests of a person without capacity, since the procedures and their aftermath often carry considerable risk for the donor. There is, however, authority from another jurisdiction that where a transplant would ensure the survival of a close family member it may be in the best interests of a person without capacity to make such a donation.[10]

> **We recommend that any treatment or procedure to facilitate the donation of non-regenerative tissue or bone marrow should require court authorisation. (Draft Bill, clause 7(2)(b).)[11]**

6.6   There was support on consultation for our provisional view[12] that the Secretary of State should be able to add to any statutory list of treatments, so that changes in medical science may be taken into account without the need for primary amending legislation.[13]

> **We recommend that the Secretary of State should have power to prescribe further treatments requiring court authorisation. (Draft Bill, clause 7(2)(c).)[14]**

**Treatments requiring a second doctor's certificate**

6.7   The BMA, the Royal Colleges and the Department of Health all offer guidance to doctors about seeking a second doctor's opinion as a matter of good clinical

---

[9]   Consultation Paper No 129, para 6.9.

[10]   *Strunk v Strunk* (1969) 445 SW 2d 145.

[11]   The Human Organ Transplants (Unrelated Persons) Regulations 1989 (SI 1989 No 2480) require that an unrelated donor must consent to donation while having capacity so to do (reg 3(2)(b)). These Regulations will require consequential amendment upon implementation of our recommendations.

[12]   Consultation Paper No 129, para 6.33.

[13]   The Association of the British Pharmaceutical Industry referred us to two relatively new procedures, partial hepatectomy and leucophoresis for stem cell isolation. Although these involve *regenerative* tissue, they may be so risky for the donor that independent supervision should be imposed where the prospective donor lacks capacity to consent.

[14]   Regulations should be made by statutory instrument under the negative resolution procedure (draft Bill, clause 7(3)).

practice.[15] Statute imposes a requirement for an independent second medical opinion in relation to certain treatments for mental disorder.[16] This means of supervision, much quicker and cheaper than the full procedure of a court hearing, could also usefully be applied to certain complex medical procedures where a patient lacks capacity. One advantage would be that consistency in relation to the treatments for mental disorder specified in section 58 of the Mental Health Act 1983 could be introduced by this means, regardless of whether a patient was "liable to be detained" or not.

6.8 The treatments suitable for a second opinion category all share the characteristic that they are being proposed by the treating doctor to relieve an existing medical condition of the patient concerned. In this sense, they pose a clearer and more focused question than do the treatments in the court category.[17] The second opinion doctor should be one specially appointed by the Secretary of State to fulfil the role of confirming whether the patient lacks capacity to consent to the procedure, and if so whether it would be in that patient's best interests.[18] As with "court category" treatments, a decision by a properly authorised attorney or court-appointed manager will displace the need for the statutory second opinion to be obtained. Unlike the treatments in the court category, those in the second opinion category may be accompanied by emergency circumstances. It should therefore be stipulated that action to preserve life or prevent deterioration is permitted, while the second opinion doctor's certificate (or the consent of a person with authority to consent) is being obtained.[19]

> **We recommend that the general authority should not authorise certain listed treatments or procedures, which should require a certificate from an independent doctor appointed for that purpose by the Secretary of State or the consent of an attorney or manager. The independent doctor should certify that the person concerned is without capacity to consent but that it is in his or her best interests for the treatment or procedure to be carried out. This should not preclude action necessary to prevent the death of the person concerned or a serious deterioration in**

---

[15] See for example the Department of Health's evidence to the House of Lords Select Committee on Medical Ethics, referring to the need to seek a second opinion if it is thought a patient lacks capacity to take a treatment decision ((1993-94) HL 21-II Oral Evidence p 6).

[16] Mental Health Act 1983, ss 57 - 58.

[17] See paras 6.3 and 6.6 above.

[18] See para 3.25 above and draft Bill, clause 3.

[19] Compare the analogous stipulation where it is believed that an advance refusal may affect matters, para 5.36 above and draft Bill, clause 9(7)(b).

**his or her condition while the certificate or consent is sought.**
(Draft Bill, clause 8(1), (2) and (6).)

*(1) Sterilisation*

6.9 Although we have concluded that a sterilisation operation designed to relieve a patient of any existing pain and harmful effects connected with menstruation should not require authorisation by the court, many of our respondents expressed concern about operations being labelled "for menstrual management", with the result that no independent supervision at all is required. A consultant in developmental psychiatry who has made a special study of sterilisation of people with learning disabilities suggested that the level of menstrual distress is often misrepresented, and that further investigation can reveal less drastic means of coping with the problem than a sterilisation operation. There is a clear need for independent supervision in such circumstances.[20]

> *We recommend* **that any treatment or procedure intended or reasonably likely to render the person concerned permanently infertile should require should require a certificate from an independent medical practitioner where it is for relieving the existing detrimental effects of menstruation.** (Draft Bill, clause 8(3)(d).)

*(2) Abortion*

6.10 There is already a statutory second opinion procedure designed to protect the interests of the foetus in the Abortion Act 1967. We were extremely concerned to note, however, that a number of our expert respondents expressed the view that abortion operations are still being performed on young women with learning disabilities without a proper investigation of their capacity to consent or of their best interests (and in particular their wishes and feelings). An overwhelming majority of respondents said that abortion in such cases should attract independent supervision. It is clear that what is needed is an additional procedure to protect the interests of any mother who lacks capacity. While some respondents said that court authorisation should be required (and others objected to abortion in principle) it was also repeatedly stressed that delay is particularly undesirable where a pregnancy is to be terminated. Balancing all these factors, we take the view that abortion should be placed in the second opinion category.

> *We recommend* **that abortion should require a certificate from an independent medical practitioner.** (Draft Bill, clause 8(3)(c).)

---

[20] If the operation is intended to promote the greater convenience of carers or merely to relieve discomfort or distress then it will attract the need for court approval. The phrase, "the existing detrimental effects of menstruation", does not cover such circumstances.

*(3) Treatments for mental disorder*

6.11 Respondents welcomed our provisional proposal[21] that the new statutory scheme should apply when it is proposed to administer medical treatment *for mental disorder* to a patient without capacity to consent to that treatment. The alternative would be to introduce a requirement that in such circumstances the patient should always be detained in accordance with the Mental Health Act 1983 and treated pursuant to the statutory provisions. Respondents did not favour this option, which might radically increase the numbers of people being compulsorily detained and treated. They did, however, favour all patients having the same safeguards where special procedures are laid down in relation to particular types of treatment for mental disorder.

6.12 If the new statutory scheme can apply to treatments for mental disorder there would in some cases be an overlap between the Mental Health Act scheme and the new "incapacity" scheme. We do not believe this will cause any difficulty in practice. There is already an overlap between the Mental Health Act scheme and the common law rules in *Re F*,[22] which our scheme is intended to replace. The Mental Health Act Code of Practice stipulates that "[i]t is the personal responsibility of any doctor proposing to treat a patient to determine whether the patient has capacity to give a valid consent".[23] If the patient does not have capacity then the common law as set out in *Re F* may justify treatment in certain circumstances.[24] Where a patient is "liable to be detained" and the treatment proposed is treatment for his or her mental disorder, statute certainly provides that the treatment may be given without the patient's consent.[25] This does not, however, justify the doctor in disregarding the question of capacity, since the Code of Practice states that consent should nonetheless "always be sought".[26] It also suggests that in practice many treatments will require the patient's acceptance and active co-operation.[27] There will of course be no overlap with our scheme if the patient has capacity but refuses consent to treatment.[28]

6.13 Equally, there will be no overlap if a person who now lacks capacity has made an

---

[21] Consultation Paper No 129, para 7.7.

[22] See Consultation Paper No 129, paras 7.4 - 7.5.

[23] Mental Health Act 1983 - Code of Practice (2nd ed 1993) para 15.9.

[24] *Ibid*, para 15.19.

[25] Mental Health Act 1983, s 63.

[26] Mental Health Act 1983 - Code of Practice (2nd ed 1993) para 16.16.

[27] *Ibid*, para 16.17.

[28] Treatment for mental disorder can then be given *to detained patients only* in accordance with Part IV of the 1983 Act. *Ibid*, para 15.24.

advance refusal of treatment for mental disorder. If valid and applicable, this would preclude treatment being given pursuant to our new scheme after capacity has been lost.[29] If the person meets the statutory criteria for detention under the 1983 Act, however, then the existence of an advance refusal will not be an end of the matter. The patient can be compulsorily detained and treated in accordance with the terms of the 1983 Act.[30]

6.14      The 1983 Act already makes special provision for two forms of treatment, requiring that an independent second doctor's opinion be obtained if the patient is "liable to be detained" under the Act. These treatments are (1) electro-convulsive therapy (ECT) and (2) the administration of psychotropic medication for a period exceeding three months.[31] MIND and other respondents welcomed our suggestion[32] that all patients unable to consent to these treatments, whether or not detained under the 1983 Act, should have the same protection. Rather than requiring such patients to be compulsorily detained, our respondents agreed that it would be far preferable for them all to be given the protection of a formal second opinion.

> ***We recommend*** **that the treatments for mental disorder described in section 58(1) of the Mental Health Act 1983 should require a certificate from an independent medical practitioner.** (Draft Bill, clause 8(3)(a) and (b).)[33]

6.15      In this category too we take it to be important that the Secretary of State should have power to add further treatments or procedures to the list we have proposed.

> ***We recommend*** **that the Secretary of State should have power to prescribe that other treatments or procedures should be included in the second opinion category.** (Draft Bill, clause 8(3)(e).)[34]

---

[29]   See para 5.20 above and draft Bill, clause 9(2).

[30]   Clearly, detention will also be necessary if the patient has capacity to consent but refuses consent.

[31]   Mental Health Act 1983, s 58(1) and the Mental Health (Hospital, Guardianship and Consent to Treatment) Regulations 1983 (SI 1983 No 893), reg 16. The Secretary of State has power to specify further forms of treatment (s 58(1)) and to alter the time limit for medication (s 58(2)).

[32]   Consultation Paper No 129, para 7.11.

[33]   The meaning of "mental disorder" should match that in the 1983 Act and the Secretary of State should have a matching power to vary the time period relating to medication (draft Bill, clause 8(4)).

[34]   Regulations should be made by statutory instrument under the negative resolution procedure (draft Bill, clause 8(5)).

**Where the "best interests" criterion fails**

6.16 The court, the second opinion doctor, the attorney or the manager in the cases we have discussed above will be confirming that the proposed treatment is indeed in the best interests of the particular patient. The statutory list of "best interests" factors set out in Part III above is flexible enough to apply to these special decisions.[35] We now move on to discuss the very rare circumstances in which departure from the governing concept of the patient's "best interests" can be justified.

*(1) Withdrawing artificial nutrition and hydration*

6.17 The case of *Airedale NHS Trust v Bland*[36] established that if doctors seek to discontinue artificial nutrition and hydration for a patient in a persistent vegetative state (PVS) they should seek the prior approval of the High Court by applying for declaratory relief.[37] We suggested in the consultation paper[38] that a court exercising our proposed new jurisdiction, which is limited to making orders in the best interests of people without capacity, would be unable to approve the withdrawal of artificial feeding from a PVS patient. We quoted Lord Mustill in *Bland's* case asserting "[t]he distressing truth which must not be shirked" that such patients have "no best interests of any kind".[39] The great majority of our respondents believed that decisions to withdraw artificial feeding from those in PVS should require prior court approval, and that the court should have the power to approve or disapprove any proposed withdrawal. Few favoured our provisional proposal that a "declaration as to lawfulness"[40] might continue to be made in such circumstances.

6.18 There is not the same difficulty in relation to decisions to provide treatment, even where a patient is in PVS. Questions as to whether a particular treatment or procedure should be initiated can be decided by reference to the general authority and the best interests criterion. The particular difficulty arises where, as in the case of Anthony Bland, feeding was being provided on an ongoing basis and the doctors sought to take the positive step of terminating that provision. It may no longer be in the best interests of such a patient to be fed, but it can equally be argued that it is not in his or her best interests for the feeding to stop. The upshot may be that the

---

[35] In Consultation Paper No 129, para 6.16 we invited views on the need for special criteria. The majority of respondents accepted that the "best interests" criterion was satisfactory, although some refinements for particular treatments were suggested. Guidance or a code of practice (under clause 31(1)(b) of the draft Bill) could add refinements and detail in relation to particular procedures.

[36] [1993] AC 789.

[37] The Official Solicitor to the Supreme Court has issued a Practice Note on the procedure to be followed, [1994] 2 All ER 413.

[38] Consultation Paper No 129, para 6.23.

[39] *Airedale NHS Trust v Bland* [1993] AC 789, 897.

[40] Consultation Paper No 129, para 6.24.

status quo must continue, even though all involved in the case take the view that this is undesirable. We note that the House of Lords Select Committee on Medical Ethics expressed the opinion that a decision to withdraw nutrition and hydration would be unnecessary if an appropriate "treatment-limiting" decision, for example not to administer antibiotics, were taken at an earlier stage.[41] It did not appear from our consultation, however, that the need to discontinue nutrition could always be avoided by such means.

6.19    The recent case of *Frenchay Healthcare NHS Trust v S*[42] is a good illustration of the distinction we have just drawn. In spite of the confusing language of the applications sought, this was not in fact a case where the doctors were seeking to discontinue artificial sustenance. The patient's gastrostomy tube had become dislodged before the case came to court, so that no artificial sustenance was in fact being provided. The consultant had formed the view that to subject his patient to an operation to reinsert a new gastrostomy tube would not be in his best interests. He rightly took it to follow that carrying out the operation in such circumstances would be a criminal act.[43] If such a case came to court after the enactment of our proposed legislation there would be no difficulty at all in the court ordering, in the best interests of the patient, that no such operation should be carried out on him.[44]

6.20    Respondents with expertise in intensive care made it clear to us that decisions to terminate artificial feeding often have to be taken in acute cases. It does not follow from our analysis of the difficulty where a patient is in persistent vegetative state that *any* decision to discontinue artificial nutrition should have to go to court. In an acute case, it may well be obvious that it is in the best interests of the patient for sustenance to be withdrawn, so that he or she does not recover consciousness to live in temporary pain and distress and then die shortly thereafter of severe and incurable injuries or illness. The recommendation below is directed to those cases where the "best interests" criterion cannot be invoked to resolve the dilemma of treatment-providers. Those cases are where (1) artificial sustenance is being provided and (2) the patient's condition is such that it cannot be said to be in his or her best interests to discontinue the sustenance. The defining characteristic of such a condition is a complete inability to have any physical or emotional experience of whatever kind, whether in the present or at any future time. This can be

---

[41]    Report of the Select Committee on Medical Ethics (1993-94) HL 21-I para 257. See para 1.7 and n 13 above.

[42]    [1994] 1 WLR 601.

[43]    *Ibid*, 604. It would also be the civil wrong of battery.

[44]    There would be no necessity for the case ever to be brought to court unless there was a dispute or difficulty about whether what was proposed was reasonable and in the patient's best interests.

established by assessing whether there is any activity in the cerebral cortex.[45] In our view, a lawful route to the discontinuance of artificial sustenance in such circumstances should be provided. There should, however, be a very high level of independent supervision.

> **We recommend** that discontinuing the artificial nutrition and hydration of a patient who is unconscious, has no activity in the cerebral cortex and no prospect of recovery should be lawful if certain statutory requirements are met. (Draft Bill, clause 10(1).)

6.21 We agree with the majority of our consultees that, as at present, the discontinuance of artificial sustenance to a patient in PVS should in every case require the prior approval of the court, unless an attorney or court-appointed manager already has express authority to make that decision. Equally, if the patient has made an advance refusal of artificial sustenance in the circumstances which have arisen then that would resolve the matter and there would be no obligation to seek court approval. It was, however, suggested by the Master of the Rolls in *Bland's* case that there might come a time when a body of experience and practice had built up, such that a prior court declaration might not be necessary in every case.[46] This suggestion was reiterated in four of the five speeches in the House of Lords.[47] If, as we recommend, the matter is placed on a statutory footing then the primary legislation would require amendment if it were decided that no court approval was necessary. This would be a laborious process. In view of the comments made in *Bland's* case, we have therefore made provision for the Secretary of State by order to replace the need for court approval with a requirement for a certificate from an independent medical practitioner duly appointed for that purpose, to the effect that it is appropriate for artificial nutrition to be discontinued.[48] Before making any such order, the Secretary of State should consult with relevant organisations and with the Official Solicitor; and any order should be subject to an affirmative resolution by each House of Parliament.[49] In cases of dispute or difficulty it would of course still be possible for the decision to be referred to the court, even if the alternative of a second opinion procedure were to be brought into force.

---

[45]  It was suggested to us in the course of consultation that some doctors might not see any need to seek a declaration if the specific diagnosis of "persistent vegetative state" is not applied to a patient. We have therefore avoided this diagnostic label in defining the circumstances which require any proposed withdrawal of nutrition and hydration to be referred to the court.

[46]  *Airedale NHS Trust v Bland* [1993] AC 789, 815 - 816.

[47]  *Ibid, per* Lord Keith of Kinkel at p 859, *per* Lord Goff of Chieveley at p 873, *per* Lord Lowry at p 875 and *per* Lord Browne-Wilkinson at p 885.

[48]  The certificate should also state that the person concerned is without capacity to consent to what is proposed (draft Bill, clause 10(6)).

[49]  Draft Bill, clause 10(7) and (8). See paras 6.26 and 6.27 below.

**We recommend** that the discontinuance of artificial sustenance to an unconscious patient with no activity in the cerebral cortex and no prospect of recovery should require either (1) the approval of the court, (2) the consent of an attorney or manager or (3) if an order of the Secretary of State so provides, a certificate by an independent medical practitioner. (Draft Bill, clause 10(2).)[50]

*The criteria for discontinuing artificial sustenance*

6.22 Not all of our consultees agreed with Lord Mustill's view[51] that decisions to discontinue artificial nutrition for a patient in PVS cannot be justified by reference to the patient's "best interests". We prefer to avoid any semantic argument and confusion by disapplying the general rule where such decisions are concerned, and concentrating instead on the individual factors in the best interests checklist.[52] Some of these are equally applicable to any decision as to whether cessation of feeding and hydration should occur. This is especially true of the first factor, namely the wishes and feelings of the person, and the factors he or she would have taken into account if able to do so. Equally important may be the third factor, namely the views of any of the persons who should be consulted as to the patient's wishes and best interests.

**We recommend** that where the court, an attorney, a manager or an independent medical practitioner decides on discontinuance of artificial sustenance for an unconscious patient with no activity in the cerebral cortex and no prospect of recovery, then regard must be had to the factors in the best interests checklist. (Draft Bill, clause 10(3).)

*(2) Other procedures which will benefit others*

6.23 In the course of consultation, our attention was drawn to a number of innovative medical procedures which could be applied to patients unable to give consent to them but would appear to be unlawful under the present law. Some respondents argued that the procedures in question were ethical and reasonable and urged that they should also be rendered lawful. The procedure most often referred to by consultees is known as "interventional" or "elective" ventilation. Another is genetic screening.[53]

---

[50] The second opinion doctor should be a doctor specially appointed by the Secretary of State for the purpose of providing such certificates (draft Bill, clause 10(2)(c)).

[51] See para 6.17 above.

[52] Draft Bill, clause 3(2).

[53] Although the technology is not yet available, there was also heated public and parliamentary debate about the use of donated tissue from aborted foetuses or human ovarian tissue after the Human Fertilisation and Embryology Authority issued a paper for public consultation in January 1994. See now Criminal Justice and Public Order Act 1994,

6.24 The law and ethics relating to elective ventilation were recently comprehensively reviewed in a research report published by the King's Fund Institute.[54] The procedure involves the mechanical ventilation of an unconscious patient whose imminent death is considered inevitable, with the express aim of making effective arrangements for the retrieval and subsequent transplantation of donor organs. It has been carried out at a number of English hospitals over recent years.[55] The researchers' conclusion, with which we agree, is that ventilation in such circumstances is an unlawful battery,[56] since it is not being carried out in the best interests of the potential donor. The researchers were less certain that there was any ethical objection to the procedure, but they pointed out that the research necessary to establish whether any ethical objection is made out cannot be carried out if the procedure is unlawful. They suggested that this "Catch-22 situation" requires resolution.[57] Our recommendations for a comprehensive scheme whereby decisions could be taken in the best interests of a person without capacity do not assist if it is thought appropriate to make elective ventilation lawful.

6.25 Genetic screening or testing involves the taking of a blood or other body sample from a person in order to investigate the genetic make-up of that person. The ethics of this procedure were also comprehensively reviewed in a recent report, published by the Nuffield Council on Bioethics.[58] For the purposes of our own work we take the view that where the purpose of the procedure is to plan a treatment which will help the person concerned, then the general authority and the best interests criterion will apply in the usual way, if the person lacks capacity to consent to the procedure.[59] Sometimes, however, the purpose of the procedure is to provide information to a relative about the genetic structure of the extended family. Some screening programmes also have as their purpose the provision of statistical information to health care professionals. We take the view that the testing of a

---

s 156 which amends the Human Fertilisation and Embryology Act 1990.

[54] B New, M Solomon, R Dingwall, J McHale, *A Question of Give and Take: Improving the supply of donor organs for transplantation* (1994) King's Fund Research Report No 18, pp 55 - 56 and 63 - 66.

[55] It was pioneered at the Royal Devon and Exeter Hospital, which developed and applied its own Protocol (King's Fund Report, *op cit*, p 55).

[56] *Ibid*, p 64. In October 1994 the Department of Health issued guidelines stating that the practice would be unlawful where it is not for the patient's own benefit but to ensure that organs can be retrieved for transplantation, NHS Executive HSG(94)41.

[57] *Ibid*, p 66.

[58] *Genetic Screening: Ethical Issues* (1993). The authors explain that there is a significant, though not a completely hard and fast, distinction between "genetic testing" and "genetic screening". They suggest that the former phrase should be used where there is some prior evidence of the presence of a genetic defect in the individual being tested (para 1.9).

[59] If, as is often the case at present, the procedure is part of a research project then our specific recommendations about research will apply. See paras 6.28 - 6.39 below.

person without capacity in circumstances where the test is not in the best interests of that person is unlawful under the present law.[60] The expert view of those who recently reported on the ethics of genetic screening is, however, that it is "a matter for consideration" whether the testing of those with incapacitating conditions should be permitted where "the benefit to the family could be great and the risk of harm to the individual being tested negligible".[61] Again, law reform recommendations which are entirely dependent on a notion of "best interests" will not assist in rendering such procedures lawful.

6.26　We did not invite specific views on either elective ventilation or genetic screening in our consultation papers. While the expert reports referred to above suggest that there is a case for legalising both procedures, none of the comments which have been made to us by respondents allow us to be confident that the case has been made out. We are, however, persuaded that there may come a time when Parliament could be confident that a procedure which was not intended to be in the best interests of a person without capacity to consent to it should nevertheless be rendered lawful. We therefore consider that the Secretary of State should have power to introduce such a change in the law, after consultation and subject to an affirmative resolution by each House of Parliament.[62]

> **We recommend** that the Secretary of State may make an order providing for the carrying out of a procedure in relation to a person without capacity to consent if the procedure, although not carried out for the benefit of that person, will not cause him or her significant harm and will be of significant benefit to others. (Draft Bill, clause 10(4).)[63]

If any procedures are designated by the Secretary of State in future, there should (in accordance with the recommendations made elsewhere in this report) still be a clear prohibition against things being done to a person who objects or to a person who

---

[60]　Although the Nuffield Council Report does not deal with the legality of the procedures in question, it does state that "it is not clear that genetic testing could ever be properly conducted on someone who is mentally disabled when the purpose of the test is to benefit a family member or someone other than the person being tested" (*Genetic Screening: Ethical Issues* (1993) para 4.26).

[61]　*Ibid.* We note that the Council of Europe in its Recommendation R(92)3, *Genetic Testing and Screening for Health Care Purposes*, has ruled that testing of persons "suffering from mental disorder" or "placed under limited guardianship" should be permitted only when necessary for their own health or "if the information is imperatively needed to diagnose the existence of a genetic disease in family members" (Principle 5).

[62]　The affirmative resolution procedure is provided for in the draft Bill, clause 10(8).

[63]　This recommendation does not apply to any procedure carried out for the purposes of research (draft Bill, clause 10(5)). See paras 6.28 - 6.39.

has made an applicable advance refusal.[64]

6.27 Before making any order of the type referred to in paragraphs 6.21 or 6.26 above, the Secretary of State should be under a statutory obligation to consult with organisations representing persons with mental disability and with the Official Solicitor.[65] It may well be appropriate to consult more widely. In relation to any new designated procedures, the statutory requirements for approval or consent which we recommended in relation to discontinuance of artificial sustenance should apply. Any order made by the Secretary of State must stipulate whether the procedure requires the prior approval of the court; or alternatively, a certificate from an independent medical practitioner. It seems clear that decisions about elective ventilation would have to be taken in circumstances where it would be quite impractical to require prior court approval on every occasion. If an attorney or manager has authority to consent to the procedure then neither the court nor the second opinion doctor need be involved. As with discontinuance of sustenance, the best interests factors will be relevant and regard should be had to them.[66]

**Research procedures not intended to benefit the participant**

6.28 In the consultation paper we raised the question of people without capacity participating in research projects.[67] We referred to the widely-used distinction between "therapeutic" and "non-therapeutic" research procedures. The former covers procedures which, whether or not there is also a research objective, are intended to benefit the individual participant. The label can also be applied to "randomised controlled trials", where neither researcher nor participant knows whether a particular person is receiving the established treatment, a placebo or the experimental treatment. The ethical case for such trials is that the researcher genuinely cannot say whether the old treatment, no treatment or the new treatment is preferable, and is therefore asserting that all options are equally liable to be in the best interests of the patient.[68] These situations can very adequately be dealt with under the broad general authority which revolves around "reasonableness",[69] and the best interests criterion.

---

[64] Draft Bill, clause 10(5).

[65] Draft Bill, clause 10(7). The Official Solicitor has extensive experience in acting as next friend or guardian ad litem for litigants under a disability. The Court of Protection Rules also provide for the involvement of the Official Solicitor in special circumstances. See Court of Protection Rules 1994 (SI 1994 No 3046), rules 12, 15 and 16. The present rules came into force on 22 December 1994.

[66] Draft Bill, clause 10(3).

[67] Consultation Paper No 129, paras 6.26 - 6.29.

[68] If the researcher believes one of the treatments being given is in fact better than the others then this analysis will not apply. In our view, the trial would then fall into the category of "non-therapeutic" research.

[69] See para 4.4 above and draft Bill, clause 4(1).

6.29 "Non-therapeutic" research, on the other hand, does not claim to offer any direct or immediate benefit to the participant. Such procedures may well be scientifically and ethically acceptable to those who are qualified to decide such matters.[70] If, however, the participant lacks capacity to consent to his or her participation, and the procedure cannot be justified under the doctrine of necessity, then any person who touches or restrains that participant is committing an unlawful battery. The simple fact is that the researcher is making no claim to be acting in the best interests of that individual person and does not therefore come within the rules of law set out in *Re F*.[71] It was made abundantly clear to us on consultation, however, that non-therapeutic research projects of this nature are regularly taking place. We were told of a research project into the organic manifestations of Alzheimer's disease which involves the administration of radioactive isotopes to sufferers, followed by extensive testing of blood and bodily functions.[72] Another project was said to involve the examination of written patients' records, although they are unable to consent to this examination. In some cases relatives are asked to "consent" to what is proposed, and do so. It appears that some funding bodies and Ethics Committees stipulate for consent by a relative where the research participant cannot consent. As a matter of law, such "consent" is meaningless.[73] It appears that the question of the legality of non-therapeutic research procedures is regularly misunderstood or ignored by those who design, fund and approve the projects.[74]

6.30 A number of our respondents expressed concern about non-invasive research based on observations, photography or videoing of participants (sometimes covertly). We accept that questions of dignity and privacy arise in such situations where the project is not designed to benefit the research participant.

[70] In practice, all research involving NHS patients or premises must be approved by a Local Research Ethics Committee. See para 6.33 below.

[71] *Re F (Mental patient: Sterilisation)* [1990] 2 AC 1 and see para 3.26 above.

[72] Radioactive substances can only be administered to persons by a doctor or dentist who holds a certificate granted in accordance with the Medicine (Administration of Radioactive Substances) Regulations 1978 (SI 1978 No 1006), the Medicines (Radioactive Substances) Order 1978 (SI 1978 No 1004) and the Medicines (Committee on Radiation from Radioactive Medicinal Products) Order 1978 (SI 1978 No 1005). Ministers are advised on this topic by the Administration of Radioactive Substances Advisory Committee (ARSAC).

[73] J Neuberger reports that 25% of research ethics committees observed by her allowed proxy consent from a relative of a mentally ill or mentally handicapped person. She concludes that "this is an area where research ethics committees are uncertain, and have tended to ignore the difficulties". *Ethics and Health Care: The role of research ethics committees in the United Kingdom* (King's Fund Institute Research Report No 13) p 42.

[74] Researchers who touch a person who cannot consent to being touched may well be in danger of incurring criminal liability. There must be considerable doubt as to whether touchings in the course of non-therapeutic research would count as "reasonable surgical interference". See para 5.13 and n 31 above.

6.31    We suggested in our consultation paper[75] that the balance of expert opinion favours the participation of people unable to consent in even non-therapeutic research projects, subject to strict criteria. The majority of our consultees argued that there is an ethical case for such participation. This case turns on the desirability of eradicating painful and distressing disabilities, where progress can be achieved without harming research subjects. The wide range of guidance and expert commentary on this matter shows a striking degree of consensus over the factors which make non-therapeutic research ethical,[76] and we remarked a similar consensus in the responses submitted to us on consultation. In summary, the consensus appears to be that non-therapeutic research involving participants who cannot consent is justifiable where (1) the research relates to the condition from which the participant suffers, (2) the same knowledge cannot be gained from research limited to those capable of consenting, and (3) the procedures involve minimal risk and invasiveness. The recommendations which follow are intended to resolve the unacceptable anomaly that projects of this type, assessed by those with appropriate scientific and ethical expertise as being important and meritorious, in fact involve actionable unlawful conduct by the researchers. At the same time, our recommendations will place necessary protections for the participant without capacity on a statutory footing.

> **We recommend that research which is unlikely to benefit a participant, or whose benefit is likely to be long delayed, should be lawful in relation to a person without capacity to consent if (1) the research is into an incapacitating condition with which the participant is or may be affected and (2) certain statutory procedures are complied with.[77] (Draft Bill, clause 11(1).)**

6.32    Special considerations may apply in relation to the testing of medicinal products. The UK has implemented[78] a European Directive on the licensing and testing of medicinal products. The Directive requires compliance with "good clinical practice".[79] In 1991 the European Commission issued guidelines on "Good Clinical Practice for Trials on Medicinal Products in the European Community", one of the

---

[75]   Consultation Paper No 129, para 6.28.

[76]   See for example, the Royal College of Physicians, *Research Involving Patients* (1990) paras 7.41 and 7.65; the Royal College of Psychiatrists, "Guidelines for Research Ethics Committees on psychiatric research involving human subjects" (1990) 14 Psychiatric Bulletin 48, p 50; the Medical Research Council, *The Ethical Conduct of Research on the Mentally Incapacitated* (1991) para 6.3; the British Medical Association, *Medical Ethics Today* (1993) p 213.

[77]   See paras 6.33 - 6.37 below for the statutory procedures recommended.

[78]   The Medicines (Applications for Grant of Product Licences - Products for Human Use) Regulations 1993 (SI 1993 No 2538).

[79]   Commission Directive 91/507/EEC (OJ L270, 26.9.91, p 32) Annex, Part IV, para 1.1.

guidelines being that "consent must always be given by the signature of the subject in a non-therapeutic study".[80] If "good clinical practice" in the 1991 directive means good clinical practice as defined in the 1991 guidelines, then the directive forbids any non-therapeutic product research involving a participant without capacity to consent. One leading text book on medical law concludes that the meaning of "good clinical practice" in the directive is "a matter of conjecture".[81] Our own view is that it is not restricted to those matters set out in the 1991 guidelines and we understand that the Department of Health shares this view. In relation to those participants who lack capacity, our recommendations are designed to put good clinical practice on a proper legal footing.

*A Mental Incapacity Research Committee*

6.33    The Department of Health has instructed District Health Authorities to set up Local Research Ethics Committees (LRECs) "to advise NHS bodies on the ethical acceptability of research proposals involving human subjects".[82] LRECs have no legal standing, a decision by a LREC does not make a researcher's actions lawful, and statute cannot enable a non-statutory body to achieve such an end. In the consultation paper[83] we suggested that a judicial body should have power to make a declaration that proposed research involving persons without capacity would be lawful. Courts and the adversarial process, however, are not well adapted to cases where there are no opposing parties to present evidence. Ordinary judges will have no relevant scientific expertise. Instead, therefore, we recommend that a new statutory committee should be established. This will supplement the "extra-legal" checks and balances which already exist,[84] avoiding duplication of valuable time and effort.

> **We recommend** that there should be a statutory committee to be known as the **Mental Incapacity Research Committee.** (Draft Bill, clause 11(2).)

6.34    A non-therapeutic research procedure should only be lawful in relation to a person

---

[80]    Commission of the European Communities EC 43 1990-91, para 1.14.

[81]    I Kennedy and A Grubb, *Medical Law: Text and Materials* (2nd ed 1994) p 1048.

[82]    NHS Management Executive HSG(91)5, which has the status of Department of Health guidelines.

[83]    Consultation Paper No 129, para 6.29.

[84]    I Kennedy points out ("Research Ethics Committees and the Law" in *Manual for Research Ethics Committees* (2nd ed 1992) para 1) that not only will researchers be unable to gain access to NHS patients without LREC approval, they will be unlikely to find funding and equally unlikely to succeed in publishing any results in English journals. Another example of the power of an extra-legal check is the fact that research proposals which fail to conform to the Medical Research Council's recommendations in *The Ethical Conduct of Research on the Mentally Incapacitated* (1991) will not secure MRC funding.

who is without capacity to consent if the new Mental Incapacity Research Committee approves the research. Although most research which would otherwise be unlawful will be "medical" in the broadest sense, we do not suggest that the remit of the committee should be expressly limited to medical research. The criteria to be applied by the committee should be set out in statute. They all refer to the one particular issue of participants without capacity. Wider scientific questions will still be investigated by the relevant funding bodies. If NHS patients are involved, then the ethical advice of the LREC will be required before the Department of Health guidance will be satisfied.[85]

> **We recommend that the committee may approve proposed research if satisfied:**
>
> **(1) that it is desirable to provide knowledge of the causes or treatment of, or of the care of people affected by, the incapacitating condition with which any participant is or may be affected,**
>
> **(2) that the object of the research cannot be effectively achieved without the participation of persons who are or may be without capacity to consent, and**
>
> **(3) that the research will not expose a participant to more than negligible risk, will not be unduly invasive or restrictive of a participant and will not unduly interfere with a participant's freedom of action or privacy. (Draft Bill, clause 11(3).)**

6.35 The draft Bill makes provision for the composition and procedures of the committee.[86]

*Protection for the individual participant*

6.36 It is not realistic or practicable for the individual participation of a person without capacity in a particular project to be referred to the special statutory committee for approval. The committee's role is to approve the research protocol, and we anticipate this involving documentary submissions in most cases. There is, however, a need for a separate and individualised independent check to confirm whether any particular proposed participant should indeed be brought into the project. Our recommendations therefore involve a two-stage process. By way of example, researchers obtain the committee's approval to a project which envisages tests on those with advanced Alzheimer's Disease. The researchers should not then be under the impression that this approval means they may involve in their project all the

---

[85] See para 6.33 above.

[86] Draft Bill, Sched 2.

residents of a particular nursing home who have been diagnosed as suffering from Alzheimer's Disease without the need for any further permission. They must approach each of these proposed participants as an individual. They must ask whether this particular person does indeed have the capacity to consent to what is proposed. It may be that an explanation in simpler or more appropriate terms would be quite comprehensible to the person, especially if given by a person familiar to him or her. If, however, it appears that the proposed participant is without capacity to consent to what is proposed then an independent check is required, and we describe the nature of this check below.

6.37 In most cases the appropriate person to carry out an independent check will be a registered medical practitioner who is not involved in the research project. This need not be an independent doctor appointed to consider such matters by the Secretary of State (as recommended in relation to "second opinion category" treatments).[87] The important point is simply that this doctor should not be involved with the proposed research. The doctor who knows the person best, by virtue of having responsibility for his or her general medical care, will often be the best candidate. An attorney with express authorisation from a donor should, however, be able to consent on the donor's behalf. Similarly, a court-appointed manager may have express authority to give such consent. In some cases the court itself may have made it clear whether the person concerned may participate in non-therapeutic research. In none of these situations need the "second opinion" doctor be involved. There will also be some rare cases where the research protocol does not contemplate any direct contact between researcher and participant. These might involve covert observation or photographing, or the inspection of written records.[88] In such cases, the broad ethical issues still have to be weighed by the committee but there is no purpose in anyone else looking at individual circumstances. The committee should therefore have the power to designate a project as one which does not involve direct contact with participants, with no second-stage check then required.

*We recommend* **that, in addition to the approval of the Mental Incapacity Research Committee, non-therapeutic research in relation to a person without capacity should require either:**

**(1) court approval,**

**(2) the consent of an attorney or manager,**

---

[87] See paras 6.7 - 6.8 above.

[88] The Committee's approval would not address any problem of confidentiality if records are held by a person with a duty of confidentiality. See J V McHale, "Guidelines for Medical Research - Some Ethical and Legal Problems" (1993) 1 Med L Rev 160, 178 - 179. The Department of Health issued draft guidance for the NHS, "Confidentiality, Use and Disclosure of Personal Health Information" (August 1994), inviting comments before 9 December 1994; Section 5 of the draft specifically addresses research.

**(3) a certificate from a doctor not involved in the research that the participation of the person is appropriate, or**

**(4) designation of the research as not involving direct contact.**
(Draft Bill, clause 11(1)(c) and (4).)

6.38    Where the court, an attorney, a manager or an independent doctor is considering the question of a particular individual participating in a project then regard should be had to the factors in the best interests checklist.[89]

6.39    In accordance with the recommendations we have made elsewhere in this report, there should be a clear prohibition against anything being done to a research participant if he or she objects to what is being done. Equally, in the event that a person has made an effective advance refusal to participate in a non-therapeutic research project then no approval of the committee or third party's confirmation would have any effect.[90]

---

[89]   Draft Bill, clause 11(5) and clause 3(2).

[90]   Draft Bill, clause 11(6).

# PART VII
# CONTINUING POWERS OF ATTORNEY

## Introduction

7.1 Our prime policy aim is to encourage people to take for themselves those decisions which they are able to take.[1] This should cover "anticipatory" decisions by people who, knowing or fearing that their decision-making faculties may fail, wish to make plans for what is to happen at that time. Respondents to our consultation papers repeatedly asserted that any judicial process of substitute decision-making should be a last resort, reserved for serious or disputed cases. Anticipatory decision-making or advance planning may well obviate the need for any decision or action imposed by the state.[2] As always, however, endorsement of the autonomy principle must be balanced with the requirements of protection. A law which allows and encourages private arrangements intended to outlast the capacity of the maker to change or cancel them must also provide adequate safeguards for that person.

7.2 A power of attorney is a formal document by which one person (the donor) gives another person (the donee or attorney) authority to act on his or her behalf. The legal principles which govern powers of attorney are to be found in the general law of agency. It is an essential principle that an act done by an attorney can be treated as an act done by the donor, so as to affect the donor's legal relations with third parties.[3] It follows that the attorney only has authority to do what the donor has capacity to do,[4] and that any ordinary power of attorney terminates by operation of law when the donor loses mental capacity.

7.3 Powers of attorney have received attention from this Commission from time to time over the years. Our work[5] led to the Powers of Attorney Act 1971, which clarified the law on the effect of powers of attorney and introduced a short standard form of power. Later work[6] led to the Enduring Powers of Attorney Act 1985, which made it possible for authority granted in a special form of power of attorney to "endure" even if the donor should lose mental capacity. A series of safeguards for

---

[1] See para 2.46 above.

[2] In "Privatising Guardianship - The EPA Alternative" (1993) 15 ADEL LR 79, R Creyke regrets that "scant attention has been given to the relationship of EPAs with other protective mechanisms" (p 83). She argues that EPAs may be capable of fulfilling many of the functions of guardianship and property management and concludes that necessary legislative changes in the Australian states and territories should be considered both "achievable" and "given the financial exigencies of governments, timely" (p 102).

[3] *Bowstead on Agency* (15th ed 1985) p 1.

[4] *Ibid*, p 30.

[5] Powers of Attorney (1970) Law Com No 30 Cmnd 4473.

[6] The Incapacitated Principal (1983) Law Com No 122 Cmnd 8977.

incapacitated donors, to be administered by the Court of Protection, accompanied the introduction of the "enduring power of attorney" ("EPA") in the 1985 Act.

7.4 The perceived need for a statutory regime for EPAs was influenced by the continuing increase in the number of elderly people in our society.[7] Familiarity with the new statutory creature of the EPA appears to have increased very steadily since 1986 and some 15,000 of these documents are now registered with the Court of Protection.[8] It can safely be assumed that many others have been executed but not yet registered.[9] In this Part, we make recommendations for the extension of an enduring power of attorney scheme to a broader range of decisions, and for the reform of its procedures.

7.5 This project presents an invaluable opportunity for integrating a reformed scheme of enduring powers of attorney into a unified scheme which provides for other substitute decision-making procedures. Enduring powers of attorney will take their place in a scheme which comprises the "general authority" already described[10] and formal decision-making within a judicial forum, to be described below.[11] A number of our respondents saw greater scope for "switching jurisdictions" as between a donor-appointed attorney and a court-appointed manager.[12] Our draft Mental Incapacity Bill incorporates an improved statutory scheme for powers of attorney to continue in effect once a donor has lost capacity. Documents executed after the bringing into force of the new legislation will be able to give attorneys authority over whole new areas of decision-making, and should therefore be distinguished from those executed under the 1985 Act by the use of a new label. New safeguards, consistent with the policy aims of this project and with the lessons learned since the introduction of the 1985 Act, are provided.[13]

7.6 Two respondents to our consultation papers questioned whether the use of the terminology of "donor" and "attorney" was appropriate where personal and medical decisions are concerned, and we have considered such terms as "proxy", "agent",

---

[7]  Law Com No 122, *op cit*, para 3.2.

[8]  National Audit Office, *Looking After the Financial Affairs of People with Mental Incapacity* (1994) para 2.20.

[9]  The 1985 Act does not require the document to be registered until the donee has reason to believe that the donor is or is becoming mentally incapable (s 4). One research study suggests that the proportion of EPAs created to EPAs registered is of the order of about 20 to 1 (S Cretney, G Davis, R Kerridge and A Borkowski, *Enduring Powers of Attorney: A Report to the Lord Chancellor* (1991) para 2.19).

[10]  See Part IV above.

[11]  See Part VIII below.

[12]  This matter was raised in Consultation Paper No 128, para 5.34.

[13]  The new scheme is intended to replace the 1985 Act. See further para 7.59 below.

"substitute" or "mandate". We are conscious, however, that the Acts of 1971 and 1985 were not codifications and that the common law in relation to powers of attorney provides a solid base for the statutory provisions. We see dangers and no benefit in abandoning that base. It appears that the concept of the "enduring" power of attorney has gained great ground over the past nine years and that familiarity with this concept can usefully be exploited.

> **We recommend that a new form of power of attorney, to be called a "continuing power of attorney" ("CPA"), should be introduced. The donee of a CPA should have authority to make and implement decisions on behalf of the donor which the donor is without capacity to make.** (Draft Bill, clause 12(1) and (2).)

### Scope of a Continuing Power of Attorney

7.7 As the law now stands, the donor of an EPA can only delegate continuing decision-making authority over his or her "property and affairs".[14] In Consultation Paper No 128 we suggested that donors should be permitted to delegate authority over "personal welfare" decisions,[15] while in Consultation Paper No 129 we extended this proposal to health care decisions.[16] Our consultees almost universally supported the proposal that a donor should be able to delegate non-financial decision-making in advance, in such a way that the authority would outlast any supervening incapacity of the donor. It was said that the great advantage of appointing an attorney to take health care decisions is the ability of the attorney to respond to new situations as they arise. For this reason, some respondents who expressed reservations about the advisability of "advance directives" for health care were nonetheless enthusiastic about allowing people to appoint proxy decision-makers. In its report, the House of Lords Select Committee on Medical Ethics acknowledged "the strong current of opinion in favour of proxy decision-making" about health care matters but concluded that it did not favour the more widespread development of such a system. The committee feared that a person's choice of proxy might become out of date, that the proxy might not make the same choice the patient would have made, and that the proxy might lack objectivity whether as a result of financial self-interest or psychological stress.[17] Exactly the same arguments could be made against allowing people to delegate their financial powers. They appear to us to be arguments in favour of adequate safeguards rather than arguments against the extension of the popular EPA scheme to personal and medical matters. As the Lord Chancellor said in responding to the committee's

---

[14] 1985 Act, s 3(1) and *Re F (Mental Patient: Sterilisation)* [1990] 2 AC 1.

[15] Paragraph 7.3.

[16] Paragraph 5.3.

[17] Report of the Select Committee on Medical Ethics (1993-94) HL 21-I paras 268 - 271.

report, "some people might prefer to appoint a trusted family member rather than try to draw up a complicated living will or leave it all up to the doctors."[18] In our view, the appointment of an attorney with a range of powers should be one option available to those who wish to plan for the possibility of future incapacity. As under the present law, it should always be open to a donor to impose specific conditions or restrictions on the attorney.

> **We recommend that a CPA may extend to matters relating to a donor's personal welfare, health care and property and affairs (including the conduct of legal proceedings); and may be subject to conditions or restrictions.** (Draft Bill, clause 16(1).)

7.8     In the consultation papers we suggested that a donor should always retain power to do any act in relation to which he or she has capacity at the time.[19] Respondents all agreed with this principle.[20] The general law in relation to powers of attorney has always catered for donor and attorney having simultaneous authority to act and we see no reason to depart from this principle. The issue only merits mention because the 1985 Act restricts the ability of the donor of a registered EPA to change the terms of the document.[21] It should be noted, however, that in 1983 this Commission clearly stated that "if the donor after registration has sufficient capacity to do his shopping or run his bank account he should be able to do so independently of the attorney; and people with whom the donor deals should not be prevented from relying on his instructions just because they know that an EPA granted by him has been registered."[22] Imposing any restriction on a donor, merely because authority to act has also been given to an attorney, would conflict with the policy aim of enabling people to act for themselves whenever they have capacity to do so. We do not, therefore, recommend any statutory provision to restrict the common law power of a donor of a power of attorney to act personally where he or she has capacity to do so.

7.9     The general law in relation to powers of attorney will continue to underlie our proposed scheme for Continuing Powers of Attorney. It would, however, be confusing and unhelpful if a document intended to take effect as a CPA, but which failed to meet some of the specific statutory requirements, could be taken to operate

---

[18]   *Hansard* (HL) 9 May 1994, vol 554, col 1353.

[19]   Consultation Paper No 128, paras 7.5 - 7.10; Consultation Paper No 129, para 5.6.

[20]   We discuss the particular issue of revocation by a donor at paras 7.42 - 7.43 below.

[21]   1985 Act, s 7(1)(a) and (c) and s 7(2).

[22]   Law Com No 122, *op cit*, para 4.70.

as an ordinary power of attorney.[23] Nor does this possibility fit with the simplified procedures which we recommend,[24] whereby registration of the CPA will act as a trigger to its effectiveness. We take the view that express provision to rule out any question of an unregistered (and therefore ineffective) CPA operating as an ordinary power would be helpful.

> **We recommend that where an instrument purports to create a CPA but does not comply with the statutory requirements it should confer no powers on the donee.** (Draft Bill, clause 12(4).)

### Duties and powers of attorneys under CPAs

7.10 "An unpaid attorney need not do anything".[25] Although a number of our respondents expressed dissatisfaction with this principle, the arguments against the imposition of a duty to act[26] seem to us even stronger when the attorney may have authority over difficult and delicate personal and medical matters. An attorney with such powers may genuinely be unable to arrive at a firm decision. The new legislation we propose will of course identify others with lawful authority to act, including the court in the last resort. All our respondents, however, agreed with our provisional proposal[27] that where the attorney does exercise his or her authority to act on behalf of the donor then this should be done in the best interests of the donor, with reference to the statutory check-list.[28] This represents a slight shift in the nature of an attorney's duty, which currently depends on the law in relation to contractual and fiduciary relationships.[29] While this may have been entirely adequate when an attorney could only be involved in financial matters, the concept of "best interests" is better adapted to non-financial decisions and can equally well be applied to financial ones.

> **We recommend that an attorney acting under a Continuing Power of Attorney should act in the best interests of the donor, having regard to the statutory factors.** (Draft Bill, clause 3.)

---

[23] There has been debate as to whether a "would be" Enduring Power of Attorney can take effect as a valid ordinary power of attorney; R T Oerton, "EPAs as ordinary powers?" (1987) 131 SJ 1645.

[24] See paras 7.23 *et seq* below.

[25] T Aldridge, *Powers of Attorney* (8th ed 1991) p 72.

[26] See Law Com No 122, *op cit*, paras 4.67 - 4.69; Consultation Paper No 128, paras 7.30 - 7.31; and Consultation Paper No 129, para 5.16.

[27] Consultation Paper No 128, paras 7.30 - 7.31; Consultation Paper No 129, para 5.16.

[28] See Part III above and draft Bill, clause 3.

[29] *Bowstead on Agency* (15th ed 1985) pp 138 and 156 respectively.

7.11    The general law in relation to fiduciary obligations restricts an ordinary attorney from acting so as to benefit himself or herself. The 1985 Act, however, made specific provision relaxing the common law restriction so as to allow the attorney (1) to benefit persons other than the donor and (2) to make gifts in some circumstances.[30] In view of our recommendation that an attorney under a CPA should be subject to the same duty to act in the donor's best interests as any other decision-maker, we see no need for comparable provisions in the new legislation. The power to act in the donor's best interests is a more flexible and slightly wider power than the power of an ordinary attorney at common law. Since it requires the attorney to consider the wishes and feelings of the donor and the factors he or she would have taken into account, the attorney would in appropriate cases be quite able to meet another person's needs (including the attorney's own needs) or make seasonal or charitable gifts, while still acting within the parameters of the best interests duty.[31]

### Statutory conditions and restrictions on CPAs

7.12    While the scope of a CPA may be much wider than that of an EPA, an attorney will not be able to do anything which, under the general law, can only be done by a person acting for himself or herself.[32] Some further special restrictions should be imposed.

*(1) Confinement and coercion*

7.13    If an attorney under a CPA has powers in relation to personal and health care matters then that attorney should be bound by the general restriction against acts of confinement or coercion which we have recommended as a qualification upon the general authority of informal decision-makers.[33] It is a well-established facet of the general law in relation to powers of attorney that the donor may revoke the power either expressly or impliedly, by doing acts inconsistent with the continued existence of the power. The active objection of a donor is highly likely to be an act amounting to implied revocation. It might therefore be argued that no express restriction on the authority of attorneys under CPAs to confine or coerce donors is needed. It appears to us, however, that the arguments in favour of express provision apply to attorneys as they apply to informal decision-makers.

> **We recommend** that the restriction against coercion or confinement should apply equally to attorneys. (Draft Bill, clauses

---

[30]    Section 3(4) and (5).

[31]    This is consistent with the fact that the court might approve the donation of non-regenerative tissue by a person without capacity as being in the best interests of the donor. See para 6.5 above.

[32]    See para 4.29 above and draft Bill, clause 30.

[33]    Draft Bill, clause 5.

16(4) and 5.)

*(2) The donor has capacity to act personally*

7.14 The origins of the EPA scheme in the 1985 Act lie in the general law relating to powers of attorney and it is no part of that law that a donor or principal must lack capacity before an attorney or agent may act. We suggested in the consultation papers, however, that while no such restriction need apply to personal welfare powers,[34] an attorney should only have power to take a medical treatment decision if the donor lacks capacity to take that decision for himself or herself.[35] The difference in the health care context is that the health care provider is always under a personal obligation to assess the patient's capacity to consent to any treatment proposed. There is therefore nothing unduly burdensome in expecting both doctor and attorney to investigate whether the donor can give or refuse personal consent to any particular treatment. Respondents supported our provisional views.

**We *recommend* that no attorney may consent to or refuse any treatment unless the donor is, or is reasonably believed by the attorney to be, without capacity to give or refuse personal consent to that treatment.** (Draft Bill, clause 16(3)(a).)

*(3) Admission to hospital under the 1983 Act*

7.15 The Mental Health Act 1983 provides that persons may be compulsorily admitted to hospital to be assessed or treated for mental disorder. In fact, the vast majority of people so assessed or treated are not detained under the compulsory powers but have agreed (or at least not objected) to the hospital admission.[36] We see no objection to an attorney who holds health care powers assisting and arranging such an admission within the terms of his or her obligation to act in the donor's best interests. However, the situation is entirely different where the donor actively objects to the proposed hospital admission. We have already recommended a general restriction on attorneys where the donor actively objects to what is being done.[37] However, for the avoidance of doubt,

**we *recommend* that no attorney should have power to consent to the donor's admission to hospital for assessment or treatment for mental disorder, where such admission is against the will of the**

---

[34] Consultation Paper No 128, paras 7.8 - 7.9.

[35] Consultation Paper No 129, para 5.5.

[36] The most recent figures available (for 1989/90) indicate that less than 7% of those admitted to hospital in such circumstances were formally admitted under the civil admission provisions in the Mental Health Act 1983 (Department of Health Statistical Bulletin 2(7)92, *Inpatients Formally Detained in Hospitals under the Mental Health Act 1983 and Other Legislation, England 1984/90* (1993) Table 1).

[37] See para 7.13 above.

**donor.** (Draft Bill, clause 16(3)(b).)

This simply means that the safeguards and procedures of the 1983 Act cannot be avoided by reference to the consent of an attorney.

*(4) Basic care*

7.16 We suggested in Consultation Paper No 129[38] that no attorney with health care powers should be able to refuse, on a donor's behalf, the sort of basic care which maintains the patient in a hygienic pain-free state and provides spoon-feeding. All but one of our consultees agreed with this proposed restriction. We intend a similar restriction to apply to decisions by way of "advance refusal" and have already explained that our thinking is based on considerations of public policy.[39] We have referred to the BMA's submission to us that patients can wish to limit the amount of pain relief administered so as to retain a higher level of consciousness and interaction.[40] The definition of "basic care" adopted in our draft legislation acknowledges that not *all* forms of pain relief must be accepted, but that all "direct oral" forms of nutrition and hydration should be covered.

> *We recommend* that no attorney should be authorised to withhold basic care from the donor or refuse consent to its provision. (Draft Bill, clauses 16(3)(c) and 9(8).)

*(5) The donor has made an advance refusal*

7.17 It may be that people will wish to give written directions about their future health care, as well as appointing another person under a CPA. It follows from our discussion of advance refusals of treatment in Part V above that an attorney can have no more power than any other person (or the court) to override a valid and applicable advance refusal. In Consultation Paper No 129[41] we suggested that an attorney might override an advance refusal if the refusal itself provided for this eventuality. An example might be "I refuse cardio-pulmonary resuscitation unless my attorney consents to it". There is, however, no need for any special provision to cover the possibility of such wording; the refusal will simply not "apply in the circumstances" of the attorney consenting. The situation may be less clear and easy to resolve where a donor has granted a general power over health care matters to an attorney, but *subsequently* makes an advance refusal. We think it would be helpful to specify that, in the absence of express provision to the contrary in the CPA, the attorney may not consent to procedures covered by an advance refusal. In relation

---

[38] Paragraph 5.20 and paras 3.25 - 3.26.

[39] See para 5.34 above. We recommend a similar restriction on the powers of a court-appointed manager; see para 8.24 below.

[40] See para 5.34 above.

[41] Paragraph 5.20.

to advance statements which are not "advance refusals" the attorney, acting in the best interests of the donor, will still be obliged to consider the donor's expressed wishes and feelings. An attorney will also be able to take into account such factors as changes in medical technology and changes in the donor's outlook and attitudes. In this way the appointment of an attorney will, importantly, allow a flexible and adaptable approach to future health care issues to be constructed by a donor.

> **We recommend that, unless expressly authorised to do so, no attorney may consent to any treatment refused by the donor by an advance refusal of treatment.** (Draft Bill, clause 16(3)(d)(i).)

### (6) Procedures requiring independent supervision

7.18 In Consultation Paper No 129 we provisionally proposed that an attorney should never be able to consent to procedures requiring independent supervision.[42] In discussing such procedures in Part VI above, we recommended instead that if a donor clearly intends his or her attorney to displace the need for independent supervision then the law should respect that decision. We think this represents a sensible compromise, neither forbidding a donor to delegate a certain range of decisions nor allowing power over controversial decisions to be handed over without careful consideration. In each case, the donor must give the attorney express authority to consent to any of the "independent supervision" procedures.

> **We recommend that, unless expressly authorised to do so, no attorney may consent on a donor's behalf to:**
>
> **(1) a procedure requiring court approval,**
>
> **(2) a procedure requiring a certificate from an independent medical practitioner,**
>
> **(3) discontinuance of artificial nutrition or hydration,**
>
> **(4) procedures for the benefit of others, or**
>
> **(5) participation in non-therapeutic research.** (Draft Bill, clauses 16(3)(d)(ii) and 16(5).)

### (7) Life-sustaining treatment

7.19 Many respondents agreed with our preliminary view[43] that power over certain sorts of serious medical decision (and not only those requiring independent supervision)

---

[42] *Ibid.*

[43] Consultation Paper No 129, para 5.7.

should require express authorisation by a donor. Such decisions would never be covered by a "general" power[44] and would require express "opting-in" on the donor's part. In the consultation paper we suggested that a donor might be required to take a positive decision about granting power to refuse "life-saving treatment".[45] It was clear on consultation that many people might want to appoint a health care attorney precisely so as to ensure that someone makes appropriate "treatment-limiting" decisions for them. While there is therefore no question of preventing donors from giving attorneys such powers, it is entirely appropriate to require that the donor should have made express provision in the CPA.[46]

> **We recommend** that, unless expressly authorised to do so, no attorney may refuse consent to any treatment necessary to sustain life. (Draft Bill, clause 16(3)(d)(iii).)

**Requirements affecting the donor and donee**

*(1) The donor*

7.20 Under the current law, a donor of an EPA must be an individual with capacity to create the power. There are no other restrictions on donors, and it was stated in Law Com No 122 that minors and undischarged bankrupts would be able to create EPAs, albeit that this would be unusual and that any attorney's authority might be restricted by the general law.[47] The general law as to the effect of a minor appointing an attorney remains complex, and it may be that the appointment itself is voidable by the minor if not for his or her benefit.[48] Where CPAs are concerned, it would not be satisfactory to rely on the fact that a minor has power to "avoid" transactions by an attorney. There may be physical, emotional or psychological consequences of a personal welfare or health care decision which cannot easily be reversed by the payment of a compensatory sum of money. Since a CPA may cover personal welfare matters and health care decisions, there would also be very significant complications with the law in relation to parental responsibility and the inherent jurisdiction of the High Court if a CPA could be created by a minor. We think it entirely appropriate that the right to create a document with such far-reaching legal consequences as a Continuing Power of Attorney should be restricted to adults.

---

[44] See paras 7.25 - 7.26 below for a discussion of a general form of CPA.

[45] Consultation Paper No 129, para 5.7.

[46] We have recommended that a similar requirement should apply to a person's own "advance refusal" of life-sustaining treatment, see para 5.26 above and draft Bill, clause 9(3).

[47] Law Com No 122, *op cit*, para 4.5 n 109.

[48] See further *Bowstead on Agency* (15th ed 1985) p 31.

**We recommend** that a CPA may only be created by an individual who has attained the age of eighteen. (Draft Bill, clause 14(1).)

*(2) The donee*

7.21    The 1985 Act specifically provided that the donee executing an EPA must be either an individual (over eighteen and not bankrupt) or a trust corporation.[49] It would not be appropriate for a trust corporation to exercise personal or health care powers, but apart from that there is no need for any change in the law.[50] In the consultation papers we provisionally proposed that it should never be possible for a public official *in his or her official capacity* to be appointed attorney.[51] However, we were influenced by the views of the Public Trustee and the Association of Directors of Social Services (among others) that there might be occasions where a public official should be available to act as attorney of last resort. This would not require specific provision, since all the likely candidates will be either "individuals" or trust corporations. For the avoidance of doubt, we think the legislation should specify that an individual can be identifiable by reference to an office or position (eg, the manager for the time being of the X branch of the Y Bank, or the Director of Social Services of Z Region). The person fulfilling the description at the time of execution would have to execute the CPA as donee of the power, even though a successor might subsequently act as attorney. Appointing an office-holder is probably possible under the existing law,[52] but is uncommon. Where it is not intended to put the CPA into immediate effect, there will often be good reasons for avoiding the appointment of an office-holder. The result of local government or NHS re-organisation, or of business changes in a solicitors' firm or a financial institution, might be that there is no person fulfilling the description of the attorney when a time arrives when the CPA is needed.[53] In cases where the CPA is to be registered and put into effect at once, however, the appointment of an office-holder might be a useful facility.

**We recommend** that an individual donee of a CPA may be described as the holder for the time being of a specified office or position. (Draft Bill, clause 14(3).)

---

[49]    Enduring Powers of Attorney Act 1985, s 2(7). "Trust corporation" is defined in the Trustee Act 1925, s 68(18), and the definition includes the Public Trustee. The Treasury Solicitor and Official Solicitor are included by virtue of the Law of Property (Amendment) Act 1926, s 3. The rules for qualifying corporations are contained in the Public Trustee Rules 1912 (SR & O 1912/348) (as amended).

[50]    See draft Bill, clause 14(2) and (4). In relation to revocation by supervening bankruptcy see para 7.47 below.

[51]    Consultation Paper No 128, para 7.27; Consultation Paper No 129, para 5.14.

[52]    S Cretney, *Enduring Powers of Attorney* (3rd ed 1991) para 2.3.3.

[53]    See para 7.56 below for the power of the court to appoint a replacement attorney.

*(3) Multiple donees*

7.22 The present law makes special provision for multiple attorneys, specifically allowing joint or "joint and several" attorneys.[54] We suggested in the consultation papers that, in contrast with the present law, donors should also be permitted to appoint an "alternate" attorney to act if the original fails or ceases to act for some reason.[55] Respondents agreed that there would be advantages in allowing for such a possibility. In order to ensure consistency with the registration system we describe below, replacement attorneys should only be available in circumstances where the original donee has ceased to act for a reason which can be established by objective evidence.

> **We recommend that a donor may, in a CPA, appoint a person to replace the donee in the event of the donee disclaiming, dying, becoming bankrupt or becoming divorced from the donor. (Draft Bill, clause 20(1)).**

It should also be possible to appoint joint or joint and several attorneys under a CPA.[56] Our draft Bill applies the rules in relation to CPAs to the case of multiple attorneys.[57]

**Formalities and safeguards**

7.23 We will now deal with the formal and procedural aspects of our proposed scheme for Continuing Powers of Attorney. In the consultation papers we proposed some radical departures from the formalities and safeguards constructed by the 1985 Act.[58] We have reconsidered our original suggestions in the light of helpful comments, and significant reservations, expressed by those whom we consulted. We believe that our recommendations now strike the right balance between protection for donors who may come to lack capacity and procedural simplicity, encouraging ever greater use of the provisions.[59]

---

[54] 1985 Act, s 11(1). Joint attorneys must all join together in any decision. "Joint and several" attorneys may each act independently, or all together.

[55] Consultation Paper No 128, para 7.25; Consultation Paper No 129, para 5.13. It seems that appointing an attorney to act only if the original attorney never takes up the appointment is possible under the present law (S Cretney, *Enduring Powers of Attorney* (3rd ed 1991) para 7.2.1)). This would also appear to follow from the discussion in Law Com No 122, *op cit*, paras 4.91 n 211 and 4.92 n 214.

[56] Draft Bill, clause 20(2).

[57] Draft Bill, clause 20(3) and (4).

[58] Consultation Paper No 128, paras 7.12 - 7.23; Consultation Paper No 129, paras 5.7 - 5.11.

[59] See the discussion on balancing these two requirements in Law Com No 122, *op cit*, paras 3.9 - 3.13.

*(1) A prescribed form*

7.24 We see no need to depart from the principle that a power of attorney which is going to outlast the donor's incapacity must be in a form prescribed by the Lord Chancellor, and include prescribed explanatory information.[60] This should describe the general effect of creating and accepting the power.[61] The form should include a statement by the donor that he or she intends the power to continue in spite of supervening mental incapacity and that he or she has read (or had read to him or her) the explanatory information.[62] The 1985 Act stipulates that the form must include a statement by the attorney in relation to the duty to register the EPA.[63] No such duty will apply to donees of CPAs but

> **we recommend that a CPA must contain a statement by the donee that he or she understands the duty to act in the best interests of the donor in relation to any decision which the donor is, or is reasonably believed by the donee to be, without capacity to make.** (Draft Bill, clause 13(3)(b)(ii).)

7.25 In Consultation Paper No 128 we expressed reservations about a "general" power of attorney being used in relation to personal welfare matters.[64] Numerous respondents, however, saw disadvantages in requiring donors to use a more complex prescribed form. Few agreed that a more complex form would offer any significant protection to vulnerable donors. Some recalled the days before the 1971 Act, when every power of attorney had to specify the powers being granted and many of them ran into copious pages of small print. Respondents to Consultation Paper No 129[65] were in favour of a standard form which could be adapted as required by an individual donor. We are now persuaded that there is no objection in principle to donors granting wide "general" powers so long as explanatory information makes clear the nature of the powers granted. As we have explained,[66] donors can impose their own restrictions and there will be certain conditions and restrictions imposed by law.

---

[60] 1985 Act, s 2(1)(a) and (c). Draft Bill, clause 13(1)(a) and (c) and clause 13(2). The necessary regulations should be made by statutory instrument subject to the negative resolution procedure: 1985 Act, s2(4) and draft Bill, clause 22. See para 7.55 below on a saving provision and a dispensing power.

[61] 1985 Act, s 2(2)(a); draft Bill, clause 13(3)(a).

[62] 1985 Act, s 2(2)(b); draft Bill, clause 13(3)(b)(i).

[63] 1985 Act, s 2(2)(b)(iii).

[64] Paragraphs 7.12 - 7.14.

[65] Paragraph 5.7.

[66] See para 7.7 above.

**We recommend** that a CPA may be expressed to confer general authority on a donee. (Draft Bill, clause 16(2).)

7.26 While the details of any prescribed form are for secondary legislation, we should report that both the Law Society and the BMA submitted to us that a power of attorney for health care decisions should always be a completely separate document from one dealing with personal welfare or property and affairs. We are not ourselves persuaded, in the context of the unified scheme we recommend throughout this report, that people need be put to the trouble and expense of preparing and executing two separate documents. We take it that a great many people would find it entirely appropriate to give power over all three areas to a spouse, life-partner or other relative. A single form with separate sections in relation to (1) personal welfare matters (2) health care matters and (3) property and affairs might be a possible solution.

*(2) Execution requirements*

7.27 In the consultation papers, we proposed creating much more stringent formalities for execution than those which have been imposed in relation to EPAs.[67] The 1985 Act stipulates that an EPA must be executed in the prescribed manner.[68] At present, the relevant regulations require signature by both donor and donee, each in the presence of a single witness.[69] Our provisional proposal that the donor's capacity to execute should be certified by a solicitor and a doctor at the time of execution did not commend itself to the majority of our consultees. Numerous respondents said that any such requirement would present practical difficulties and force donors to incur extra costs. Concern focused on the idea that *both* a doctor *and* a lawyer need be involved in every case. It should in any event be a matter of good practice for all health professionals not to witness a signature without considering the question of the person's capacity to execute the document. Lawyers involved in drawing up powers of attorney should also, as a matter of good practice, be very clear that the client to whom the duty of care is owed is the donor of the power and no-one else. In appropriate cases good practice already demands that an appropriate medical certificate should be obtained and/or appropriate records kept on file. The provisional proposal for a certification procedure was a corollary to the proposed abolition of any form of registration, which, as we explain below, we are no longer pursuing. In those circumstances, the draft Bill simply provides that a CPA (like an EPA) must be executed in the prescribed manner by both donor and donee.[70]

---

[67] Consultation Paper No 128, para 7.15; Consultation Paper No 129, para 5.8.

[68] 1985 Act, s 2(1)(b).

[69] Enduring Powers of Attorney (Prescribed Form) Regulations 1990 (SI 1990 No 1376), reg 3(1).

[70] Clause 13(1)(b).

*(3) Registration of Continuing Powers of Attorney*

7.28 The 1985 Act requires an attorney under an EPA to notify a listed set of relatives and then apply to register the EPA with the Court of Protection, once the donor "is or is becoming" mentally incapable.[71] In the consultation papers we suggested that the 1985 registration scheme was flawed, and should be abandoned and replaced with a different set of safeguards for donors.[72] Consultees who commented on this were evenly divided between those who wanted some form of registration scheme retained and those who did not. Although many of those with detailed knowledge of the workings of the present scheme subscribed to our provisional view, others were convinced that registration operated as a significant protection for donors. We have carefully reconsidered this matter in the light of the many helpful comments made on consultation.

7.29 We have also been assisted in our deliberations by discussions with our colleagues in the Scottish Law Commission. They, in a sense, approach the matter from the opposite direction. As a temporary measure, pending a full review of the various options by the Commission, Scots law simply provides that no power of attorney is revoked by the donor's mental incapacity.[73] There are no special formalities and no registration requirements. The Scottish Law Commission originally proposed that adequate safeguards ensuring that a donor had capacity to execute a CPA would be preferable to any form of registration.[74] The Commission's consultees, however, favoured a simple scheme of registration with an administrative body, and we understand that some form of registration procedure is likely to be recommended by our Scottish counterparts.

7.30 A straightforward administrative registration procedure can have the merit of bringing a document into the public domain and establishing its formal validity. A mark of validity can be of benefit to both donor and donee. A process of registration involving a public body will undoubtedly discourage some people who might abuse powers which remain in the private domain and will provide a point of reference for those who have queries or concerns about the status of a particular document. Registration can also serve to distinguish CPAs from ordinary powers of attorney. We therefore considered whether every CPA should be registered under such a scheme at the time of execution. Some donors, however, currently execute their EPAs well in advance of any loss of capacity. These are sometimes called "insurance

---

[71] 1985 Act, s 4.

[72] Consultation Paper No 128, paras 7.20 - 7.23; Consultation Paper No 129, para 5.11.

[73] Law Reform (Miscellaneous Provisions) (Scotland) Act 1990, s 71. This section only has effect in relation to those powers of attorney "granted on or after the date on which this section comes into force"; s 71 came into force on 1 January 1991.

[74] Discussion Paper No 94, Mentally Disabled Adults: Legal Arrangements for Managing their Welfare and Finances (1991), para 5.50. Criticisms of the registration scheme in the Enduring Powers of Attorney Act 1985 are made at paras 5.45 - 5.50.

policy" EPAs; the need for the attorney to exercise any of the powers granted might never materialise. A requirement to register upon execution might needlessly burden a well-organised donor, as well as the registration authority.

7.31 Any registration scheme should direct its benefits towards those donors who are in need of them. Under the scheme in the 1985 Act, this leads to the requirement to register only when the donor "is or is becoming" mentally incapable. In the consultation paper[75] we expressed particular concern about the fact that this requirement leads on to a statutory assumption that the donor of a registered EPA lacks capacity, and in particular capacity to revoke the EPA. We take the view that registration should no longer purport to identify those donors who are losing their capacity, but should instead apply to those donors of CPAs whose attorneys wish to *use* the powers granted in the instrument. A firm distinction should therefore be drawn between an "ordinary power of attorney" and one which is in the prescribed form for a CPA, and in particular contains the essential statement by the donor that it is intended to last beyond incapacity. It should no longer be possible to operate an unregistered CPA as if it were an ordinary power of attorney.[76] Every potential CPA must be a *registered* CPA before the donee can exercise any of the powers conferred in the document.

> **We recommend that no document should create a Continuing Power of Attorney until it has been registered in the prescribed manner.** (Draft Bill, clause 15(1).)

7.32 The 1985 Act allocated numerous administrative and judicial functions in relation to EPAs to the Court of Protection. Many of the administrative functions, especially those concerned with registration,[77] have in reality been carried out in the Public Trust Office rather than by the Court itself. New Rules which have been brought into force now that the Public Trust Office has acquired agency status[78] provide for the division of functions between the Court of Protection and the Public Trustee.[79] The registration scheme we now recommend will be purely administrative in nature and we would expect it to be operated by the Public Trust Office, many of whose staff have been performing administrative functions in relation to EPAs for the past

---

[75] Consultation Paper No 128, paras 7.7 and 7.20.

[76] In Law Com No 122 it was envisaged that an EPA could be "operable like an ordinary power" during the donor's capacity, although EPAs would be "by no means interchangeable with other powers" (Law Com No 122, *op cit*, paras 4.32 and 4.33). See our recommendation at para 7.9 above.

[77] 1985 Act, s 6.

[78] On 1 July 1994.

[79] The Court of Protection (Enduring Powers of Attorney) Rules 1994 (SI 1994 No 3047). Functions relating to registration of EPAs are allocated to the Public Trustee (rule 6).

eight years.[80] It will, however, be for the Lord Chancellor to determine which administrative body should discharge the functions described in our Bill.

**We recommend that a registration authority appointed by the Lord Chancellor should register CPAs. (Draft Bill, clause 15(1).)[81]**

7.33 Any donee of a CPA who seeks to *use* the powers granted in the document will be obliged to apply for registration of the document. Questions about the donor's capacity will not concern the registration authority, which will register the power upon the donee making an application for registration in the prescribed form, subject only to the CPA complying with the prescribed formalities.[82] If the document is an "insurance policy" CPA then the donee will probably not wish to go to the trouble of registration until the need arises.

*(4) Notification to the donor*

7.34 We favour the retention of a requirement that a donee must notify a donor of his or her intention to register a CPA.[83] It may be some time since the document was executed and, in any event, the act of registration will significantly alter matters by triggering the attorney's power to act. The donor must be warned that this is in prospect and be given an opportunity to prevent registration. The registration authority will have no power to determine disputes and such matters will always have to go to the court. Thus, if the registration authority is informed by a donor that he or she objects to registration of a CPA then the registration authority will have no power to register it in the absence of a direction from the court. There is no need to specify any particular grounds on which a donor may object to registration.[84]

**We recommend that if a donor objects to registration of a CPA then the registration authority should inform the donee and should not register the document unless the court directs it to do so. (Draft Bill, clause 15(4).)**

7.35 As at present, the court should have power to dispense with notification if it would

---

[80] The 1985 Act came into force on 10 March 1986 (Enduring Powers of Attorney Act 1985 (Commencement) Order 1986 (SI 1986 No 125)).

[81] The draft Bill makes the necessary provision for office copies of registered instruments to be issued (clause 15(8)) and for copies to be proved by other authorised means (clause 15(9)).

[82] Draft Bill, clause 15(2).

[83] 1985 Act, s 4(3) and Sched 1, para 4(1); draft Bill, clause 15(3).

[84] Contrast 1985 Act, s 6(5).

serve no useful purpose.[85] Examples would be where the donor is in a coma or severely demented. We were told on consultation that at present an attorney is often embarrassed by having to spell out for the donor the attorney's belief that he or she is becoming mentally incapacitated. In future, there will be no necessary link between the intention to register and incipient incapacity. We therefore see no need to reproduce the extremely wide power in the 1985 Act for notification to the donor to be dispensed with because it would be "undesirable" or "impractical".[86]

7.36 The fact that a CPA has been registered will not necessarily signify any loss of capacity on the donor's part. It is therefore only right that notice should also be given to the donor once registration takes place.

> *We recommend* **that once a CPA has been registered the registration authority should give notice of that fact in the prescribed form to the donor.** (Draft Bill, clause 15(6)(a).)

*(5) Notification to relatives or others*

7.37 In Consultation Paper No 128 we suggested that requiring an attorney to notify listed relatives of the donor was hard to justify in the context of "least restrictive intervention".[87] Many respondents endorsed this view. There was particular concern about the fact that the statutory list makes no acknowledgment that close and important relationships may exist outside of legal marriage and blood ties. It conflicts with the autonomy principle to require, regardless of the donor's wishes, that certain relatives must be notified of a private arrangement to govern future decision-making. Our respondents strongly supported the idea that a donor should be able to choose who might be notified about his or her power of attorney.[88]

7.38 We see a place for the notification of relatives or others as part of the "publicity" facet of the new registration scheme. It should, however, differ in two marked respects from the present notification scheme. First, it should be a notification that a CPA *has been* registered rather than a notification of an intention to register. We see no reason for the law to assume that the donor's actions are such that his or her relatives should have a right to object. The assumption should be that the donor has made valid arrangements, although properly concerned relatives will be able to take

---

[85] 1985 Act, s 4(3) and Sched 1 paras 4(2) and 3(2)(b); draft Bill, clause 15(5).

[86] 1985 Act, s 4(3) and Sched 1 paras 3(2)(a) and 4(2).

[87] Paragraph 7.16.

[88] See Consultation Paper No 128, paras 7.17 - 7.18 and Consultation Paper No 129, para 5.9. Our provisional proposal was to abolish registration so that any notification would take place on execution of the document.

positive steps to challenge those arrangements.[89] Secondly, it is for the donor to say who should be notified and not for statute to lay down a list.

> **We recommend** that once a CPA has been registered the registration authority should give notice of that fact in the prescribed form to a maximum of two people (not including the donee) as specified in the CPA. (Draft Bill, clause 15(6)(b).)

7.39 Although some respondents expressed concern about donors who had no friends or relatives to name for the purposes of notification, the same problem arises under the present statutory list arrangements. Notification can only ever be one small part of the protection afforded to donors. We note that more than one respondent to Consultation Paper No 129 suggested that a GP would be an appropriate person to be notified about a health care power of attorney.

### Termination of Continuing Powers of Attorney

7.40 At common law a power of attorney comes to an end when (1) disclaimed by the attorney, (2) revoked (expressly or impliedly) by the donor or (3) terminated by operation of law (for example, upon the incapacity, death or bankruptcy of the parties). It can also terminate by expiry, having been granted for a fixed term or until the happening of a particular event. It seems most unlikely that a donor of a CPA, whose whole purpose is to provide for a future time when he or she will lack capacity, would wish to fix an expiry date for his or her CPA. We will now deal with the circumstances in which Continuing Powers of Attorney will terminate. As we will explain later,[90] the court will also have power to terminate a CPA in certain circumstances.

*(1) Disclaimer by the donee*

7.41 The donee of a CPA is under no duty to act on behalf of the donor and, until the CPA is registered, has no power so to act.[91] There is no scope for any special disclaimer rules in relation to unregistered (and therefore ineffective) CPAs. Once a CPA is registered, however, a disclaiming attorney should notify both the donor (since registration does not signify that the donor lacks capacity) and the registration authority.

> **We recommend** that no disclaimer of a registered CPA should be

---

[89] See para 7.58 below.

[90] See para 7.58 below.

[91] This should be contrasted with the position of a donee of an Enduring Power of Attorney who is under a duty to register the power when he or she has reason to believe that the donor is becoming mentally incapable (1985 Act, s 4(1) and (2)). It follows from this duty to register that the donee of an EPA can be obliged to notify the donor of any disclaimer, even if the donor has not yet lost capacity (1985 Act, s 2(12)).

**valid unless notice is given to the donor and the registration authority.** (Draft Bill, clause 15(7).)

*(2) Revocation by the donor*

7.42   There is a common law principle that a donor of a power can revoke all or any of it, either expressly (for example by saying so, or by tearing up the document) or impliedly, by doing an act which is inconsistent with the continuation of the power (for example, concealing the whereabouts of all assets from the attorney). The general rule as to capacity applies to revocation and a donor's revocation is only effective if he or she has capacity to revoke, in other words understands the nature and effect of the action being taken. The 1985 Act does not affect the common law position until the attorney makes an application for registration, whereupon it radically alters it. Our predecessors recommended that the ability of a donor of an EPA to deal in any way with *a registered power* should be curtailed, in order to preserve "the 'sanctity' of registration".[92] The 1985 Act therefore provides that "no revocation of...[a registered] power by the donor shall be valid unless and until the court confirms the revocation... ".[93]

7.43   We suggested in the consultation papers that a donor with capacity to do so should always be able to revoke a power of attorney.[94] Respondents unanimously agreed with this policy and some of them mentioned that it was particularly important not to restrict, and not even to impose any delay upon, a donor's ability to revoke a health care power. In relation to CPAs covering health care decisions, we have explained that no attorney's authority will ever coincide with that of a donor who is still able personally to consent to or refuse any treatment offered.[95] Where a donor does, however, lack capacity to take the decision in question, he or she may still have capacity to revoke the CPA ("I don't want X deciding things for me any more"). It would be most unappealing to require that a treatment-provider must continue to honour the decision of an attorney when faced with a donor who is now revoking the authority granted. We therefore think it necessary to stress, by way of an explicit provision, that a donor should always retain the power to revoke his or her CPA.

> *We recommend* **an express provision that nothing in the legislation should preclude the donor of a CPA from revoking it at any time when he or she has the capacity to do so.** (Draft Bill,

---

[92]   Law Com No 122, *op cit*, para 4.73.

[93]   1985 Act, s 7(1)(a). Subsection (2) stresses that subsection (1) applies "for so long as the instrument is registered...whether or not the donor is for the time being mentally incapable."

[94]   Consultation Paper No 128, para 7.10; Consultation Paper No 129, para 5.6.

[95]   See para 7.14 above.

clause 12(3).)

7.44    Some of our expert legal consultees, however, raised the matter of protection for attorneys and third parties. The clear effect of the 1985 Act is that an attorney or third party can confidently ignore any purported revocation by a donor if "confirmation" has not been received from the court. This provision conflicts with the principles underlying our project.[96] Can adequate protection for attorneys or third parties be provided by some other means? As we mentioned in Consultation Paper No 128,[97] the Powers of Attorney Act 1971 already provides protection for attorneys and third parties where revocation may be an issue. For attorneys, it states that:

> " A donee of a power of attorney who acts in pursuance of the power at a time when it has been revoked shall not, by reason of the revocation, incur any liability (either to the donor or to any other person) if at that time he did not know that the power had been revoked".[98]

For third parties, it states that:

> "Where a power of attorney has been revoked and a person, without knowledge of the revocation, deals with the donee of the power, the transaction between them shall, in favour of that person, be as valid as if the power had then been in existence".[99]

We take the view that these provisions, looking at the *knowledge* of the attorney or third party, provide clear and adequate protection for them in all the circumstances where it is appropriate. They should apply equally to Continuing Powers of Attorney.

> ***We recommend*** **that section 5 of the Powers of Attorney Act 1971 should apply to Continuing Powers of Attorney.** (Draft Bill, clause 19(6).)

*(3) Termination by operation of law*

7.45    The rules about bankruptcy in relation to CPAs need to distinguish between the grant of powers over "property and affairs" and the grant of powers over personal

---

[96]    See para 2.46 above.

[97]    Paragraph 7.10.

[98]    1971 Act, s 5(1).

[99]    1971 Act, s 5(2).

and health care matters. Although the existing rules whereby a bankrupt cannot act as an attorney should continue to apply to any powers over "property and affairs", we see no reason for an absolute rule that a bankrupt may not act as an attorney in relation to personal and health care matters. Those parts of a CPA which relate to personal or health care matters need not, therefore, be revoked by the donee's bankruptcy.

7.46    A bankrupt may not be appointed as a donee of powers over property and financial affairs in a CPA.[100] The supervening bankruptcy of a donee revokes an EPA[101] and so should the supervening bankruptcy of a donee of powers over property and affairs in a CPA revoke his or her appointment as the donee of such powers.[102] The 1985 Act provides that where two or more attorneys are appointed to act jointly then the bankruptcy of any one should revoke the powers of all; where they may act jointly and severally, however, the bankruptcy of any one of them does not revoke the powers of the others.[103] Similar provision is made in the draft Bill.[104]

7.47    The authority of an attorney is revoked by the later bankruptcy of the donor.[105] This rule applies to transactions relating to property of which the donor is divested by the vesting of it in the trustee in bankruptcy[106] and it would not therefore apply to personal or health care matters. The 1985 Act did not give the rule a statutory form. In view of the fact that CPAs can extend beyond financial matters, express provision in the new legislation would be helpful.

> **We recommend that any part of a CPA which relates to matters other than property and financial affairs should not be revoked by the donor's bankruptcy.** (Draft Bill, clause 16(6).)

Our draft legislation provides for the consequences of the partial revocation of a CPA so far as the registration of the document is concerned.[107]

7.48    The 1985 Act makes no specific provision for cases where a donor and donee who

---

[100]  See para 7.21 above.

[101]  1985 Act, s 2(10).

[102]  Draft Bill, clause 14(4).

[103]  1985 Act, Sched 3 paras 2 and 7 respectively.

[104]  Draft Bill, clause 20(3)(d).

[105]  *Markwick v Hardingham* (1880) 15 Ch 339.

[106]  It should be noted that the Insolvency Act 1986, s 337 now provides that a bankrupt has certain rights of occupation in his dwelling house as against the trustee of his estate.

[107]  Draft Bill, clause 18(2) and see para 7.49 below.

were married at the time the donee was appointed have subsequently divorced. Since a CPA cannot take effect immediately, but must first be registered, we think it appropriate to provide for such circumstances. The law already makes provision for the situation where a testator appointed a divorced spouse executor or beneficiary under his or her will.[108] A donor of a CPA may be equally unable to remedy the original, now inappropriate, appointment.

> **We recommend that, in the absence of a contrary intention, the appointment of the donee's spouse as an attorney under a CPA should be revoked by the subsequent dissolution or annulment of the parties' marriage. (Draft Bill, clause 14(5).)**

A reminder might helpfully be placed on the standard form decree absolute of divorce. By analogy with the case where one attorney becomes bankrupt but multiple attorneys have been appointed to act jointly and severally, the divorce between the donor and one of multiple joint and several donees should not terminate the powers of other donees to act.[109]

## Powers of the registration authority

7.49 The role of the registration authority should simply be (1) to register CPAs and give notice of registration, (2) to cancel registrations and (3) to amend registrations in cases of partial revocation or the appointment of replacement attorneys. Since the registration authority will be an administrative rather than a judicial body, cancellation or amendment should only be effected on the receipt of specified types of objective evidence. If a change to the registration requires a determination of some disputed fact, or the exercise of discretion, then the court will make the necessary determination and then give instructions to the registration authority.

> **We recommend that the registration authority should cancel the registration of a CPA on receipt of a revocation by the donor, a disclaimer by the donee or evidence that the power has expired or been revoked by death, bankruptcy, winding up or the dissolution of the parties' marriage. (Draft Bill, clause 18(1).)**

> **The registration authority should attach an appropriate note to any registered CPA which has been partially revoked, or in relation to which a replacement donee has gained power to act. (Draft Bill, clause 18(2) and (5).)**

---

[108] Wills Act 1837, s 18A. In our report, Family Law: The Effect of Divorce on Wills (1993) Law Com No 222 Cm 2322 we recommended a technical amendment to this provision. The Government have accepted this recommendation (Written Answer *Hansard* (HC) 14 July 1994, vol 246, col 696).

[109] Draft Bill, clause 20(3)(d).

The draft Bill provides that the registration authority should give notice to the donee in appropriate cases,[110] and that instruments should be delivered up to the registration authority for cancellation.[111]

### Powers of the court

7.50 Under the 1985 Act, the Court of Protection was given some judicial control over attorneys acting under registered EPAs,[112] and over attorneys where the donor is or is becoming mentally incapable.[113] Although our scheme for CPAs distinguishes very clearly between the administrative powers of the registration authority and the judicial powers of the court, many of the court's powers over CPAs will mirror the powers of the Court of Protection in relation to EPAs. We will simply mention such powers here for the sake of completeness.

7.51 The court should have power to determine any question as to the meaning or effect of a CPA, whether the donor had capacity to create or revoke it, and whether it has been effectively revoked.[114]

7.52 It will be remembered that the fact that a CPA has been registered will in future signify only that the attorney expects to seek to use it, rather than that the donor is losing capacity. The powers of the court to direct or control the attorney should only arise in relation to matters where the donor no longer has capacity, and the draft Bill therefore provides that the court should have power to give directions to the attorney and to give any consent or authorisation which the donor might have given had he or she had capacity.[115]

7.53 The court should also retain some supervisory powers where donors of CPAs lack capacity. Thus, the court should have power to give directions to an attorney in relation to reports, accounts and records;[116] to require an attorney to produce information, documents or things;[117] to give directions to an attorney in relation to remuneration or expenses;[118] and to relieve an attorney from liability for breach of

---

[110] Draft Bill, clause 18(3).

[111] Draft Bill, clause 18(6).

[112] 1985 Act, s 8.

[113] 1985 Act, s 5.

[114] 1985 Act, s 8(2)(a), s 4(5) and s 8(3); draft Bill, clause 17(2).

[115] 1985 Act, s 8(2)(b)(i) and (d); draft Bill, clause 17(3)(a) and (b).

[116] 1985 Act, s 8(2)(b)(ii); draft Bill, clause 17(5)(a).

[117] 1985 Act, s 8(2)(c); draft Bill, clause 17(5)(b).

[118] 1985 Act, s 8(2)(b)(iii); draft Bill, clause 17(5)(c).

duty.[119] Where the court finds that fraud or undue pressure was used to induce the donor to create a purported CPA, it should have power to direct that the document shall not be registered, or to revoke it if it has been registered.[120] Where it follows from the decision of the court that the registration of the CPA should be cancelled, then the court should have power to direct the registration authority to cancel the registration.[121]

7.54    We suggested in the consultation papers[122] that it might be appropriate to extend the powers which the Court of Protection has possessed in relation to EPAs. All those who responded supported our provisional proposals and we now recommend that the court should have certain new and additional powers in relation to CPAs.

*(1) A dispensing power*

7.55    A number of our respondents expressed concern about the rejection of EPAs on "pettifogging" technical grounds. In some cases the donor will have suffered irreversible loss of capacity by the time the rejection of registration is made, with the result that a technically valid EPA can no longer be executed. The 1985 Act does provide that a document which "differs in an immaterial respect" from the prescribed form shall be treated as sufficient.[123] This is a useful provision of general application and we have retained it in our draft Bill.[124] Respondents did, however, give an enthusiastic welcome to our provisional proposal for a wider power whereby a judicial forum could "cure" technical defects in a document.[125] This would enable the court to look to the intention of the donor in executing any document which fails to conform to all the prescribed formalities.

> **We recommend** that the court should have power to declare that a document not in the prescribed form shall be treated as if it were in that form if the court is satisfied that the persons executing it intended it to create a CPA. (Draft Bill, clause 17(1).)

*(2) Power to appoint a new attorney*

7.56    We suggested in the consultation papers that the court might appoint a replacement

---

[119]  1985 Act, s 8(2)(f); draft Bill, clause 17(5)(d).

[120]  1985 Act, s 8(4)(f) and (5); draft Bill, clause 17(6)(a).

[121]  Draft Bill, clause 18(4).

[122]  Consultation Paper No 128, paras 7.35 - 7.37; Consultation Paper No 129, para 5.21.

[123]  1985 Act, s 2(6).

[124]  Draft Bill, clause 13(4).

[125]  Consultation Paper No 128, para 7.37; Consultation Paper No 129, para 5.21.

attorney for an attorney who is unable or unwilling to act.[126] Although this may appear to be a radical departure from the pure concepts of agency law which underlie the law on powers of attorney, none of our consultees expressed opposition to the suggestion. This suggests a general acceptance of the fact that strict agency principles have already been fundamentally altered by the statutory provision that an agency granted in an EPA can survive the incapacity of the principal. In the context of special statutory rules for CPAs, a donor may be better served by changes being made to a CPA which contains clear and valuable guidance to the attorney, than by the CPA being disregarded and a court-appointed manager being given a new set of powers. We would note that a number of our respondents saw no objection to the court simply "appointing" an "attorney" even where no attempt to appoint one has been made by the person concerned. This, we think, offends too greatly against the personal and contractual elements of the donor-donee relationship. On balance, however, we believe that the creation of a power in the court to appoint a new attorney can be justified. The question will be whether it is in the best interests of the donor to build on the provisions of the CPA even though the basis on which it was made has altered or, alternatively, to put the CPA on one side and appoint a manager.[127] This is an example of the flexibility which can be achieved when the same judicial forum has jurisdiction over both CPAs and court-based decision-making. The court should not be able to act in this way if the donor has stipulated that it should not have power to appoint a new attorney.

> **We recommend** that, subject to any contrary intention expressed in the document, the court should have power to appoint a donee in substitution for or in addition to the donee mentioned in a CPA. The court may act where the donor is without capacity to act and the court thinks it desirable to do so. (Draft Bill, clause 17(3)(c)(i).)[128]

*(3) Power to modify or extend the scope of CPA*

7.57    In the consultation papers we suggested that the court might be given power to modify or extend the scope of an attorney's powers, though only if the donor had specifically directed that the court could do so.[129] Few respondents commented specifically on this suggestion. The arguments which have to be balanced are similar to those discussed above in relation to a power to appoint a new attorney. Again, we take the view that a power to modify or extend the scope of the powers would

---

[126] *Ibid.*

[127] For the appointment of managers see Part VIII below.

[128] Where the court exercises this power it should also have power to direct the registration authority to register the amended instrument and the amendment should not take effect until the registration formalities have been completed. (Draft Bill, clause 17(4).)

[129] Consultation Paper No 128, para 7.37; Consultation Paper No 129, para 5.21.

sometimes be a useful one for the court to deploy in the best interests of the donor. For example, a donor may have appointed her husband as attorney with comprehensive financial powers over substantial assets. Once the donor has lost capacity, it may then transpire that a series of decisions will have to be taken about her medical treatment or about where she should live. Another family member may seek authority to take those decisions as a court-appointed manager. If the court takes the view that the husband should in fact take the personal and medical decisions as well then there would seem little objection to the scope of the existing CPA being extended to cover them. Again, however, the donor should be able to exclude the possibility of the court exercising the power to modify or extend the scope of the power.

> *We recommend* that, subject to any contrary intention expressed in the document, the court should have power to modify or extend the scope of the donee's power to act. The court may act where the donor is without capacity to act and the court thinks it desirable to do so. (Draft Bill, clause 17(3)(c)(ii).)[130]

*(4) Power to revoke based on the donee's behaviour*

7.58 The 1985 Act provides that the court shall cancel the registration of, and revoke, an EPA if "the attorney is unsuitable to be the donor's attorney".[131] In Consultation Paper No 129[132] we suggested that this power to revoke should be linked to the question of whether the attorney was acting in the donor's best interests. Respondents supported this proposal, with some seeking reassurance that the court should not be able to override a patient's advance decisions about health care by revoking the appointment of an attorney. We have already recommended that an attorney under a CPA should be under a duty to act in the donor's best interests.[133] It is therefore logical to use this terminology, rather than that of "unsuitability", in relation to the court's power to displace an attorney. Express provision should also be made for revocation by the court where an attorney's acts contravene the terms of the authority granted by the donor.

> *We recommend* that the court may, on behalf of a donor without capacity to do so, either direct that a purported CPA should not be registered or revoke a CPA where the donee or intended donee has behaved, is behaving or proposes to behave in a way

---

[130] Where the court exercises this power it should also have power to direct the registration authority to register the amended instrument and the amendment should not take effect until the registration formalities have been completed. (Draft Bill, clause 17(4).)

[131] 1985 Act, s 8(4)(g) and (5).

[132] Paragraph 5.22.

[133] See para 7.10 above.

**that (1) contravenes or would contravene the authority granted in the CPA or (2) is not or would not be in the donor's best interests.** (Draft Bill, clause 17(6)(b).)[134]

### Transitional provisions in relation to EPAs

7.59 Our scheme for CPAs is designed to supplant the EPA scheme in the 1985 Act and it should not be possible to execute an EPA once the CPA scheme comes into force. The Enduring Powers of Attorney Act 1985 should be repealed in its entirety. Many donors of EPAs who still have capacity may prefer to destroy any EPA and execute a CPA under the new statutory provisions. Some donors, however, will not have capacity to make a CPA and others will omit, or choose not, to do so. The expectations of donors of EPAs, whether registered or not, must continue to be met and our draft legislation makes comprehensive transitional provisions to ensure that this is achieved. Minor amendments to the 1985 scheme to take account of the fact that the court should in future only exercise judicial functions, while the registration authority exercises administrative functions, have been made. Subject to these amendments, the old law in relation to EPAs has been preserved.

> *We recommend* that no EPA should be created after the coming into force of the new law in relation to CPAs. Transitional provisions should apply to any EPAs made prior to repeal of the 1985 Act. (Draft Bill, clause 21(1) and (3); Schedule 3, Parts II to V.)

*An option to convert*

7.60 If our reformed CPA scheme is brought into force, many donors of "insurance policy" EPAs might find it helpful to be able to opt in to the new provisions. They might be happy to give up the additional notification procedures of the 1985 Act and to adopt the amended registration requirements we have described. They might also be happy for the court to gain the additional powers which it will have in relation to CPAs. Although we tend to the view that the best solution would be for the EPA to be destroyed and a new CPA executed, we believe that donors of EPAs who have capacity to exercise an option to convert their EPA into a CPA should be given such an option. There should be a prescribed form for the exercise of the option to convert, on which the donee will be required to state that he or she has no reason to believe that the donor is or is becoming mentally incapable. Both donor and donee will be required to state that they have read the explanatory information. Both donor and donee will be required to execute the form.

7.61 If the option to convert is exercised, then the donee will have no power to act until the document is registered. The new registration procedures and the new extended powers of the court will apply. The document will take effect as a CPA within the

---

[134] The court shall then direct cancellation of the registration if appropriate. (Draft Bill, clause 18(4)(c).)

meaning of the new Act.

**We recommend** **that an unregistered EPA may be converted into**
**a CPA by the donor and donee executing a prescribed form and**
**by registration.** (Draft Bill, clause 21(2); Schedule 3, Part I.)

### Miscellaneous

#### (1) Trustee powers

7.62    Section 3(3) of the 1985 Act specifically provides that an attorney acting under an EPA may exercise any of the donor's functions as a trustee. This was not part of the Bill drafted by this Commission and was introduced at a late stage in the Act's passage through Parliament. The section conflicts with other common law and statutory provisions in ways examined in detail in our recent report, The Law of Trusts: Delegation by Individual Trustees.[135] We have recommended its repeal, and the draft Trustee Delegation Bill attached to our recent report makes all necessary and consequential amendments to the law. We will not recapitulate those recommendations and, for present purposes, we need only say that we have assumed, for the purposes of drafting the legislation appended to this Report, that the recommendations in Law Com No 220 will have been implemented.[136]

#### (2) Invalid registered CPAs

7.63    The 1985 Act made provision for the possibility that a document registered as an EPA might later transpire to have been invalid. It was thought only fair that the fact of registration should give some protection to innocent attorneys and third parties in such circumstances.[137] Attorneys and third parties who rely on invalid registered CPAs deserve similar protection and we have reproduced the effect of the 1985 Act provisions in our own draft legislation.[138]

---

[135]  (1994) Law Com No 220.

[136]  The minor amendments to the resulting law which would be required on implementation of the draft Mental Incapacity Bill appended to the present report are not, in the circumstances, dealt with in Sched 8 to the Bill.

[137]  Law Com No 122, *op cit*, paras 4.86 - 4.88.

[138]  1985 Act, s 9; draft Bill, clause 19(1) - (5).

# PART VIII
# DECISION-MAKING BY THE COURT

## Introduction

8.1 In this Part, we make recommendations for a court-based jurisdiction to resolve the many different problems or disputes which may arise because a person lacks decision-making capacity. This jurisdiction will have a number of new and distinctive features. It will provide a single integrated framework for the making of personal welfare decisions, health care decisions and financial decisions. It will provide for both "one-off" orders or, where necessary, for the appointment of a "manager" with continuing powers. We also propose that it should be operated by a range of judges within the normal judicial hierarchy, according to the seriousness and complexity of the issues in any case; this is discussed in Part X below.

8.2 At present the Court of Protection only has jurisdiction over the "property and affairs" of those subject to its jurisdiction. Respondents to Consultation Paper No 128 overwhelmingly supported our provisional proposal[1] that a new jurisdiction should combine new functions in relation to "personal welfare" matters with functions in relation to financial matters. Those who responded to Consultation Paper No 129 almost universally welcomed our proposal[2] that a new statutory jurisdiction should be created with powers to make orders and declarations about health care issues. A number of respondents also expressed the view that any such jurisdiction should be integrated with a jurisdiction governing personal and financial decisions. There was general agreement with our suggestion[3] that most difficulties would continue to be resolved, as they are at present, by discussion and agreement, with the new jurisdiction being provided as a last resort in cases of dispute or controversy. A number of respondents also asserted that the existence of a framework within which decisive judgments could, if necessary, be made would in fact promote fruitful negotiation and the likelihood of agreement.[4]

8.3 We have identified a need for a court to make three kinds of determination: (1) a declaration, (2) an order and (3) the appointment of a manager. These powers should be exercisable in three broad areas: (1) personal welfare, (2) health care and (3) property and affairs. The court will have flexibility to make the most appropriate determination in relation to the relevant area of decision-making. The same court

---

[1] Paragraph 4.7.

[2] Paragraph 4.4.

[3] Consultation Paper No 128, para 6.6; Consultation Paper No 129, para 4.1.

[4] It is noteworthy that in *Re C (Mental Patient: Contact)* [1993] 1 FLR 940, for example, agreement was reached only after the preliminary judgment of Eastham J had established that the High Court did have jurisdiction to deal with the issue of contact which was disputed between the parties.

will have jurisdiction in relation to Continuing Powers of Attorney, and the same principles will apply to the CPA jurisdiction. The two governing concepts[5] will be the nature and extent of the decision-making capacity of the person concerned, and the principle that any decision must be taken in his or her best interests. The recommendations made in this Part are implemented by Chapter IV of the draft Mental Incapacity Bill.

8.4 In our consultation papers we suggested that the "last resort" nature of court proceedings could be stressed by requiring the court to be satisfied that "the making of an order will bring greater benefit to the incapacitated person than making no order at all."[6] In the context of our revised "best interests" factors, the fourth of which points to the need to choose the least restrictive option,[7] we see no need for a specific restriction introducing the different criterion of "greater benefit". The option of making no order will always be available to the court. As we argued in Part II, however, the new incapacity jurisdiction should not be assumed to be inherently negative, but rather to require a balance to be struck between autonomy (non-intervention) and protection (which may require positive steps by way of a court order or appointment).

8.5 We also suggested in the consultation papers that the court should be able to make "recommendations".[8] Our consultees pointed out, however, that large numbers of recommendations will inevitably have been made before a case involving a person without capacity ever gets as far as an application to the court. The purpose of such an application is to obtain an authoritative ruling, and to blur the distinction between a court's judicial powers and the rights of other agencies to recommend particular courses of action would not, we accept, be helpful.

8.6 The new jurisdiction is designed to provide for decisions to be made by the court in circumstances where that role has recently been taken - if at all[9] - by the inherent jurisdiction of the High Court, in cases such as *Re F (Mental Patient: Sterlisation)*,[10] *Airedale NHS Trust v Bland*,[11] *Re C (Mental Patient: Contact)*,[12] *Re C (Adult: Refusal*

---

[5] See Part III above.

[6] Consultation Paper No 128, paras 4.10 - 4.12; Consultation Paper No 129, para 4.9.

[7] Draft Bill, clause 3(2)(d).

[8] Consultation Paper No 128, para 6.15; Consultation Paper No 129, para 4.13.

[9] In the case of *Cambridgeshire County Council v R and others* [1994] 2 FCR 973 it was held that the court had no power to grant the declaratory relief applied for, which would interfere with rather than protect the legal rights of the person concerned.

[10] [1990] 2 AC 1.

[11] [1993] AC 789.

*of Treatment)*[13] and *Re S.*[14] The use of the declaratory jurisdiction which has been developed in the course of these cases will, to that extent, be replaced by the introduction of the new statutory jurisdiction. It has been clear at least since *Re F* that the High Court no longer has any general inherent jurisdiction to look after the welfare of mentally disabled adults (as it has in relation to children). It will, of course, always retain its normal inherent jurisdiction to make declarations as to lawfulness where remedies are not provided under any statutory scheme. Although we hope that very few matters concerning decision-making for those who lack capacity need in future be referred to the costly uncertainties of judge-made law, this inherent jurisdiction is always in place as a valuable safeguard.

**Declarations**

8.7    The development of the High Court's declaratory jurisdiction in cases involving people without capacity has been a reflection of the fact that there is, at present, a yawning gap where a decision-making jurisdiction might usefully exist. Once that gap is filled, declarations will still be called for in relation to two particular matters. First, since the court will only be able to exercise its decision-making jurisdiction if the person concerned is without capacity, it ought to have a power to make declarations about questions of capacity. A person who is being treated as if he or she lacked capacity must be able to challenge that treatment by seeking a declaration as to capacity. One of our respondents aptly labelled this a necessary "escape route" for people who seek to establish that they are in fact able take their own decisions.

8.8    Secondly, the court should be able to make a declaration as to the validity or applicability of an advance refusal of treatment. The recommendations we have already made seek to clarify, for the benefit of both doctors and patients, the circumstances in which a patient can make an anticipatory refusal of particular treatments.[15] It is inevitable, however, that in some cases doubt will arise as to the following questions:

> (1) whether the patient had capacity to make the refusal at the time when it was made,

> (2) whether the patient has effectively withdrawn or altered the refusal, or can now do so,

> (3) whether the refusal is valid, and

[12]   [1993] 1 FLR 940.

[13]   [1994] 1 WLR 290.

[14]   26 September 1994, Family Division, unreported judgment of Hale J.

[15]   See Part V above and draft Bill, clause 9.

(4) whether the refusal applies to the treatment proposed in the circumstances.

In such cases, the court should have power to establish whether the refusal effectively restricts the doctor's authority to act. As we have already explained, however, the court should not have power to override a valid and applicable advance refusal.[16]

> *We recommend* that the court should have power to make a declaration in relation to: (1) the capacity of a person; (2) the validity or applicability of an advance refusal of treatment. (Draft Bill, clause 23.)

### Orders and appointments

8.9 Decision-making for people without capacity has traditionally been achieved by appointing a proxy decision-maker. The Court of Protection will only make a short order instead of appointing a receiver where the property in question does not exceed £5,000 or where "it is otherwise appropriate".[17] Those of our respondents who commented on financial decision-making arrangements were very supportive of our provisional proposal[18] that there should be no restriction on the making of specific orders (as opposed to appointments), and that their use should be encouraged. Respondents also warmly welcomed the broader proposals[19] for a flexible jurisdiction with power to make one-off orders where appropriate. Most of them agreed that we had identified the main kinds of order that a judicial forum might wish to make in relation to personal welfare,[20] health care[21] and financial matters.[22] Some, however, also argued for a broad "catch-all" provision. Taking note of these comments, and of the model of Part VII of the 1983 Act, we have arrived at the view that the court's jurisdiction should be expressed in broad general terms. There should then be a non-exhaustive list of the matters which might be covered by an order.[23] On this basis, the draft Bill devotes a clause to each of the three broad areas of personal welfare, health care and property and affairs.

---

[16] See para 5.36 above.

[17] The Court of Protection Rules 1994 (SI 1994 No 3046), rule 9.

[18] Consultation Paper No 128, para 5.31.

[19] Consultation Paper No 128, para 4.13; Consultation Paper No 129, para 4.4.

[20] See Consultation Paper No 128, para 6.12.

[21] See Consultation Paper No 129, paras 4.12 and 4.14.

[22] See Consultation Paper No 128, paras 5.29 - 5.31.

[23] This is in fact the method adopted in the Mental Health Act 1983, ss 95 and 96.

**We recommend** that the court may

**(1) make any decision on behalf of a person who lacks capacity to make that decision or**

**(2) appoint a manager to be responsible for making a decision on behalf of a person who lacks capacity to make it.** (Draft Bill, clause 24(1).)

**The decisions in question may extend to any matter relating to the personal welfare, health care, property or affairs of the person concerned, including the conduct of legal proceedings.** (Draft Bill, clause 24(3).)

8.10 In this report and in our draft Bill we have called any court-appointed decision-maker a "manager". No more suitable alternative term was put to us during our extensive consultations. We considered, but rejected, the option of introducing different terms for different sorts of powers.[24] It would be unsatisfactory for a single person to be appointed as "administrator" in relation to a series of financial matters, "guardian" in relation to residence decisions and "proxy" in relation to medical decisions. The substitute decision-maker will have the particular powers granted in the particular case, and a single general term which can apply to all the areas of the court's jurisdiction is preferable.

8.11 The court should have power to make any orders and directions that may be necessary so that effect can be given to any orders or appointments made. The orders made after proper enquiry by a judicial body should be capable of enforcement in the normal way, and the draft Bill makes the necessary provision.[25]

*General principles in relation to orders and appointments*

8.12 We suggested in our consultation papers[26] that continuing powers of management over another person should only be granted where the issue in the case cannot be resolved by a "one-off" order. A number of respondents pointed out that, where money is concerned, the need for an ongoing authority will often be made out. Similar considerations may also apply if a person has a progressive illness which will involve a series of medical decisions being made over a period of time. Nevertheless, the important general principle that a single issue order is preferable to a management appointment was widely supported on consultation.

---

[24] As in Victoria's Guardianship and Administration Board Act 1986 and New Zealand's Protection of Personal and Property Rights Act 1988.

[25] Draft Bill, clauses 24(4) and 50.

[26] Consultation Paper No 128, para 4.13; Consultation Paper No 129, para 4.11.

> *We recommend* **that a specific decision by the court is to be preferred to the appointment of a manager.** (Draft Bill, clause 24(2).)

8.13   We also suggested in the consultation papers that any management powers should be as limited as possible.[27] There is a worldwide trend towards "partial guardianship", in acknowledgment of the fact that many disabled people living in the community have capacity to take many day-to-day decisions and only need help and protection in relation to a limited range of matters. Again, we accept the arguments of those respondents who pointed out that extended powers will sometimes still be needed. We see merit, however, in setting down the general principle which we suggested on consultation and which was warmly supported by our consultees.

> *We recommend* **that the powers conferred on a manager should be as limited in scope and duration as possible.** (Draft Bill, clause 24(2).)

8.14   The court will be bound by the general requirement to act in the best interests of the person without capacity, taking into account the statutory "best interests" factors.[28] It is therefore important that it should have power to act of its own motion even if no application for the most appropriate type of order has been made.

> *We recommend* **that the court may make any order or appointment which is in the best interests of the person concerned, regardless of the terms of the application made to the court.** (Draft Bill, clause 24(5).)

**Personal welfare matters**

8.15   A number of matters are listed in the draft Bill as requiring a personal decision, and the court will have no power to deal with those matters.[29]

8.16   In Consultation Paper No 128[30] we specifically mentioned orders about the place where the person concerned should live, and what contact he or she should have with others. Respondents agreed that these are likely to be the main issues in the personal welfare field. One said that these issues cause great difficulties in practice and that a clear power to take such decisions would be "a godsend".

---

[27]   *Ibid.*

[28]   Draft Bill, clause 3. In the case of the court the obligation will not be qualified by reference to a reasonable belief (clause 3(3)).

[29]   See para 4.29 above and draft Bill, clause 30.

[30]   Paragraph 6.12.

137

> **We recommend** that the court's powers should cover (1) where the person concerned is to live and (2) what contact, if any, the person concerned is to have with specified persons. (Draft Bill, clause 25(1)(a) and (b).)

8.17 A person with capacity obviously has power to tell someone else to stay away, or to refuse to have any contact with a person who may wish to visit or otherwise stay in contact with him or her. Some people, however, may lack capacity to take such decisions. It was precisely this issue which could not be resolved under the declaratory jurisdiction in the recent case of *Cambridgeshire County Council v R and others*.[31] Respondents agreed with our preliminary view[32] that restraining orders against third parties may therefore be needed in some cases. It may be found that the third party presents a risk of abuse, or that continued contact between that person and the person who lacks capacity will harm or distress the person concerned. In the exercise of its general jurisdiction to make decisions in the best interests of a person without capacity, the court should have power to make orders restraining a third party. The power of the court to restrain a third party would not extend to any interference with other rights of that person, such as a right to occupy property, unless justified by other principles of law.

> **We recommend** that the court should have power to make an order restraining a person from having contact with or molesting the person without capacity. (Draft Bill, clause 25(3).)

8.18 Respondents also agreed with our provisional view[33] that the power to make residence decisions should not cover any decision that the person concerned should "live in" a hospital to receive assessment or treatment for mental disorder, where he or she objects to doing so.[34] The draft Bill includes a provision to clarify this point.[35]

8.19 Some consultees asked whether the court's power to make an order about where the person should live might provide a route to challenge a care plan made by a local social services authority under the National Health Service and Community Care Act 1990. We trust it is clear from the draft Bill that the court only has power to

---

[31] [1994] 2 FCR 973 and see para 8.6 and n 9 above. Quite apart from the issue as to the court's jurisdiction, there was in any event insufficient evidence to establish whether the person concerned did in fact lack capacity to take the decisions in question.

[32] Consultation Paper No 128, para 6.12.

[33] *Ibid*, para 6.14.

[34] See our discussion of this issue in relation to attorneys acting under CPAs at para 7.15 above.

[35] Draft Bill, clause 25(2).

make any decision which the person without capacity could have made. Its role is to stand in the shoes of the person concerned. If that person has no power, under the community care legislation, to demand the provision of particular services then the court can do no such thing on his or her behalf.

8.20 Consultees suggested a number of other "personal welfare" powers which might be specifically mentioned as within the court's jurisdiction, and we have included two of these in the non-exhaustive list in the draft Bill. The first arises because several recent statutes and regulations have granted new powers to citizens in relation to records or information held about them.[36] Unfortunately, provision has not normally been made for the exercise of such rights by a substitute if the person named in the record lacks or has lost capacity to make the relevant application. A manager may well require access to certain personal information which the person concerned could have applied for, in order to exercise the powers granted by the court in an effective manner.

> **We recommend that the court's powers should cover the exercise of a person's statutory rights to information.** (Draft Bill, clause 25(1)(c).)

8.21 The court should also be able to deal with the rights of the person concerned to apply for and obtain any benefits and services. In many situations "substitute" applications are readily accepted by service- or benefit-providers. In one recent case, however, it was held that an application for housing under the homelessness provisions of the Housing Act 1985 need not be considered by a housing authority where it was made by the father of a disabled adult without capacity to make it for herself.[37] The broad power conferred on the court in our scheme would give a substitute claim or application on behalf of a person without capacity the judicial authority of the court.

> **We recommend that the court's powers should cover obtaining statutory benefits and services which may be available to the person concerned.** (Draft Bill, clause 25(1)(d).)

**Health care matters**

8.22 We suggested in Consultation Paper No 129 that two kinds of order would be required in relation to health care, namely an order approving (or not) a particular

---

[36] See for example the Data Protection Act 1984, the Local Government (Access to Information) Act 1985, the Access to Personal Files Act 1987, the Access to Medical Reports Act 1988 and The Education (School Records) Regulations 1989 (SI 1989 No 1261) made under the Education Reform Act 1988, s 218.

[37] *R v Tower Hamlets London Borough Council, ex parte Ferdous Begum* [1993] AC 509.

treatment and an order transferring the care of the patient to another person.[38] Our consultees approved these suggestions, acknowledging that a power in the court to approve or disapprove proposed actions would be a great advance on the current declaration procedure. Attention could then focus on whether the thing *should* be done, rather than on its legality if it were to be done. In the case of a manager, it is more appropriate to refer to the manager consenting to treatment (or not), rather than approving it. The concern of one respondent that certain other decisions relating to health care might sometimes be required is met by our policy of defining the jurisdiction in broad general terms, and referring to specific types of order in a non-exhaustive list. The BMA sought reassurance that the court would not have power to order a treatment provider to act contrary to his or her conscience or clinical judgment. Again, it must be remembered that the general jurisdiction is simply to make decisions which the person without capacity could have made. No patient can decide that a doctor should provide treatment against his or her clinical judgment or conscience.[39] A patient can, however, request a transfer to a different doctor. It follows that the court, standing in that patient's shoes, can order such a transfer.

> *We recommend* that the court's powers in relation to health care matters should cover (1) approving or refusing approval for particular forms of health care (2) appointing a manager to consent or refuse consent to particular forms of health care, (3) requiring a person to allow a different person to take over responsibility for the health care of the person concerned. (Draft Bill, clause 26(1)(a) and (b).)

8.23 We provisionally suggested that any proxy with health care powers should be able to exercise the rights of the person without capacity to access personal health records.[40] Respondents agreed with this proposal, pointing out that access to records would often be essential to allow the manager to make a valid informed decision. We would expect it to be standard for any manager given health care powers also to be given authority to obtain access to health records.

> *We recommend* that the court's powers should cover obtaining access to the health records of the person concerned. (Draft Bill, clause 26(1)(c).)

---

[38] Paragraphs 4.12 and 4.14.

[39] Nor will the court order a doctor to provide treatment in such circumstances, see *Re J (A Minor) (Child in Care: Medical Treatment)* [1993] Fam 15. A patient's valid and applicable refusal of treatment will, however, be effective even if the doctor objects to the patient's point of view (see further para 5.28 above).

[40] Consultation Paper No 129, para 4.27. The relevant enactments are the Data Protection Act 1984 and the Access to Health Records Act 1990.

*Excluded powers*

*(1) Basic care and advance refusals*

8.24 It follows from our policy in relation to advance refusals of treatment that neither the court nor a manager may approve any treatment which the patient has already refused. In that connection, however, it should also be made clear that, since no advance refusal of "basic care" by a patient who now lacks capacity can be effective, neither the court nor the manager may authorise the withholding of that type of care.[41] Our consultation revealed overwhelming support for an exclusion in relation to both advance refusals and basic care.[42]

> **We recommend that the court may not approve, nor a manager consent to, (1) the withholding of basic care, or (2) any treatment refused by an advance refusal of treatment.** (Draft Bill, clause 26(2)(b).)

*(2) Procedures requiring independent supervision*

8.25 We have already recommended that certain kinds of medical decision should require independent supervision.[43] In Consultation Paper No 129 we suggested[44] that no court-appointed manager should ever be able to take such decisions. We no longer see the need for a blanket restriction of this type. It may be, for example, that the court has been asked whether sterilisation by hysterectomy would be in the patient's best interests, and it is then agreed to attempt a less intrusive method of contraception. Nonetheless, the court feels quite able to decide that the patient's sister is an appropriate person to make decisions about her health care, including any decision to consent to a sterilisation at a later stage. In such circumstances, there would be little merit in requiring everyone to return to court when that later stage is reached. Equally, the second opinion procedure is intended to ensure some supervision of serious decisions by someone independent of the responsible doctor. The court might sometimes be satisfied that a "health care manager" who was a family member, citizen advocate or friend was quite capable of providing the necessary independent input. Although we would not anticipate power over "court category" or "second opinion category" treatments being granted to managers as a matter of course, we are now persuaded that there could be cases where this was an appropriate step. Any such authority should be expressly granted by the court.

---

[41] See draft Bill, clause 9(8) for the definition of "basic care".

[42] As proposed in Consultation Paper No 129, para 4.28.

[43] See Part VI above.

[44] Paragraph 4.28.

*(3) Non-therapeutic procedures and research*

8.26   We have recommended the adoption of special procedures where it is proposed to carry out a procedure or a research project which will not bring direct benefit to the person without capacity.[45] Again, there might be rare circumstances where the court may determine that a manager should in future have power to consent to such matters. Any such authority should, however, be expressly granted by the court. In relation to non-therapeutic research, no decision of the court could ever obviate the need for prior approval of the project by the statutory committee.[46]

> **We recommend** that the court may grant a manager express authority to consent to the carrying out of treatments which would otherwise require court approval or a certificate from an independent medical practitioner; or to consent to the carrying out of non-therapeutic procedures or research. (Draft Bill, clause 26(3).)

*(4) Admission to hospital as if under the Mental Health Act 1983*

8.27   The Mental Health Act 1983 sets out the circumstances in which people can be detained and treated for their mental disorder. It does not require any consideration of their capacity to take decisions about such treatment.[47] Many would argue that most of those who are detained and treated under the compulsory powers do in fact lack capacity to make decisions about their treatment. Others would dispute this. We have already recommended that the safeguards for detained patients in relation to ECT and prolonged medication should also apply to non-detained patients without capacity to consent to such treatments.[48] We have also recommended that no manager should have power to arrange the coercive admission of a person to a psychiatric institution.[49]

8.28   The vast majority of those in hospital for psychiatric assessment or treatment have gone there without compulsory powers being used,[50] if with varying degrees of volition. Others have been admitted pursuant to the compulsory procedures laid down in the 1983 Act. It might be argued that, in pursuance of its general power to make decisions in the best interests of those who cannot decide for themselves (and irrespective of the criteria set out in the Mental Health Act 1983), the court

---

[45]   See Part VI above and draft Bill, clauses 10 and 11.

[46]   See para 6.34 above.

[47]   Only treatment under s 57 (currently psycho-surgery or hormone treatment) requires personal consent and therefore capacity.

[48]   See para 6.14 above.

[49]   See para 8.18 and n 35 above and draft Bill clauses 25(2) and 26(2)(a).

[50]   See para 7.15 and n 36 above.

should have power to order that a person should be admitted and detained in hospital. This, however, would be to introduce a wholly new category of compulsory psychiatric patients and to depart from the safeguards in the mental health legislation. On the other hand, there is no reason why the court exercising the incapacity jurisdiction should not have power to order admission to hospital on the *same* criteria, with the *same* safeguards and with the effect being the *same* as for other compulsory admissions.

8.29   The general terms of the court's incapacity jurisdiction would require it to be established that the person concerned lacks capacity to decide whether to be admitted to hospital for assessment or treatment. In addition, the medical criteria which would otherwise apply to a civil admission would have to be met, with the production of two medical certificates, one of them prepared by a specialist in mental disorder.[51] It would not be sensible to apply the "best interests" criterion to orders of the kind proposed. One of the criteria for admission under the 1983 legislation is "the protection of other persons" and the grounds for the new order should simply mirror those criteria. The "best interests" factors[52] will still be of assistance, but the court's power should be one of determining whether it is appropriate to make an order, having regard to those factors.

> **We recommend** that the court should have power to order the admission to hospital for assessment or treatment for mental disorder of a person without capacity, if satisfied on the evidence of two doctors that:
>
> **(1) the grounds for admission specified in sections 2 or 3 respectively of the Mental Health Act 1983 exist, and**
>
> **(2) it is appropriate, having regard to the "best interests" factors, that the person concerned should be admitted to hospital.** (Draft Bill, clause 26(4) and (5).)

8.30   Once a person has been admitted to hospital under an order of the incapacity court he or she should be in exactly the same position as anyone admitted under the civil procedures. However, in recognition of the fact that a judicial determination has been made, the right to apply to the Mental Health Review Tribunal (and the right of the nearest relative to discharge) should not arise during the first period of

---

[51]   There is an analogy with the way in which the criminal courts have power to make orders which achieve a result similar to civil admission for treatment, on conditions similar to those for civil admission, Mental Health Act 1983, ss 37 - 40.

[52]   See Part III above and draft Bill, clause 3.

detention.[53]

## Property and affairs

8.31 As far as the powers of the court or a manager in relation to a person's financial affairs are concerned, the existing provisions in Part VII of the 1983 Act are a helpful starting-point. As we have already explained,[54] we recommend the repeal of Part VII of the 1983 Act in its entirety, in order that provisions about financial matters (many of which will closely resemble those of the old law) can be integrated with the entirely new provisions about personal and health care matters which are needed. We hope that the introduction of the new integrated jurisdiction will be accompanied by significant changes in attitude and practice so far as financial decision-making for those who lack capacity is concerned.

8.32 In relation to property and affairs, the court should be able to exercise its powers even if the person concerned is under 16, if it is likely that the young person will still lack capacity on attaining his or her majority. There is no lower age limit on the exercise of the current powers of the Court of Protection, and we were persuaded on consultation (in particular by the comments of the present Master) that it is sometimes important for a long-term view to be taken at an early stage of a patient's life. This is particularly true where a child with a mental disability has been awarded a large sum of damages and there is no prospect of the child ever gaining the capacity to manage that money.

> *We recommend* that the court's powers in relation to property and affairs may be exercised where the person concerned is under 16, if it is likely that the person will still lack capacity on attaining his or her majority. (Draft Bill, clause 27(3).)

8.33 The non-exhaustive list of powers in relation to property and affairs can, for the most part, mirror the list in section 96(1) of the 1983 Act. One difference, however, relates to gifts made on behalf of the person without capacity.[55] The relevant provisions of the 1983 Act[56] rely on the concept of "benefit" to the person without capacity rather than the concept of his or her "best interests". This means that a special provision was required to cover the giving of gifts.[57] The new "best interests" factors go wider than "benefit", and specific reference is made in clause 3 of the

---

[53] Draft Bill, clause 26(6). Similar restrictions apply to persons admitted pursuant to an order of a criminal court under the 1983 Act.

[54] See para 2.51 above.

[55] See our discussion of the similar point in relation to EPAs and CPAs at para 7.11 above.

[56] Section 95(1)(a).

[57] Section 96(1)(d) and s 95(1)(b) and (c).

draft Bill to the factors the person without capacity would take into account if able to do so. There is therefore no need for a special clause about gifts. The court making an order or appointing a manager might, of course, impose a restriction on gifts being given, according to the circumstances of the case.

> *We recommend* **that the court's powers over the property and affairs of a person without capacity should cover:**
>
> - **the control and management of any property**
>
> - **the disposal of any property**
>
> - **the acquisition of any property**
>
> - **the carrying on of a business, trade or profession**
>
> - **the dissolution of any partnership**
>
> - **the carrying out of any contract**
>
> - **the discharge of any debt or obligation.** (Draft Bill, clause 27(1)(a) - (g).)

All these powers can be exercised either by the court making an order or by the court appointing a manager to take decisions in future.[58]

8.34 There are, however, a number of financial matters with which only the court itself should be able to deal. The Court of Protection already has similar powers to those we now recommend, including the power to make a settlement of the patient's property. We mentioned in our consultation paper that it is not common for the Court of Protection to make settlements for the benefit of a patient himself or herself, and expressed the provisional view that there would be little advantage in providing any new power for a trust (for the benefit of a person without capacity) to be set up.[59] A number of our expert consultees, however, argued that such a trust might sometimes be the best solution for the person concerned, and we are persuaded that the court should certainly have this option available to it. It is likely to be attractive only where substantial assets are involved or perhaps where issues of tax planning are important. It may be necessary for a financial manager to be appointed at the same time as property is ordered to be settled. Alternatively, the

---

[58] See para 8.12 above and draft Bill, clause 24(2) for the general principle that a decision by the court itself is to be preferred to the appointment of a manager.

[59] Consultation Paper No 128, para 5.37.

making of the settlement may mean that there is no need for anyone to hold management powers and responsibilities.[60]

> *We recommend* that the court's powers should also extend to:
>
> - **making a settlement of any property, whether with the person concerned or with others as beneficiary or beneficiaries**
>
> - **making a will**
>
> - **exercising powers vested in the person concerned. These powers should not be exercisable by any manager.** (Draft Bill, clause 27(1)(h) - (j) and (2).)

8.35 There need be no other restriction on the financial powers which the court *may* award to a manager. The order or appointment which is in the best interests of the person without capacity must be made in each case, remembering the general principles that (1) a specific order is preferable to the appointment of a manager and (2) the powers of any manager should be as limited in scope and duration as possible.[61] To take one common case, an elderly lady who has lost capacity to deal with her finances might be the owner of a house and have a small state pension. She has been assessed as requiring residential care and an order is therefore needed approving the sale of the house, and the investment of the proceeds in an appropriate deposit account from which the residential care costs can be met by direct debit. If an appointment under the Social Security Regulations then deals with the pension income there might be no need for any manager to be appointed. Even if the court perceives a need for ongoing management powers to be granted to a relative it might set a limit to those powers. The option of settling the proceeds of sale on trustees would also be available.

8.36 We anticipate that courts may wish to depart from the types of order and appointment which have traditionally been made by the Court of Protection in its present form. The minimal changes we have recommended to the substantive law for financial decision-making could be accompanied by significant changes in the actual handling of cases in future. A brief discussion of the present procedures of the Court of Protection and Public Trust Office may clarify this point.

8.37 The present jurisdiction of the Court of Protection, as set out in sections 95 and 96

---

[60] Compare the possibility under the present law that the Court might discharge a receiver on the grounds that a settlement has been executed (*Heywood & Massey, Court of Protection Practice* (12th ed 1991) p 63).

[61] See paras 8.12 - 8.13 above.

of the 1983 Act, is extremely wide and flexible in its terms. In the vast majority of cases, however, the Court of Protection exercises its jurisdiction by appointing a receiver to whom it grants specified powers over the patient's income.[62] Control over capital is retained by the Public Trust Office, which invests each patient's capital on his or her behalf.[63] A receiver can request the release of sums of capital. In the language of our proposed scheme, the reality at present is that the Public Trust Office is "financial manager" in every case.

8.38    We suggested in Consultation Paper No 128[64] that a financial manager appointed by the court might be given powers over capital and power to make investment decisions. There was broad agreement from our consultees that this should be an option open to the court. It was said that the practice of retaining control over capital was a hangover from a bygone era. Considerable concern was also expressed about the fees charged by the Public Trust Office for the service provided.[65] The central question here is whether there is, in every case, a need for a public administrative body staffed by civil servants to manage the capital assets of persons without capacity. Could not a solicitor, an accountant, an investment manager, a commercial trust company or even a relative perform such a management function equally well in some cases? Management of this type should be clearly distinguished (as it is not at present) from a supervisory function which may well require the involvement of a centralised state-run body.[66]

8.39    We have found it instructive to study the Annual Reports of the Guardianship and Administration Board of the Australian state of Victoria. There, as here, it was

---

[62] If there is no other suitable candidate the Public Trustee will be appointed receiver. These cases are handled in the Receivership Division of the Public Trust Office, while those where there is a "private" receiver are handled in the Protection Division.

[63] The National Audit Office reported that the Public Trust Office usually invests capital of less than £50,000 in cash accounts run by the Office. In only 8% of those cases where securities were held had the Public Trust Office delegated powers to manage investments to receivers and their nominated brokers. In all other cases the Public Trust Office was itself managing the investment of the patient's capital. National Audit Office, *Looking after the Financial Affairs of People with Mental Incapacity* (1994) paras 3.21 - 3.26.

[64] Paragraph 5.28.

[65] Earlier this year, the Public Trustee informed the Public Accounts Committee that about 80% of complaints received were about fees, Committee of Public Accounts, Thirty-ninth Report, *Looking After the Financial Affairs of People with Mental Incapacity* (1993-94) HC 308 para 49. It must be stressed, however, that the Public Trust Office's fees are set so as to recover costs. The Office's main objectives are to avoid any major distortion between the cost of a case and the fee; to pitch fees at a reasonable level; and to ensure that fees are calculated accurately and collected promptly (National Audit Office, *Looking after the Financial Affairs of People with Mental Incapacity* (1994) para 3.35). The Public Trust Office informed the National Audit Office that it strives to operate as economically as possible and the fees have to cover more work than many receivers may realise (*ibid*, para 3.41).

[66] See paras 8.48 - 8.50 below.

previously the case that only the Public Trustee[67] could "manage" the affairs of the mentally incapacitated. Legislation passed in 1986 broke this monopoly, making provision for "any other person... suitable to act" to be appointed as administrator of the estate of a "represented person" who lacks capacity.[68] Such an administrator has any powers which are specifically granted in the order of appointment and also the general powers of a trustee under the jurisdiction's Trustee Act 1958. In its most recent Annual Report, the Guardianship and Administration Board reported that in 1992/3 the State Trustees were appointed administrators in 54.9% of cases and "relatives and others" in 42.9% of cases, with solicitors, accountants and private trustee companies making up the small balance. By way of contrast, in 1987/88 the State Trustees had been appointed in 67% of cases, and "relatives and others" in only 30%. The Board concluded that "the increase in private administrator appointments over the six year period reflects some six years experience by the Board with a range of possible appointees, the increased confidence of the Board in relatives handling both small and large estates...and a concern by the Board with the standard of administration by State Trustees in some estates." It added that the possibility of appointing private trust companies, solicitors and accountants is particularly important for persons living outside the metropolis, since the State Trustees have no regional offices.[69]

8.40 We have no reason to think that the relatives of persons without capacity in England and Wales are any less able to manage their affairs for them than such relatives in Victoria. We take the view that there are cases where full management powers, including powers over capital, could be granted to suitable individuals or trust corporations. The Public Trustee will be one candidate and there will continue to be cases where the only appropriate financial manager is the Public Trustee, reflecting a need for a level of ongoing control at least over the capital assets of the person without capacity. The Public Trustee may, as manager acting in the best interests of the person without capacity, choose to delegate certain powers to a carer or family member but the level and nature of delegation would be a matter for the Public Trustee in the exercise of his or her discretion.[70] There is no need for any statutory provision to deal with this. The possibility of appointing someone other than the Public Trustee as manager should not, of course, mean that there should be any diminution in protection and safeguards for the estate of the person without capacity. A manager will have to provide security against the possibility of loss to the estate and will have to file reports and accounts with the Public Trustee, who

---

[67] Now renamed the "State Trustees".

[68] Guardianship and Administration Board Act 1986, s 47.

[69] Victoria, Guardianship and Administration Board, *Annual Report 1992-1993* p 36.

[70] Clearly, delegation of this sort would not relieve the Public Trustee of any liability to the person concerned for loss to the estate.

will have monitoring functions.[71] Where a manager is a solicitor, accountant or other professional person then further safeguards will be provided by professional indemnity insurance schemes.

> **We recommend that a manager may be appointed to take possession or control of all or any specified part of the property of the person concerned and to exercise all or any specified powers in respect of it including such powers of investment as the court may determine.** (Draft Bill, clause 28(7).)

In Schedule 4 to our draft Bill various detailed supplementary provisions in relation to wills and settlements are reproduced from Part VII of the Mental Health Act 1983 without amendment.[72] Schedule 5 lists some old enactments whose provisions should not apply to those in relation to whom the court has exercised its powers; this matches the list in Schedule 3 to the 1983 Act.[73]

**Managers appointed by the court**

8.41 This concludes our recommendations as to the powers of the judicial forum in relation to declarations, orders and appointments whether in relation to personal welfare, health care or financial decisions. We now turn to the need for certain common provisions in relation to persons appointed as managers.

*Who can be a manager?*

8.42 A manager should be an individual of eighteen or over or, in relation to financial matters only, a trust corporation.[74] We consulted on the question whether public officials should be allowed to act as managers.[75] Respondents pointed out that managers who were also public office-holders would have to ensure that they could act in the best interests of the person concerned and avoid any conflict of interest. Equally, however, it was argued that public officials might be appropriate managers and that, in creating the new system, it should not be assumed that private unpaid carers would always step in to fill any breach. The court should be left with the widest possible choice of manager and we do not favour a ban on any particular candidates.

---

[71] See paras 8.48 - 8.50 below.

[72] Draft Bill, clause 27(4).

[73] Draft Bill, clause 29.

[74] Draft Bill, clause 28(2). See para 7.21 and n 49 above for the definition of a trust corporation. As a trust corporation, the Public Trustee may be appointed manager in relation to property and affairs.

[75] Consultation Paper No 128, para 6.19; Consultation Paper No 129, para 5.14.

**We recommend** that an individual appointed as manager may be described as the holder for the time being of an office or position. (Draft Bill, clause 28(2).)

8.43    We suggested in our consultation papers[76] that it might sometimes be appropriate for more than one manager to be appointed. Respondents agreed that this might be useful. Experience in Victoria indicates that the joint appointment of a social services worker and a family member to take personal welfare decisions can work very well.[77] It may also be that the best candidate is already elderly and wishes to be sure that someone will take over at a time in the future. If there is a suitable person to take over then the court should be able to make such provision at the time when it is looking at the case. Some foreign jurisdictions also provide for a "standby" manager to be appointed, to take over on a temporary basis if the manager should die or become incapable of acting.[78] This is only likely to be necessary in the rare case of a disabled person who should not be left for however short a period without a manager to exercise certain powers. Provision for a standby manager may, however, allay the fears of those respondents who pointed out that many elderly carers of younger disabled persons experience great anxiety about what will become of the younger person once they, the carers, have "gone".[79]

**We recommend** that the court may appoint joint, joint and several, successive or standby managers. (Draft Bill, clause 28(5).)

No-one should be appointed a manager without his or her consent.[80]

*Duties and powers of managers*

8.44    We proposed in the consultation papers that a manager should be under a duty to act in the best interests of the person concerned.[81] Respondents agreed that it was reasonable to impose such a duty on a person appointed by the court to take decisions, when he or she has consented to that appointment. The draft Bill therefore provides that the court may appoint a manager *to be responsible for* making

---

[76]    Consultation Paper No 128, para 6.20; Consultation Paper No 129, para 5.13.

[77]    T Carney and D Tait, *Balanced Accountability: An Evaluation of the Victorian Guardianship and Administration Board* (1991) p 79.

[78]    See for example the standby guardianship provisions in Florida Statute 744.304.

[79]    The vast majority of respondents agreed with our provisional view that powers of management over another human being should not be passed on by testamentary writing as if they were an item of property (Consultation Paper No 128, para 6.21).

[80]    Draft Bill, clause 28(3).

[81]    Consultation Paper No 128, para 6.26; Consultation Paper No 129, para 4.25.

particular decisions.[82] Unlike an attorney, a manager who failed to act at all when a decision within the scope of his or her authority was called for could be in breach of duty.[83] The manager's duty will otherwise match that of all those who act under the new legislation, being a duty to act in the best interests of the person concerned, having regard to the statutory factors. The court will have power to vary or discharge the order appointing a manager who fails to do so.[84] Any manager who wishes to receive further directions or seeks a further order will be entitled to apply to the court without first seeking leave.[85]

> **We recommend that a manager should act in the best interests of the person without capacity, having regard to the statutory factors.** (Draft Bill, clause 3.)

8.45    We take the view that it would be helpful to specify the precise legal status of a court-appointed manager. Case law has established that the sort of person now known as a "receiver", and now appointed by the Court of Protection, is a statutory agent of the patient.[86] The property of the person without capacity does not vest in the receiver.[87] The receiver is not personally liable for the costs of those he employs in the course of acting for the person concerned.[88] We do not propose any change to these rules of law. As we have already explained, the draft Bill provides that a manager may take *possession or control* of the property of the person concerned.[89] For the avoidance of doubt, however, we favour an express provision to the effect that a manager is an agent for the person concerned. We would expect any guidance issued to managers[90] to recommend that they should always notify any third party with whom they are dealing of the fact that they are acting as manager for a person without capacity.[91]

---

[82]   Draft Bill, clause 24(1)(b).

[83]   See para 7.10 above for the position of attorneys under CPAs.

[84]   Draft Bill, clause 24(6).

[85]   See para 10.20 below and draft Bill, clauses 24(4) and 47(3)(b).

[86]   *Re EG* [1914] 1 Ch 927.

[87]   *Ibid*, p 933.

[88]   *Ibid*, p 935.

[89]   See para 8.40 above and draft Bill, clause 28(7).

[90]   See para 8.54 below.

[91]   It is a general principle of the law of agency that an agent is personally liable on any contract made where the principal is undisclosed at the time of contracting (*Bowstead on Agency* (15th ed 1985) p 432). In *Re EG* [1914] 1 Ch 927, 933 Cozens-Hardy MR said that where a principal tells an agent to retain a solicitor then the principal, not the agent, is the solicitor's client. He was careful to add, however, "I assume, of course, that the

> ***We recommend*** **that a manager should be regarded as the agent of the person for whom he or she is appointed.** (Draft Bill, clause 28(8).)

8.46 There may be cases where an attorney has certain decision-making powers and a manager has others. Each will be under a duty to act in the best interests of the person without capacity, and the statutory factors provide that they should consult each other.[92] If there is a conflict which cannot be resolved then the attorney, who was appointed by the donor, is entitled to take precedence. It should therefore be made clear that no manager has power to make a decision inconsistent with the decision of an attorney who is operating within the scope of his or her authority. A dissatisfied manager in such circumstances must apply to the court for the powers of the attorney to be revoked.[93]

> ***We recommend*** **that no manager should have power to make a decision which is inconsistent with a decision made within the scope of his or her authority by the donee of a CPA.** (Draft Bill, clause 28(10).)

*A time limit on appointment*

8.47 There is no time limit to a determination that a person is a "patient" within the meaning of Part VII of the Mental Health Act 1983, nor are appointments of receivers under section 99 of that Act made subject to any time limit. In the consultation papers we suggested that appointments should expire after six or twelve months.[94] These are the time periods for detention in hospital or guardianship found in the rest of the 1983 Act. Although many of our respondents supported the proposal that there should be a time limit on appointments, the majority argued that periods of six or twelve months were unrealistically and unnecessarily short. The making of a management appointment as opposed to a specific order will itself reflect a need for continuing authority to be exercised, suggesting that the person's disability is either unlikely to disappear or likely to worsen. The time-scale in such cases can reasonably differ from the time-limits for detention under the Mental Health Act, where it is thought that the patient's psychiatric illness may be treated and the symptoms thereby relieved. We now suggest a much longer maximum time-limit, namely five years. A manager could, thereafter, be re-appointed for a further term where this was in the best interests of the person concerned. The principle that

solicitor knows the limited authority of the agent".

[92] Draft Bill, clause 3(2)(c).

[93] See para 7.58 above and draft Bill, clause 17(6)(b).

[94] Consultation Paper No 128, paras 5.26 and 6.23; Consultation Paper No 129, para 4.23.

152

*any* appointment should be as limited as possible will, however, always apply.[95]

> **We recommend that no manager should be appointed for longer than five years.** (Draft Bill, clause 28(4).)

*Protection for the person concerned*

8.48 Apart from the expedient of retaining control over the bulk of a patient's capital, the Court of Protection currently seeks to protect patients against loss incurred by receivers in two main ways. First, it requires receivers to give security for the possibility of loss to the estate (this being most often provided by the purchase of a guarantee bond on the payment of a single premium). Secondly, it requires receivers to file accounts, usually on an annual basis.[96] Both forms of protection should remain under our new scheme. The court making any management appointment will consider what controls to order when it appoints the manager. We would expect that anyone given substantial property powers would have to give security and file an annual account, as at present. The Public Trust Office deals with security and accounts at present, and we suggest it should continue to do so. In some cases no powers in relation to financial matters will be given and security is unlikely to be required. A regular report would, however, still be appropriate in the majority of cases. It is more appropriate to refer to the filing of "reports" rather than "accounts", to cover cases where no financial powers have been granted.

> **We recommend that the court may require a manager to give to the Public Trustee such security as the court thinks fit, and to submit to the Public Trustee such reports at such intervals as the court thinks fit.** (Draft Bill, clause 28(6)(a).)

*Monitoring by the Public Trustee*

8.49 We appreciate that the Public Trust Office does not at present supervise anyone who possesses powers in relation to personal or health care matters. In the consultation papers we proposed that the Mental Health Act Commission might be given certain supervisory powers in relation to managers with personal welfare powers, although we did not see a need for supervision of managers with health care powers.[97] A number of consultees expressed doubts about the relevance of the expertise of the Mental Health Act Commission to supervisory work of this sort. Some suggested that local social services authorities would have the appropriate skills in relation to personal welfare matters (but not in relation to financial matters). A clear majority expressed the view that some supervisory mechanism should be in place for all managers. We have recommended in paragraph 8.48 above

---

[95] See para 8.13 above and draft Bill, clause 24(2).

[96] Mental Health Act 1983, s 107.

[97] Consultation Paper No 128, para 6.25; Consultation Paper No 129, para 4.24.

that security should be given and reports filed in every case where the court has made such an order. It appears to us that the Public Trust Office already has the necessary skills to supervise financial decision-makers and is perhaps best placed to develop the skills applicable to personal and medical managers. We think it likely that a single manager might have powers ranging across the three areas and that it would be wasteful and confusing for different reports to be submitted to different bodies. In many cases no clear or significant lines can be drawn between "personal", "medical" and "financial" decisions.

8.50 Under the present Court of Protection Rules the Public Trustee is allocated a series of functions, all of which depend on the fact that the Public Trustee can currently exercise all the functions conferred on the judge by Part VII of the Mental Health Act 1983.[98] The Public Trustee will have no judicial powers under our new scheme, which carefully distinguishes between judicial and administrative functions. At present, the drawing of this vital distinction is left to Rules made by the Lord Chancellor. Some of the existing functions of the Public Trustee should, however, be retained under the new scheme. The Public Trustee may in future act as manager if appointed to do so. In cases where some other manager has been appointed the Public Trustee will have the function of receiving any security and reports which the court has ordered. For the effective discharge of either function, the Public Trustee should also have certain powers of a supervisory nature similar to some of those currently specified in the Court of Protection Rules. Although the precise nature of the necessary supervisory powers should be a matter for the Lord Chancellor (who already has power to make rules about the powers of the Public Trustee under the Public Trustee Act 1906) we would expect the following powers to be specified: (1) the power to raise requisitions on a manager's reports; (2) the power to direct a Lord Chancellor's Visitor or any other appropriate person to visit the person concerned and report whether it is desirable for the Public Trustee to exercise any of his or her functions; (3) the power to inspect any property of the person concerned or direct some other appropriate person to do so and report; and (4) the power to make or cause to be made any other inquiries which may be necessary or expedient for the proper discharge of his or her functions.[99]

> **We recommend that the Public Trustee should have such supervisory functions in relation to other managers as are laid down in Rules.** (Draft Bill, clause 28(6)(b).)

8.51 In his or her capacity as a manager, or as an adjunct to the function of monitoring other managers, the Public Trustee should be able to apply as of right to the court

---

[98]   Mental Health Act 1983, s 94.

[99]   Compare Court of Protection Rules 1994 (SI 1994 No 3046), rules 63, 69(3), 70 and 73 respectively.

for the making of an order under clause 24 of the draft Mental Incapacity Bill.[100]

*Expenses and remuneration for the manager*

8.52 We proposed in the consultation papers[101] that managers should be able to recover out-of-pocket expenses, and this was accepted by consultees. We do not recommend any change to the present situation whereby remuneration may be payable to a manager from the estate of the person concerned. The court in making the appointment should direct whether or not remuneration is to be paid. Any professional person, including the Public Trustee, will expect to be remunerated for acting on behalf of a person without capacity. The level of remuneration claimed will be one matter which the court will take into account when deciding who should be appointed to act as manager. It remains to be seen whether, as some of our respondents maintained, commercial trust corporations could do the same work as the Public Trust Office does more effectively and at a lower cost to individual estates.[102] Remuneration is most unlikely to be approved where personal and health care powers are concerned, since professional skills are unlikely to be involved in those cases.

> **We recommend that a manager should be entitled to be reimbursed for the reasonable expenses of discharging his or her functions. If the court so directs when appointing a manager, he or she shall be entitled to remuneration for discharging those functions.** (Draft Bill, clause 28(9).)

8.53 Where the Public Trustee acts as financial manager then he or she will seek remuneration for doing so. Provision will also be made for the Public Trustee to charge an appropriate fee for the discharge of the separate supervisory function involved in taking security and receiving a report from a manager.

**Managers: a code of practice**

8.54 In view of the fact that managers may have powers in relation to personal welfare and health care decision-making, and may have more powers than receivers have traditionally had over financial decisions, there is a clear need for guidance to be issued to those who are appointed as managers. The recent National Audit Office report drew attention to the fact that many existing receivers would like more

---

[100] See para 10.20 below and draft Bill, clause 47(3)(c).

[101] Consultation Paper No 128, para 6.31; Consultation Paper No 129, para 4.26.

[102] It should be noted that the fees currently charged to patients with private receivers are inflated by an element of cross-subsidisation to keep down the fees charged to patients for whom the Public Trustee is receiver. The Committee of Public Accounts reported that this was "basically unacceptable", (Thirty-ninth Report, *op cit*, para 3(xii)).

information and practical guidance about their role and responsibilities.[103]

> ***We recommend*** **that the Secretary of State should issue and from time to time revise a code of practice for the guidance of people who act as managers.** (Draft Bill, clause 31(1)(c).)

---

[103] National Audit Office, *Looking After the Financial Affairs of People with Mental Incapacity* (1994) paras 2.14 - 2.16.

# PART IX
# PUBLIC LAW PROTECTION FOR VULNERABLE PEOPLE AT RISK

## Introduction

9.1 In our 1991 overview paper[1] we examined certain "emergency powers" which are available under the National Assistance Acts 1947 and 1951 and the Mental Health Act 1983. These give public officials power to intervene in the lives of persons with certain types of disability, including power to arrange that they be forcibly removed from their homes. Part of the background to our review was public concern about the death of Beverley Lewis, a severely disabled young woman whose mentally ill mother had obstructed the efforts of the authorities to provide the services she needed.[2] We invited comment on how the balance between protection from harm and respect for individual rights, which is particularly delicate in this area of our project, should be struck and maintained.[3] To the basic question of whether any reform of these emergency powers was needed our consultees responded with a resounding affirmative. The existing law was said to be ineffective in protecting elderly, disabled and other vulnerable people from abuse and neglect, and inadequate in its approach to issues of autonomy and individual rights. It appeared to be counter-productive, being so draconian that it was rarely used.

9.2 In Consultation Paper No 130 we therefore made provisional proposals to up-date and rationalise the powers of local authorities to intervene when they have concerns for the safety of incapacitated or vulnerable people living in the community. The proposals were designed to be consistent with relevant provisions of the National Health Service and Community Care Act 1990 and the new community care system which that Act brought into effect from 1 April 1993. They also took account of growing public and professional anxiety about both "elder abuse"[4] and the abuse (particularly sexual abuse) of adults with learning disabilities.[5] We proposed[6] that local social services authorities should have a new duty to investigate, together with a series of short-term powers for use in cases where the adult at risk or some third

---

[1] Consultation Paper No 119, paras 3.20 - 3.23.

[2] *Ibid*, para 3.20 and n 82.

[3] *Ibid*, para 7.9.

[4] Community Care magazine ran a major campaign on "elder abuse" in the summer of 1993. In July 1993 the Social Services Inspectorate of the Department of Health issued Practice Guidelines addressing the problem of elder abuse, *No Longer Afraid : The Safeguard of older people in domestic settings*. In September 1993 a national organisation, "Action on Elder Abuse" was launched. See para 2.42 above.

[5] See para 2.43 above.

[6] Consultation Paper No 130, Part III.

party refuses to co-operate with the investigation. We went on[7] to consider the long-term powers currently available to local authorities under the guardianship scheme contained in the Mental Health Act 1983. The Scottish Law Commission has published a Discussion Paper which draws on the proposals in our own consultation paper and makes a number of very similar proposals.[8]

9.3 Many of our respondents, including the Association of Directors of Social Services, the British Association of Social Workers and representatives of voluntary organisations, were enthusiastic in their support for the law reform proposals in the consultation paper. Reservations were expressed by some carers' organisations, notably the Alzheimer's Disease Society. Their concerns appear, however, to be based on an understandable concern that priority should be given to understanding, assessing and providing for the needs of carers. We have borne in mind the need for any new system to be more sensitive to the needs of carers and less intrusive of their own rights, while providing for the needs of vulnerable people who are being cared for.

9.4 In view of the broad support for the suggestions in the consultation paper, the recommendations in this Part bear a close resemblance to our provisional proposals. We begin by recommending new protective powers, and we conclude by showing how their use will quickly feed into one of several longer-term solutions, as appropriate. Our recommendations are implemented in Part II of the draft Mental Incapacity Bill.

**Defining the client group**

9.5 In the title of Consultation Paper No 130 we referred not to mentally incapacitated adults but to "mentally incapacitated and other vulnerable adults". In the context of emergency investigative powers, it seemed sensible to extend the scope of our project to include all those who might need emergency protection.[9] We provisionally suggested a very broad definition of vulnerability, namely that "a person is vulnerable if by reason of old age, infirmity or disability (including mental disorder within the meaning of the Mental Health Act 1983) he is unable to take care of himself or to protect himself from others".[10] Throughout the consultation paper, we suggested that our proposals should apply to (1) persons without capacity (according to the definition proposed in relation to the private law jurisdiction), (2) mentally disordered persons (according to the definition in the Mental Health Act 1983) and (3) vulnerable persons (according to our new definition). Although

---

[7] *Ibid*, Parts IV and V.

[8] Discussion Paper No. 96, Mentally Disordered and Vulnerable Adults: Public Authority Powers (August 1993).

[9] See further Consultation Paper No 130, paras 2.21 - 2.29.

[10] *Ibid*, para 2.29.

respondents were overwhelmingly in favour of extending the client group beyond the narrow category of those who lack mental capacity, some were confused by the overlap between the three categories. In the light of the many helpful comments of consultees, it has proved possible to develop a single definition of vulnerability which will apply to all those who should be brought within the scope of the reformed emergency powers.[11]

9.6 It is vital to stress that the reformed emergency powers which will be recommended in this Part are not an end in themselves. They are all linked to an investigation by the public authorities into an individual's need for services or protection. In the great majority of cases there will be no question at all of exercising coercive powers in order to carry out such an investigation. People will be only too keen to have a proper assessment of their needs carried out. Similarly, most people will positively want to be protected from harm. The powers need only be invoked in relation to a small number of people who are not able to furnish themselves with effective protection from harm. This may be because of their own frailty or disability. It is important to emphasise, however, that the need for coercive intervention is likely to be most pressing where some third party has decided to block the way of the caring agencies.

> **We recommend that a "vulnerable person" should mean any person of 16 or over who (1) is or may be in need of community care services by reason of mental or other disability, age or illness and who (2) is or may be unable to take care of himself or herself, or unable to protect himself or herself against significant harm or serious exploitation.** (Draft Bill, clause 36(2).)

*Age*

9.7 Respondents agreed with our provisional view[12] that vulnerable people who have attained the age of sixteen should be included in the client group. This would result in some overlap with the emergency protection scheme in the Children Act 1989 but there is already a similar overlap with the emergency powers which we propose to replace. The fact is that a person can require protection either because he or she is a child or because he or she has a special vulnerability unconnected with age. It would not be right to suggest that these two possibilities are mutually exclusive, especially as a young person approaches the age of majority. We prefer to acknowledge this, and also to maintain consistency within the draft Mental Incapacity Bill, by providing that the protective scheme, like the new jurisdiction in

---

[11] As will be seen, the exercise of any powers will be triggered by the person being "at risk". "Vulnerability" is a threshold criterion, or a first hurdle of two. See further, para 9.16 below.

[12] Consultation Paper No 130, para 2.30.

general,[13] can apply to those sixteen and over. The draft Bill therefore provides that, in relation to those under eighteen, the definition of "community care services" should be extended to include relevant services governed by the Children Act 1989.[14]

### The meaning of "harm"

9.8 In the consultation paper,[15] we suggested that the concept of "significant harm" used in the Children Act 1989 might also be helpful in the context of adults at risk. This suggestion was welcomed on consultation. "Harm" should be defined in such a way as to stress that it can arise not only from physical or sexual ill-treatment, but also where a person's development is being impaired. This might be especially relevant where a younger person with a learning disability (mental handicap) is kept away from social and educational provision. Equally, and in particular in relation to older people, it should be made clear that "harm" is caused where an avoidable deterioration in a person's health or welfare is allowed to occur.

> **We recommend that "harm" should be defined to mean ill-treatment (including sexual abuse and forms of ill-treatment that are not physical); the impairment of, or an avoidable deterioration in, physical or mental health; and the impairment of physical, intellectual, emotional, social or behavioural development.** (Draft Bill, clause 36(5).)

### Exploitation

9.9 In response to a suggestion in our consultation paper,[16] many of our respondents urged that, in addition to "harm", the problem of "exploitation" should be specifically mentioned in any new legislation. They told us that financial abuse of the elderly was extremely prevalent and they wished to be sure that this form of abuse was explicitly covered. We shall make recommendations accordingly.[17]

### The objecting client

9.10 Throughout our consultation paper it was stressed that "merely vulnerable" clients, as opposed to mentally disordered clients or those who lack capacity, should be able

---

[13] See para 2.52 above; but note the exceptions to the general rule discussed at paras 5.18, 7.20 and 8.32 respectively.

[14] Clause 36(3). Such services are provided by local authorities in the exercise of functions conferred by the 1989 Act, s 17.

[15] Consultation Paper No 130, para 3.16.

[16] *Ibid.*

[17] See for example para 9.16 below.

to reject intervention by the authorities.[18] By making this clear, we intended to strike the necessary balance between the need to protect people with disabilities or frailties and the need to respect individual autonomy. It is clear that some physically frail and vulnerable people choose, in the exercise of their free will, to refuse services which might (in the view of most people) benefit them. Others choose to remain in situations which appear to others to be causing them unnecessary harm. Just as a person with capacity may refuse medical treatment which a doctor believes would be efficacious and beneficial, so a person with capacity is entitled to refuse community care or other protective services if he or she wishes.

9.11    At present, the National Assistance Act 1948 further qualifies one's right to autonomy, if grave chronic disease, age, infirmity or physical incapacity (conjoined in the three latter cases to insanitary conditions) are linked to inability to care for oneself.[19] There was almost unanimous agreement among our respondents that these provisions get the balance between protection and autonomy wrong, are counter-productive and should be repealed and replaced.[20] Other emergency powers are found in the Mental Health Act 1983, and therefore use the existence of mental disorder (rather than any lack of decision-making capacity) as the justification for protective action being taken. A number of respondents agreed with our provisional view[21] that the power in section 135(1) of the 1983 Act was, however, "of little help in practice".

9.12    The opportunity should now be taken to create a unified set of emergency powers, tied to principled and acceptable criteria, to help protect vulnerable people. The outdated and ineffective provisions that exist at present should be repealed. Mentally disordered people who are also vulnerable should be covered by the new powers. It would be nonsense to exclude such people from our recommendations or to reduce the ability of local authorities to offer them help and protection. We have concluded that no bar to intervention which is based on the objections of a person who is or may be suffering from "mental disability" can be justified in relation to short-term measures designed merely to protect and assess the person concerned. This conclusion clarifies and simplifies the provisional view we set out in our consultation paper[22] and which was very widely supported by our consultees. Since there is to be a single client group of vulnerable persons, protection for the autonomy of those who do not want help should be expressed as a proviso to the effect that the new powers may not be exercised where the person concerned objects, unless that person

[18]   Consultation Paper No 130, para 3.30.

[19]   National Assistance Act 1948, s 47.

[20]   As proposed in Consultation Paper No 130, para 2.10.

[21]   *Ibid*, para 2.12.

[22]   *Ibid*, especially paras 1.16 and 2.29.

is believed to suffer from mental disability. "Mental disability" will have the same wide definition as in the test for incapacity.[23] This proviso will be found to apply to all the new powers recommended in this Part.

**Mandatory reporting, case conferences and registers**

9.13 In relation to a few other issues canvassed in the consultation paper, the responses we received have not led us to make any recommendations for reform of the law in those areas. The first was the idea of a "mandatory reporting" law, making it a criminal offence to fail to report any information about the abuse of a vulnerable adult. In view of the growing concern about the abuse of vulnerable adults, three respondents urged us to reconsider our preliminary rejection of any such reform.[24] It was said that care workers operate in a norm of non-reporting which stops them "blowing the whistle" on abuses being perpetrated by colleagues. The concern was not to punish those who did not report but rather to protect those who did. We understand this concern, but we see it as a matter for the employer-employee relationship. Contractual clauses can require that workers report abuses and that they will not be discriminated against for doing so. Professional codes of practice can give appropriate guidance.

9.14 We also asked whether there was a need for guidance on suitable case conference procedures, equivalent or similar to those in use for the protection of children.[25] And we invited views on the desirability of setting up registers of the incapacitated or vulnerable people about whom the local authority were concerned.[26] It was clear from our consultation that a growing number of local social services authorities already have internal guidelines and procedures about both case conferences and some form of register for adults at risk, while many more are in the process of developing their policy in this field. Both issues have also been addressed by the Department of Health since the publication of our paper. In relation to abused elderly persons, the Social Services Inspectorate of the Department of Health has published guidelines which cover case conferences and registers.[27] In addition, in relation to certain mentally disordered persons, the Secretary of State has issued

---

[23] See draft Bill, clause 2(2).

[24] See Consultation Paper No 130, para 3.18.

[25] *Ibid*, para 3.20.

[26] *Ibid*, para 3.22.

[27] *No Longer Afraid: The Safeguard of older people in domestic settings* (1993). Paragraph 5.18 states that "[i]n complex cases, or where intervention is being refused, a multi-disciplinary meeting will be needed to arrive at a suitable care plan." Paragraph 5.23 deals with registers by stating that "[a] systematic approach to monitoring and review will reduce the need for 'at-risk' registers."

guidance requiring the maintenance of "at risk" registers.[28] Among our respondents, all those who commented on this point saw multi-disciplinary case conferences as essential. There was, on the other hand, no consensus about the merits of setting up registers. Even those who supported the establishment of registers said that there must be clear procedures for challenging and reviewing any entry made.

**A duty to investigate**

9.15 The prime proposal in our consultation paper was that local social services authorities should be placed under a duty to investigate allegations of abuse or neglect of an incapacitated, mentally disordered or vulnerable person.[29] Many respondents said that the proposed new duty would merely strengthen existing duties (especially the duty to assess needs) which are already placed on local authorities under community care arrangements, but would have the merit of focusing attention on abuse, neglect and harm. Most respondents also agreed with our provisional view[30] that any new statutory duty should be imposed only on local social services authorities. Of course other bodies, such as the police, hospital managers or the trustees of charities may have their own independent responsibilities, whether arising from statute or contract, to investigate such allegations. As one expert respondent pointed out, however, the introduction of concurrent powers to initiate proceedings might lead to indecision and a failure to protect the client.

9.16 The fact that a person is vulnerable, as defined in the draft Bill, only means that he or she *may* need services and has a *potential* for suffering significant harm or serious exploitation. The bridge to the exercise of the new emergency powers must be provided by the concept of the client suffering or being likely to suffer such harm or exploitation. A shorthand for this concept is that the client must be "at risk".[31] All the new powers, like the new duty we set out below, will depend on the existence of risk as well as vulnerability.

> *We recommend* that where a local authority have reason to believe that a vulnerable person in their area is suffering or likely to suffer significant harm or serious exploitation they shall make such enquiries as they consider necessary to enable them to decide:

---

[28] NHS Management Executive HSG(94)5, requiring health authorities to introduce supervision registers which identify those people with a severe mental illness who may be a significant risk to themselves or to others from 1 April 1994.

[29] Consultation Paper No 130, paras 3.11 - 3.16.

[30] *Ibid*, para 3.11.

[31] *Ibid*, para 3.16.

**(1) whether the person is in fact suffering or likely to suffer such harm or exploitation and**

**(2) if so, whether community care services should be provided or arranged or other action taken to protect the person from such harm or exploitation.** (Draft Bill, clause 37(1).)

In the consultation paper,[32] we proposed that the enquiries made by the local authority should always include taking steps to gain access to the client. The draft Bill provides that the local authority should take steps to gain access to the client unless they already have sufficient information to enable them to decide what action, if any, they should take.[33] We discuss the sorts of protective action local authorities might take later in this Part,[34] one example being the making of an application for an order of the type discussed in Part VIII above.

9.17 A number of our respondents stressed that other agencies, particularly health authorities, might hold relevant information and should be consulted where appropriate. The draft Bill provides that a variety of statutory bodies should be under a duty to assist a local authority in its investigation unless this would be unreasonable.[35] It also provides that where the client is ordinarily resident in a different local authority area then the authority for that area should be consulted and may undertake the enquiries.[36]

**Authorised officers**

9.18 We suggested in the consultation paper that local social services authorities should authorise certain officers to exercise any new emergency intervention powers.[37] Such officers would have relevant training and experience, without necessarily having to be "approved social workers" or their equivalent, with statutory powers of their own. Our draft Bill adopts this notion of an authorised officer of the local social services authority, and provides that the officer should produce identification on request.[38]

---

[32] *Ibid*, para 3.16.

[33] Draft Bill, clause 37(2).

[34] See paras 9.42 - 9.53 below.

[35] Draft Bill, clause 37(3) - (5).

[36] Draft Bill, clause 37(6).

[37] Consultation Paper No 130, para 3.13.

[38] Draft Bill, clauses 36(4) and 38(2).

### Step-by-step emergency intervention

*(1) Power to enter premises and interview a person*

9.19 The local authority may find obstacles preventing them from discharging their duty to investigate a client's level of risk and his or her need for services or protection. We therefore proposed in the consultation paper[39] that an officer of the local authority should have a power (adapted from the existing power in section 115 of the Mental Health Act 1983) to enter premises.[40] There was overwhelming support from respondents for including such a power within the new legislation. Although our original proposal did not suggest that there should be a right to see the person concerned, we suggested such an extension[41] and now propose that this would be a sensible improvement on the model provided by section 115 of the 1983 Act. The power to enter should be restricted, as it is at present, to reasonable times of the day, since a balance is required between the right of the vulnerable person to protection and the rights of occupiers of property not to have their own rights infringed at unreasonable hours. We did not originally propose any proviso to this power. It follows, however, from our final policy decisions in relation to clients who are known or believed to object[42] that there should be a proviso to protect the rights of those who are not believed to be suffering from mental disability, but are believed to object. It seems sensible to apply the proviso at this first step of our step-by-step approach.

> *We recommend* that where an authorised officer of the local authority has reasonable cause to believe that a vulnerable person living in premises in the local authority's area is "at risk", the officer may at any reasonable time enter and inspect those premises and interview the person concerned in private. These powers should not be exercised if the officer knows or believes that the person concerned objects or would object unless the officer has reasonable cause to believe that the person concerned is or may be suffering from mental disability. (Draft Bill, clause 38(1) and (3).)

The power of entry in section 115 of the 1983 Act would become redundant and

---

[39] Consultation Paper No 130, para 3.25.

[40] The power in s 115 of the 1983 Act permits an approved social worker to enter any premises in which a mentally disordered patient is living, if he has reasonable cause to believe that the patient is not under proper care. In Consultation Paper No 130 (para 3.24) we noted that this provision is limited in its usefulness as the term "mentally disordered patient" would seem to require a prior assessment of the patient and a diagnosis of mental disorder.

[41] Consultation Paper No 130, para 3.25.

[42] See paras 9.10 - 9.12 above.

should be repealed once this new power is enacted.[43]

9.20 The local authority officer may be able to complete the necessary enquiries simply by invoking the new power to enter and by interviewing the person about whom there is concern. That person may be happy to co-operate with the enquiry and may also be happy to accept any services or suggestions offered. The objections of any third party who has been obstructing access to him or her may be overcome.

*(2) Entry warrants*

9.21 There may, however, be occasions when the person believed to be at risk, or that person's carer, continues to refuse entry and access to the investigating authority. We therefore proposed that there should be power to apply to the court for a warrant to enter premises.[44] The majority of respondents agreed that such a power was a necessary adjunct to the new investigative duty.

> **We recommend** that, on the application of an authorised officer, the court should have power to issue a warrant authorising a constable, accompanied by such an officer, to enter specified premises if:
>
> **(1) the applicant has reasonable cause to believe that a vulnerable person living in those premises is "at risk";**
>
> **(2) granting the warrant is necessary to enable the officer to gain access to the vulnerable person, and**
>
> **(3) (unless there is reasonable cause to believe that the person is or may be suffering from mental disability) the applicant does not know or believe that the person objects or would object.**
> (Draft Bill, clause 39.)

9.22 As we explained in the consultation paper,[45] the Mental Health Act 1983 already provides for the issue of a warrant to enter premises where a person is suffering from mental disorder. In sharp contrast to our step-by-step approach, however, the present law provides that a single warrant can contain authority both to enter premises and to remove a mentally disordered person from them. In our view, any process of forcible removal should come at the conclusion of a process of investigation. The existing power in the Mental Health Act 1983 will have no

---

[43] See draft Bill, Sched 9.

[44] Consultation Paper No 130, para 3.30. As with the power to enter, this was modelled on a provision of the Mental Health Act 1983, namely s 135(1).

[45] Consultation Paper No 130, para 3.28.

remaining function and should be repealed, upon the introduction of the new provision for the issue of an entry warrant.[46]

9.23 Once the officer has gained entry to the premises where the vulnerable person is living, it may become possible for the local authority to decide whether the vulnerable person is indeed at risk and, if so, whether community care services should be arranged or other protective action taken without the use of any further statutory powers. It may become clear that the client has no form of mental disability and simply wants to be left alone. Even if the position is less clear, the client may willingly co-operate with a lengthier assessment procedure.

*(3) Assessment orders*

9.24 In a small number of cases, however, the client or some third party may refuse to participate in an assessment process which is considered to be necessary. We therefore proposed in the consultation paper[47] that the local authority should be able to apply for an order authorising them to carry out an assessment of the client. On consultation, there was wide support for the introduction of such an order, for which there is no equivalent in the present law. It would be a necessary adjunct to the duty to investigate risk and a vital component in the step-by-step approach we favour.

**We *recommend* that, on the application of an authorised officer the court should have power to make an assessment order if:**

**(1) the applicant has reasonable cause to believe that a vulnerable person is "at risk", and**

**(2) the order is required so that the local authority can assess whether the person is in fact "at risk" and if so whether community care services should be provided or arranged, or other protective action taken, and**

**(3) (unless there is reasonable cause to believe that the person is or may be suffering from mental disability) the applicant does not know or believe that the person objects or would object.**
**(Draft Bill, clause 40(1) and (2).)**

9.25 This new power is still one which is designed to address short-term problems arising in a crisis or emergency. For this reason we suggested[48] that an assessment order

---

[46] See draft Bill, Sched 9.

[47] Consultation Paper No 130, paras 3.33 - 3.34.

[48] *Ibid*, para 3.34.

should be subject to a time-limit of seven days. Some respondents believed that the necessary assessments could be completed more quickly, but few argued for a *maximum* time-limit shorter than seven days. We were not persuaded by those who argued that renewal for a further week should be permitted since, in order to cater for any difficulty in making appointments with medical and other professionals, the order will specify the date by which the assessment should begin. The time-limit will run from that time, rather than from the date of the making of the order.

> **We recommend that an assessment order should specify (1) the date by which the assessment is to begin, and (2) the period for which it will remain in force, being the shortest period necessary for the purposes of the assessment, not exceeding eight days.** (Draft Bill, clause 40(4).)

9.26 We invited comments on whether an assessment order should include the power to examine the client.[49] A medical examination may be necessary, *inter alia* to satisfy the requirements of the European Convention of Human Rights that longer term detention is only justifiable where a diagnosis of mental disorder has been made.[50] Several respondents argued that a power to examine might be required in exceptional circumstances, while another suggested that additional criteria should be met before the judicial forum can grant a power to examine. We would expect, as is the case with child assessment orders under the Children Act 1989, that the applicant would have to set out in detail the components of the proposed assessment for the court, and to make a case for each of them. There will undoubtedly be circumstances in which a medical and/or psychiatric assessment should be included. The question is, however, whether an examining doctor (and indeed any other "assessor") should have power to carry out an examination where the person concerned objects to it. Few doctors will ever seek to do so. For the avoidance of doubt, it should be provided that any objections by the person concerned may only be overridden with the express authorisation of the court. This may be done either on the making of the order, if sufficient information is available at that time, or else by a direction made while the order is in force. Any court which is asked to make such an authorisation will wish to consider the issue of the person's capacity to decide about the matter to which objection is being taken.

> **We recommend that nothing to which the person concerned objects should be done pursuant to the assessment order unless the court has authorised it to be done notwithstanding that objection.** (Draft Bill, clause 40(3).)

---

[49] *Ibid*, para 3.35.

[50] For a fuller discussion of these requirements see Consultation Paper No 130, paras 3.36 - 3.37.

9.27 An assessment order should not usually be used to remove the person from home, and the legislation should reinforce this point. A separate power will be available if there is a need to take a person away from home.[51] There may, however, be rare occasions where, in order to complete the assessment itself, it is found necessary to remove the vulnerable person from his or her place of residence. Again, we would envisage most of the difficulties arising from the activities of an obstructive third party.

> **We recommend that a vulnerable person may only be removed from his or her place of residence pursuant to an assessment order in accordance with specific directions and for such period or periods as are specified in the order, and only if it is necessary for the purposes of the assessment.** (Draft Bill, clause 40(5).)

*(4) Temporary protection orders*

9.28 In exceptional circumstances it may also be necessary to remove a person to a safe place for a short time, simply in order to ensure that he or she is adequately protected from risk. An obvious case is where the vulnerable person is living with someone who is a suspected abuser. Under the National Assistance Acts 1948 and 1951, the court can issue an order authorising the removal of a person to suitable premises. There are also powers under the Mental Health Act 1983[52] to remove a person to "a place of safety". We discussed these powers in our consultation paper[53] and suggested[54] that a new "emergency protection order" was called for. Respondents supported the introduction of a new and more principled power to remove, although several disapproved of the adoption of the terms "emergency protection order" and "place of safety" which are used in the Children Act 1989. Older people and organisations which represent them are understandably sensitive to "infantilising" terminology. Those who work with adults with learning difficulties have a similar sensitivity, especially when references to the unhelpful concept of "mental age" are still rife.[55] Our draft Bill therefore uses new vocabulary, instead of adopting the terms used in child law.

> **We recommend that, on the application of an authorised officer, the court should have power to make a temporary protection order if:**

[51] See paras 9.28 - 9.33 below.

[52] Sections 135 and 136.

[53] Consultation Paper No 130, paras 2.9 - 2.14.

[54] *Ibid*, para 3.37.

[55] See para 3.22 and n 33 above.

**(1) a vulnerable person is likely to be "at risk" unless removed to or kept in protective accommodation for a short period, and**

**(2) (unless there is reasonable cause to believe that the person is or may be suffering from mental disability) the applicant does not know or believe the person objects or would object to the order.** (Draft Bill, clause 41(1) and (2).)

9.29   We provisionally proposed[56] that a removal order should last for a maximum period of seven days. We were not persuaded by those respondents who wanted a provision that this initial period might be extended for a further eight days. The fact that ostensibly "emergency" procedures are used to effect long-term changes is one of the chief objections to the provisions in the National Assistance Acts. A temporary protection order should provide a necessary breathing-space during which a variety of long-term options for the client can be considered, while he or she is safely protected from whichever form of harm was being suffered.

> *We recommend* that a temporary protection order should authorise removal to protective accommodation for a specified period being the shortest possible necessary for achieving the purpose of the order, with a maximum of eight days. (Draft Bill, clause 41(3).)

The draft clause also caters for the less common situation of a client who is already in protective accommodation, but who should be prevented from leaving it. This will usefully complement the more usual power to remove.

9.30   We anticipate that the applicant for a temporary protection order will have identified an appropriate destination for the client and that this will, wherever possible, be specified in the order. Although we recommend the use of the new phrase "protective accommodation", only minor amendments to the old definition of "place of safety" in the 1983 Act are required. The opportunity should be taken to replace the phrase "residential home for mentally disordered persons" with "residential care home".[57] Nor is there any need to provide for accommodation in a police station. Subject to those two changes, the definition of "protective accommodation" should mirror that of "place of safety" in section 135(6) of the 1983 Act.[58]

---

[56]   Consultation Paper No 130, para 3.39.

[57]   The survival of this outdated wording, which used to have a precise meaning in a statute which has now been repealed, appears to be an oversight.

[58]   Draft Bill, clause 41(7). The power of the police (under the Mental Health Act 1983, s 136) to detain a person found in a public place can sometimes be useful and will remain intact. For technical reasons, the draft Bill repeals s 135(6) of the Mental Health Act 1983, which defines "place of safety", and inserts a new s 136(3) into the 1983 Act,

9.31    Clearly, the need for a temporary protection order may coincide with the need for an assessment, in that the long-term options cannot be given adequate consideration until an assessment of risk and need is performed.

> **We recommend that the court may, on making a temporary protection order, give directions for assessment as it may when making an assessment order.** (Draft Bill, clause 41(4).)

It is important that the court should be able to make the most appropriate order in the particular circumstances and the draft Bill therefore provides that an application for an assessment order can be treated as an application for a temporary protection order, and vice versa.[59]

9.32    We provisionally proposed that if a person is removed from home then the local authority should have a duty to return him or her as soon as it appears that there will be no remaining risk if this is done.[60] There was general support for this proposal, a number of respondents confirming that where a person is taken from home inadequate consideration is often given to the possibility of a quick return. It was suggested that many elderly people quickly fail in health once they are removed from familiar environments, and that keeping the person in his or her own home should always be the first option. This is consistent with the Government's stated policy in relation to community care.[61] The order will, in any event, only last for a maximum of eight days and the authority will then have no power to prevent the person returning home if he or she wishes and is able to do so. Any duty to return must cater for cases where the client may not wish to return home, or may not be entitled to do so, or may lack the capacity to decide where to live. Since the place where the person was suffering harm may not always be his or her own "home", our draft legislation refers to a duty to return to the place from which the person was removed.

> **We recommend that where a person has been removed to protective accommodation it shall be the duty of the local authority to return the person to the place from which he or she was removed as soon as that is practicable and consistent with his or her interests.** (Draft Bill, clause 41(8).)

defining "place of safety" as protective accommodation or also a police station. See draft Bill, Scheds 8 and 9.

[59]    Draft Bill, clauses 40(6) and 41(6).

[60]    Consultation Paper No 130, para 3.41.

[61]    One of the six "key objectives" in the White Paper *Caring for People: Community Care in the Next Decade and Beyond* (1989) Cm 849 was "to promote the development of domiciliary, day and respite services to enable people to live in their own homes wherever feasible and sensible" (para 1.11).

9.33    Since a temporary protection order is intended to be available where there is an urgent need for removal, it must clearly be possible to grant the order *ex parte*. Respondents supported our proposal to this effect.[62] We originally proposed[63] that someone with whom the person was living immediately before the order was made should be able to apply to have the order varied or discharged. Respondents, however, expressed concern that the person with whom the client has been residing would often be the person whose care of the client has been inadequate. It appears appropriate instead to limit the right to apply for the discharge of an ex parte order to those directly concerned with the client's decision-making powers, namely the client, any donee of a CPA and any court-appointed manager.

> **We recommend** that an application for a temporary protection order may be made ex parte. The person concerned, any donee of a CPA and any court-appointed manager should be entitled to apply for the discharge of an ex parte order. (Draft Bill, clause 41(5).)

9.34    The new temporary protection order will supersede the provisions of section 47 of the National Assistance Act 1948, of the National Assistance (Amendment) Act 1951 and of section 135(1) and (3) of the Mental Health Act 1983. These provisions should be repealed as soon as our recommendations are implemented.[64]

**Appeals**

9.35    We took the provisional view[65] that it would not be practicable to allow for appeals against the making of a protection order, in view of the short time-limit we proposed. Most of our legal respondents agreed, although representatives of the social work profession argued for the availability of an appeal against a *refusal* to make an order. We are not convinced of the need for any such appeal, since the local authority will also be able to apply to the long-term jurisdiction or to renew their application for a temporary protection order if new or additional facts come to light. These considerations apply equally to assessment orders and accordingly we have made no provision for appeals in either case.[66]

---

[62]    Consultation Paper No 130, para 3.38.

[63]    *Ibid*, para 3.44.

[64]    Draft Bill, Sched 9. Schedule 7 Parts III and IV, makes necessary transitional and saving provision for orders already made and executed.

[65]    Consultation Paper No 130, para 3.43.

[66]    General provisions for appeals on a point of law by way of case stated from a magistrates' court will apply. Challenges might also be mounted by way of judicial review.

### An offence of obstruction

9.36 In the consultation paper we proposed[67] an offence of refusing without reasonable cause to allow an authorised person to enter and inspect premises, or to have access to the person believed to be at risk, or otherwise to obstruct the exercise of the power to enter.[68] All those who responded in writing supported the creation of such an offence. Two respondents argued that it should not be an offence if it is the person believed to be at risk who is refusing entry or obstructing access, and we agree that it is important to make this clear. It also appears to us that the proposed new obstruction offence should be extended to include within its scope anyone who is carrying out the terms of an assessment or temporary protection order, and not only authorised officers of the local authority. These offences should be summary only, punishable by fine or imprisonment for a maximum of three months.[69] The local authority should have power to prosecute.

> **We recommend that it should be an offence for any person (other than the person concerned) without reasonable cause to obstruct (1) an authorised officer of a local authority in the exercise of his or her powers, or (2) any person who is acting pursuant to an assessment or temporary protection order. (Draft Bill, clause 42.)**

### Miscellaneous

*Power to assist in legal proceedings*

9.37 We asked consultees to comment on various other mechanisms, specifically aimed at cases of suspected abuse by a third party, whereby the local authority might afford protection to the vulnerable adult.[70] Respondents were generally in favour of there being a power to assist a vulnerable person to bring proceedings for a non-molestation or ouster order under the private law.[71] Assistance could range from referral to legal advisers, financial assistance with legal costs, providing "in house" advice or assistance, or acting as the "next friend" of a litigant without capacity.

> **We recommend that local authorities should have power to assist a vulnerable person in bringing proceedings for an order under the private law. (Draft Bill, clause 43.)**

---

[67] Consultation Paper No 130, para 3.26.

[68] The proposal was based on an analogous offence in s 129 of the Mental Health Act 1983.

[69] At an appropriate time it may be desirable to bring together the different offences of obstructing officials in the exercise of their powers into a single place on the statute book, but this is beyond the compass of the present project.

[70] Consultation Paper No 130, paras 3.45 - 3.48.

[71] *Ibid*, para 3.47.

We also asked[72] whether there should also be an associated power, like that available to local authorities under the Children Act 1989,[73] to assist an alleged abuser in finding alternative accommodation. This whole question is bound up, however, with the general question of local authorities' responsibilities towards carers and it might be thought wrong to single out suspected abusers for special help. On balance, therefore, we make no recommendation on this point.

9.38 A third suggestion (modelled on a recommendation which the Commission has already made in relation to child protection[74]) was that the court might include an exclusion requirement in any assessment or temporary protection order.[75] Respondents expressed concern, however, about any order, especially one made *ex parte*, requiring a person to leave his or her own home on mere suspicion of causing harm. It was pointed out that the suspected person might himself or herself be a hard-pressed family carer in need of services. There would be nothing to stop a social worker who goes to remove a vulnerable person to a safe place from advising the suspected person that the removal would not be effected if that person chose to leave the premises for the short duration of the order. It is difficult to judge what additional effect a condition imposed by the court would have. On balance, taking into account the very short time periods for which assessment or temporary protection orders may last, we make no recommendation on this point.

*The protection of property*

9.39 Local authorities already have a duty to protect the movable property of people admitted to hospital or "Part III accommodation",[76] or removed under section 47 of the National Assistance Act 1948.[77] That duty should obviously be amended to refer instead to removal under an assessment or temporary protection order. Logically, it should also extend to cases where, at the instance of the local authority, an order has been made by the court with jurisdiction under the new incapacity jurisdiction that the person concerned is to be admitted to accommodation arranged or provided by the authority.

**We *recommend* that the existing duty to protect the movable**

---

[72] *Ibid.*

[73] 1989 Act, Sched 2 para 5.

[74] *Family Law: Domestic Violence and Occupation of the Family Home* (1992) Law Com No 207, paras 6.15 - 6.22. The Government has accepted this recommendation (Written Answer, *Hansard* (HC) 15 June 1994, vol 244, col 562).

[75] Consultation Paper No 130, para 3.47.

[76] That is, residential accommodation provided by a local authority in accordance with Part III of the National Assistance Act 1948.

[77] National Assistance Act 1948, s 48.

**property of a person removed from his or her place of residence should apply where a person is removed (1) pursuant to the local authority applying for an order under Part I of the Mental Incapacity Bill and (2) pursuant to an assessment or temporary protection order.** (Draft Bill, clause 44.)

9.40 In the consultation paper we asked for views on whether local authorities should be placed under a new and more extensive duty to protect the "property and affairs" of all "incapacitated persons" for whom they provide or arrange accommodation away from home.[78] Respondents pointed out that this could oblige the authority to act as appointee under the Social Security Regulations,[79] or to apply to the court for the appointment of a manager, or to accept appointment as manager if there is no other suitable candidate willing to serve. Although a number of respondents urged upon us the need to impose such obligations, in spite of their resource implications, we have so far taken the view that decisions about the level of services which ought to be provided are outside the scope of a law reform exercise like this.[80] Some respondents also pointed out that carers and family members have a role to play where property needs to be protected, and that this role should not be displaced by the imposition of a duty on the local social services authority. It will, in our view, be more helpful to establish in clear terms that a local authority which provides or arranges accommodation for a person should have *power* to take steps to protect that person's property, if he or she lacks capacity to take such steps personally.

> **We recommend that local authorities should have power to take reasonable steps for the protection of the property and affairs of a person who is without capacity to protect them and for whom they provide or arrange accommodation.** (Draft Bill, clause 35.)

**Resource implications**

9.41 We expressed the provisional view in our consultation paper that our proposals would not have major resource implications for local authorities, and invited views.[81] Some respondents, including the British Association of Social Workers, agreed that local authorities were already working with the clients identified in the paper and that clearer and more rational powers would simply increase the efficiency and effectiveness of work which was already being done. The Social Services Inspectorate guidelines on safeguarding older people in domestic settings certainly assume that local social services authorities have responsibilities to that client group

---

[78] Consultation Paper No 130, para 5.10.

[79] See paras 4.22 - 4.28 above.

[80] See Consultation Paper No 119, para 1.15 and Consultation Paper No 130, para 1.4.

[81] Consultation Paper No 130, para 1.7.

when they state that "[a]gencies need to consider carefully both the preventive and protective aspects of intervention".[82] A number of respondents did express concern about present levels of funding and told us that new duties could not realistically be taken on without the provision of additional resources. No-one, however, suggested that the resource implications for local authorities in what we have proposed would be enormous, and many expressed the view that there should be speedy implementation of the much-needed reforms.

**Long-term solutions**

9.42 Throughout this Part, we have stressed that the new powers we are recommending will address a particular short-term need. This is the need to ascertain whether a vulnerable person is "at risk" and, if so, whether services or protection are required. Even if an assessment or temporary protection order is required and obtained, it will expire after a maximum period of eight days. If it is decided that there is risk and also a need for services and protection, then the question of recourse to one of a number of longer-term solutions arises.

*(1) Consensual solutions*

9.43 The client may very well have capacity to agree to, and accept, services or advice offered by the local authority at the conclusion of their investigation. If the problem has been self-neglect the client may accept community care services, including alternative accommodation, or health services. If the problem has been financial abuse, a power of attorney could be executed or banking and financial arrangements restructured. If there has been physical abuse then assistance in relation to legal proceedings may be welcome. If offences have been committed against the client then the police may commence criminal proceedings. If the client has capacity to make decisions about services or protection offered by the local authority then the need for compulsory steps has ended. This will be the case whether the client accepts or rejects what is offered. Many people choose environments, companions and life-styles which would not appeal to others.

*(2) Advocacy*

9.44 If the client is isolated, lacks information or has difficulty asserting himself or herself then a citizen advocacy project may provide the answer. We have already referred to the important role of citizen advocacy services, while explaining that the focus of our own project is on law reform issues where a legally effective substitute decision is required.[83] Advocacy deals with the quite different issue of assisting and encouraging disabled people to speak up for themselves.

---

[82] *No Longer Afraid: The Safeguard of older people in domestic settings* (1993) para 1.8.

[83] See para 2.44 above.

*(3) Detention and treatment under the Mental Health Act 1983*

9.45    In some cases it may become clear in the course of the local authority's investigation that the client is suffering from mental disorder and requires treatment in hospital. Sections 2 and 3 of the Mental Health Act 1983 provide for compulsory detention in such circumstances, although the vast majority of those who receive treatment for mental disorder do so informally.

*(4) Guardianship under the Mental Health Act 1983*

9.46    The client's mental disorder may be of a nature and degree which makes reception into guardianship under the Mental Health Act 1983 appropriate. Under section 7 of the 1983 Act, a local social services authority can, by administrative act (subject to review by a Mental Health Review Tribunal), acquire limited powers over certain mentally disordered people. The guardian is usually the local authority, but is occasionally a private individual. Both the powers and the persons to whom the scheme applies are strictly limited. We provisionally proposed[84] that (subject to a few minor amendments) guardianship under the 1983 Act should stay in place as a structure for supervising and supporting in the community certain mentally disordered people who would otherwise have to be detained in hospital. Linked to this, we provisionally rejected any extension of guardianship so as to bring in all persons who lack decision-making capacity.[85] The great majority of our respondents agreed with these provisional views. We do not, therefore, make any recommendations which would fundamentally alter the nature of the existing guardianship scheme.[86] Our consultation does, however, encourage us to recommend minor alterations to the scheme, and in particular those needed to reflect the introduction of the new jurisdiction described in this report.

9.47    The authors of the Department of Health's internal review on *Legal Powers on the Care of Mentally Ill People in the Community*[87] reviewed the purpose and current use of guardianship and concluded that they "would like to see active consideration given to its use for a wider range of patients".[88] More recently, however, the Department of Health issued a letter and discussion paper setting out views on

---

[84]  Consultation Paper No 130, para 4.16.

[85]  *Ibid*, para 4.16.

[86]  We anticipate that our conclusions in this regard will differ from those of the Scottish Law Commission, which may recommend a new "guardianship" scheme superseding the scheme in the Mental Health (Scotland) Act 1984. The parameters of the existing Scottish scheme are, however, already much wider than that in England and Wales, in particular because it can apply to all those with mental handicap. See Scottish Law Commission Discussion Paper No 94, Mentally Disabled Adults: Legal Arrangements for Managing their Welfare and Finances (1991) paras 2.49 - 2.53.

[87]  Department of Health, August 1993.

[88]  Paragraph 7.14.

Mental Health Act guardianship, and inviting comments.[89] The Government's view is that the combined effects of the proposed supervised discharge procedure, the new discharge guidance and the new supervision registers should be monitored before any consideration is given to amending the Mental Health Act guardianship provisions. The Government is not, therefore, convinced of the need for any amendments "*at this stage*". In view of the Department of Health's continuing work on this issue, we have not included in our draft Bill any provisions implementing our own very restricted recommendations. These will no doubt be taken into account when the Department considers the results of its own consultation process.

*Renaming "guardianship"*

9.48 First, it was suggested in some of our meetings that the name "guardianship" was not appropriate to the present scheme, which only gives a guardian three "essential powers". We see merit in the proposal that guardianship should be renamed to reflect the reality, perhaps as an "essential powers" or "community powers" order. It might then be asked whether the "managers" referred to in our draft Bill might instead be termed "guardians".

*Guardians*

9.49 In our consultation paper we proposed that individuals should no longer be appointed as guardians and that new appointments should be restricted to social services authorities.[90] Views were invited on whether health authorities might also be guardians.[91] The majority of our respondents agreed that, with the introduction of the new jurisdiction, there would be no need for private individuals to act as guardians under the Mental Health Act 1983. It is more appropriate for supervision and control of adults to be effected by public authorities rather than private individuals. A slim majority of our respondents opposed the possibility of a health authority acting as guardian. We see force in their argument that the primary guardianship power is to decide on the person's residence, and that accommodation outside hospital is not within the scope of a health authority's powers or duties. It appears to us that the Department of Health's proposals for a new supervised discharge scheme would satisfy any need for continuing control by health workers.[92] In that context, Mental Health Act guardianship can appropriately be the preserve of local social services authorities.

---

[89] Letter from Department of Health, Health Care (Administration) dated 21 October 1994 with annex, "Mental Health Act Guardianship: A Discussion Paper". Comments invited until 31 January 1995.

[90] Consultation Paper No 130, paras 4.6 - 4.8.

[91] *Ibid*, para 4.9.

[92] Report of the Internal Review, *op cit*, paras 8.10 - 8.19. See para 2.4 and n 13 and 14 above.

**We recommend** that section 7(5) of the Mental Health Act 1983 should be amended so that only a local social services authority may be named as guardian.

*Powers*

9.50 We took note in our consultation paper of the long-standing argument that the powers of a guardian should be extended to include a power to convey a person to the residence chosen by the guardian, and we proposed such an extension.[93] The Government's present view, as expressed in the letter of October 1994, is that the evidence to justify such a change is not at present clear enough.[94] As we said in the consultation paper, however, the introduction of a power to convey appears to be a minor and logical amendment which can be justified on the simple basis that, without it, the *existing* power to require residence at a particular place[95] is of little use. Our respondents were unanimous in supporting the introduction of a power to convey, saying this was a serious omission from the existing scheme.

**We recommend** that section 8(1) of the Mental Health Act 1983 should be amended to give a guardian an additional power to convey the patient to a residence specified by the guardian.

*Reviews and supervision*

9.51 We also invited comments[96] on whether the guardianship scheme should provide for automatic reference to a Mental Health Review Tribunal. Automatic reference for detained patients was introduced by the 1983 Act to ensure periodic independent review for long-term patients.[97] Although guardianship clients live in the community and have rights to apply to the Tribunal, a number of our respondents saw a case for automatic reference. The case in favour of such a provision was not particularly strong, and the level of support shown for it on consultation was certainly not sufficient to justify us in making any recommendation.

9.52 Our last provisional proposal was that the powers of the Mental Health Act Commission (to deal with complaints and make visits) should be extended to cover those under guardianship.[98] All those who responded to this proposal, including the Commission itself, supported it.

---

[93] Consultation Paper No 130, para 4.12.

[94] See para 9.47 and n 89 above.

[95] Mental Health Act 1983, s 8(1)(a).

[96] Consultation Paper No 130, para 4.17.

[97] L Gostin, *Mental Health Services - Law and Practice* (1986) para 18.05.

[98] Consultation Paper No 130, para 4.18.

*We recommend* that the powers of the Mental Health Act Commission should be extended to include those received into guardianship.

*(5) The new jurisdiction*

9.53 The last long-term option available to the local authority brings us back to our draft Mental Incapacity Bill and the recommendations made earlier in this report. The investigation carried out by the local authority in accordance with the new duty to investigate may conclude that the client lacks decision-making capacity in relation to a single matter or to a number of matters. It may be thought necessary that arrangements should be made for decisions on those matters to be taken either on a "one-off" or on a continuing basis. In such circumstances, those involved should consider applying to the court for the exercise of powers under the new decision-making jurisdiction described in Part VIII above.[99] Appropriate orders of the court, or the appointment of a manager with decision-making powers, will then provide for the necessary decisions to be made.

[99] See Part I Chapter IV of the draft Bill. See also draft Bill, clause 48 for the power of the court to make orders or give directions in an emergency.

# PART X
# THE JUDICIAL FORUM

### Introduction and background

10.1 Throughout this report we have referred to decisions being made or authorisations given by "the court". In this Part we offer our views about what this court might look like, who its members should be and how it should operate. These jurisdictional questions are ancillary to the substantive reform of the law with which this report is concerned. Our consultation process did, however, provoke respondents to express helpful views about them and we have been able to formulate certain recommendations which are implemented in Part III of the draft Mental Incapacity Bill appended to this report.

10.2 The three consultation papers published in 1993 referred to decisions by a "judicial forum" but made no specific proposals about the location or nature of this forum. We said in Consultation Paper No 128[1] that decisions about the judicial forum could best be made once the nature and scope of the new jurisdiction had become clearer. Only in an appendix to our final consultation paper did we invite views on the type of judicial forum which should operate the jurisdiction which had been proposed.[2] We identified three options. First, the new jurisdiction could be exercised by the ordinary courts, perhaps with the existing Court of Protection integrated into the system.[3] Secondly, administrative tribunals could be given power to decide all the issues which might arise under the new jurisdiction.[4] Thirdly, there could be a hybrid system, with medical treatment issues being decided by an appropriately constituted tribunal but others being dealt with in the ordinary courts.[5] Respondents, especially those with practical experience of the working of the Court of Protection, submitted some very useful reactions to these preliminary views. We also had very helpful discussions with officials from the Lord Chancellor's Department, with the Master of the Court of Protection and with the Official Solicitor.

### Courts or tribunals?

10.3 Our original view[6] was that the coercive nature of the new public law orders

---

[1] Paragraph 4.1.

[2] Consultation Paper No 130, Appendix.

[3] *Ibid*, para 11.

[4] *Ibid*, para 13.

[5] *Ibid*, para 14. In Consultation Paper No 129, para 4.6, we had invited views on whether a judicial forum with power to make medical decisions need be the same as the forum dealing with questions of personal welfare or finances.

[6] Consultation Paper No 130, Appendix para 11.

proposed in Consultation Paper No 130 was such that they should only be exercised by courts, a view which was supported by all those who commented on the options set out in the appendix. It was also noticeable that the option of a "hybrid" system found very little support among respondents.

10.4 Many respondents favoured an informal and inquisitorial approach to the issues which would arise under the new jurisdiction. There was also a very loud and clear call for the jurisdiction to be locally based and easily accessible. A number of respondents favoured tribunals for these reasons. Few, however, asserted that the Mental Health Review Tribunal could deal with the requisite range of issues. It is quite clear that the present expertise of the Mental Health Review Tribunal would have to be fundamentally altered and enormously extended before it could deal with the new jurisdiction.

10.5 There remains the option of a new and specially constituted tribunal, as suggested by various organisations over recent years and examined in our 1991 overview paper.[7] Now that the scope of the new, unified jurisdiction has become clear, however, this option seems much less compelling. The perceived advantages of informality and an inquisitorial approach could in fact be worked into a court-based system. It is true that a tribunal can include non-lawyers with relevant expertise in the process of adjudication. However, the very wide range of decisions covered by the new "incapacity" jurisdiction would make it hard to identify which non-legal specialism was relevant in a particular case. Decisions about financial matters, personal and social matters and complex medical decisions will all fall to be made. Even if the only decision to be made was about a health care question, the relevant specialism might be neurology, gynaecology, learning disability or psycho-geriatrics. In any event, there was a widespread view on consultation that certain very serious medical decisions should continue to be taken by senior members of the judiciary. There is, moreover, little doubt that the type of property and finance issues currently being resolved in the Court of Protection will continue to be the major part of the workload. Jurisdiction over new-style Continuing Powers of Attorney should also be integrated with the broad decision-making powers of the judicial forum which is chosen. All these factors make the use of the court system seem increasingly appropriate.

10.6 We have benefitted from the deliberations of the House of Lords Select Committee on Medical Ethics. Although strongly attracted at first to the idea of using tribunals to decide difficult medical issues, the committee took account of the fact that we intended a new decision-making forum to discharge a wider range of functions. The

---

[7] Consultation Paper No 119, paras 6.41 - 6.46. The use of multi-disciplinary committees was also favoured by a number of those who responded to the overview paper. See also the BMA's *Proposals for the Establishment of a Decision-Making Procedure on Behalf of the Mentally Incapable* (1990).

committee acknowledged that "it would not be practical or desirable to establish two separate systems of decision-making, one for medical matters and another for dealing with, say, an incompetent person's financial affairs. Indeed it would no doubt sometimes be difficult to distinguish between different types of decision, or to separate one element of a person's affairs from others".[8] The committee concluded that, in broad terms, it would support decision-making for incompetent patients being located within a new court-based system comprising High Court, circuit and district judges.[9] It stressed that any such system should make full use of independent advice, should be locally based, accessible and able to deal with emergency applications. The committee also urged appeal procedures, monitoring for consistency and public hearings with published judgments.[10]

10.7    The Select Committee was not alone in stressing the need for the widest possible dissemination of judgments given and orders made in the new jurisdiction proposed in our consultation papers. Professor Michael Freeman questioned whether, in relation to "life and death decisions", tribunal decisions would have the necessary authority in the eyes of the public.[11] He concluded that it is time for the law to play its role in habilitating and normalising people with intellectual disability, "and right that courts should be part of this educative function."[12] Authoritative case-law can guide those seeking to act in the best interests of people without capacity and stimulate public awareness of the ethical, social and legal issues involved in decision-making on behalf of those without capacity to decide matters for themselves.

10.8    We now consider that the use of existing court structures and personnel, albeit arranged so as to meet the needs of those without capacity, is the most responsible and practical way forward. The new statutory jurisdiction to make decisions on behalf of persons lacking capacity and to grant orders for the protection of vulnerable persons should be exercised by courts, both by an expanded and reconstituted Court of Protection and, in relation to the public law powers only, by magistrates' courts.

### A new Court of Protection

10.9    As was made clear in Parts VII and VIII respectively, a single court should in future exercise jurisdiction in relation to Continuing Powers of Attorney; and in relation to personal, health care and financial decisions for a person who lacks capacity. The

---

[8]    Report of the Select Committee on Medical Ethics (1993-94) HL 21-I para 247. For the Committee and its terms of reference see para 1.7 n 13 above.

[9]    *Ibid*, para 246.

[10]   *Ibid*, paras 248 and 249.

[11]   M Freeman, "Deciding for the Intellectually Impaired" (1994) 2 Med L Rev 77, 81.

[12]   *Ibid*, p 91.

expertise of the existing Court of Protection, especially in relation to financial matters and powers of attorney, should be retained and built upon. At the same time, the opportunity should be taken to change the anomalous nature of the present Court of Protection, an "office" of the Supreme Court with a single location in central London. The types of decisions which the judicial forum will be called upon to make are decisions which should be taken in a properly constituted court, whose decisions can contribute to a body of case-law.

> **We recommend** that a new superior court of record called the Court of Protection should be established, and that the office of the Supreme Court known as the Court of Protection should be abolished. (Draft Bill, clause 46(1).)

### Magistrates' courts

10.10 Magistrates' courts (and individual justices of the peace) are well placed to respond quickly to emergency situations. They currently issue removal orders under the National Assistance Acts 1948 and 1951 and they grant entry warrants under a great variety of enactments, including section 135(1) of the Mental Health Act 1983. They are the natural forum for the short-term protective orders described in Part IX above. Our respondents did not, however, favour magistrates' courts having jurisdiction over complex financial or medical cases, many of which might involve copious written evidence. The role of magistrates' courts should be confined to dealing with warrants and short-term orders in respect of the care and protection of vulnerable people who are at risk.[13]

> **We recommend** that magistrates' courts and single justices of the peace should have jurisdiction to deal with applications under Part II of the draft Bill only. (Draft Bill, clause 45(1)(b).)

10.11 Within magistrates' courts, family proceedings courts[14] now exercise a specialist jurisdiction in relation to children and other family cases. This is a specialism which can be built upon. The specially trained magistrates are very familiar with the concept of "significant harm" in the Children Act 1989, a concept adopted in our recommendations for new public law powers.

> **We recommend** that proceedings under Part II of the draft Bill should be treated as "family proceedings". (Draft Bill, clause 45(2).)

---

[13] The new Court of Protection should also have jurisdiction over the public law powers in Part II of the draft Bill. See para 10.12 below.

[14] For the constitution of family proceedings courts see Magistrates' Courts Act 1980, ss 66-68, s 69(1) and s 70.

**The jurisdiction of the Court of Protection**

10.12    The new Court of Protection will have jurisdiction to deal with all of the matters with which this Report is concerned, including the same powers as magistrates' courts to issue entry warrants or make other orders for the care and protection of the vulnerable.[15] The latter powers would not often be exercised by the Court of Protection, but the necessity for an entry warrant, an assessment order or a temporary protection order might arise during Court of Protection proceedings. It would not be sensible for the Court of Protection to have to refer any such matters to the magistrates' court.[16]

*Court of Protection judges*

10.13    The Court of Protection should consist of an appropriate number of judges nominated by the Lord Chancellor to exercise the jurisdiction of the Court. These judges will build up special expertise in cases involving people who may lack mental capacity. The availability of a range of judicial personnel should mean that cases, depending on their subject matter or complexity, are heard at the appropriate level by a judge with the appropriate experience and expertise. The range of judges should include district and circuit judges, and judges from the Chancery and Family Divisions of the High Court. Judges of the Chancery Division are currently nominated to deal with cases concerning the property and affairs of patients under Part VII of the Mental Health Act 1983 and their experience in this area should be retained. Judges of the Family Division deal with such cases as arise at present concerning the personal welfare or medical treatment of persons without capacity to consent.

> **We recommend** **that the jurisdiction of the Court of Protection should be exercised by judges nominated by the Lord Chancellor, whether Chancery Division or Family Division High Court judges, circuit judges or district judges.** (Draft Bill, clause 46(2).)

10.14    The office of Master of the Court of Protection has a long history.[17] It would seem useful for there to continue to be a member of the judiciary with special responsibility for the jurisdiction governing issues of mental incapacity, and with power to take necessary administrative decisions about the operation of the Court of Protection. Senior District Judges carry out comparable functions in other spheres. The present exercise presents a useful opportunity to update the existing terminology.

---

[15]    Draft Bill, clause 45(1).

[16]    See para 10.18 below for the power of the Lord Chancellor to make allocation orders about where proceedings should be commenced.

[17]    The title replaced the former title of "Master in Lunacy". The present "Master" is Mrs A B Macfarlane.

185

**We recommend** that the Lord Chancellor should designate one of the judges nominated as a Court of Protection judge to be Senior Judge of the Court of Protection. (Draft Bill, clause 46(4).)

10.15    There may come a time when it would be useful to have a President of the Court of Protection, perhaps if the workload and profile of the Court should increase.

**We recommend** that the Lord Chancellor may appoint one of the judges of the High Court nominated as a Court of Protection judge to be President of the Court of Protection. (Draft Bill, clause 46(3).)

*The location of the Court of Protection*

10.16    Respondents to every one of our consultation papers consistently bemoaned the fact that the present Court of Protection has no regional presence at all. Obviously, it is hard to quantify the effect of this on those who might otherwise have recourse to the jurisdiction of the Court of Protection. We ourselves can have no doubt, based on the many comments made by social workers, care workers, experts from voluntary organisations and solicitors who responded to our consultation papers, that the present Court of Protection seems to many a remote and inaccessible institution which offers no solution to the problems they face. We are persuaded that provision should be made for the new Court of Protection to sit in different parts of England and Wales. There is ample precedent for the Lord Chancellor designating courts to exercise specialist statutory jurisdictions,[18] in sufficient numbers to meet the demand for accessibility while not diluting the need for special expertise in the judges. We ourselves would anticipate a need for at least one venue to be designated for each of the six court circuits in England and Wales. Clearly, however, it will be for the Lord Chancellor's Department to assess the need for more or fewer.

**We recommend** that the Court of Protection should be able to sit at any place in England and Wales designated by the Lord Chancellor. (Draft Bill, clause 46(6).)

10.17    Although it is not for us to guess how many regional centres might be required to administer the incapacity jurisdiction, we do consider that the Court of Protection should retain a central office in London where proceedings could be commenced regardless of where the parties to the proceedings live.[19] Respondents who supported

---

[18]    See for example Children Act 1989, s 92(6) and Sched 11, Part I; The Civil Courts Order 1983 (SI 1983 No 713).

[19]    Compare the role of the Principal Registry of the Family Division which, as well as being the central administrative office of the Family Division of the High Court, is also a divorce county court and a nominated care and family hearing centre. It is therefore able to hear all types of family proceedings. This has enabled the Principal Registry to become a centre

using the existing Court of Protection as the central decision-making forum for all issues concerning the personal welfare, health care or property and affairs of persons without capacity urged that the expertise which that Court now has in dealing with complex financial matters or large estates should not be lost. This can be achieved by ensuring that a central London registry is retained, while allowing for the designation of regional registries as thought fit.

> **We recommend that the Court of Protection should have a central office and registry in London. The Lord Chancellor should have power to designate additional registries outside London.** (Draft Bill, clause 46(7).)

*Allocation and transfer of proceedings*

10.18 Cases should be heard by a judge of appropriate standing within the Court of Protection. This can be achieved by giving the Lord Chancellor power to allocate and transfer proceedings. The Lord Chancellor's order could set criteria, such as complexity or the possibility of delay, whereby cases begun at one level should be transferred to another. Provision for transfer on geographical grounds would also be possible.

> **We recommend that the Lord Chancellor should have power to provide by order for which kind of judge of the Court of Protection should deal with any particular proceedings and for the transfer of proceedings between the different kinds of judges.** (Draft Bill, clause 46(5).)

In view of the fact that both the Court of Protection and magistrates' courts (as well as single justices) may exercise the emergency protective jurisdiction, the Lord Chancellor should also have power to provide by order for where such proceedings should be instituted.[20] We would anticipate any such order requiring the proceedings to be instituted in a magistrates' court unless there are particular reasons for application being made to the Court of Protection.

*Relationship with the Children Act 1989*

10.19 In general, the new statutory decision-making jurisdiction will be exercisable in respect of persons without capacity who have attained the age of sixteen.[21] There will therefore be an overlap between the Children Act 1989 jurisdiction and the new incapacity jurisdiction. In respect of 16 and 17 year olds, applicants will be able to

of expertise and has provided a forum to which cases, either because of their complexity or because of delays in other court centres throughout the country, can be transferred.

[20] Draft Bill, clause 45(2).

[21] Draft Bill, clauses 1(2) and 36(2).

choose to apply to the jurisdiction which seems most appropriate to the circumstances of the case. In view of this overlap it is sensible to make provision for whichever court is seised of an application to decline to exercise its jurisdiction if it considers that the case can be more suitably dealt with under the alternative jurisdiction. It would also be advisable for the Lord Chancellor to have power to make orders about the transfer of proceedings from a court having jurisdiction under the Children Act 1989 to a court with jurisdiction under the mental incapacity legislation.

> **We recommend that the Lord Chancellor should have power to provide by order, in relation to persons who have not attained the age of eighteen, for the transfer of proceedings between a court having jurisdiction under the Mental Incapacity Act and a court having jurisdiction under the Children Act 1989. A court with either jurisdiction may decline to exercise it in respect of those under eighteen if the court considers that the issue can be more suitably dealt with by a court exercising the other jurisdiction.** (Draft Bill, clause 45(3).)

## Applicants

10.20 Applications for public law orders may only be made by authorised officers of a local authority.[22] In the consultation papers we suggested that some applicants for private law orders should be able to apply as of right, while others would require leave.[23] Respondents supported the idea of a filtering mechanism, but tended to suggest more and more categories of persons who should be able to apply as of right. It became clear that it would be extremely difficult to create an acceptable list of relatives who should have an automatic right to apply. We have concluded that the category of persons with an automatic right to apply should be restricted to those who have *existing* decision-making powers, or are mentioned in an *existing* order. It should be specifically provided that the Public Trustee may apply without leave where he or she has any functions exercisable by virtue of an existing order.[24] The leave requirement can then be used in a positive and helpful way, to direct prospective applicants towards the factors which are likely to be relevant to the determination of any application for which leave is given.

> **We recommend that leave should be required before an application to the Court of Protection can be made. In granting leave the court should have regard to:**

---

[22] I.e. for entry warrants, assessment orders or temporary protection orders. See Part IX above and draft Bill, Part II.

[23] Consultation Paper No 128, para 6.16; Consultation Paper No 129, para 4.30.

[24] See para 8.51 above.

**(1) the applicant's connection with the person concerned,**

**(2) the reasons for the application,**

**(3) the benefit to the person concerned of any proposed order,**

**(4) whether that benefit can be achieved in any other way.**

**No leave should be required for any application to the court by**

**(1) a person who is or is alleged to be without capacity, or, in respect of such a person who is under 18 years old, any person with parental responsibility for that person,**

**(2) a donee of a CPA granted by the person without capacity or a court-appointed manager,**

**(3) the Public Trustee as respects any functions exercisable by virtue of an existing order, and**

**(4) any person mentioned in an existing order of the court. (Draft Bill, clause 47.)**

### Emergency orders

10.21 As is the case under Part VII of the Mental Health Act 1983[25] we consider that it would be useful for the Court of Protection to be able to make an order or give directions even if it cannot yet determine whether the person concerned actually lacks the capacity to take the decision in question. In exercising this emergency jurisdiction the court would only be able to make the order or give the directions sought if it is of the opinion that the order or direction is in the best interests of the person concerned.

> **We recommend that the Court of Protection should have power to make an order or give directions on a matter, pending a decision on whether the person concerned is without capacity in relation to that matter. (Draft Bill, clause 48.)**

### Rights of appeal

10.22 We have already explained[26] that we see no justification for an appeals procedure in relation to the short-term public law orders. The new Court of Protection will be

---

[25] Section 98.

[26] See para 9.35 above.

staffed by district, circuit and High Court judges and the usual civil appeal system should form the basis of its appeals system.

**We recommend** that appeals should lie:
**(1) from a decision of a district judge to a circuit judge or a judge of the High Court;**

**(2) from a decision of a circuit judge or judge of the High Court given in the exercise of his or her original or appellate jurisdiction to the Court of Appeal.** (Draft Bill, clause 49(1).)

10.23 The judges of the Court of Protection may, in addition to substantive decisions, also make decisions about the transfer of proceedings. The Lord Chancellor should have power to provide by order for the transfer of proceedings, and this power should cover any arrangements about appeals from transfer decisions.[27] We see no need to provide for an appeal to be made against a decision to decline jurisdiction in favour of the overlapping Children Act jurisdiction.[28]

## Rules of court

10.24 One of the advantages which tribunals are said to have over courts is that tribunal proceedings are more informal, less adversarial and more user-friendly than the procedures which operate in the ordinary courts. Respondents to all four of our consultation papers stressed the need for any proceedings under the decision-making jurisdiction to be relaxed and non-technical. The existing Court of Protection Rules provide for cases to be considered in an informal way, with many issues dealt with by correspondence without the need for a formal hearing before the Master. This precedent should be adapted in the preparation of Rules for the new Court of Protection. The draft Bill sets out a non-exhaustive list of the types of issue for which the rules should cater. These include arrangements for cases to be heard in private, for cases to be disposed of without a hearing, for evidence to be admitted notwithstanding any rule of law to the contrary and for permitting a person with a mental disability to conduct his or her own case. There should also be provision for the appointment of the Official Solicitor or a private solicitor to represent the person concerned where this is desirable.

**We recommend** that proceedings under the new jurisdiction should be conducted in accordance with rules made by the Lord Chancellor. (Draft Bill, clause 51.)

The new Court of Protection should have all the same powers as the High Court

---

[27] Draft Bill, clause 49(2).

[28] Draft Bill, clause 49(3).

in relation to witnesses, documents and the enforcement of orders.[29]

### Independent reports

10.25 Decisions taken by the court on behalf of a person without capacity must be taken in that person's "best interests". The court will be obliged to have regard to the wishes and feelings of the person concerned, and the factors he or she would have considered. It may not always be appropriate for the person concerned to be present in court, whether because of physical or mental frailty.[30] Other parties and witnesses to the proceedings may offer conflicting assessments of the situation. It should be expected that an independent report should be prepared in such circumstances.

> *We recommend* **that, where the person concerned is neither present nor represented, the court should (unless it considers it unnecessary) obtain a report on his or her wishes.** (Draft Bill, clause 52(2).)

10.26 The decisions which the court is asked to make may not depend purely on legal points. Arriving at the solution which is in the best interests of the person concerned might require evidence from expert professionals, and the House of Lords Select Committee particularly urged that "some mechanism should be adopted whereby the new court will make full use of appropriate independent medical and ethical advice."[31] The most appropriate mechanism, adapting existing procedures and personnel, is to involve court welfare officers and local authority officers where necessary.[32]

> *We recommend* **that the Court of Protection should have power to ask a probation officer to report to the court, and power to ask a local authority officer to report or arrange for another person to report, on such matters as the court directs, relating to the person concerned.** (Draft Bill, clause 52(1).)

### Lord Chancellor's Visitors

10.27 In proceedings under Part VII of the Mental Health Act 1983, the Court of Protection has power to direct a Lord Chancellor's Visitor to visit a person

---

[29] Draft Bill, clause 50.

[30] We have recommended that Rules may make provision for determining whether the person concerned need be present. See para 10.24 above and draft Bill, clause 51(2)(e).

[31] Report of the Select Committee on Medical Ethics (1993-94) HL 21-I para 248.

[32] These officers already perform a reporting function in relation to proceedings under the Children Act 1989. Court welfare officers are in fact probation officers and we recognise that Government may wish to review the extent to which the Probation Service should become further involved in work which has no connection with the criminal justice system.

incapable of managing his property and affairs and to report back to the Court.[33] The officials exercising the functions of Lord Chancellor's Visitors are civil servants whose main job is to look after the welfare of employees of the Lord Chancellor's Department. The role of Lord Chancellor's Visitors has been the subject of comment in two recent reports[34] and the present arrangements are now under review by the Department. Pending the outcome of this review, we have provided that the panels of Lord Chancellor's Visitors should be retained and their role preserved.[35]

**Privacy of proceedings**

10.28 A number of our respondents expressed anxiety about the need to protect the privacy of any person concerned in proceedings where it is alleged that decision-making capacity is lacking. The present Rules of the Court of Protection make appropriate provision.[36] The Lord Chancellor's power to make Rules for the new Court of Protection should cover provision for proceedings to be held in private and for enabling the court to determine who may be admitted when it sits in private and who may be excluded when it sits in public.[37] Further protection for the privacy of parties to such proceedings can best be achieved by making it an offence to publish identifying information about a person involved in incapacity proceedings, as it is in relation to proceedings under the Children Act.[38] In addition, the provisions of the existing law which render publicity a contempt of court in certain circumstances should apply to incapacity proceedings, as they presently do to proceedings under Part VII of the 1983 Act.[39]

> *We recommend* that it should be an offence to publish any material intended or likely to identify any person in respect of whom proceedings are brought under the new incapacity

---

[33] Section 103.

[34] National Audit Office, *Looking after the Financial Affairs of People with Mental Incapacity* (1994) and the Committee of Public Accounts Thirty-ninth Report, *Looking after the Financial Affairs of People with Mental Incapacity* (1993-94) HC 308.

[35] Draft Bill, clause 53 and Sched 6.

[36] Court of Protection Rules 1994 (SI 1994 No 3046), rule 39.

[37] Draft Bill, clause 51(2)(g).

[38] Children Act 1989, s 97(2)-(6).

[39] By virtue of the Administration of Justice Act 1960, s 12(1)(b). Although this protection is already afforded in relation to proceedings under the Mental Health Act 1983, it does not apply to proceedings under the Enduring Powers of Attorney Act 1985. This anomaly appears to be accidental. See now draft Bill, Sched 8.

**legislation.** (Draft Bill, clause 54.)[40]

---

[40] As under the existing law, there should be a defence if the accused person proves that he or she did not know and had no reason to suspect that the material published was intended or was likely to identify the person in respect of whom the proceedings are brought. (Draft Bill, clause 54(2).)

# PART XI
# COLLECTED RECOMMENDATIONS

11.1 In this Part we set out our principal recommendations, referring where appropriate to the paragraphs of the report where the recommendations are discussed and to the corresponding provisions of the draft Bill at Appendix A.

## PART II - THE CONTEXT AND THE BASIC APPROACH TO REFORM

11.2 We recommend the introduction of a single piece of legislation to make new provision for people who lack mental capacity: and to confer new functions on local authorities in relation to people in need of care or protection. (Paragraph 2.51 and draft Mental Incapacity Bill.)

11.3 The provisions of the legislation should in general apply to those aged 16 and over. (Paragraph 2.52 and Draft Bill, clauses 1(2) and 36(2).)

11.4 The Secretary of State should prepare and from time to time revise a code or codes of practice to give guidance in connection with the legislation. There should be consultation before any code is prepared or revised, and preparation of any part of any code may be delegated. (Paragraph 2.53 and draft Bill, clause 31(1) and (2).)

## PART III - TWO FUNDAMENTAL CONCEPTS: LACK OF CAPACITY AND BEST INTERESTS

11.5 There should be a presumption against lack of capacity and any question whether a person lacks capacity should be decided on the balance of probabilities. (Paragraph 3.2 and draft Bill, clause 2(6).)

11.6 The expression "mental disability" in the new legislation should mean any disability or disorder of the mind or brain, whether permanent or temporary, which results in an impairment or disturbance of mental functioning. (Paragraphs 3.8 to 3.12 and draft Bill, clause 2(2).)

11.7 Legislation should provide that a person is without capacity if at the material time he or she is:

    (1) unable by reason of mental disability to make a decision on the matter in question, or

    (2) unable to communicate a decision on that matter because he or she is unconscious or for any other reason. (Paragraph 3.14 and draft Bill, clause 2(1).)

11.8 A person should be regarded as unable to make a decision by reason of mental disability if the disability is such that, at the time when the decision needs to be made, he or she is unable to understand or retain the information relevant to the decision, including information about the reasonably foreseeable consequences of deciding one way or another or failing to make the decision. (Paragraph 3.16 and draft Bill, clause 2(2)(a).)

11.9    A person should be regarded as unable to make a decision by reason of mental disability if the disability is such that, at the time when the decision needs to be made, he or she is unable to make a decision based on the information relevant to the decision, including information about the reasonably foreseeable consequences of deciding one way or another or failing to make the decision. (Paragraph 3.17 and draft Bill, clause 2(2)(b).)

11.10   A person should not be regarded as unable to understand the information relevant to a decision if he or she is able to understand an explanation of that information in broad terms and simple language. (Paragraph 3.18 and draft Bill, clause 2(3).)

11.11   A person should not be regarded as unable to make a decision by reason of mental disability merely because he or she makes a decision which would not be made by a person of ordinary prudence. (Paragraph 3.19 and draft Bill, clause 2(4).)

11.12   A person should not be regarded as unable to communicate his or her decision unless all practicable steps to enable him or her to do so have been taken without success. (Paragraph 3.21 and draft Bill, clause 2(5).)

11.13   The Secretary of State should prepare and from time to time revise a code of practice for the guidance of persons assessing whether a person is or is not without capacity to make a decision or decisions on any matters. (Paragraph 3.22 and draft Bill, clause 31(1)(a).)

11.14   Anything done for, and any decision made on behalf of, a person without capacity should be done or made in the best interests of that person. (Paragraph 3.25 and draft Bill, clause 3(1).)

11.15   In deciding what is in a person's best interests regard should be had to:-

(1) the ascertainable past and present wishes and feelings of the person concerned, and the factors that person would consider if able to do so;

(2) the need to permit and encourage the person to participate, or to improve his or her ability to participate, as fully as possible in anything done for and any decision affecting him or her;

(3) the views of other people whom it is appropriate and practicable to consult about the person's wishes and feelings and what would be in his

or her best interests;

(4) whether the purpose for which any action or decision is required can be as effectively achieved in a manner less restrictive of the person's freedom of action. (Paragraphs 3.26 to 3.37 and draft Bill, clause 3(2).)

## PART IV - GENERAL AUTHORITY TO ACT REASONABLY

11.16     It should be lawful to do anything for the personal welfare or health care of a person who is, or is reasonably believed to be, without capacity in relation to the matter in question if it is in all the circumstances reasonable for it to be done by the person who does it. (Paragraphs 4.1 to 4.4 and draft Bill, clause 4(1).)

11.17     Where necessary goods are supplied to, or necessary services are provided for, a person without capacity to contract, he or she must pay a reasonable price for them. (Paragraph 4.9 and draft Bill, clause 34(1).)

11.18     Where reasonable actions for the personal welfare or health care of the person lacking capacity involve expenditure, it shall be lawful for the person who is taking the action (1) to pledge the other's credit for that purpose or (2) to apply money in the possession of the person concerned for meeting the expenditure; and if the person taking the action bears the expenditure then he or she is entitled to be reimbursed or otherwise indemnified from the money of the person concerned. (Paragraph 4.10 and draft Bill, clause 4(2).)

11.19     There should be a statutory scheme enabling certain payments which would otherwise be made to a person without capacity to be made instead to a person acting on his or her behalf. (Paragraphs 4.12 to 4.21 and draft Bill, clause 4(4) and Schedule 1.)

11.20     No person should be able to make decisions about the following matters on behalf of a person without capacity:

(1) consent to marriage, (2) consent to have sexual relations, (3) consent to a divorce petition on the basis of two years separation, (4) agreement to adoption or consent to freeing a child for adoption, (5) voting at an election for any public office or (6) discharging parental responsibilities except in relation to a child's property. (Paragraph 4.29 and draft Bill, clause 30.)

11.21     The general authority to provide care to a person without capacity should not authorise the use or threat of force to enforce the doing of anything to which that person objects; nor should it authorise the detention or confinement of that person, whether or not he or she objects. This provision is not to preclude the taking of steps which are necessary to avert a substantial risk of serious harm to the person concerned. (Paragraphs 4.30 to 4.33 and draft Bill, clause 5.)

11.22 The general authority should not authorise the doing of anything which is contrary to the directions of, or inconsistent with a decision made by, an attorney or manager acting within the scope of his or her authority. However, this restriction will not apply to actions necessary to prevent the death of, or a serious deterioration in the condition of, the person concerned while an order is being sought from the court. (Paragraph 4.34 and draft Bill, clause 6.)

11.23 The Secretary of State should prepare and from time to time revise a code of practice for the guidance of persons acting in pursuance of the general authority to act and the statutory restrictions which apply to it. (Paragraph 4.37 and draft Bill, clause 31(1)(b).)

11.24 It should be an offence for anyone to ill-treat or wilfully neglect a person in relation to whom he or she has powers by virtue of the new legislation. (Paragraph 4.38 and draft Bill, clause 32(1).)

## PART V - ADVANCE STATEMENTS ABOUT HEALTH CARE

11.25 An "advance refusal of treatment" should be defined as a refusal made by a person aged eighteen or over with the necessary capacity of any medical, surgical or dental treatment or other procedure and intended to have effect at any subsequent time when he or she may be without capacity to give or refuse consent. (Paragraph 5.16 and draft Bill, clause 9(1).)

11.26 The general authority should not authorise any treatment or procedure if an advance refusal of treatment by the person concerned applies to that treatment or procedure in the circumstances of the case. (Paragraph 5.20 and draft Bill, clause 9(2).)

11.27 In the absence of any indication to the contrary it shall be presumed that an advance refusal of treatment does not apply in circumstances where those having the care of the person who made it consider that the refusal (a) endangers that person's life or (b) if that person is a woman who is pregnant, the life of the foetus. (Paragraphs 5.23 to 5.26 and draft Bill, clause 9(3).)

11.28 No person should incur liability (1) for the consequences of withholding any treatment or procedure if he or she has reasonable grounds for believing that an advance refusal of treatment applies; or (2) for carrying out any treatment or procedure to which an advance refusal applies unless he or she knows or has reasonable grounds for believing that an advance refusal applies. (Paragraph 5.27 and draft Bill, clause 9(4).)

11.29 In the absence of any indication to the contrary it should be presumed that an advance refusal was validly made if it is in writing, signed and witnessed. (Paragraphs 5.29 to 5.30 and draft Bill, clause 9(5).)

11.30    An advance refusal of treatment may at any time be withdrawn or altered by the person who made it, if he or she has capacity to do so. (Paragraphs 5.31 to 5.32 and draft Bill, clause 9(6).)

11.31    An advance refusal of treatment should not preclude the provision of "basic care", namely care to maintain bodily cleanliness and to alleviate severe pain, as well as the provision of direct oral nutrition and hydration. (Paragraph 5.34 and draft Bill, clause 9(7)(a) and (8).)

11.32    An advance refusal should not preclude the taking of any action necessary to prevent the death of the maker or a serious deterioration in his or her condition pending a decision of the court on the validity or applicability of an advance refusal or on the question whether it has been withdrawn or altered. (Paragraph 5.36 and draft Bill, clause 9(7)(b).)

11.33    It should be an offence punishable with a maximum of two years imprisonment to conceal or destroy a written advance refusal of treatment with intent to deceive. (Paragraph 5.38 and draft Bill, clause 33.)

## PART VI - INDEPENDENT SUPERVISION OF MEDICAL AND RESEARCH PROCEDURES

11.34    The general authority should not authorise certain listed treatments or procedures, which will require authorisation by the court or the consent of an attorney or manager. (Paragraph 6.3 and draft Bill, clause 7(1).)

11.35    Any treatment or procedure intended or reasonably likely to render the person permanently infertile should require court authorisation unless it is to treat a disease of the reproductive organs or relieve existing detrimental effects of menstruation. (Paragraph 6.4 and draft Bill, clause 7(2)(a).)

11.36    Any treatment or procedure to facilitate the donation of non-regenerative tissue or bone marrow should require court authorisation. (Paragraph 6.5 and draft Bill, clause 7(2)(b).)

11.37    The Secretary of State should have power to prescribe further treatments requiring court authorisation. (Paragraph 6.6 and draft Bill, clause 7(2)(c).)

11.38    The general authority should not authorise certain listed treatments or procedures, which should require a certificate from an independent doctor appointed for that purpose by the Secretary of State or the consent of an attorney or manager. The independent doctor should certify that the person concerned is without capacity to consent but that it is in his or her best interests for the treatment or procedure to be carried out. This should not preclude action necessary to prevent the death of the person concerned or a serious deterioration in his or her condition while the certificate or consent is sought. (Paragraphs 6.7 to 6.8 and draft Bill, clause 8(1), (2) and (6).)

11.39 Any treatment or procedure intended or reasonably likely to render the person concerned permanently infertile should require a certificate from an independent medical practitioner where it is for relieving the existing detrimental effects of menstruation. (Paragraph 6.9 and draft Bill, clause 8(3)(d).)

11.40 Abortion should require a certificate from an independent medical practitioner. (Paragraph 6.10 and draft Bill, clause 8(3)(c).)

11.41 The treatments for mental disorder described in section 58(1) of the Mental Health Act 1983 should require a certificate from an independent medical practitioner. (Paragraphs 6.11 to 6.14 and draft Bill, clause 8(3)(a) and (b).)

11.42 The Secretary of State should have power to prescribe that other treatments or procedures should be included in the second opinion category. (Paragraph 6.15 and draft Bill, clause 8(3)(e).)

11.43 Discontinuing the artificial nutrition and hydration of a patient who is unconscious, has no activity in the cerebral cortex and no prospect of recovery should be lawful if certain statutory requirements are met. (Paragraphs 6.17 to 6.20 and draft Bill, clause 10(1).)

11.44 The discontinuance of artificial sustenance to an unconscious patient with no activity in the cerebral cortex and no prospect of recovery should require either (1) the approval of the court, (2) the consent of an attorney or manager or (3) if an order of the Secretary of State so provides, a certificate by an independent medical practitioner. (Paragraph 6.21 and draft Bill, clause 10(2).)

11.45 Where the court, an attorney, a manager or an independent medical practitioner decides on discontinuance of artificial sustenance for an unconscious patient with no activity in the cerebral cortex and no prospect of recovery, then regard must be had to the factors in the best interests checklist. (Paragraph 6.22 and draft Bill, clause 10(3).)

11.46 The Secretary of State may make an order providing for the carrying out of a procedure in relation to a person without capacity to consent if the procedure, although not carried out for the benefit of that person, will not cause him or her significant harm and will be of significant benefit to others. (Paragraphs 6.23 to 6.26 and draft Bill, clause 10(4).)

11.47 Research which is unlikely to benefit a participant, or whose benefit is likely to be long delayed, should be lawful in relation to a person without capacity to consent if (1) the research is into an incapacitating condition with which the participant is or may be affected and (2) certain statutory procedures are complied with. (Paragraphs 6.28 to 6.31 and draft Bill, clause 11(1).)

11.48 There should be a statutory committee to be known as the Mental Incapacity Research Committee. (Paragraph 6.33 and draft Bill, clause 11(2).)

11.49 The committee may approve proposed research if satisfied:

(1) that it is desirable to provide knowledge of the causes or treatment of, or of the care of people affected by, the incapacitating condition with which any participant is or may be affected,

(2) that the object of the research cannot be effectively achieved without the participation of persons who are or may be without capacity to consent, and

(3) that the research will not expose a participant to more than negligible risk, will not be unduly invasive or restrictive of a participant and will not unduly interfere with a participant's freedom of action or privacy. (Paragraph 6.34 and draft Bill, clause 11(3).)

11.50 In addition to the approval of the Mental Incapacity Research Committee, non-therapeutic research in relation to a person without capacity should require either:

(1) court approval,

(2) the consent of an attorney or manager,

(3) a certificate from a doctor not involved in the research that the participation of the person is appropriate, or

(4) designation of the research as not involving direct contact. (Paragraphs 6.36 to 6.37 and draft Bill, clause 11(1)(c) and (4).)

## PART VIII - CONTINUING POWERS OF ATTORNEY

11.51 A new form of power of attorney, to be called a "continuing power of attorney" ("CPA"), should be introduced. The donee of a CPA should have authority to make and implement decisions on behalf of the donor which the donor is without capacity to make. (Paragraphs 7.1 to 7.6 and draft Bill, clause 12(1) and (2).)

11.52 A CPA may extend to matters relating to a donor's personal welfare, health care and property and affairs (including the conduct of legal proceedings); and may be subject to conditions or restrictions. (Paragraph 7.7 and draft Bill, clause 16(1).)

11.53 Where an instrument purports to create a CPA but does not comply with the statutory requirements it should confer no powers on the donee. (Paragraph 7.9 and draft Bill, clause 12(4).)

11.54 An attorney acting under a Continuing Power of Attorney should act in the best interests of the donor, having regard to the statutory factors. (Paragraph 7.10 and draft Bill, clause 3.)

11.55 The restriction against coercion or confinement should apply equally to attorneys. (Paragraph 7.13 and draft Bill, clauses 16(4) and 5.)

11.56 No attorney may consent to or refuse any treatment unless the donor is, or is reasonably believed by the attorney to be, without capacity to give or refuse personal consent to that treatment. (Paragraph 7.14 and draft Bill, clause 16(3)(a).)

11.57 No attorney should have power to consent to the donor's admission to hospital for assessment or treatment for mental disorder, where such admission is against the will of the donor. (Paragraph 7.15 and draft Bill, clause 16(3)(b).)

11.58 No attorney should be authorised to withhold basic care from the donor or refuse consent to its provision. (Paragraph 7.16 and draft Bill, clauses 16(3)(c) and 9(8).)

11.59 Unless expressly authorised to do so, no attorney may consent to any treatment refused by the donor by an advance refusal of treatment. (Paragraph 7.17 and draft Bill, clause 16(3)(d)(i).)

11.60 Unless expressly authorised to do so, no attorney may consent on a donor's behalf to:

(1) a procedure requiring court approval,

(2) a procedure requiring a certificate from an independent medical practitioner,

(3) discontinuance of artificial nutrition or hydration,

(4) procedures for the benefit of others, or

(5) participation in non-therapeutic research. (Paragraph 7.18 and draft Bill, clause 16(3)(d)(ii) and (5).)

11.61 Unless expressly authorised to do so, no attorney may refuse consent to any treatment necessary to sustain life. (Paragraph 7.19 and draft Bill, clause 16(3)(d)(iii).)

11.62    A CPA may only be created by an individual who has attained the age of eighteen. (Paragraph 7.20 and draft Bill, clause 14(1).)

11.63    An individual donee of a CPA may be described as the holder for the time being of a specified office or position. (Paragraph 7.21 and draft Bill, clause 14(3).)

11.64    A donor may, in a CPA, appoint a person to replace the donee in the event of the donee disclaiming, dying, becoming bankrupt or becoming divorced from the donor. (Paragraph 7.22 and draft Bill, clause 20(1)).

11.65    A CPA must contain a statement by the donee that he or she understands the duty to act in the best interests of the donor in relation to any decision which the donor is, or is reasonably believed by the donee to be, without capacity to make. (Paragraph 7.24 and draft Bill, clause 13(3)(b)(ii).)

11.66    A CPA may be expressed to confer general authority on a donee. (Paragraph 7.25 and draft Bill, clause 16(2).)

11.67    No document should create a Continuing Power of Attorney until it has been registered in the prescribed manner. (Paragraphs 7.28 to 7.31 and draft Bill, clause 15(1).)

11.68    A registration authority appointed by the Lord Chancellor should register CPAs. (Paragraph 7.32 and draft Bill, clause 15(1).)

11.69    If a donor objects to registration of a CPA then the registration authority should inform the donee and should not register the document unless the court directs it to do so. (Paragraph 7.34 and draft Bill, clause 15(4).)

11.70    Once a CPA has been registered the registration authority should give notice of that fact in the prescribed form to the donor. (Paragraph 7.36 and draft Bill, clause 15(6)(a).)

11.71    Once a CPA has been registered the registration authority should give notice of that fact in the prescribed form to a maximum of two people (not including the donee) as specified in the CPA. (Paragraph 7.38 and draft Bill, clause 15(6)(b).)

11.72    No disclaimer of a registered CPA should be valid unless notice is given to the donor and the registration authority. (Paragraph 7.41 and draft Bill, clause 15(7).)

11.73    There should be an express provision that nothing in the legislation should preclude the donor of a CPA from revoking it at any time when he or she has the capacity to do so. (Paragraphs 7.42 to 7.43 and draft Bill, clause 12(3).)

11.74    Section 5 of the Powers of Attorney Act 1971 should apply to Continuing Powers of Attorney. (Paragraph 7.44 and draft Bill, clause 19(6).)

11.75    Any part of a CPA which relates to matters other than property and financial affairs should not be revoked by the donor's bankruptcy. (Paragraph 7.47 and draft Bill, clause 16(6).)

11.76    In the absence of a contrary intention, the appointment of the donee's spouse as an attorney under a CPA should be revoked by the subsequent dissolution or annulment of the parties' marriage. (Paragraph 7.48 and draft Bill, clause 14(5).)

11.77    The registration authority should cancel the registration of a CPA on receipt of a revocation by the donor, a disclaimer by the donee or evidence that the power has expired or been revoked by death, bankruptcy, winding up or the dissolution of the parties' marriage. (Paragraph 7.49 and draft Bill, clause 18(1).)

The registration authority should attach an appropriate note to any registered CPA which has been partially revoked, or in relation to which a replacement donee has gained power to act. (Paragraph 7.49 and draft Bill, clause 18(2) and (5).)

11.78    The court should have power to declare that a document not in the prescribed form shall be treated as if it were in that form if the court is satisfied that the persons executing it intended it to create a CPA. (Paragraph 7.55 and draft Bill, clause 17(1).)

11.79    Subject to any contrary intention expressed in the document, the court should have power to appoint a donee in substitution for or in addition to the donee mentioned in a CPA. The court may act where the donor is without capacity to act and the court thinks it desirable to do so. (Paragraph 7.56 and draft Bill, clause 17(3)(c)(i).)

11.80    Subject to any contrary intention expressed in the document, the court should have power to modify or extend the scope of the donee's power to act. The court may act where the donor is without capacity to act and the court thinks it desirable to do so. (Paragraph 7.57 and draft Bill, clause 17(3)(c)(ii).)

11.81    The court may, on behalf of a donor without capacity to do so, either direct that a purported CPA should not be registered or revoke a CPA where the donee or intended donee has behaved, is behaving or proposes to behave in a way that (1) contravenes or would contravene the authority granted in the CPA or (2) is not or would not be in the donor's best interests. (Paragraph 7.58 and draft Bill, clause 17(6)(b).)

11.82    No EPA should be created after the coming into force of the new law in relation to CPAs. Transitional provisions should apply to any EPAs made prior to repeal of the

1985 Act. (Paragraph 7.59 and draft Bill, clause 21(1) and (3); Schedule 3, Parts II to V.)

11.83  An unregistered EPA may be converted into a CPA by the donor and donee executing a prescribed form and by registration. (Paragraph 7.61 and draft Bill, clause 21(2); Schedule 3, Part I.)

## PART VIII - DECISION-MAKING BY THE COURT

11.84  The court should have power to make a declaration in relation to: (1) the capacity of a person; (2) the validity or applicability of an advance refusal of treatment. (Paragraph 8.8 and draft Bill, clause 23.)

11.85  The court may

> (1) make any decision on behalf of a person who lacks capacity to make that decision or

> (2) appoint a person to be responsible for making a decision on behalf of a person who lacks capacity to make it. (Paragraph 8.9 and draft Bill, clause 24(1).)

The decisions in question may extend to any matter relating to the personal welfare, health care, property or affairs of the person concerned including the conduct of legal proceedings. (Paragraph 8.9 and draft Bill, clause 24(3).)

11.86  A specific decision by the court is to be preferred to the appointment of a manager. (Paragraph 8.12 and draft Bill, clause 24(2).)

11.87  The powers conferred on a manager should be as limited in scope and duration as possible. (Paragraph 8.13 and draft Bill, clause 24(2).)

11.88  The court may make any order or appointment which is in the best interests of the person concerned, regardless of the terms of the application made to the court. (Paragraph 8.14 and draft Bill, clause 24(5).)

11.89  The court's powers should cover (1) where the person concerned is to live and (2) what contact, if any, the person concerned is to have with specified persons. (Paragraph 8.16 and draft Bill, clause 25(1)(a) and (b).)

11.90  The court should have power to make an order restraining a person from having contact with or molesting the person without capacity. (Paragraph 8.17 and draft Bill, clause 25(3).)

11.91  The court's powers should cover the exercise of a person's statutory rights to information. (Paragraph 8.20 and draft Bill, clause 25(1)(c).)

11.92    The court's powers should cover obtaining statutory benefits and services which may be available to the person concerned. (Paragraph 8.21 and draft Bill, clause 25(1)(d).)

11.93    The court's powers in relation to health care matters should cover (1) approving or refusing approval for particular forms of health care (2) appointing a manager to consent or refuse consent to particular forms of health care, (3) requiring a person to allow a different person to take over responsibility for the health care of the person concerned. (Paragraph 8.22 and draft Bill, clause 26(1)(a) and (b).)

11.94    The court's powers should cover obtaining access to the health records of the person concerned. (Paragraph 8.23 and draft Bill, clause 26(1)(c).)

11.95    The court may not approve, nor a manager consent to, (1) the withholding of basic care, or (2) any treatment refused by an advance refusal of treatment. (Paragraph 8.24 and draft Bill, clause 26(2)(b).)

11.96    The court may grant a manager express authority to consent to the carrying out of treatments which would otherwise require court approval or a certificate from an independent medical practitioner; or to consent to the carrying out of non-therapeutic procedures or research. (Paragraph 8.26 and draft Bill, clause 26(3).)

11.97    The court should have power to order the admission to hospital for assessment or treatment for mental disorder of a person without capacity, if satisfied on the evidence of two doctors that:

        (1) the grounds for admission specified in sections 2 or 3 respectively of the Mental Health Act 1983 exist, and

        (2) it is appropriate, having regard to the "best interests" factors, that the person concerned should be admitted to hospital. (Paragraphs 8.27 to 8.29 and draft Bill, clause 26(4) and (5).)

11.98    The court's powers in relation to property and affairs may be exercised where the person concerned is under 16, if it is likely that the person will still lack capacity on attaining his or her majority. (Paragraph 8.32 and draft Bill, clause 27(3).)

11.99    The court's powers over the property and affairs of a person without capacity should cover:

        -   the control and management of any property

- the disposal of any property

- the acquisition of any property

- the carrying on of a business, trade or profession

- the dissolution of any partnership

- the carrying out of any contract

- the discharge of any debt or obligation. (Paragraph 8.33 and draft Bill, clause 27(1)(a) - (g).)

11.100  The court's powers should also extend to:

- making a settlement of any property, whether with the person concerned or with others as beneficiary or beneficiaries

- making a will

- exercising powers vested in the person concerned.

These powers should not be exercisable by any manager. (Paragraph 8.34 and draft Bill, clause 27(1)(h) - (j) and (2).)

11.101  A manager may be appointed to take possession or control of all or any specified part of the property of the person concerned and to exercise all or any specified powers in respect of it including such powers of investment as the court may determine. (Paragraph 8.40 and draft Bill, clause 28(7).)

11.102  An individual appointed as manager may be described as the holder for the time being of an office or position. (Paragraph 8.42 and draft Bill, clause 28(2).)

11.103  The court may appoint joint, joint and several, successive or standby managers. (Paragraph 8.43 and draft Bill, clause 28(5).)

11.104  A manager should act in the best interests of the person without capacity, having regard to the statutory factors. (Paragraph 8.44 and draft Bill, clause 3.)

11.105  A manager should be regarded as the agent of the person for whom he or she is appointed. (Paragraph 8.45 and draft Bill, clause 28(8).)

11.106  No manager should have power to make a decision which is inconsistent with a decision made within the scope of his or her authority by the donee of a CPA.

(Paragraph 8.46 and draft Bill, clause 28(10).)

11.107 No manager should be appointed for longer than five years. (Paragraph 8.47 and draft Bill, clause 28(4).)

11.108 The court may require a manager to give to the Public Trustee such security as the court thinks fit, and to submit to the Public Trustee such reports at such intervals as the court thinks fit. (Paragraph 8.48 and draft Bill, clause 28(6)(a).)

11.109 The Public Trustee should have such supervisory functions in relation to other managers as are laid down in Rules. (Paragraph 8.50 and draft Bill, clause 28(6)(b).)

11.110 A manager should be entitled to be reimbursed for the reasonable expenses of discharging his or her functions. If the court so directs when appointing a manager, he or she shall be entitled to remuneration for discharging those functions. (Paragraph 8.52 and draft Bill, clause 28(9).)

11.111 The Secretary of State should issue and from time to time revise a code of practice for the guidance of people who act as managers. (Paragraph 8.54 and draft Bill, clause 31(1)(c).)

## PART IX - PUBLIC LAW PROTECTION FOR VULNERABLE PEOPLE AT RISK

11.112 A "vulnerable person" should mean any person of 16 or over who (1) is or may be in need of community care services by reason of mental or other disability, age or illness and who (2) is or may be unable to take care of himself or herself, or unable to protect himself or herself against significant harm or serious exploitation. (Paragraph 9.6 and draft Bill, clause 36(2).)

11.113 "Harm" should be defined to mean ill-treatment (including sexual abuse and forms of ill-treatment that are not physical); the impairment of, or an avoidable deterioration in, physical or mental health; and the impairment of physical, intellectual, emotional, social or behavioural development. (Paragraph 9.8 and draft Bill, clause 36(5).)

11.114 Where a local authority have reason to believe that a vulnerable person in their area is suffering or likely to suffer significant harm or serious exploitation they shall make such enquiries as they consider necessary to enable them to decide:

(1) whether the person is in fact suffering or likely to suffer such harm or exploitation and

(2) if so, whether community care services should be provided or

arranged or other action taken to protect the person from such harm or exploitation. (Paragraph 9.16 and draft Bill, clause 37(1).)

11.115 Where an authorised officer of the local authority has reasonable cause to believe that a vulnerable person living in premises in the local authority's area is "at risk", the officer may at any reasonable time enter and inspect those premises and interview the person concerned in private. These powers should not be exercised if the officer knows or believes that the person concerned objects or would object unless the officer has reasonable cause to believe that the person concerned is or may be suffering from mental disability. (Paragraph 9.19 and draft Bill, clause 38(1) and (3).)

11.116 On the application of an authorised officer, the court should have power to issue a warrant authorising a constable, accompanied by such an officer, to enter specified premises if:

(1) the applicant has reasonable cause to believe that a vulnerable person living in those premises is "at risk";

(2) granting the warrant is necessary to enable the officer to gain access to the vulnerable person, and

(3) (unless there is reasonable cause to believe that the person is or may be suffering from mental disability) the applicant does not know or believe that the person objects or would object. (Paragraph 9.21 and draft Bill, clause 39.)

11.117 On the application of an authorised officer the court should have power to make an assessment order if:

(1) the applicant has reasonable cause to believe that a vulnerable person is "at risk", and

(2) the order is required so that the local authority can assess whether the person is in fact "at risk" and if so whether community care services should be provided or arranged, or other protective action taken, and

(3) (unless there is reasonable cause to believe that the person is or may be suffering from mental disability) the applicant does not know or believe that the person objects or would object. (Paragraph 9.24 and draft Bill, clause 40(1) and (2).)

11.118 An assessment order should specify (1) the date by which the assessment is to begin, and (2) the period for which it will remain in force, being the shortest period necessary for the purposes of the assessment, not exceeding eight days. (Paragraph 9.25 and draft Bill, clause 40(4).)

11.119  Nothing to which the person concerned objects should be done pursuant to the assessment order unless the court has authorised it to be done notwithstanding that objection. (Paragraph 9.26 and draft Bill, clause 40(3).)

11.120  A vulnerable person may only be removed from his or her place of residence pursuant to an assessment order in accordance with specific directions and for such period or periods as are specified in the order, and only if it is necessary for the purposes of the assessment. (Paragraph 9.27 and draft Bill, clause 40(5).)

11.121  On the application of an authorised officer, the court should have power to make a temporary protection order if:

(1) a vulnerable person is likely to be "at risk" unless removed to or kept in protective accommodation for a short period, and

(2) (unless there is reasonable cause to believe that the person is or may be suffering from mental disability) the applicant does not know or believe the person objects or would object to the order. (Paragraph 9.28 and draft Bill, clause 41(1) and (2).)

11.122  A temporary protection order should authorise removal to protective accommodation for a specified period being the shortest possible necessary for achieving the purpose of the order, with a maximum of eight days. (Paragraph 9.29 and draft Bill, clause 41(3).)

11.123  The court may, on the making of a temporary protection order, give directions for assessment as it may when making an assessment order. (Paragraph 9.31 and draft Bill, clause 41(4).)

11.124  Where a person has been removed to protective accommodation it shall be the duty of the local authority to return the person to the place from which he or she is removed as soon as that is practicable and consistent with his or her interests. (Paragraph 9.32 and draft Bill, clause 41(8).)

11.125  An application for a temporary protection order may be made ex parte. The person concerned, any donee of a CPA and any court-appointed manager should be entitled to apply for the discharge of an ex parte order. (Paragraph 9.33 and draft Bill, clause 41(5).)

11.126  It should be an offence for any person (other than the person concerned) without reasonable cause to obstruct (1) an authorised officer of a local authority in the exercise of his or her powers, or (2) any person who is acting pursuant to an assessment or temporary protection order. (Paragraph 9.36 and draft Bill, clause 42.)

11.127 Local authorities should have power to assist a vulnerable person in bringing proceedings for an order under the private law. (Paragraph 9.37 and draft Bill, clause 43.)

11.128 The existing duty to protect the movable property of a person removed from his or her place of residence should apply where a person is removed (1) pursuant to the local authority applying for an order under Part I of the Mental Incapacity Bill and (2) pursuant to an assessment or temporary protection order. (Paragraph 9.39 and draft Bill, clause 44.)

11.129 Local authorities should have power to take reasonable steps for the protection of the property and affairs of a person without capacity to protect them and for whom they provide or arrange accommodation. (Paragraph 9.40 and draft Bill, clause 35.)

11.130 Section 7(5) of the Mental Health Act 1983 should be amended so that only a local social services authority may be named as guardian. (Paragraph 9.49.)

11.131 Section 8(1) of the Mental Health Act 1983 should be amended to give a guardian an additional power to convey the patient to a residence specified by the guardian. (Paragraph 9.50.)

11.132 The powers of the Mental Health Act Commission should be extended to include those received into guardianship. (Paragraph 9.52.)

## PART X - THE JUDICIAL FORUM

11.133 A new superior court of record called the Court of Protection should be established, and the office of the Supreme Court known as the Court of Protection should be abolished. (Paragraph 10.9 and draft Bill, clause 46(1).)

11.134 Magistrates' courts and single justices of the peace should have jurisdiction to deal with applications under Part II of the draft Bill only. (Paragraph 10.10 and draft Bill, clause 45(1)(b).)

11.135 Proceedings under Part II of the draft Bill should be treated as "family proceedings". (Paragraph 10.11 and draft Bill, clause 45(2).)

11.136 The jurisdiction of the Court of Protection should be exercised by judges nominated by the Lord Chancellor, whether Chancery Division or Family Division High Court judges, circuit judges or district judges. (Paragraph 10.13 and draft Bill, clause 46(2).)

11.137 The Lord Chancellor should designate one of the judges nominated as a Court of Protection judge to be Senior Judge of the Court of Protection. (Paragraph 10.14 and draft Bill, clause 46(4).)

11.138 The Lord Chancellor may appoint one of the judges of the High Court nominated as a Court of Protection judge to be President of the Court of Protection. (Paragraph 10.15 and draft Bill, clause 46(3).)

11.139 The Court of Protection should be able to sit at any place in England and Wales designated by the Lord Chancellor. (Paragraph 10.16 and draft Bill, clause 46(6).)

11.140 The Court of Protection should have a central office and registry in London. The Lord Chancellor should have power to designate additional registries outside London. (Paragraph 10.17 and draft Bill, clause 46(7).)

11.141 The Lord Chancellor should have power to provide by order for which kind of judge of the Court of Protection should deal with any particular proceedings and for the transfer of proceedings between the different kinds of judges. (Paragraph 10.18 and draft Bill, clause 46(5).)

11.142 The Lord Chancellor should have power to provide by order, in relation to persons who have not attained the age of eighteen, for the transfer of proceedings between a court having jurisdiction under the Mental Incapacity Act and a court having jurisdiction under the Children Act 1989. A court with either jurisdiction may decline to exercise it in respect of those under eighteen if the court considers that the issue can be more suitably dealt with by a court exercising the other jurisdiction. (Paragraph 10.19 and draft Bill, clause 45(3).)

11.143 Leave should be required before an application to the Court of Protection can be made. In granting leave the court should have regard to:

> (1) the applicant's connection with the person concerned,

> (2) the reasons for the application,

> (3) the benefit to the person concerned of any proposed order,

> (4) whether that benefit can be achieved in any other way.

No leave should be required for any application to the court by

> (1) a person who is or is alleged to be without capacity, or, in respect of such a person who is under 18 years old, any person with parental responsibility for that person,

(2) a donee of a CPA granted by the person without capacity or a court-appointed manager,

(3) the Public Trustee as respects any functions exercisable by virtue of an existing order, and

(4) any person mentioned in an existing order of the court. (Paragraph 10.20 and draft Bill, clause 47.)

11.144 The Court of Protection should have power to make an order or give directions on a matter, pending a decision on whether the person concerned is without capacity in relation to that matter. (Paragraph 10.21 and draft Bill, clause 48.)

11.145 Appeals should lie:

(1) from a decision of a district judge to a circuit judge or a judge of the High Court;

(2) from a decision of a circuit judge or judge of the High Court given in the exercise of his or her original or appellate jurisdiction to the Court of Appeal. (Paragraph 10.22 and draft Bill, clause 49(1).)

11.146 Proceedings under the new jurisdiction should be conducted in accordance with rules made by the Lord Chancellor. (Paragraph 10.24 and draft Bill, clause 51.)

11.147 Where the person concerned is neither present nor represented, the court should (unless it considers it unnecessary) obtain a report on his or her wishes. (Paragraph 10.25 and draft Bill, clause 52(2).)

11.148 The Court of Protection should have power to ask a probation officer to report to the court, and power to ask a local authority officer to report or arrange for another person to report, on such matters as the court directs, relating to the person concerned. (Paragraph 10.26 and draft Bill, clause 52(1).)

11.149 It should be an offence to publish any material intended or likely to identify any person in respect of whom proceedings are brought under the new incapacity legislation. (Paragraph 10.28 and draft Bill, clause 54.)


*(Signed)* HENRY BROOKE, *Chairman*
ANDREW BURROWS
DIANA FABER
CHARLES HARPUM
STEPHEN SILBER

MICHAEL SAYERS, *Secretary*
13 December 1994

# APPENDIX A

# MENTAL INCAPACITY BILL

# INDEX

This index shows alongside each clause and subsection of the draft Bill the paragraph(s) in the report where the provision is discussed.

## CHAPTER III
## CONTINUING POWERS OF ATTORNEY

# CHAPTER IV
## GENERAL POWERS OF THE COURT AND APPOINTMENT OF MANAGERS

## CHAPTER V
## MISCELLANEOUS AND SUPPLEMENTARY

# PART II
# PERSONS IN NEED OF CARE OR PROTECTION

# PART III
# JURISDICTION

## PART IV
## GENERAL

These clauses deal mainly with such matters as the introduction of the Schedules to the Bill and the technical measures by which the legislation comes into effect. These are not discussed in the report.

# Mental Incapacity Bill

## ARRANGEMENT OF CLAUSES

DRAFT

OF A

# B I L L

TO

Make new provision in relation to mentally incapacitated persons; to confer new functions on local authorities in relation to persons in need of care or protection; and for connected purposes.

**B**E IT ENACTED by the Queen's most Excellent Majesty, by and with the advice and consent of the Lords Spiritual and Temporal, and Commons, in this present Parliament assembled, and by the authority of the same, as follows:—

PART I

MENTAL INCAPACITY

CHAPTER I

PRELIMINARY

**1.**—(1) This Part of this Act has effect—

Purpose of Part I.

(a) for conferring statutory authority, subject to specified restrictions, for things done for the personal welfare or health care of a person without capacity; and

(b) for enabling decisions to be made on behalf of such a person by the donee of a power of attorney (in this Act referred to as a "continuing power of attorney") which complies with the requirements of this Part of this Act, by the court or by a manager appointed by the court.

(2) Except as otherwise provided, this Part of this Act does not enable anything to be done for, or a decision to be made on behalf of, a person who has not attained the age of sixteen.

**2.**—(1) For the purposes of this Part of this Act a person is without capacity if at the material time—

Persons without capacity.

(a) he is unable by reason of mental disability to make a decision for himself on the matter in question; or

(b) he is unable to communicate his decision on that matter because he is unconscious or for any other reason.

(2) For the purposes of this Part of this Act a person is at the material time unable to make a decision by reason of mental disability if the disability is such that at the time when the decision needs to be made— 5

    (a) he is unable to understand or retain the information relevant to the decision, including information about the reasonably foreseeable consequences of deciding one way or another or of failing to make the decision; or

    (b) he is unable to make a decision based on that information, 10

and in this Act "mental disability" means a disability or disorder of the mind or brain, whether permanent or temporary, which results in an impairment or disturbance of mental functioning.

(3) A person shall not be regarded as unable to understand the information referred to in subsection (2)(a) above if he is able to 15 understand an explanation of that information in broad terms and in simple language.

(4) A person shall not be regarded as unable to make a decision by reason of mental disability merely because he makes a decision which would not be made by a person of ordinary prudence. 20

(5) A person shall not be regarded as unable to communicate his decision unless all practicable steps to enable him to do so have been taken without success.

(6) There shall be a presumption against lack of capacity and any question whether a person lacks capacity shall be decided on the balance 25 of probabilities.

Actions to be in
best interests of
persons without
capacity.

**3.**—(1) Anything done for, and any decision made on behalf of, a person by virtue of this Part of this Act shall be done or made in his best interests.

(2) In deciding what is in a person's best interests regard shall be had to 30 the following—

    (a) so far as ascertainable, his past and present wishes and feelings and the factors which he would consider if he were able to do so;

    (b) the need to permit and encourage that person to participate, or to improve his ability to participate, as fully as possible in 35 anything done for and any decision affecting him;

    (c) if it is practicable and appropriate to consult them, the views as to that person's wishes and feelings and as to what would be in his best interests of—

        (i) any person named by him as someone to be consulted 40 on those matters;

        (ii) anyone (whether his spouse, a relative, friend or other person) engaged in caring for him or interested in his welfare;

        (iii) the donee of any continuing power of attorney granted by him; 45

        (iv) any manager appointed for him by the court;

(d) whether the purpose for which any action or decision is required can be as effectively achieved in a manner less restrictive of his freedom of action.

(3) In the case of anything done or a decision made by a person other 5 than the court it shall be a sufficient compliance with subsection (1) above if that person reasonably believes that what he does or decides is in the best interests of the person concerned.

## CHAPTER II

### CARE OF PERSON WITHOUT CAPACITY

10 *General authority*

**4.**—(1) Subject to the provisions of this Chapter, it shall be lawful to do anything for the personal welfare or health care of a person who is, or is reasonably believed to be, without capacity in relation to the matter in question ("the person concerned") if it is in all the circumstances 15 reasonable for it to be done by the person who does it.

Power to provide care.

(2) Where what is done by virtue of this section involves expenditure it shall be lawful—

(a) for that purpose to pledge the credit of the person concerned; and

(b) to apply money in the possession of the person concerned for 20 meeting the expenditure;

and if the expenditure is borne for him by another person that person shall be entitled to reimburse himself out of any such money or to be otherwise indemnified by the person concerned.

(3) Subsection (2) above is without prejudice to any power to spend 25 money for the benefit of the person concerned which is exercisable apart from this section by virtue of having lawful control of money or other property of his.

(4) Schedule 1 to this Act shall have effect for enabling certain payments which would otherwise be made to a person without capacity to 30 be made instead to a person acting on his behalf or to be otherwise dealt with as provided in that Schedule.

### *Restrictions on general authority*

**5.**—(1) Subject to subsection (2) below, section 4 above does not authorise—

No powers of coercion.

35 (a) the use or threat of force to enforce the doing of anything to which the person concerned objects; or

(b) the detention or confinement of that person whether or not he objects.

(2) This section does not preclude the taking of any steps necessary to 40 avert a substantial risk of serious harm to the person concerned.

**6.**—(1) Subject to subsection (2) below, section 4 above does not authorise the doing of anything for the person concerned which is contrary to directions given, or inconsistent with a decision made, within the scope of his authority by the donee of a continuing power of attorney 45 granted by him or by a manager appointed for him by the court.

No power to overrule authority of manager or attorney.

(2) This section does not preclude any action necessary to prevent the death of the person concerned or a serious deterioration in his condition while an order as respects the matter in question is sought from the court.

Treatment
requiring
approval of the
court or delegated
consent.

**7.**—(1) Section 4 above does not authorise any treatment or procedure to which this section applies unless—

5

   (a) it has been approved by the court; or

   (b) consent to the treatment or procedure has been given within the scope of his authority by the donee of a continuing power of attorney granted by the person concerned or by a manager appointed for him by the court.

10

(2) This section applies to—

   (a) any treatment or procedure intended or reasonably likely to render the person concerned permanently infertile except where it is for disease of the reproductive organs or for relieving existing detrimental effects of menstruation;

15

   (b) any treatment or procedure to facilitate the donation of non-regenerative tissue or bone marrow;

   (c) such other treatments or procedures (including treatments or procedures to facilitate the donation of tissue not within paragraph (b) above) as may be prescribed for the purposes of this section by regulations made by the Secretary of State.

20

(3) The power to make regulations under subsection (2)(c) above shall be exercisable by statutory instrument subject to annulment in pursuance of a resolution of either House of Parliament.

Treatment
requiring second
opinion or
delegated
consent.

**8.**—(1) Section 4 above does not authorise any treatment or procedure to which this section applies unless—

25

   (a) a registered medical practitioner other than the one who will be responsible for carrying it out has certified in writing—

      (i) that the person concerned is without capacity to consent to the treatment or procedure; and

30

      (ii) his opinion that it is in the best interests of the person concerned for the treatment or procedure to be carried out; or

   (b) consent to the treatment or procedure has been given within the scope of his authority by the donee of a continuing power of attorney granted by the person concerned or by a manager appointed for him by the court.

35

(2) The practitioner giving the certificate must be one appointed for the purposes of this section by the Secretary of State.

(3) This section applies to—

   (a) any form of treatment for the time being specified under section 58(1)(a) of the Mental Health Act 1983;

40

1983 c.20

   (b) the administration to the person concerned by any means of medicine for mental disorder if three months or more have elapsed since the first occasion when medicine was administered to him by any means for his mental disorder;

45

(c) abortion;

(d) any treatment or procedure intended or reasonably likely to render the person concerned permanently infertile where it is for relieving existing detrimental effects of menstruation;

5 (e) such other treatments or procedures as may be prescribed for the purposes of this section by regulations made by the Secretary of State.

(4) In paragraph (b) of subsection (3) above "mental disorder" has the same meaning as in the said Act of 1983 and the Secretary of State may by 10 order vary the length of the period mentioned in that paragraph.

(5) The power to make regulations under subsection (3)(e) or an order under subsection (4) above shall be exercisable by statutory instrument subject to annulment in pursuance of a resolution of either House of Parliament.

15 (6) This section does not preclude any action necessary to prevent the death of the person concerned or a serious deterioration in his condition while the necessary certificate or consent is sought.

**9.**—(1) In this Act an "advance refusal of treatment" means a refusal by a person who has attained the age of eighteen and has the necessary 20 capacity of any medical, surgical or dental treatment or other procedure, being a refusal intended to have effect at any subsequent time when he may be without capacity to give or refuse his consent.

(2) Section 4 above does not authorise any such treatment or procedure as is mentioned in subsection (1) above if an advance refusal of treatment 25 by the person concerned applies to that treatment or procedure in the circumstances of the case.

(3) In the absence of any indication to the contrary, it shall be presumed that an advance refusal of treatment does not apply in circumstances where those having the care of the person who made it 30 consider that the refusal—

(a) endangers that person's life; or

(b) if that person is a woman who is pregnant, the life of the foetus.

(4) No person shall incur any liability—

(a) for the consequences of withholding any treatment or procedure if 35 he has reasonable grounds for believing that an advance refusal of treatment by the person concerned applies to that treatment or procedure; or

(b) for carrying out any treatment or procedure to which an advance refusal of treatment by the person concerned applies unless he 40 knows, or has reasonable grounds for believing, that an advance refusal of treatment by the person concerned applies to the treatment or procedure.

(5) Without prejudice to any other method of expressing an advance refusal of treatment, such a refusal may take the form of an instrument in 45 writing; and, in the absence of any indication to the contrary, it shall be presumed that an advance refusal of treatment was validly made if it takes the form of an instrument in writing which is signed by the person

by whom it is made and by at least one other person as a witness to his signature.

(6) An advance refusal of treatment may at any time be withdrawn or altered by the person who made it if he then has the capacity to do so.

(7) Notwithstanding the foregoing provisions, an advance refusal of    5
treatment shall not preclude—

    (a) the provision for the person who made it of basic care; or

    (b) the taking of any action necessary to prevent his death or a serious deterioration in his condition pending a decision of the court on the validity or applicability of an advance refusal of   10 treatment or on the question whether it has been withdrawn or altered.

(8) In subsection (7)(a) above "basic care" means care to maintain bodily cleanliness and to alleviate severe pain and the provision of direct oral nutrition and hydration.    15

### Non-therapeutic procedures

Termination of life support and procedures of benefit to others.

**10.**—(1) It shall be lawful, if one of the requirements specified in subsection (2) below is satisfied, to discontinue artificial nutrition or hydration for a person who is unconscious, has no activity in his cerebral cortex and has no prospect of recovery from his condition.    20

(2) The requirements referred to above are—

    (a) the approval of the court;

    (b) the consent given within the scope of his authority by the donee of a continuing power of attorney granted by the person concerned or by a manager appointed for him by the court;    25

    (c) if an order made by the Secretary of State so provides either generally or in cases of a specified description, a certificate in writing by a registered medical practitioner appointed by him for the purposes of this section (not being the one who is to take the proposed action) that it is appropriate for that action to be   30 taken.

(3) Section 3 above shall not apply to a decision made for the purposes of this section by the court, the donee of a power, a manager or the practitioner referred to in subsection (2)(c) above but in making the decision regard is to be had to the matters mentioned in subsection (2) of   35 that section.

(4) The Secretary of State may by an order applying either generally or in cases of a specified description authorise the carrying out, subject to one of the requirements specified in subsection (2) above being satisfied, of any medical or surgical procedure in relation to a person without   40 capacity to consent which, though not carried out for his benefit, will in the opinion of the Secretary of State not cause him significant harm and be of significant benefit to others.

(5) Subsection (4) above does not apply to any procedure carried out for the purposes of research and nothing shall be done by virtue of an   45 order under that subsection if the person concerned objects or it would be contrary to an advance refusal of treatment by that person.

(6) In relation to any procedure to which an order under subsection (4) above applies the requirement in subsection (2)(c) above shall have effect as if it required the certificate to state also that the person concerned is without capacity to consent.

5 (7) Before making an order under this section the Secretary of State shall consult such organisations as appear to him to represent persons affected by mental disability and shall also consult the Official Solicitor.

(8) The power to make orders under this section shall be exercisable by statutory instrument and no such order shall be made unless a draft of it 10 has been laid before and approved by a resolution of each House of Parliament.

**11.**—(1) It shall be lawful to carry out in relation to a person without capacity to consent a procedure for the purposes of research notwithstanding that the research is unlikely to be of benefit to him or 15 that its benefit to him is likely to be long delayed if—

  (a) the research is into an incapacitating condition with which he is or may be affected;

  (b) the committee established by subsection (2) below has approved the research in accordance with subsection (3) below; and

20  (c) one of the requirements specified in subsection (4) below is satisfied.

(2) For the purposes of this section the Secretary of State shall appoint a committee to be known as the Mental Incapacity Research Committee.

(3) The committee may approve any proposed research for the 25 purposes of this section if satisfied—

  (a) that it is desirable in order to provide knowledge of the causes or treatment of, or of the care of persons affected by, mental disability;

  (b) that its object cannot be effectively achieved without the
30    participation of persons who are or may be without capacity to consent; and

  (c) that it will not expose such a person participating in the research to more than negligible risk and that what is done in relation to such a person for the purposes of the research will not be unduly
35    invasive or restrictive and will not unduly interfere with his freedom of action or privacy.

(4) The requirements referred to in subsection (1)(c) above are—

  (a) the approval of the court;

  (b) the consent given within the scope of his authority by the donee
40    of a continuing power of attorney granted by the person concerned or by a manager appointed for him by the court;

  (c) a certificate in writing by a registered medical practitioner not involved in the research that the person concerned is without capacity to consent and that his participation in the research is
45    appropriate;

  (d) the designation by the committee of the research as not involving direct contact with the person concerned.

(5) Section 3 above shall not apply to a decision made for the purposes of this section by the court, the donee of a power, a manager or the practitioner referred to in subsection (4)(c) above but in making the decision regard shall be had to the matters mentioned in subsection (2) of that section.                                        5

(6) Notwithstanding any of the foregoing provisions, nothing shall be done under this section in relation to a person without capacity to consent if he objects or if it would be contrary to an advance refusal of treatment by that person.

(7) Schedule 2 to this Act shall have effect in relation to the committee  10 mentioned in this section.

## CHAPTER III

### CONTINUING POWERS OF ATTORNEY

**12.**—(1) A power of attorney created by an individual is a continuing power of attorney if the requirements of this Chapter are complied with in  15 respect of the power.

(2) The rule of law whereby a power of attorney is revoked by the subsequent mental incapacity of the donor shall not apply to a continuing power of attorney and, accordingly, the decisions which the donee of the power has authority to make and implement on behalf of the donor  20 include decisions which the donor is without capacity to make.

(3) Nothing in this Chapter precludes the donor of a continuing power of attorney from revoking it at any time when he has the capacity to do so.

(4) Subject to sections 13(4) and 17(1) below, an instrument which  25 purports to create a continuing power of attorney but in respect of which all or any of the requirements of this Chapter are not complied with confers no powers on the donee.

**13.**—(1) An instrument creating a continuing power of attorney must be—                                                                    30

  (a) in the prescribed form;

  (b) executed in the prescribed manner by the donor and the donee;

  (c) include at the time of execution by the donor the prescribed explanatory information.

(2) In this Chapter, "prescribed" means prescribed by regulations made  35 by the Lord Chancellor.

(3) The regulations made by him for the purposes of this section shall contain such provision as appears to him to be appropriate for securing—

  (a) that no instrument is used to create a continuing power of attorney which does not include the prescribed information  40 explaining the general effect of creating and accepting the power; and

  (b) that any instrument used to create a continuing power of attorney includes—

      (i) a statement by the donor to the effect that he intends the  45 power to continue in spite of any supervening mental incapacity of his and that he has read (or had read to him) the information explaining the effect of creating the power;

(ii) a statement by the donee to the effect that he understands his duty under section 3 above as respects any decision made by him which the donor is, or is reasonably believed by him to be, without capacity to make.

(4) Where an instrument differs in an immaterial respect in form or mode of expression from the prescribed form the instrument shall be treated as sufficient in point of form and expression.

**14.**—(1) The donor of a continuing power of attorney must have attained the age of eighteen when he executes the instrument creating the power.

(2) The donee of a continuing power of attorney must be—

(a) an individual who has attained the age of eighteen; or

(b) if the power relates only to the property or financial affairs of the donor, either such an individual or a trust corporation.

(3) An individual donee may be described as the holder for the time being of a specified office or position.

(4) An individual who is bankrupt cannot be appointed as donee of a continuing power of attorney relating wholly or partly to the property or financial affairs of the donor; and the appointment of an individual as donee of such a power is revoked by his subsequent bankruptcy whatever its circumstances.

(5) Unless the instrument creating the power otherwise provides, the appointment of the donor's spouse as donee is revoked by the dissolution or annulment of the marriage.

**15.**—(1) An instrument does not create a continuing power of attorney unless, after execution, it is registered in the prescribed manner by such authority (in this Part of this Act referred to as the "registration authority") as the Lord Chancellor may appoint.

(2) Subject to the provisions of sections 13 and 14 above, section 17(6) below and of this section, an instrument shall be registered if an application in that behalf is made in the prescribed form by the donee of the power.

(3) Subject to subsection (5) below, the donee shall before applying for registration of the instrument give notice in the prescribed form to the donor of his intention to do so, and the application shall be accompanied by a certificate that the required notice has been given.

(4) The donor may within the prescribed period (which shall be specified in the notice) inform the registration authority that he objects to the instrument being registered and, if he does so—

(a) the registration authority shall notify the donee; and

(b) the instrument shall not be registered unless the court, on the application of the donee, directs the registration authority to register it.

(5) The court may, on the donee's application, dispense with the requirement in subsection (3) above if satisfied that no useful purpose would be served by giving the notice.

(6) Where an instrument is registered under this section the registration authority shall give notice of that fact in the prescribed form— 5

(a) to the donor of the power; and

(b) if the instrument contains a requirement to that effect, to the person or persons (not exceeding two and not being or including the donee) specified for that purpose in the instrument.

(7) After an instrument has been registered under this section no 10 disclaimer of the power conferred by the instrument shall be valid unless and until notice of the disclaimer is given to the donor of the power and to the registration authority.

(8) A document purporting to be an office copy of an instrument registered under this section shall, in any part of the United Kingdom, be 15 evidence of the contents of the instrument and of the fact that it has been registered.

1971 c.27

(9) Subsection (8) above is without prejudice to section 3 of the Powers of Attorney Act 1971 (proof by certified copy) and to any other method of proof authorised by law. 20

Scope of
continuing power
of attorney.

**16.**—(1) Subject to the provisions of this section, a continuing power of attorney may—

(a) extend to all or to any specified matters relating to the donor's personal welfare, health care, property or affairs, including the conduct of legal proceedings; and 25

(b) be subject to conditions or restrictions.

(2) Where the instrument creating a continuing power of attorney is expressed to confer general authority on the donee it shall, subject to the provisions of this section, be construed as extending to all the matters mentioned in subsection (1)(a) above but without prejudice to such 30 conditions or restrictions (if any) as are specified in the instrument.

(3) So much of a continuing power of attorney as relates to the health care of the donor shall not authorise the donee—

(a) to consent or refuse consent to any treatment or procedure unless the donor is then, or is then reasonably believed by the donee to 35 be, without capacity to give or refuse his own consent to the treatment;

(b) to consent to the donor's admission to hospital against his will for assessment or treatment for mental disorder within the meaning of the Mental Health Act 1983; 40

1983 c.20

(c) to withhold basic care as defined in section 9(8) above from the donor or refuse consent to its provision for him;

(d) unless the donee is expressly authorised to do so by the instrument creating the power—

(i) to consent to any treatment or procedure refused by the 45 donor by an advance refusal of treatment;

(ii) to consent to any treatment or procedure to which section 7 or 8 above applies; or

(iii) to refuse consent to any treatment or procedure necessary to sustain life.

(4) The authority conferred by a continuing power of attorney shall be subject to the same restriction as is imposed by section 5 above on the authority given by section 4.

(5) Express authority is required in the instrument creating the power if the donee is to have power to give his consent to the doing of anything in relation to the donor under section 10 or 11 above.

(6) A continuing power of attorney which relates only to matters other than the donor's property or financial affairs, and so much of a continuing power of attorney as relates to matters in addition to the donor's property or financial affairs, shall not be revoked by his bankruptcy.

**17.**—(1) The court may declare that an instrument which is not in the form prescribed for the purposes of section 13(1)(a) above shall be treated as if it were in that form if the court is satisfied that the persons executing it intended it to create a continuing power of attorney.

Powers of court in relation to continuing power of attorney.

(2) The court may determine any question as to the meaning or effect of a continuing power of attorney, as to whether the donor had capacity to create it or has or had capacity to revoke it or as to whether it has been effectively revoked.

(3) The court may—

(a) give directions with respect to decisions to be made by the donee of a continuing power of attorney in relation to the matters to which it extends, being decisions which the donor is without capacity to make;

(b) give any consent or authorisation to act which the donee would have to obtain from the donor if he had capacity to give it;

(c) unless the instrument creating the continuing power of attorney otherwise provides—

(i) appoint a person to be the donee of the power in substitution for or in addition to the donee mentioned in the instrument;

(ii) modify or extend the scope of the donee's power to act in relation to any of the matters to which the power could extend,

in any case in which the court thinks it desirable to do so and the donor is without capacity to act in the matter.

(4) Where the court exercises its powers under subsection (3)(c) above it shall—

(a) order the instrument in question to be delivered up for amendment to give effect to the appointment, modification or extension; and

(b) direct the registration authority to register the amended instrument in substitution for the instrument in its previous form;

and the appointment, modification or restriction shall not have effect until the amended instrument is registered.

(5) The court may on behalf of a donor without capacity to do so—

   (a) give directions to the donee with respect to the rendering by him of reports or accounts and the production of records kept by him for that purpose;

   (b) require the donee to furnish information or produce documents or things in his possession as donee;

   (c) give directions with respect to the remuneration or expenses of the donee;

   (d) relieve the donee wholly or partly from any liability which he has or may have incurred on account of a breach of his duty as donee.

(6) The court may direct that an instrument purporting to create a continuing power of attorney shall not be registered or, on behalf of a donor without capacity to do so, revoke a continuing power of attorney if satisfied—

   (a) that fraud or undue pressure was used to induce the donor to execute the instrument or create the power; or

   (b) that the donee or intended donee has behaved, is behaving or proposes to behave, in a way that contravenes or would contravene his authority or is or would otherwise not be in the donor's best interests.

Cancellation of registration.

**18.**—(1) The registration authority shall cancel the registration of the instrument creating a continuing power of attorney—

   (a) on receipt of a revocation in the prescribed form signed by the donor;

   (b) on receipt of a disclaimer in the prescribed form signed by the donee;

   (c) if satisfied that the power has expired or has been revoked—

      (i) by the death or bankruptcy of the donor;

      (ii) by the death or bankruptcy of the donee or, if the donee is a body corporate, by its winding up or dissolution; or

      (iii) by the dissolution or annulment of the marriage between the donor and the donee.

(2) Where in the case of a registered instrument it appears to the registration authority—

   (a) that the donor or donee is bankrupt; but

   (b) that the instrument relates to matters in addition to the donor's property and financial affairs (so that the bankruptcy does not wholly revoke the power),

the authority shall attach to the instrument a note to the effect that it is revoked so far as relating to the donor's property and financial affairs.

(3) Where the registration authority cancels the registration of an instrument under subsection (1)(a) or (c)(i) above or attaches a note to an instrument under subsection (2) above it shall give notice of the cancellation or note to the donee of the power.

(4) The court shall direct the registration authority to cancel the registration of the instrument creating a continuing power of attorney—

   (a) if the court determines under section 17(2) above that the donor has or had capacity to revoke the power and has done so; or

5    (b) if the court is satisfied—

      (i) that the donee is without capacity to act as donee; or

      (ii) that the power was not valid and subsisting when it was registered; or

   (c) if the court revokes the power under section 17(6) above.

10   (5) Where in the case of a registered instrument it appears to the registration authority that the donee has been replaced pursuant to a power in that behalf in the instrument it shall attach to the instrument a note to that effect; and where the donee is replaced in consequence of having disclaimed the instrument shall not by reason of the disclaimer be 15 cancelled under subsection (1)(b) above.

(6) On the cancellation of the registration of an instrument the instrument shall be delivered up to be cancelled.

**19.**—(1) Subsections (2) and (3) below apply where an instrument which did not create a valid continuing power of attorney has been 20 registered under section 15 above (whether or not the registration has been cancelled at the time of the act or transaction in question).

Protection of donee and third persons when power is invalid or revoked.

(2) A donee who acts in pursuance of the power shall not incur any liability (either to the donor or to any other person) by reason of the non-existence of the power unless at the time of acting he knows—

25    (a) that the instrument did not create a valid continuing power of attorney; or

   (b) that an event has occurred which, if the instrument had created a valid continuing power of attorney, would have had the effect of revoking it; or

30    (c) that, if the instrument had created a valid continuing power of attorney, the power would have expired before that time.

(3) Any transaction between the donee and another person shall, in favour of that person, be as valid as if the power had been in existence unless at the time of the transaction that person has knowledge of any of 35 matters mentioned in subsection (2) above.

(4) Where the interest of a purchaser depends on whether a transaction between the donee and the other person was valid by virtue of subsection (3) above, it shall be conclusively presumed in favour of the purchaser that the transaction was valid if—

40    (a) the transaction between that person and the donee was completed within twelve months of the date on which the instrument was registered; or

   (b) that person makes a statutory declaration, before or within three months after the completion of the purchase, that he had no 45 reason at the time of the transaction to doubt that the donee had authority to dispose of the property which was the subject of the transaction.

(5) In subsection (4) above "purchaser" and "purchase" have the meaning given in section 205(1) of the Law of Property Act 1925.

(6) In its application to a continuing power of attorney which relates to matters in addition to the donor's property and financial affairs section 5 of the Powers of Attorney Act 1971 (protection where power is revoked) 5 shall have effect as if references to revocation included references to the cessation of the power in relation to the donor's property and financial affairs.

Substituted and joint and several donees.

**20.**—(1) An instrument creating a continuing power of attorney—

    (a) cannot give the donee power to appoint a substitute or successor; 10 but

    (b) may itself appoint a person to replace the donee in the event of his disclaiming or in any such event as is mentioned in section 18(1)(c)(ii) or (iii) above.

(2) An instrument creating a continuing power of attorney may appoint 15 two or more persons as donees whether to act jointly or jointly and severally.

(3) Where two or more donees are appointed—

    (a) references to the donee in subsection (1) above and in sections 13 and 14 above shall be read as referring to each of them and 20 regulations made for the purposes of section 13 may make provision which differs according to whether only one or more than one donee is to be appointed;

    (b) references to the donee in sections 15 and 16 above shall be read, if they are to act jointly, to them acting jointly and otherwise to 25 any one of them;

    (c) references to the donee in sections 17 and 19 above shall be read as referring to all or any of them;

    (d) references to the donee in section 18 above shall be read, if they are to act jointly, as references to any of them but if— 30

        (i) they are to act jointly and severally, and

        (ii) the condition for cancellation of the registration in subsection (1)(b) or (c)(ii) or (iii) or (4)(b)(i) is satisfied in the case of any but not all of them,

    the registration authority shall, instead of cancelling (or being 35 directed to cancel) the registration, attach (or be directed to attach) to the instrument a note to the effect that the power has ceased to be exercisable by the donee or donees in whose case the condition is satisfied.

(4) Where two or more donees are appointed to act jointly and 40 severally, a failure, as respects any one of them, to comply with the requirements of section 13, 14 or 15 above shall prevent the instrument in question from creating a continuing power of attorney in his case but without affecting its efficacy for that purpose as respects the other or others. 45

Enduring powers of attorney.

1985 c.29

**21.**—(1) No enduring power of attorney within the meaning of the Enduring Powers of Attorney Act 1985 shall be created after the coming into force of this Act.

(2) An existing enduring power of attorney which has not been registered under that Act before the coming into force of this Act may be converted into a continuing power of attorney by—

    (a) the execution by the donor and the attorney (or, if more than one, all the attorneys), in accordance with Part I of Schedule 3 to this Act, of a declaration stating their desire that the instrument creating the enduring power should be treated as creating a continuing power; and

    (b) the registration of that instrument in accordance with section 15 above.

(3) The provisions of Parts II to V of Schedule 3 to this Act shall have effect in place of the said Act of 1985 in relation to any enduring power of attorney which has been created before the coming into force of this Act and not converted into a continuing power by virtue of subsection (2) above.

**22.**—(1) The power of the Lord Chancellor to make regulations under this Chapter shall be exercisable by statutory instrument subject to annulment in pursuance of a resolution of either House of Parliament.

Regulations.

(2) Regulations which amend or revoke previous regulations may contain such savings or other transitional provisions as the Lord Chancellor thinks necessary or expedient.

## CHAPTER IV

### GENERAL POWERS OF THE COURT AND APPOINTMENT OF MANAGERS

**23.** The court may make a declaration on any of the following matters—

Power of court to make declarations.

    (a) the capacity of a person to make a particular decision or decisions on particular matters;

    (b) whether an advance refusal of treatment has been validly made, withdrawn or altered, including any question as to the capacity to make, withdraw or alter it, and whether it is applicable in particular circumstances.

**24.**—(1) The court may—

Power of court to make decisions and to appoint a manager.

    (a) by making orders or giving directions make a decision or decisions on behalf of a person without capacity to make the decision or decisions; or

    (b) subject to the subsequent provisions of this Chapter, appoint a person (in this Act referred to as "a manager") to be responsible for making a decision or decisions on behalf of a person without capacity to make the decision or decisions.

(2) In exercising its powers under this section the court shall have regard to the principle that a decision by the court is to be preferred to the appointment of a manager to make a decision and that the powers conferred on a manager should be as limited in scope and duration as possible.

(3) The decisions to which the powers conferred by or under this section apply extend to any matter relating to the personal welfare, health care, property or affairs of the person concerned, including the conduct of legal proceedings, but subject to the subsequent provisions of this Chapter in respect of particular matters.                                              5

(4) The court may make such further orders or give such directions, and confer on a manager such powers, as it thinks necessary or expedient for giving effect to any order or appointment made by it under subsection (1) above.

(5) The court may make an order, or appoint a manager, on any terms it   10 considers in the best interests of the person concerned even though the application before the court is not for an order or an appointment on those terms.

(6) Any order of the court may be varied or discharged by a subsequent order but this does not apply to an order under section 26(4) below and   15 has effect subject to the provisions of Schedule 4 to this Act with respect to settlements.

Personal welfare matters.

**25.**—(1) The powers conferred by or under section 24 above as respects the personal welfare of the person concerned extend in particular to the following matters—                                              20

   (a)  where the person concerned is to live;

   (b)  what contact, if any, he is to have with any specified persons;

   (c)  the exercise of the rights conferred on him by or under any enactment to obtain information;

   (d)  obtaining the benefits and services to which he is entitled, or   25 which are available to him, by virtue of any enactment.

(2) The powers as to where the person concerned is to live shall not be construed as including power to require or authorise him to be admitted to hospital against his will for assessment or treatment for mental

1983 c.20

disorder within the meaning of the Mental Health Act 1983.            30

(3) The powers as to what persons are to have contact with the person concerned include power to make an order restraining a named person from having contact with or molesting the person concerned.

Health care matters.

**26.**—(1) The powers conferred by or under section 24 above as respects the health care of the person concerned extend in particular to   35 the following matters—

   (a)  approving or refusing approval for (or in the case of a manager consenting to or refusing consent for) the giving, withholding or cessation of particular forms of health care;

   (b)  requiring a person responsible for the health care of the person   40 concerned to allow a different person to take over that responsibility;

   (c)  obtaining access to the health records of the person concerned in

1984 c.35
1990 c.23

        accordance with the Data Protection Act 1984 or the Access to Health Records Act 1990.                                              45

(2) The powers conferred by or under section 24 above as respects the health care of the person concerned do not extend to—

    (a) approving (or in the case of a manager consenting to) the admission of the person concerned to hospital for assessment or treatment for mental disorder within the meaning of the Mental Health Act 1983 except as provided in subsection (4) below;

    (b) approving (or in the case of a manager consenting to)—

        (i) the withholding from the person concerned of basic care as defined in section 9(8) above; or

        (ii) any treatment refused by an advance refusal of treatment.

(3) The powers of a manager extend to giving his consent to the doing of anything under section 7, 8, 10 or 11 above in relation to the person for whom he is appointed if, and only if, that power is expressly conferred on him by the court.

(4) If the court is satisfied on the written or oral evidence of two registered medical practitioners of whom at least one is approved for the purposes of section 12 of the Mental Health Act 1983 that in the case of the person concerned—

    (a) the grounds specified in section 2(2)(a) and (b) of that Act or those specified in section 3(2)(a), (b) and (c) of that Act exist; and

    (b) that it is appropriate that he should be admitted to hospital for assessment or, as the case may be, for treatment,

the court may order his admission to hospital for assessment or, as the case may be, for treatment.

(5) Section 3 above shall not apply to a decision of the court under subsection (4)(b) above but in determining whether admission to hospital is appropriate the court shall have regard to the matters mentioned in subsection (2) of that section.

(6) The Mental Health Act 1983 shall apply in relation to a person admitted to hospital in pursuance of an order under subsection (4) above as if he had been admitted under section 2 or, as the case may be, section 3 of that Act except that no order for his discharge may be made under section 23 of that Act by his nearest relative and that no application may be made by him to the Mental Health Review Tribunal under section 66(1)(a) or (b) of that Act.

**27.**—(1) The powers conferred by or under section 24 above as respects the property and affairs of the person concerned extend in particular to the following matters—

    (a) the control and management of his property;

    (b) the sale, exchange, charging, gift or other disposition of his property;

    (c) the acquisition of property in his name or on his behalf;

    (d) the carrying on on his behalf of any profession, trade or business;

    (e) the dissolution of a partnership of which he is a member;

(f) the carrying out of any contract entered into by him;

(g) the discharge of his debts and of any of his obligations, whether legally enforceable or not;

(h) the settlement of any of his property, whether for his own benefit or for the benefit of others;                                                                        5

(i) the execution for him of a will;

(j) the exercise of any power (including a power to consent) vested in him whether beneficially or as trustee or otherwise.

(2) The court shall not confer on a manager powers with respect to the matters mentioned in subsection (1)(h), (i) or (j) above.                                          10

(3) The powers conferred by or under section 24 above as respects any matter relating to the property or affairs of the person concerned may be exercised notwithstanding that he has not attained the age of sixteen if the court considers it likely that he will still lack capacity to make decisions in respect of that matter when he attains the age of eighteen.                                    15

(4) Schedule 4 to this Act shall have effect for supplementing the provisions of this section.

Managers.

**28.**—(1) This section has effect in relation to the appointment of managers by the court under section 24 above and to managers appointed by it.                                                                                                       20

(2) The manager must be—

(a) an individual who has attained the age of eighteen; or

(b) as respects powers in relation to property or financial affairs, either an individual or a trust corporation;

and where the court appoints an individual he may be described as the 25 holder for the time being of a specified office or position.

(3) A person shall not be appointed as a manager without his consent.

(4) No appointment of a manager shall be for a period exceeding five years.

(5) The court may appoint two or more managers to act jointly or 30 jointly and severally and when appointing a manager or managers it may at the same time—

(a) appoint one or more other persons to succeed that manager or those managers after a specified period;

(b) appoint one or more other persons to be, pending a fresh 35 appointment, a manager or managers in the event of an existing manager dying or becoming incapable of acting.

(6) Where the manager is a person other than the Public Trustee—

(a) the court may require him to give to the Public Trustee such security as the court thinks fit for the due discharge of his 40 functions, and to submit to the Public Trustee such reports at such times or at such intervals as the court may direct; and

(b) the Public Trustee shall have such supervisory functions in relation to the manager as are provided by rules under section 14 of the Public Trustee Act 1906.                                                                         45

1906 c.55

(7) Without prejudice to the generality of section 24(4) above, a manager may be appointed to take possession or control of all or any specified part of the property of the person concerned and to exercise all or any specified powers in respect of it including such powers of investment
5 as the court may determine.

(8) A manager shall, as respects anything done by him in his capacity as such, be regarded as the agent of the person for whom he is appointed.

(9) A manager shall be entitled to be reimbursed out of the property of the person concerned for his reasonable expenses in discharging his
10 functions and, if the court so directs when appointing him, remuneration out of that property for discharging them.

(10) A manager shall not have power to make any decision on behalf of another person which is inconsistent with a decision made within the scope of his authority by the donee of a continuing power of attorney
15 granted by that person.

**29.** The provisions of the Acts described in Schedule 5 to this Act which are specified in the third column of that Schedule, so far as they make specific provision for persons without capacity, shall not have effect in relation to persons as to whom powers have been exercised
20 under this Chapter or section 48 below.

Disapplication of other enactments.

## CHAPTER V

### MISCELLANEOUS AND SUPPLEMENTARY

**30.** Nothing in this Part of this Act shall be construed as enabling a decision on any of the following matters to be made on behalf of a person
25 without capacity to make it for himself—

Excluded decisions.

(a) consent to marriage;

(b) consent to have sexual relations;

(c) consent to a divorce petition on the basis of two years' separation;

30 (d) agreement to the making of an adoption order or consent to an application for an order freeing a child for adoption;

(e) voting at an election for any public office;

(f) discharging parental responsibilities in matters not relating to a child's property.

35 **31.**—(1) The Secretary of State shall prepare and from time to time revise a code or codes of practice—

Codes of practice.

(a) for the guidance of persons assessing whether a person is or is not without capacity to make a decision or decisions on any matters;

(b) for the guidance of persons acting in pursuance of Chapter II of
40 this Part of this Act;

(c) for the guidance of persons acting as managers appointed by the court; and

(d) with respect to such other matters concerned with this Part of this Act as he thinks fit.

(2) Before preparing a code under this section or revising such a code the Secretary of State shall consult such persons as he thinks appropriate and may delegate the preparation of the whole or any part of any code so far as he considers expedient.

(3) The Secretary of State shall publish any code under this section as for the time being in force and lay copies of it before Parliament.   5

(4) It shall be the duty of any person acting under this Part of this Act in relation to a person without capacity to have regard to any relevant code in force under this section if he is acting in a professional capacity or for remuneration.   10

(5) The provisions of any code in force under this section shall be admissible in evidence in any civil or criminal proceedings and may be taken into account by the court if it considers them relevant in determining any question arising in the proceedings.

Ill-treatment of mentally disabled persons and persons unable to communicate.

**32.**—(1) It is an offence for any person to whom this section applies to   15
ill-treat or wilfully neglect a person in relation to whom he has powers by virtue of this Part of this Act.

(2) This section applies to—

(a) any person having the care of, or in lawful control of property of, the person concerned;   20

(b) any donee of a continuing power of attorney granted by him;

(c) any person appointed by the court to be his manager.

(3) A person guilty of an offence under this section is liable—

(a) on summary conviction, to imprisonment for a term not exceeding six months or a fine not exceeding the statutory   25
maximum or both;

(b) on conviction on indictment, to imprisonment for a term not exceeding two years or a fine or both.

Concealing or destroying advance refusal of treatment.

**33.**—(1) It is an offence for a person with intent to deceive to conceal or destroy a written advance refusal of treatment made by another person.   30

(2) A person guilty of an offence under this section is liable—

(a) on summary conviction, to imprisonment for a term not exceeding six months or a fine not exceeding the statutory maximum or both;

(b) on conviction on indictment, to imprisonment for a term not   35
exceeding two years or a fine or both.

Payment for necessary goods and services.

**34.**—(1) Where necessary goods are supplied to, or necessary services are provided for, a person without capacity to contract, he must pay a reasonable price for them.

(2) In this section "necessary" means suitable to the condition in life of   40
the person concerned and to his actual requirements at the time when the goods are supplied or the services provided.

**35.** A local authority shall have power to take reasonable steps for the protection of the property and affairs of a person who is without capacity to protect them and for whom they provide or arrange accommodation.

PART I
CHAPTER V
Protection of property and affairs of incapacitated person accommodated by local authority.

## PART II

5 ### PERSONS IN NEED OF CARE OR PROTECTION

**36.**—(1) This Part of this Act has effect for conferring powers and duties on local authorities and their officers for the protection of vulnerable persons against significant harm or serious exploitation.

*Preliminary.*

(2) In this Part of this Act "vulnerable person" means any person who
10 has attained the age of sixteen and—

  (a) is or may be in need of community care services by reason of mental or other disability, age or illness; and

  (b) is or may be unable to take care of himself or to protect himself against significant harm or serious exploitation.

15 (3) In this Part of this Act "community care services" means services which a local authority may provide or arrange to be provided under any of the following provisions—

  (a) Part III of the National Assistance Act 1948;

  (b) section 45 of the Health Services and Public Health Act 1968;

20 (c) section 21 of and Schedule 8 to the National Health Service Act 1977;

  (d) section 117 of the Mental Health Act 1983;

*1948 c.29*

*1968 c.46*

*1977 c.49*

*1983 c.20*

and, in relation to a person who has not attained the age of eighteen, includes services provided by a local authority in the exercise of
25 functions conferred by section 17 of the Children Act 1989.

*1989 c.41*

(4) In this Part of this Act "authorised officer of a local authority", in relation to any action to be taken by such an officer, means an officer of the authority authorised by them to take actions of that description.

(5) In this Part of this Act "harm", in relation to a vulnerable person,
30 means ill-treatment of that person (including sexual abuse and forms of ill-treatment that are not physical), the impairment of, or an avoidable deterioration in, the physical or mental health of that person or the impairment of his physical, intellectual, emotional, social or behavioural development.

35 **37.**—(1) Where a local authority have reasonable cause to believe that a vulnerable person in their area is suffering or likely to suffer significant harm or serious exploitation the authority shall make such enquiries as they consider necessary to enable them to decide—

*Investigations.*

  (a) whether that person is in fact suffering or likely to suffer such
40 harm or exploitation; and

(b) if so, whether they should provide or arrange for the provision for that person of community care services or take any other action (including action under the subsequent provisions of this Part of this Act) to protect that person from such harm or exploitation.

(2) Where enquiries are made under subsection (1) above with respect 5 to any person the local authority shall (with a view to enabling them to decide what action, if any, to take with respect to that person) take such steps as are reasonably practicable to enable an authorised officer of the authority to gain access to that person unless the authority are satisfied that they already have sufficient information with respect to that person. 10

(3) Where a local authority are conducting enquiries under this section it shall be the duty of any person mentioned in subsection (5) below to assist the authority with those enquiries (in particular by providing relevant information and advice) if called upon to do so by the authority.

(4) Subsection (3) above does not oblige a person to assist the local 15 authority where doing so would be unreasonable in all the circumstances.

(5) The persons referred to in subsection (3) above are—

(a) any local authority;

(b) any local education authority;

(c) any local housing authority; 20

(d) any health authority; and

(e) any person authorised by the Secretary of State for the purposes of this section.

(6) Where a local authority are conducting enquiries under this section with respect to a person who appears to be ordinarily resident in the area of 25 another authority, they shall consult that other authority, who may undertake the necessary enquiries in their place.

Officer's powers of entry.

**38.**—(1) If an authorised officer of a local authority has reasonable cause to believe that a vulnerable person living in any premises in the authority's area is suffering or likely to suffer significant harm or serious 30 exploitation he may at any reasonable time—

(a) enter and inspect those premises; and

(b) interview that person in private.

(2) The officer shall, if requested to do so, produce some duly authenticated document showing that he is an authorised officer of the 35 local authority.

(3) The powers conferred by this section shall not be exercised in respect of any person if the officer knows or believes that the person objects or would object to their exercise but that restriction shall not apply if he has reasonable cause to believe that the person is or may be 40 suffering from mental disability.

1977 c.49

(4) This section does not confer any powers of entry to a health service hospital within the meaning of the National Health Service Act 1977 or any accommodation provided by a local authority and used as a hospital by or on behalf of the Secretary of State under that Act. 45

**39.**—(1) The court may, on the application of an authorised officer of a local authority, issue a warrant authorising a constable, accompanied by such an officer, to enter any premises in the authority's area which are specified in the warrant if satisfied—

5     (a) that the applicant has reasonable cause to believe that a vulnerable person living in those premises is suffering or likely to suffer significant harm or serious exploitation;

    (b) that granting the warrant is necessary to enable the officer to gain access to that person; and

10     (c) that the application is competent under subsection (2) below.

(2) An authorised officer shall not make an application under this section in respect of any person if he knows or believes that the person objects or would object to entry being obtained but that restriction shall not apply if he has reasonable cause to believe that the person is or may be 15 suffering from mental disability.

**40.**—(1) The court may, on the application of an authorised officer of a local authority, make an order under this section (an "assessment order") in respect of any person in the authority's area if satisfied—

    (a) that the applicant has reasonable cause to believe that the person 20       concerned is a vulnerable person suffering or likely to suffer significant harm or serious exploitation;

    (b) that the order is required so that all or any of the matters referred to in section 37(1)(a) and (b) above can be properly assessed; and

    (c) that the application is competent under subsection (2) below.

25     (2) An authorised officer shall not make an application under this section in respect of any person if he knows or believes that the person objects or would object to the making of the order but that restriction shall not apply if he has reasonable cause to believe that the person is or may be suffering from mental disability.

30     (3) An assessment order shall specify the steps to be taken for carrying out the assessment but nothing to which the person concerned objects shall be done pursuant to the order unless the court when making the order, or at any time while it is in force, expressly authorises it to be done notwithstanding the objection.

35     (4) An assessment order shall—

    (a) specify the date by which the assessment is to begin; and

    (b) specify a period beginning with that date for which the order is to be in force, being the shortest period considered by the court to be necessary for the purposes of the assessment and not in any 40       event exceeding eight days.

(5) The person to whom an assessment order relates may only be removed from his place of residence pursuant to the order—

    (a) in accordance with directions specified in the order;

    (b) if it is necessary for the purposes of the assessment; and

45     (c) for such period or periods as are specified in the order.

(6) The court may treat an application for an assessment order as an application for a temporary protection order if the requirements for the making of such an order are satisfied and the court considers that such an order is more appropriate than an assessment order.

**41.**—(1) The court may, on the application of an authorised officer of a 5
local authority, make an order under this section (a "temporary protection order") in respect of any person in the authority's area if satisfied—

    (a) that the person concerned is a vulnerable person;

    (b) that he is likely to suffer significant harm or serious exploitation
        unless removed to and kept in, or prevented from leaving, 10
        protective accommodation for a short period; and

    (c) that the application is competent under subsection (2) below.

(2) An authorised officer shall not make an application under this section in respect of any person if he knows or believes that the person objects or would object to the making of the order but that restriction 15
shall not apply if he has reasonable cause to believe that the person is or may be suffering from mental disability.

(3) A temporary protection order shall authorise the removal of the person concerned to protective accommodation specified in the order and the keeping of that person in that accommodation or, as the case may be, 20
preventing that person from leaving the accommodation, for such period as is so specified, being the shortest period considered by the court to be necessary for achieving the purpose of the order and not in any event exceeding eight days.

(4) On the making of a temporary protection order or at any time while it 25
is in force the court may give directions for the assessment of all or any of the matters mentioned in section 37(1)(a) and (b) above and, if such directions are given, section 40(3) above shall have effect in relation to the directions as it has effect in relation to an assessment order.

(5) An application for a temporary protection order may be made ex 30
parte but the person in respect of whom it is made on any such application, and any person who is the donee of a continuing power of attorney granted by him or appointed by the court to be his manager, may apply for the order to be discharged.

(6) The court may treat an application for a temporary protection order 35
as an application for an assessment order if the requirements for the making of such an order are satisfied and the court considers that such an order is more appropriate than a temporary protection order.

(7) In this section "protective accommodation" means—

    (a) residential accommodation provided by a local social services 40
        authority under Part III of the National Assistance Act 1948;

    (b) a health service hospital within the meaning of the National
        Health Service Act 1977 or accommodation provided by a local
        authority and used as a hospital by or on behalf of the Secretary of
        State under that Act; 45

    (c) a residential care home within the meaning of Part I of the
        Registered Homes Act 1984, a nursing home as defined in

section 21 or a mental nursing home as defined in section 22 of that Act;

PART II

(d) any other suitable place the occupier of which is willing temporarily to receive the person concerned.

5 (8) Where a person has been removed to protective accommodation pursuant to a temporary protection order it shall be the duty of the local authority to return him to the place from which he was removed as soon as that is practicable and consistent with his interests.

**42.**—(1) It is an offence for a person without reasonable excuse to 10 obstruct an authorised officer of a local authority in the execution of his powers under this Part of this Act.

Offences.

(2) It is an offence for a person without reasonable excuse to obstruct any person acting pursuant to an assessment order or a temporary protection order or to any directions given in connection with such an 15 order.

(3) Subsections (1) and (2) above do not apply to the person for whose benefit the powers are sought to be exercised or, as the case may be, in respect of whom the order is made or the directions are given.

(4) A person guilty of an offence under this section is liable on 20 summary conviction to imprisonment for a term not exceeding three months or a fine not exceeding level 4 on the standard scale or both.

(5) Proceedings for an offence under this section may be brought by a local authority.

**43.** A local authority may assist a vulnerable person, whether by 25 advice, financial assistance or otherwise, in bringing proceedings for relief under—

Assistance for<br>vulnerable person<br>in legal<br>proceedings.

(a) the Domestic Violence and Matrimonial Proceedings Act 1976;

(b) section 16 of the Domestic Proceedings and Magistrates' Courts Act 1978;

1976 c.50<br>1978 c.22

30 (c) the Matrimonial Homes Act 1983;

1983 c.19

[(d) section 7 or 13 of the Family Homes and Domestic Violence Act 1995.]

1995 c.00

**44.** In section 48 of the National Assistance Act 1948 (duty of local authority to protect property of person removed from home) after 35 subsection (1)(b) there shall be inserted—

Protection of<br>property of<br>persons removed<br>from home.<br>1948 c.29

"(ba) is admitted to accommodation provided or arranged by a council in pursuance of an order made on the application of the authority under Part I of the Mental Incapacity Act 1995, or

40 (bb) is removed from his place of residence in pursuance of an assessment order or a temporary protection order under Part II of that Act,".

## PART III

### JURISDICTION

Meaning of "the court".

**45.**—(1) Subject to the provisions of this section "the court" means—

(a) as respects Part I of this Act, the Court of Protection established by section 46 below; and    5

(b) as respects Part II of this Act, that Court, a magistrates' court or a single justice of the peace.

(2) The Lord Chancellor may by order make provision for determining whether proceedings under Part II of this Act are to be instituted in the Court of Protection, in a magistrates' court or before a single justice; and 10 proceedings under that Part shall be treated as family proceedings for the purposes of sections 66 to 68, 69(1) and 70 of the Magistrates' Courts Act 1980.

1980 c.43.

(3) The Lord Chancellor may by order make provision, in relation to persons who have not attained the age of eighteen, for the transfer of 15 proceedings between a court having jurisdiction under this Act and a court having jurisdiction under the Children Act 1989; and a court having either of those jurisdictions may decline to exercise it in a matter concerning such a person if it considers that it can more suitably be dealt with by a court exercising the other jurisdiction.    20

1989 c.41

(4) The power to make orders under subsection (2) or (3) above shall be exercisable by statutory instrument subject to annulment in pursuance of a resolution of either House of Parliament.

The Court of Protection.

**46.**—(1) There shall be a superior court of record known as the Court of Protection and the office of the Supreme Court called by that name shall 25 cease to exist.

(2) Subject to subsection (4) below, the jurisdiction of the Court shall be exercisable by any judge nominated for that purpose by the Lord Chancellor, being—

(a) a judge of the Chancery Division of the High Court;    30

(b) a judge of the Family Division of the High Court;

(c) a circuit judge; or

(d) a district judge.

(3) The Lord Chancellor may, if he thinks fit, appoint one of the nominated judges of the High Court to be president of the court.    35

(4) The Lord Chancellor shall appoint one of the nominated judges to be Senior Judge of the Court of Protection with such administrative functions in relation to the Court as the Lord Chancellor may direct and with such additional remuneration in respect of that appointment as the Lord Chancellor may with the consent of the Treasury determine.    40

(5) The Lord Chancellor may by order make provision for determining which kind of judge mentioned in subsection (2) above is to deal with any particular proceedings in the Court of Protection and for the transfer of proceedings between judges of the different kinds mentioned in that subsection.    45

(6) The Court may sit anywhere in England and Wales at places appointed by the Lord Chancellor.

(7) The Court shall have a central office and registry in London but the Lord Chancellor may designate as additional registries of the Court any district registry of the High Court and any county court office.

(8) The power to make orders under subsection (5) above shall be exercisable by statutory instrument subject to annulment in pursuance of a resolution by either House of Parliament.

**47.**—(1) Subject to subsection (3) below, no application shall be made to the Court of Protection for the exercise of any of its powers under Part I of this Act except with the leave of the court.

(2) In deciding whether to grant leave the court shall in particular have regard to the following matters—

  (a) the applicant's connection with the person in relation to whom this application is made;

  (b) the reasons for the application;

  (c) the benefit to the person concerned of the proposed order, directions or authority;

  (d) whether that benefit can be achieved in any other way.

(3) No leave shall be required for any application made to the court—

  (a) by a person who is or alleged to be without capacity or, where such a person has not attained the age of eighteen, by anyone with parental responsibility for him within the meaning of the Children Act 1989;

  (b) by the donee of a continuing power of attorney granted by, or a manager appointed for, the person in relation to whom the application is made;

  (c) by the Public Trustee as respects any functions exercisable by him by virtue of an order of the court; or

  (d) where any other person is named in an existing order of the court, by that person in respect of an application made by him which relates to that order.

**48.** Where on an application to the Court of Protection—

  (a) it is shown that there is reason to believe that a person may be without capacity in relation to any matter in respect of which the court has power to make an order or give directions under Part I of this Act; and

  (b) the court is of the opinion that it is in that person's best interests that an order or directions in respect of that matter should be made or given forthwith,

the court may make an order or give directions in relation to that matter pending a decision whether that person is in fact without capacity in relation to it.

**49.**—(1) Subject to the provisions of this section, there shall be the following rights of appeal in proceedings under this Act from and to the judges nominated under section 46—

>   (a) from a decision of a district judge to a circuit judge or a judge of the High Court;

>   (b) from a decision of a circuit judge or judge of the High Court given in the exercise of his original or appellate jurisdiction to the Court of Appeal. 5

(2) An order under section 45(3) above may make provision as to the circumstances in which appeals may be made against decisions arising in connection with the transfer of proceedings.

(3) No appeal shall lie against a decision to decline jurisdiction as mentioned in section 45(3) above. 10

Supplementary powers and effect of orders etc.

**50.**—(1) In relation to the attendance of witnesses, the production and inspection of documents, the enforcement of its orders and directions and all other matters incidental to its jurisdiction the Court of Protection shall have the like powers, rights, privileges and authority as the High Court. 15

1925 c.20

(2) Section 204 of the Law of Property Act 1925 (orders of High Court conclusive in favour of purchasers) shall apply in relation to orders and directions of the Court of Protection as it applies to orders of the High Court.

(3) Office copies of orders made, directions given or other instruments issued by the Court of Protection and sealed with its official seal shall be 20 admissible in all legal proceedings as evidence of the originals without any further proof.

Rules.

**51.**—(1) The Lord Chancellor may make rules with respect to the conduct of proceedings under this Act; and rules under section 144 of the 25

1980 c.43

Magistrates' Courts Act 1980 shall not apply to such proceedings in a magistrates' court.

(2) Rules under this section may in particular make provision—

>   (a) as to the manner and form in which proceedings are to be commenced; 30

>   (b) as to the persons entitled to be notified of, and to attend and take part in, the proceedings;

>   (c) for enabling the person to whom the proceedings relate to conduct his case without a next friend or guardian ad litem;

>   (d) for enabling an application to the court to be disposed of without a 35 hearing;

>   (e) for enabling the court to proceed with, or with any part of, a hearing in the absence of the person to whom the proceedings relate;

>   (f) for enabling the court to appoint the Official Solicitor (with his 40 consent) or a solicitor in private practice who is willing to act to represent the person to whom the proceedings relate if he is not legally represented and the court considers that it is desirable that he should be;

>   (g) for enabling or requiring the proceedings or any part of them to 45 be conducted in private and for enabling the court to determine

who is to be admitted when the court sits in private and to exclude specified persons when it sits in public;

(h) as to what may be received as evidence (whether or not admissible apart from the rules) and the manner in which it is to be presented;

(i) for the enforcement of orders made and directions given in the proceedings.

(3) The rules may contain such incidental and supplementary provisions as the Lord Chancellor thinks necessary or expedient for the purposes of the rules.

**52.**—(1) The court considering any question in proceedings under Part I of this Act may—

(a) ask a probation officer; or

(b) ask a local authority to arrange for—

(i) an officer of the authority; or

(ii) such other person (not being a probation officer) as it considers appropriate,

to report to the court on such matters as the court directs relating to the person to whom the proceedings relate.

(2) Where the person to whom proceedings under Part I of this Act relate is not present or represented before the court it shall, unless it considers it unnecessary to do so, exercise its power under subsection (1) above to obtain a report as to that person's wishes so far as relevant to the proceedings.

(3) A report under this section may be made in writing or orally as the court may require.

(4) It shall be the duty of any person requested by a court to produce a report under this section to comply with the request.

*Reports for assistance of the court.*

**53.**—(1) There shall continue to be panels of Lord Chancellor's Visitors constituted in accordance with Schedule 6 to this Act.

(2) The court may direct a Visitor to visit a person in respect of whom proceedings under Part I of this Act are before the court and to make to the court such report on the visit as the court may require.

(3) A Visitor making a visit under this section may interview the person concerned in private.

(4) A visit shall be made by a General Visitor unless the court directs that it is to be made by a Medical or Legal Visitor.

(5) A Medical Visitor making a visit under this section shall, if the court so directs, carry out in private a medical examination of the person concerned and may require the production of, and inspect, any medical records relating to that person.

*Lord Chancellor's Visitors.*

**54.**—(1) No person shall publish any material which is intended or likely to identify any person in respect of whom proceedings are brought under this Act.

*Restriction on publicity for proceedings.*

PART III

(2) In any proceedings for an offence under this section it is a defence for the accused to prove that he did not know, and had no reason to suspect, that the published material was intended or likely to identify the person concerned.

(3) In this section "publish" includes broadcast by radio, television or 5 cable television and cause to be published and "material" includes any picture or representation.

(4) A person who contravenes this section is guilty of an offence and liable on summary conviction to a fine not exceeding level 4 on the standard scale. 10

## PART IV

### GENERAL

Interpretation.

**55.** In this Act—

"advance refusal of treatment" has the meaning given in section 9 above; 15

"continuing power of attorney" has the meaning given in section 12 above;

"the court" has the meaning given in section 45 above;

"local authority" means the council of a county, a metropolitan district or a London borough or the Common Council of the 20 City of London;

"manager" means a person appointed as such under section 24(1)(b) above;

"mental disability" has the meaning given in section 2(2) above;

"person without capacity" shall be construed in accordance with 25 section 2 above;

"property" includes any thing in action and any interest in real or personal property;

1925 c.19

"trust corporation" has the same meaning as in the Trustee Act 1925;

"will" includes codicil. 30

Expenses.

**56.** There shall be paid out of money provided by Parliament—

(a) any expenses of the Lord Chancellor or the Secretary of State under this Act; and

(b) any increase attributable to this Act in the sums so payable under any other Act. 35

Transitional provisions and savings.

**57.** The transitional provisions and savings in Schedule 7 to this Act shall have effect in relation to the provisions superseded by this Act.

Amendments and repeals.

**58.**—(1) The enactments mentioned in Schedule 8 to this Act shall be amended in accordance with that Schedule, being amendments consequential on the provisions of this Act. 40

(2) In Schedule 1 to the Local Authority Social Services Act 1970 there shall be inserted at the end—

> "Mental Incapacity Act 1995 (c.00)
>
> 5  Part II                 Protection    of    vulnerable persons.
>
>    Section 52              Reports in proceedings."

(3) The enactments mentioned in Schedule 9 to this Act are repealed to the extent specified in the third column of that Schedule, being repeals
10 consequential on the provisions of this Act.

**59.**—(1) This Act shall come into force on such day as the Secretary of State may appoint by an order made by statutory instrument; and different days may be appointed for different provisions.

Commencement.

(2) Any reference in any provision to the coming into force of this Act is
15 a reference to the coming into force of that provision.

**60.**—(1) This Act may be cited as the Mental Incapacity Act 1995.

Short title and extent.

(2) Except for section 15(8) and paragraph 11(3) of Schedule 3, which extend to the whole of the United Kingdom, this Act extends to England and Wales only.

# SCHEDULES

Section 4(4).

## SCHEDULE 1

PAYMENTS DUE TO PERSONS WITHOUT CAPACITY

### PART I

PAYMENT TO RECIPIENT ACTING FOR PERSON WITHOUT CAPACITY          5

*Payments to which this Part of this Schedule applies*

1. This Part of this Schedule applies to—

(a) payments to a customer by an institution authorised by the Bank of
England under Part I of the Banking Act 1987;

1987 c.22

(b) payments to a member or depositor by a building society within the 10
meaning of the Building Societies Act 1986;

1986 c.53

(c) payments to a policyholder by a body authorised under section 3 or 4 of the
Insurance Companies Act 1982 to carry on insurance business;

1982 c.50

(d) payments by a company of dividends or interest on shares in or
securities of the company;                                       15

(e) payments to or in respect of a member by a trade union as defined in
section 1 of the Trade Union and Labour Relations (Consolidation)
Act 1992;

1992 c.52

(f) payments of such other descriptions (not falling within Part II of this
Schedule) as may be specified for the purposes of this Part of this 20
Schedule by an order made by the Secretary of State.

*Payment agreements*

2.—(1) A body by which payments to which this Part of this Schedule
applies fall to be made may, in accordance with the requirements of this Part of this
Schedule, enter into an agreement under which the payments (or any 25
description of those payments) are to be made to the person with whom the
agreement is made ("the recipient") instead of to the person who would
otherwise be entitled to receive them.

(2) A body making a payment pursuant to an agreement in respect of which
those requirements are complied with shall not by making it incur any liability to 30
the person who would otherwise be entitled to receive it unless that body has
reasonable cause to believe that the recipient is likely to apply the money he
receives otherwise than in that person's best interests or that person has
informed the body that the payment is not to be made.

*Requirements for entering into agreement*                      35

3.—(1) A body shall not enter into an agreement under this Part of this
Schedule in respect of any payments if the person who would, apart from this Part of
this Schedule, be entitled to receive them has informed that body that he does not
wish such an agreement to be made.

(2) A body shall not enter into an agreement under this Part of this Schedule in 40
respect of any payments to which a person would, apart from this Part of this
Schedule, be entitled unless the proposed recipient has furnished that body
with—

(a) a certificate signed by a registered medical practitioner stating that the
person concerned is without capacity to manage his financial affairs; 45
and

(b) a statement in writing by the proposed recipient to the effect—

(i) that he understands his duty to apply the money he receives in the best interests of the person who would otherwise be entitled to it;

(ii) that he is aware that he may incur civil or criminal liability if he misapplies the money; and

(iii) that, so far as he is aware, no other person has authority to receive the money by virtue of a power of attorney or an order or appointment made by the court.

(3) If the proposed recipient is unable to comply with sub-paragraph (2)(b)(iii) above he shall instead supply with his statement the written consent to his being the recipient of the other person concerned.

### Requirements as to contents of agreement

4.—(1) An agreement under this Part of this Schedule may specify the payments to which it applies and must specify—

(a) the period for which it is to remain in force; and

(b) the amount or maximum amount of the payments that are to be made under it, either as a single amount or as separate amounts for different periods or payments of different descriptions.

(2) No agreement shall remain in force for more than two years but without prejudice to the making of a new agreement in accordance with paragraph 3 above.

(3) The aggregate of the payments to be made under an agreement shall not exceed £2000 in any year but where the agreement applies to payments of different descriptions (such as payments referable to different accounts or to different shares or securities) that maximum shall apply separately to payments of each description.

### Payments direct to provider of accommodation, goods or services

5.—(1) An agreement under this Part of this Schedule may enable the recipient to make arrangements with the body concerned whereby payments under the agreement are to be made by it direct to persons other than the recipient in consideration of their providing the person for whom the recipient acts with accommodation, goods or services.

(2) Paragraph 2(2) above shall have effect as if the reference to the recipient included a reference to any person receiving money pursuant to such arrangements; and the maximum referred to in paragraph 4(3) above shall not apply to payments made pursuant to such arrangements.

### Power to alter prescribed maxima

6. The Secretary of State may by order alter the maximum duration and maximum amount for the time being specified in paragraph 4(2) and (3) above.

### Orders

7. The power to make orders under paragraph 1(f) or 6 above shall be exercisable by statutory instrument subject to annulment in pursuance of a resolution of either House of Parliament.

## PART II

PAYMENT OF PUBLIC SERVICE PAY AND PENSIONS

*Payments to which this Part of this Schedule applies*

8. This Part of this Schedule applies to any periodic payment which falls to be made to a person by way of pay or pension or otherwise in connection with the    5
service or employment of that or any other person if the payment falls to be made directly—

    (a) out of money provided by Parliament or the Consolidated Fund; or

    (b) out of other money administered by or under the control or supervision of a government department other than a department of the government of   10 Northern Ireland.

*Application of sums*

9. The authority by which the sum in question is payable may apply it in accordance with paragraph 10 below if satisfied, after considering medical evidence, that the person to whom it is payable ("the person entitled") is   15
without capacity to manage his financial affairs.

10. The authority may pay the sum, or such part of it as it thinks fit, to the institution or person having the care of the person entitled, to be applied for his benefit, and may pay the remainder (if any), or such part of the remainder as it thinks fit—                                                                        20

    (a) to or for the benefit of persons who appear to the authority to be members of the family of the person entitled or other persons for whom he might be expected to provide if he were not without capacity; or

    (b) in reimbursement, with or without interest, of money applied by any   25 person either in payment of the debts (whether legally enforceable or not) of the person entitled or for the maintenance or other benefit of that person or of such persons as are mentioned in (a) above.

## SCHEDULE 2

THE MENTAL INCAPACITY RESEARCH COMMITTEE                                  30

*Composition*

1.—(1) The committee shall consist of a chairman, a deputy chairman and such number of other members not exceeding twelve as the Secretary of State may determine.

(2) Neither the chairman nor the deputy chairman shall be a person who is or has   35 been—

    (a) concerned in the carrying out of research involving persons affected by mental disability; or

    (b) directly concerned with commissioning or funding such research.

*Remuneration and expenses*                                                 40

2. The Secretary of State may, with the approval of the Treasury, pay—

    (a) to members of the committee such sums in respect of expenses incurred by them in the performance of their duties; and

    (b) to the chairman and deputy chairman such remuneration,

as the Secretary of State may determine.                                     45

*Applications for approval*

3. A person applying for the committee's approval for any proposed research shall pay to the committee such fees as may be prescribed by regulations made by the Secretary of State.

*Register of research proposals*

4.—(1) The committee shall maintain a register of the proposals submitted to the committee with an indication of whether or not they have been approved.

(2) Information contained in the register shall be available for inspection in accordance with regulations made by the Secretary of State.

*Procedure*

5.—(1) The committee shall determine its own procedure and may make provision for the discharge of any of its functions by designated members of the committee.

(2) The committee may act notwithstanding a vacancy among its members.

*Annual report*

6. The committee shall in each year make a report to the Secretary of State on its activities and the Secretary of State shall lay copies of the report before each House of Parliament.

*Regulations*

7. The power to make regulations under paragraph 3 or 4(2) above shall be exercisable by statutory instrument subject to annulment in pursuance of a resolution of either House of Parliament.

## SCHEDULE 3

### ENDURING POWERS OF ATTORNEY

Section 21(2), (3).

### PART I

#### CONVERSION OF ENDURING INTO CONTINUING POWER OF ATTORNEY

1. A declaration for the purposes of section 21(2)(a) of this Act must be—
   (a) in the prescribed form;
   (b) executed in the prescribed manner;
   (c) include at the time of execution the prescribed explanatory information.

2. In this Part of this Schedule "prescribed" means prescribed by regulations made by the Lord Chancellor by statutory instrument subject to annulment in pursuance of a resolution of either House of Parliament.

3. The regulations made by him shall contain such provision as appears to him appropriate for securing—
   (a) that no instrument is used as a declaration for the purposes mentioned in paragraph 1 above which does not include the prescribed information explaining the general effect of converting an enduring into a continuing power of attorney;
   (b) that any instrument used as such a declaration includes the statements mentioned in paragraphs 4 and 5 below.

4. The attorney (or, if more than one, each of them) must state—
   (a) that he has no reason to believe that the donor is or is becoming incapable by reason of mental disorder of managing and administering his property and affairs;

    (b) that he understands that he will have no authority to act under the power until the instrument creating it is registered in accordance with section 15 of this Act;

    (c) that he understands that he will be subject to the duty in section 3 of this Act as respects any decision made by him under the power which the donor is, or is reasonably believed by him to be, without capacity to make.

5. The donor must state—

    (a) that he understands that the attorney will be under no duty to register the instrument creating the power;

    (b) that he understands that no relatives of the donor will be notified before registration;

    (c) that he understands that, unless he otherwise provides, the court will have power—

        (i) to appoint a person as donee of the power of attorney in substitution for or in addition to the attorney mentioned in the instrument; and

        (ii) to modify or extend the scope of the donee's power to act in relation to any of the matters to which the power of attorney could extend,

    in any case in which the court thinks it desirable to do so and the donor is without capacity to act in the matter;

    (d) that he has read (or had read to him) the information referred to in paragraph 3(a) above.

## PART II

### PROVISIONS APPLYING TO EXISTING UNCONVERTED ENDURING POWERS OF ATTORNEY

*Enduring power of attorney to survive mental incapacity of donor*

6.—(1) Where an individual has created a power of attorney which is an enduring power within the meaning of this Schedule then—

    (a) the power shall not be revoked by any subsequent mental incapacity of his; but

    (b) upon such incapacity supervening the donee of the power may not do anything under the authority of the power except as provided by sub-paragraph (2) below unless or, as the case may be, until the instrument creating the power is registered under paragraph 10 below; and

    (c) section 5 of the Powers of Attorney Act 1971 (protection of donee and third persons) so far as applicable shall apply if and so long as paragraph (b) above operates to suspend the donee's authority to act under the power as if the power had been revoked by the donor's mental incapacity.

(2) Notwithstanding sub-paragraph (1)(b) above, where the attorney has made an application for registration of the instrument then, until it is registered, the attorney may take action under the power—

    (a) to maintain the donor or prevent loss to his estate; or

    (b) to maintain himself or other persons in so far as paragraph 8(3) below permits him to do so.

(3) Where the attorney purports to act as provided by sub-paragraph (2) above then, in favour of a person who deals with him without knowledge that the attorney is acting otherwise than in accordance with sub-paragraph (a) or (b) of

that paragraph, the transaction between them shall be as valid as if the attorney were acting in accordance with sub-paragraph (a) or (b).

### Characteristics of an enduring power of attorney

7.—(1) Subject to sub-paragraphs (5) and (6) below and paragraph 16, a power of attorney is an enduring power within the meaning of this Schedule if the instrument which creates the power—

(a) is in the prescribed form; and

(b) was executed in the prescribed manner by the donor and the attorney; and

(c) incorporated at the time of execution by the donor the prescribed explanatory information.

(2) In this paragraph "prescribed" means prescribed by whichever of the following regulations applied when the instrument was executed—

(a) the Enduring Powers of Attorney (Prescribed Form) Regulations 1986;   S.I.1986/126

(b) the Enduring Powers of Attorney (Prescribed Form) Regulations 1987;   S.I.1987/1612

(c) the Enduring Powers of Attorney (Prescribed Form) Regulations 1990.   S.I.1990/1376

(3) An instrument in the prescribed form purporting to have been executed in the prescribed manner shall be taken, in the absence of evidence to the contrary, to be a document which incorporated at the time of execution by the donor the prescribed explanatory information.

(4) Where an instrument differs in an immaterial respect in form or mode of expression from the prescribed form the instrument shall be treated as sufficient in point of form and expression.

(5) A power of attorney cannot be an enduring power unless, when he executes the instrument creating it, the attorney is—

(a) an individual who has attained eighteen years and is not bankrupt; or

(b) a trust corporation.

(6) A power of attorney which gives the attorney a right to appoint a substitute or successor cannot be an enduring power.

(7) An enduring power shall be revoked by the bankruptcy of the attorney whatever the circumstances of the bankruptcy.

(8) No disclaimer of an enduring power, whether by deed or otherwise, shall be valid unless and until the attorney gives notice of it to the donor or, where paragraph 9(6) or 11(1) below applies, to the registration authority.

### Scope of authority etc. of attorney under enduring power

8.—(1) An enduring power may confer general authority (as defined in sub-paragraph (2) below) on the attorney to act on the donor's behalf in relation to all or a specified part of the property and affairs of the donor or may confer on him authority to do specified things on the donor's behalf and the authority may, in either case, be conferred subject to conditions and restrictions.

(2) Where an instrument is expressed to confer general authority on the attorney it operates to confer, subject to the restriction imposed by sub-paragraph (4) below and to any conditions or restrictions contained in the instrument, authority to do on behalf of the donor anything which the donor can lawfully do by an attorney.

(3) Subject to any conditions or restrictions contained in the instrument, an attorney under an enduring power, whether general or limited, may (without obtaining any consent) act under the power so as to benefit himself or other persons than the donor to the following extent but no further, that is to say—

(a) he may so act in relation to himself or in relation to any other person if the donor might be expected to provide for his or that person's needs respectively; and

SCH. 3          (b) he may do whatever the donor might be expected to do to meet those
                    needs.

(4) Without prejudice to sub-paragraph (3) above but subject to any
conditions or restrictions contained in the instrument, an attorney under an
enduring power, whether general or limited, may (without obtaining any  5
consent) dispose of the property of the donor by way of gift to the following
extent but no further, that is to say—

    (a) he may make gifts of a seasonal nature or at a time, or on an
        anniversary, of a birth or marriage, to persons (including himself)
        who are related to or connected with the donor, and          10

    (b) he may make gifts to any charity to whom the donor made or might be
        expected to make gifts,

provided that the value of each such gift is not unreasonable having regard to all the
circumstances and in particular the size of the donor's estate.

### *Duties of attorney in event of actual or impending incapacity of donor*          15

9.—(1) If the attorney under an enduring power has reason to believe that the
donor is or is becoming mentally incapable sub-paragraphs (2) to (6) below
shall apply.

(2) The attorney shall, as soon as practicable, make an application to the
registration authority for the registration of the instrument creating the power.          20

(3) Before making an application for registration the attorney shall comply
with the provisions as to notice set out in Part III of this Schedule.

(4) An application for registration shall be made in the prescribed form and
shall contain such statements as may be prescribed.

(5) The attorney may, before making an application for the registration of the          25
instrument, refer to the court for its determination any question as to the
validity of the power and he shall comply with any direction given to him by the
court on that determination.

(6) No disclaimer of the power shall be valid unless and until the attorney
gives notice of it to the registration authority and the authority shall notify the          30
donor if it receives a notice under this sub-paragraph.

(7) Any person who, in an application for registration, makes a statement
which he knows to be false in a material particular shall be liable—

    (a) on summary conviction, to imprisonment for a term not exceeding six
        months or a fine not exceeding the statutory maximum or both;          35

    (b) on conviction on indictment, to imprisonment for a term not exceeding
        two years or a fine, or both.

(8) In this paragraph "prescribed" means prescribed by rules under section 51 of
this Act.

### *Registration of instrument creating power*          40

10.—(1) In any case where an application is made in accordance with
paragraph 9(3) and (4) above the registration authority shall, subject to the
provisions of this paragraph, register the instrument to which the application
relates.

(2) The court may, on the application of the attorney, direct the registration          45
authority to register an instrument notwithstanding that notice has not been
given as required by paragraph 9(3) above and Part III of this Schedule to a
person entitled to receive it if the court is satisfied—

    (a) that it was undesirable or impracticable for the attorney to give notice to
        that person; or          50

(b) that no useful purpose is likely to be served by giving him notice.

(3) Any person entitled by virtue of paragraph 17 below to receive notice of an application for the registration of an instrument may, by notice in writing before the expiry of the period of four weeks beginning with the day on which the
5  notice under Part III of this Schedule was given to him, object to the registration by applying to the court for an order directing the registration authority not to register the application.

(4) If, in the case of an application for registration, a valid notice of objection to the registration of the instrument to which the application relates is
10  received by the court before the expiry of the period of five weeks beginning with the date or, as the case may be, latest date on which the attorney gave notice to any person under Part III of this Schedule, the court shall inform the authority of that fact and the authority shall not register the instrument except in accordance with the court's directions.

15  (5) Any objection under sub-paragraph (3) above is valid if made on one or more of the following grounds—
  (a) that the power purported to have been created by the instrument was not valid as an enduring power of attorney;
  (b) that the power created by the instrument no longer subsists;
20  (c) that the application is premature because the donor is not yet becoming mentally incapable;
  (d) that fraud or undue pressure was used to induce the donor to create the power;
  (e) that, having regard to all the circumstances and in particular the
25  attorney's relationship to or connection with the donor, the attorney is unsuitable to be the donor's attorney.

(6) If any of those grounds is established to the satisfaction of the court it shall direct the registration authority not to register the instrument, but if not so satisfied it shall direct its registration.

30  (7) Where the court directs the authority not to register an instrument because it is satisfied that the ground in sub-paragraph (5)(d) or (e) is established it shall by order revoke the power created by the instrument.

(8) Where the court directs the authority not to register an instrument because it is satisfied that any ground in sub-paragraph (5) except that in (c) is
35  established the instrument shall be delivered up to be cancelled unless the court otherwise directs.

*Effect and proof of registration*

11.—(1) The effect of the registration of an instrument under paragraph 10 above is that—
40  (a) no revocation of the power by the donor is valid unless and until the court confirms the revocation under paragraph 12(3) below;
  (b) no disclaimer of the power is valid unless and until the attorney gives notice of it to the registration authority;
  (c) the donor may not extend or restrict the scope of the authority
45  conferred by the instrument and no instruction or consent given by him after registration shall, in the case of a consent, confer any right and, in the case of an instruction, impose or confer any obligation or right on or create any liability of the attorney or other persons having notice of the instruction or consent.

50  (2) Sub-paragraph (1) above applies for so long as the instrument is registered under paragraph 10 above whether or not the donor is for the time being mentally incapable.

(3) A document purporting to be an office copy of an instrument registered under this Schedule shall, in any part of the United Kingdom, be evidence of the contents of the instrument and of the fact that it has been so registered.

(4) Sub-paragraph (3) above is without prejudice to section 3 of the Powers of Attorney Act 1971 (proof by certified copies) and to any other method of proof    5
authorised by law.

*Functions of court with regard to registered power*

12.—(1) Where an instrument has been registered under paragraph 10 above, the court shall have the following functions with respect to the power and the donor of and the attorney appointed to act under the power.                          10

(2) The court may—

(a) determine any question as to the meaning or effect of the instrument;

(b) give directions with respect to—

   (i) the management or disposal by the attorney of the property and affairs of the donor;                                                            15

   (ii) the rendering of accounts by the attorney and the production of the records kept by him for the purpose;

   (iii) the remuneration or expenses of the attorney whether or not in default of or in accordance with any provision made by the instrument, including directions for the repayment of excessive or   20 the payment of additional remuneration;

(c) require the attorney to furnish information or produce documents or things in his possession as attorney;

(d) give any consent or authorisation to act which the attorney would have to obtain from a mentally capable donor;                                        25

(e) authorise the attorney to act so as to benefit himself or other persons than the donor otherwise than in accordance with paragraph 8(3) and (4) above (but subject to any conditions or restrictions contained in the instrument);

(f) relieve the attorney wholly or partly from any liability which he has or   30 may have incurred on account of a breach of his duties as attorney.

(3) On application made for the purpose by or on behalf of the donor, the court shall confirm the revocation of the power if satisfied that the donor has done whatever is necessary in law to effect an express revocation of the power and was mentally capable of revoking a power of attorney when he did so (whether or   35 not he is so when the court considers the application).

(4) The court shall direct the registration authority to cancel the registration of an instrument registered under paragraph 10 above in any of the following circumstances, that is to say—

(a) on confirming the revocation of the power under sub-paragraph (3)   40 above;

(b) on being satisfied that the donor is and is likely to remain mentally capable;

(c) on being satisfied that the power has expired or has been revoked by the mental incapacity of the attorney;                                             45

(d) on being satisfied that the power was not a valid and subsisting enduring power when registration was effected;

(e) on being satisfied that fraud or undue pressure was used to induce the donor to create the power; or

(f) on being satisfied that, having regard to all the circumstances and in   50 particular the attorney's relationship to or connection with the donor, the attorney is unsuitable to be the donor's attorney.

(5) Where the court directs the registration authority to cancel the registration of an instrument on being satisfied of the matters specified in paragraph (e) or (f) of sub-paragraph (4) above it shall by order revoke the power created by the instrument.

5    (6) Where the court directs the cancellation of the registration of an instrument under sub-paragraph (4) above except paragraph (b) the instrument shall be delivered up to the registration authority to be cancelled, unless the court otherwise directs.

### *Cancellation of registration by registration authority*

10    13. The registration authority shall cancel the registration of an instrument creating an enduring power of attorney—

    (a)  on receipt of a disclaimer signed by the attorney;

    (b)  if satisfied that the power has been revoked by the death or bankruptcy of the donor or attorney or, if the attorney is a body corporate, by its

15        winding up or dissolution;

    (c)  on receipt of notification from the court that the court has revoked the power;

    (d)  on confirmation from the court that the donor has revoked the power.

### *Protection of attorney and third persons where power is invalid or revoked*

20    14.—(1) Sub-paragraphs (2) and (3) below apply where an instrument which did not create a valid power of attorney has been registered under paragraph 10 above (whether or not the registration has been cancelled at the time of the act or transaction in question).

(2) An attorney who acts in pursuance of the power shall not incur any
25    liability (either to the donor or to any other person) by reason of the non-existence of the power unless at the time of acting he knows—

    (a)  that the instrument did not create a valid enduring power; or

    (b)  that an event has occurred which, if the instrument had created a valid enduring power, would have had the effect of revoking the power; or

30        (c)  that, if the instrument had created a valid enduring power, the power would have expired before that time.

(3) Any transaction between the attorney and another person shall, in favour of that person, be as valid as if the power had then been in existence, unless at the time of the transaction that person has knowledge of any of the matters mentioned in
35    sub-paragraph (2) above.

(4) Where the interest of a purchaser depends on whether a transaction between the attorney and another person was valid by virtue of sub-paragraph (3) above, it shall be conclusively presumed in favour of the purchaser that the transaction was valid if—

40        (a)  the transaction between that person and the attorney was completed within twelve months of the date on which the instrument was registered; or

    (b)  that person makes a statutory declaration, before or within three months after the completion of the purchase, that he had no reason at the
45        time of the transaction to doubt that the attorney had authority to dispose of the property which was the subject of the transaction.

(5) For the purposes of section 5 of the Powers of Attorney Act 1971 (protection of attorney and third persons where action is taken under the power of attorney in ignorance of its having been revoked) in its application to an
50    enduring power the revocation of which by the donor is by virtue of paragraph 11 above invalid unless and until confirmed by the court under paragraph 12

*Mental Incapacity*

above, knowledge of the confirmation of the revocation is, but knowledge of the unconfirmed revocation is not, knowledge of the revocation of the power.

(6) In this section "purchaser" and "purchase" have the meanings specified in section 205(1) of the Law of Property Act 1925.

15.—(1) Where—

    (a) an instrument framed in a form prescribed as mentioned in paragraph 7(2) above creates a power which is not a valid enduring power; and

    (b) the power is revoked by the mental incapacity of the donor,

sub-paragraphs (2) and (3) below shall apply, whether or not the instrument has been registered.

(2) An attorney who acts in pursuance of the power shall not, by reason of the revocation, incur any liability (either to the donor or to any other person) unless at the time of acting he knows—

    (a) that the instrument did not create a valid enduring power, and

    (b) that the donor has become mentally incapable.

(3) Any transaction between the attorney and another person shall, in favour of that person, be as valid as if the power had then been in existence, unless at the time of the transaction that person knows—

    (a) that the instrument did not create a valid enduring power; and

    (b) that the donor has become mentally incapable.

(4) Paragraph 14(4) above shall apply for the purpose of determining whether a transaction was valid by virtue of sub-paragraph (3) above as it applies for the purpose or determining whether a transaction was valid by virtue of paragraph 14(3).

*Joint and several attorneys*

16.—(1) An instrument which appoints more than one person to be an attorney cannot create an enduring power unless the attorneys are appointed to act jointly or jointly and severally.

(2) This Part of this Schedule, in its application to joint attorneys, applies to them collectively as it applies to a single attorney but subject to the modifications specified in paragraph 25 below.

(3) This Part of this Schedule, in its application to joint and several attorneys, applies with the modifications specified in sub-paragraphs (4) to (7) below and in paragraph 26 below.

(4) A failure, as respects any one attorney, to comply with the requirements for the creation of enduring powers, shall prevent the instrument from creating such a power in his case without however affecting its efficacy for that purpose as respects the other or others or its efficacy in his case for the purpose of creating a power of attorney which is not an enduring power.

(5) Where one or more but not both or all the attorneys makes or joins in making an application for registration of the instrument then—

    (a) an attorney who is not an applicant as well as one who is may act pending the registration of the instrument as provided in paragraph 6(2) above;

    (b) notice of the application shall also be given under Part III of this Schedule to the other attorney or attorneys; and

    (c) objection may validly be taken to the registration on a ground relating to an attorney or to the power of an attorney who is not an applicant as well as to one or the power of one who is an applicant.

(6) The registration authority shall not be precluded by sub-paragraph (4) of paragraph 10 above from registering an instrument and the court shall not direct it not to do so under sub-paragraph (6) of that paragraph if an enduring power subsists as respects some attorney who is not affected by the ground or grounds of the objection in question.

(7) Sub-paragraph (6) above shall not preclude the court from revoking a power in so far as it confers a power on any other attorney in respect of whom the ground in paragraph 10(5)(d) or (e) is established; and where any ground in paragraph 10(5) affecting any other attorney is established the court shall direct the registration authority to make against the registration an entry in such form as may be prescribed by rules under section 51 of this Act.

(8) In sub-paragraph (4) above "the requirements for the creation of enduring powers" means the provisions of paragraph 7 above other than sub-paragraphs (7) and (8) and of the regulations mentioned in that paragraph.

## Part III

### Notification prior to registration

#### *Duty to give notice to relatives*

17. Subject to paragraph 19 below, before making an application for registration the attorney shall give notice of his intention to do so to all those persons (if any) who are entitled to receive notice by virtue of paragraph 18 below.

18.—(1) Subject to the limitations contained in sub-paragraphs (2) to (4) below, persons of the following classes (referred to in this Part of this Schedule as "relatives") are entitled to receive notice under paragraph 17 above—

    (a) the donor's husband or wife;

    (b) the donor's children;

    (c) the donor's parents;

    (d) the donor's brothers and sisters, whether of the whole or half blood;

    (e) the widow or widower of a child of the donor;

    (f) the donor's grandchildren;

    (g) the children of the donor's brothers and sisters of the whole blood;

    (h) the children of the donor's brothers and sisters of the half blood;

    (i) the donor's uncles and aunts of the whole blood; and

    (j) the children of the donor's uncles and aunts of the whole blood.

(2) A person is not entitled to receive notice under paragraph 17 above if—

    (a) his name or address is not known to the attorney and cannot be reasonably ascertained by him; or

    (b) the attorney has reason to believe that he has not attained eighteen years or is mentally incapable.

(3) Except where sub-paragraph (4) below applies, no more than three persons are entitled to receive notice under paragraph 17 above and, in determining the persons who are so entitled, persons falling within class (a) of sub-paragraph (1) above are to be preferred to persons falling within class (b) of that sub-paragraph, persons falling within class (b) are to be preferred to persons falling within class (c) of that sub-paragraph; and so on.

(4) Notwithstanding the limit of three specified in sub-paragraph (3) above, where—

    (a) there is more than one person falling within any of classes (a) to (j) of sub-paragraph (1) above, and

(b) at least one of those persons would be entitled to receive notice under paragraph 17 above,

then, subject to sub-paragraph (2) above, all the persons falling within that class are entitled to receive notice under paragraph 17 above.

19.—(1) An attorney shall not be required to give notice under paragraph 17 5 above to himself or to any other attorney under the power who is joining in making the application, notwithstanding that he or, as the case may be, the other attorney is entitled to receive notice by virtue of paragraph 18 above.

(2) In the case of any person who is entitled to receive notice under paragraph 17 above, the attorney, before applying for registration, may make an 10 application to the court to be dispensed from the requirement to give him notice; and the court shall grant the application if it is satisfied—

(a) that it would be undesirable or impracticable for the attorney to give him notice; or

(b) that no useful purpose is likely to be served by giving him notice.　　15

### Duty to give notice to donor

20.—(1) Subject to sub-paragraph (2) below, before making an application for registration the attorney shall give notice of his intention to do so to the donor.

(2) Paragraph 19 (2) above shall apply in relation to the donor as it applies in 20 relation to a person who is entitled to receive notice under paragraph 17 above.

### Contents of notices

21. A notice to relatives under this Part of this Schedule—

(a) shall be in the prescribed form;

(b) shall state that the attorney proposes to make an application to the 25 registration authority for the registration of the instrument creating the enduring power in question;

(c) shall inform the person to whom it is given of his right to object to the registration under paragraph 10(3) above.

22. A notice to the donor under this Schedule—　　　　　　　　　　　　30

(a) shall be in the prescribed form;

(b) shall contain the statement mentioned in paragraph 21(b) above; and

(c) shall inform the donor that, whilst the instrument remains registered, any revocation of the power by him will be ineffective unless and until the revocation is confirmed by the court.　　　　　　　　35

### Duty to give notice to other attorneys

23.—(1) Subject to sub-paragraph (2) below, before making an application for registration an attorney under a joint and several power shall give notice of his intention to do so to any other attorney under the power who is not joining in making the application; and paragraphs 19(2) and 21 above shall apply in 40 relation to attorneys entitled to receive notice by virtue of this paragraph as they apply in relation to persons entitled to receive notice by virtue of paragraph 18 above.

(2) An attorney is not entitled to receive notice by virtue of this paragraph if—　　　　　　　　　　　　　　　　　　　　　　　　　45

(a) his address is not known to the applying attorney and cannot reasonably be ascertained by him; or

(b) the applying attorney has reason to believe that he has not attained eighteen years or is mentally incapable.

*Supplementary*

24.—(1) For the purposes of this Part of this Schedule an illegitimate child shall be treated as if he were the legitimate child of his mother and father.

(2) Notwithstanding anything in section 7 of the Interpretation Act 1978   1978 c.30
(construction of references to service by post), for the purposes of this Part of this Schedule a notice given by post shall be regarded as given on the date on which it was posted.

(3) In this Part of this Schedule "prescribed" means prescribed by rules under section 51 of this Act.

## PART IV

### JOINT AND SEVERAL ATTORNEYS

#### *Joint attorneys*

25.—(1) In paragraph 7(5) above, the reference to the time when the attorney executes the instrument shall be read as a reference to the time when the second or last attorney executes the instrument.

(2) In paragraph 7(6) and (7) above, the reference to the attorney shall be read as a reference to any attorney under the power.

(3) Paragraph 10 above shall have effect as if the ground of objection to the registration of the instrument specified in sub-paragraph (5)(e) applied to any attorney under the power.

(4) In paragraph 12(2) above, references to the attorney shall be read as including references to any attorney under the power.

(5) In paragraph 12(4) above, references to the attorney shall be read as including references to any attorney under the power.

#### *Joint and several attorneys*

26.—(1) In paragraph 7(7) above, the reference to the bankruptcy of the attorney shall be construed as a reference to the bankruptcy of the last remaining attorney under the power; and the bankruptcy of any other attorney under the power shall cause that person to cease to be attorney, whatever the circumstances of the bankruptcy.

(2) The restriction upon disclaimer imposed by paragraph 9(6) above applies only to those attorneys who have reason to believe that the donor is or is becoming mentally incapable.

## PART V

### INTERPRETATION

27.—(1) In this Schedule—

"the court" means the Court of Protection;

"enduring power" is to be construed in accordance with paragraph 7 above;

"mentally incapable" or "mental incapacity", except where it refers to revocation at common law, means in relation to any person, that he is incapable by reason of mental disorder of managing and administering his property and affairs and "mentally capable" and "mental capacity" shall be construed accordingly;

"mental disorder" has the same meaning as it has in the Mental Health Act   1983 c.20
1983;

"notice" means notice in writing;

"registration authority" means the authority appointed under section 15 of this Act;

"trust corporation" has the same meaning as in the Trustee Act 1925.

(2) Any question arising under or for the purposes of this Schedule as to     5
what the donor of the power might at any time be expected to do shall be
determined by assuming that he had full mental capacity at the time but
otherwise by reference to the circumstances existing at that time.

## SCHEDULE 4

PROPERTY AND AFFAIRS: SUPPLEMENTARY PROVISIONS                10

### *Wills*

1.—(1) A will made by virtue of section 27 of this Act on behalf of a person
without capacity to make it himself may make any provision, whether by
disposing of property or exercising a power or otherwise, which could be made by a
will executed by him if he had capacity to make it.                          15

(2) No will shall be made by virtue of that section at a time when the person
concerned is a minor.

(3) Where under section 27 of this Act the court makes an order or gives
directions requiring or authorising a person ("the authorised person") to
execute a will for the person concerned, any will executed in pursuance of the   20
order or direction shall be expressed to be signed by the person concerned
acting by the authorised person and shall be—

    (a) signed by the authorised person with the name of the person concerned,
        and with his own name, in the presence of two or more witnesses
        present at the same time; and                                      25

    (b) attested and subscribed by those witnesses in the presence of the
        authorised person.

(4) The Wills Act 1837 shall have effect in relation to any such will as if it
were signed by the person concerned by his own hand except that in relation to any
such will—                                                                   30

    (a) section 9 of that Act (requirements as to signing and attestation) shall not
        apply; and

    (b) in the subsequent provisions of that Act any reference to execution in the
        manner required by the previous provisions shall be construed as a
        reference to execution in the manner required by sub-paragraph (3)   35
        above.

(5) Subject to sub-paragraph (6) below, any such will executed in
accordance with sub-paragraph (3) above, shall have the same effect for all
purposes as if the person concerned were capable of making a valid will and the will
had been executed by him in the manner required by the said Act of 1837.      40

(6) So much of sub-paragraph (5) above as provides for such a will to have
effect as if the person concerned were capable of making a valid will—

    (a) shall not have effect in relation to such a will in so far as it disposes of any
        immovable property other than immovable property in England and
        Wales; and                                                          45

    (b) where at the time when such a will is executed the person concerned is
        domiciled in Scotland or Northern Ireland or in a country of territory
        outside the United Kingdom, shall not have effect in relation to that
        will in so far as it relates to any other property or matter except any
        property or matter in respect of which, under the law of his domicile, any   50
        question of his testamentary capacity would fall to be determined in
        accordance with the law of England and Wales.

*Vesting orders ancillary to settlement etc.*

2. If under section 27 of this Act provision is made for the settlement of any property of the person concerned, or the exercise of a power vested in him of appointing trustees or retiring from a trust, the court may also make as respects the
5 property settled or the trust property such consequential vesting or other orders as the case may require, including (in the case of the exercise of such a power) any order which could have been made in such a case under Part IV of the Trustee Act 1925.

1925 c.19

*Variation of settlements*

10     3. Where the court has under section 27 of this Act ordered a settlement to be made it may by a further order vary or revoke the settlement if—

    (a) the settlement makes provision for its variation or revocation;

    (b) the court is satisfied that a material fact was not disclosed when the settlement was made; or

15     (c) the court is satisfied that there has been any substantial change of circumstances,

and any such further order may give such consequential directions as the court thinks fit.

*Vesting of stock in curator appointed outside England and Wales*

20     4.—(1) Where the court is satisfied—

    (a) that under the law prevailing in a place outside England and Wales a person has been appointed to exercise powers in respect of the property or affairs of any other person on the ground (however formulated) that the other person is without capacity to make
25     decisions with respect to the management and administration of his property and affairs; and

    (b) that, having regard to the nature of the appointment and to the circumstances of the case, it is expedient that the court should exercise its powers under this paragraph,

30 the court may direct any stocks standing in the name of the person without capacity or the right to receive dividends from the stock to be transferred into the name of the person so appointed or otherwise dealt with as required by that person, and may give such directions as the court thinks fit for dealing with accrued dividends from the stock.

35     (2) In this paragraph "stock" includes shares and also any funds, annuity or security transferable in the books kept by any body corporate or unincorporated company or society or by an instrument of transfer either alone or accompanied by other formalities and "dividends" shall be construed accordingly.

*Preservation of interests in property disposed of on behalf of person without*
40     *capacity*

    5.—(1) Where the property of a person ("the person concerned") has been disposed of in the exercise of powers conferred by section 27 of this Act and under his will or intestacy, or by a gift perfected or nomination taking effect on his death, any other person would have taken an interest in the property but for the
45 disposal—

    (a) he shall take the same interest, if and so far as circumstances allow, in any property belonging to the estate of the deceased which represents the property disposed of; and

    (b) if the property disposed of was real property, any property representing it
50     shall so long as it remains part of his estate be treated as if it were real property.

SCH. 4

(2) The court, in ordering or directing under section 27 of this Act any disposal of property which apart from this paragraph would result in the conversion of personal property into real property, may direct that property representing the property disposed of shall, so long as it remains the property of the person concerned or forms part of his estate, be treated as if it were personal 5 property.

(3) References in sub-paragraphs (1) and (2) above to the disposal of property are references to—

(a) the sale, exchange, charging of or other dealing (otherwise than by will) with property other than money; 10

(b) the removal of property from one place to another;

(c) the application of money in acquiring property;

(d) the transfer of money from one account to another;

and references to property representing property disposed of shall be construed accordingly and as including the result of successive disposals. 15

(4) The court may give such directions as appear to it necessary or expedient for the purpose of facilitating the operation of sub-paragraph (1) above, including the carrying of money to a separate account and the transfer of property other than money.

(5) Where the court has ordered or directed the expenditure of money for the 20 carrying out of permanent improvements on, or otherwise for the permanent benefit of, any property of the person concerned, it may order that the whole or any part of the money expended or to be expended shall be a charge on the property, whether without interest or with interest at a specified rate; and an order under this sub-paragraph may provide for excluding or restricting the 25 operation of sub-paragraph (1) above.

(6) A charge under sub-paragraph (5) above may be made in favour of such person as may be just and, in particular, where the money charged is paid out of the general estate of the person concerned, may be made in favour of a person as trustee for him; but no charge under that sub-paragraph shall confer any right of sale 30 or foreclosure during his lifetime.

*Powers as patron of benefice*

6. Only the Lord Chancellor shall have power to exercise on behalf of a person without capacity his powers as patron of a benefice.

Section 29.

## SCHEDULE 5 35

ENACTMENTS DISAPPLIED IN RESPECT OF PERSONS WITHIN JURISDICTION UNDER CHAPTER IV OF PART I AND SECTION 48

| Session and Chapter | Short Title | Enactments |
|---|---|---|
| 13 Geo.3 c.81. | The Inclosure Act 1773. | Sections 22 and 24. 40 |
| 7 Geo.4 c.16. | The Chelsea and Kilmainham Hospitals Act 1826. | Sections 44 to 48. |
| 2 & 3 Will.4 c.80. | The Ecclesiastical Corporations Act 1832. | Section 3. 45 |

| Session and Chapter | Short Title | Enactments |
|---|---|---|
| 1 & 2 Vict. c.106. | The Pluralities Act 1838. | Section 127. |
| 4 & 5 Vict. c.38. | The School Sites Act 1841. | Section 5. |
| 5 & 6 Vict. c.26. | The Ecclesiastical Houses of Residence Act 1842. | Section 12. |
| 5 & 6 Vict. c.108. | The Ecclesiastical Leasing Act 1842. | Section 24. |
| 8 & 9 Vict. c.16. | The Companies Clauses Consolidation Act 1845. | Section 79. |
| 8 & 9 Vict. c.18. | The Lands Clauses Consolidation Act 1845. | Section 9. |
| 8 & 9 Vict. c.118. | The Inclosure Act 1845. | Sections 20, 133, 134 and 137. |
| 9 & 10 Vict. c.73. | The Tithe Act 1846. | Sections 5, 9 and 10. |
| 17 & 18 Vict. c.112. | The Literary and Scientific Institutions Act 1854. | Section 5. |
| 25 & 26 Vict. c.53. | The Land Registry Act 1862. | Section 116. |
| 27 & 28 Vict. c.114. | The Improvement of Land Act 1864. | Section 24. |
| 29 & 30 Vict. c.122. | The Metropolitan Commons Act 1866. | Section 28. |
| 31 & 32 Vict. c.109. | The Compulsory Church Rate Abolition Act 1868. | Section 7. |
| 36 & 37 Vict. c.50. | The Places of Worship Sites Act 1873. | Sections 1 and 3. |
| 40 & 41 Vict. c.59. | The Colonial Stock Act 1877. | Section 6. |

## SCHEDULE 6

### LORD CHANCELLOR'S VISITORS

1. There shall be the following panels of Lord Chancellor's visitors—

    (a) a panel of Medical Visitors;

    (b) a panel of Legal Visitors; and

    (c) a panel of General Visitors (being Visitors who are not required by this Schedule to possess either a medical or legal qualification for appointment).

2. Each panel shall consist of persons appointed to it by the Lord Chancellor, the appointment of each person being for such term and subject to such conditions as the Lord Chancellor may determine.

3. A person shall not be qualified to be appointed—

(a) to the panel of Medical Visitors unless he is a registered medical practitioner who appears to the Lord Chancellor to have special knowledge and experience in cases of mental disability;

1990 c.41

(b) to the panel of Legal Visitors unless he has a 10 year general 5 qualification within the meaning of section 71 of the Courts and Legal Services Act 1990.

4. If the Lord Chancellor so determines in the case of any Visitor appointed under this Schedule he shall be paid such remuneration and allowances as the Lord Chancellor may, with the concurrence of the Treasury, determine. 10

Section 57.

## SCHEDULE 7

TRANSITIONAL PROVISIONS AND SAVINGS

### Pᴀʀᴛ I

REPEAL OF PART VII OF MENTAL HEALTH ACT 1983

*Existing receivers* 15

1.—(1) Where immediately before the day on which this Act comes into force there is in the case of any person a receiver appointed for him under
1983 c.20
section 99 of the Mental Health Act 1983 ("the 1983 Act")—

(a) the Public Trustee shall be that person's manager under Chapter IV of Part I of this Act with powers as respects the matters specified in 20 section 27(1)(a) to (g); and

(b) the person who is the receiver immediately before that day shall continue as such on and after that day with his existing functions but shall act in accordance with any directions or authority given to him by the Public Trustee in his capacity as manager. 25

(2) The court may terminate the functions exercisable by a person as receiver by virtue of sub-paragraph (1)(b) above.

(3) In sub-paragraph (1) above the reference to a receiver appointed under section 99 of the 1983 Act includes a reference to a person who by virtue of Schedule 5 to that Act was deemed to be a receiver appointed under that 30 section.

*Orders, appointments etc.*

2.—(1) Any order or appointment made, direction or authority given or other thing done which has, or by virtue of Schedule 5 to the 1983 Act was deemed to have, effect under Part VII of that Act immediately before the coming into 35 force of this Act shall continue to have effect notwithstanding the repeal of Part VII.

(2) In so far as any such order, appointment, direction, authority or thing could have been made, given or done under Chapter IV of Part I of this Act if it had then been in force it shall be treated as made, given or done under that Chapter and the powers of variation and discharge conferred by that Chapter shall apply 40 accordingly.

(3) Sub-paragraph (1) above does not apply to nominations under section 93(1) or (4) of the 1983 Act and, as respects receivers, has effect subject to paragraph 1 above.

(4) This Act does not affect the operation of section 109 of the 1983 Act 45 (effect and proof of orders etc.) in relation to orders made and directions given under Part VII of that Act.

(5) This paragraph is without prejudice to section 16 of the Interpretation Act 1978 (general savings on repeal).

SCH. 7
1978 c.30

### *Pending proceedings*

3.—(1) Any application for the exercise of a power under Part VII of the 1983 Act which is pending immediately before this Act comes into force shall, in so far as a corresponding power is exercisable under Chapter IV of Part I of this Act, be treated as an application for the exercise of that power.

(2) For the purposes of sub-paragraph (1) above an application for the appointment of a receiver shall be treated as an application for the appointment of a manager.

### *Appeals*

4.—(1) Part VII of the 1983 Act and the rules made under it shall continue to apply to any appeal brought by virtue of section 105 of that Act which has not been determined before this Act comes into force.

(2) If in the case of an appeal brought by virtue of section 105(1) (appeal to nominated judge) the judge nominated under section 93 of the 1983 Act has begun to hear the appeal he shall continue to do so but otherwise it shall be heard by a High Court judge nominated under section 46 of this Act.

### *Funds in court*

5. All investments and money which, immediately before the coming into force of this Act, constituted the funds in court of the former Court of Protection (that is, the office abolished by section 46 of this Act) shall by virtue of this paragraph, and without any transfer or assignment, be vested in the Accountant General of the Supreme Court as funds of the new Court of Protection (that is, the court established by that section).

### *Fees*

6. All fees and other payments which, having become due, have not been paid to the former Court of Protection before the coming into force of this Act shall be paid to the Public Trustee who shall pay such part of them to the new Court of Protection as the Lord Chancellor may with the consent of the Treasury direct.

### *Court records*

7. All records of the former Court of Protection shall after the coming into force of this Act be deemed to be records of the new Court of Protection and shall be dealt with accordingly under the Public Records Act 1958.

1958 c.51

### *Existing charges*

8. This Act does not affect the operation in relation to a charge created before the coming into force of this Act of—

(a) so much of section 101(6) of the 1983 Act as precludes a charge created under section 101(5) from conferring a right of sale or foreclosure during the lifetime of the patient; or

(b) section 106(6) of that Act (charge created by virtue of section 106(5) not to cause interest to fail etc.).

*Preservation of interests on disposal of property*

9. Paragraph 5(1) of Schedule 4 to this Act shall apply in relation to any disposal of property (within the meaning of that provision) by a person living on 1st November 1960, being a disposal effected under the Lunacy Act 1890 as it applies in relation to the disposal of property effected under Chapter IV of Part I of this Act.

1890 c.5

5

## PART II

### REPEAL OF ENDURING POWERS OF ATTORNEY ACT 1985

*Orders, determinations, etc.*

10.—(1) Any order or determination made or other thing done under the Enduring Powers of Attorney Act 1985 ("the 1985 Act") which has effect immediately before the coming into force of this Act shall continue to have effect notwithstanding the repeal of that Act.

1985 c.29

10

(2) In so far as any such order, determination or thing could have been made or done under Schedule 3 to this Act if it had then been in force it shall be treated as made or done under that Schedule and the powers of variation and discharge exercisable by the Court of Protection shall apply accordingly.

15

(3) Any instrument registered under the 1985 Act shall be deemed to have been registered by the registration authority under Schedule 3 to this Act.

(4) This paragraph is without prejudice to section 16 of the Interpretation Act 197 (general savings on repeal).

1978 c.30

20

*Pending proceedings*

11.—(1) Any application for the exercise of a power under the 1985 Act which is pending immediately before this Act comes into force shall, in so far as a corresponding power is exercisable under Schedule 3 to this Act, be treated as an application for the exercise of that power.

25

(2) For the purposes of sub-paragraph (1) above—

(a) a pending application under section 4(2) of the 1985 Act for the registration of an instrument shall be treated as an application to the registration authority under paragraph 9 of Schedule 3 and any notice given in connection with that application under Schedule 1 to that Act shall be treated as given under Part III of Schedule 3 to this Act;

30

(b) a notice of objection to the registration of an instrument shall be treated as an application to the court under paragraph 10(3) of that Schedule;

35

(c) pending proceedings under section 5 of that Act shall be treated as proceedings on an application for the exercise by the court of a power under paragraph 12(2) of that Schedule.

*Appeals*

12.—(1) The 1985 Act, and, so far as relevant, the provisions of Part VII of the Mental Health Act 1983 and the rules made under it as applied by section 10 of the 1985 Act, shall continue to have effect in relation to any appeal brought by virtue of section 10(1)(c) of the 1985 Act which has not been determined before this Act comes into force.

1983 c.20

40

(2) If in the case of an appeal brought by virtue of section 105(1) of the said Act of 1983 as applied by section 10(1)(c) of the 1985 Act (appeal to nominated judge) the judge nominated under section 93 of the Act of 1983 has begun to hear the appeal he shall continue to do so but otherwise the appeal shall be heard by a High Court judge nominated under section 46 of this Act.

45

PART III

REPEAL OF NATIONAL ASSISTANCE ACT 1948 S.47

13.—(1) Where immediately before the coming into force of this Act a person is being detained in pursuance of an order under subsection (3) or (4) of
5 section 47 of the National Assistance Act 1948 his detention shall not be affected by the repeal of that section but no order shall be made under subsection (4) for extending the period or under subsection (5) for varying the place of detention.

1948 c.29

(2) Where a person continues to be detained by virtue of sub-paragraph (1)
10 above—

    (a) subsections (8) and (9) of section 47 shall continue to apply to the cost of his maintenance; and

    (b) an application for the revocation of the order by virtue of which he is detained may be made under subsection (6) of that section in any case in
15         which it could have been made but for the repeal.

(3) An order made under section 47(3), (4) or (5) before this Act comes into force shall lapse if no steps to give effect to it have been taken before that time.

PART IV

REPEAL OF MENTAL HEALTH ACT 1983 S.135(1) AND (3)

20    14.—(1) Where immediately before this Act comes into force a person is detained in a place of safety, having been removed there in pursuance of a warrant issued under subsection (1) of section 135 of the Mental Health Act 1983, his detention under subsection (3) of that section shall not be affected by the repeal of those subsections.

1983 c.20

25    (2) Any warrant issued under section 135(1) before this Act comes into force but not executed shall lapse.

SCHEDULE 8

Section 58(1).

CONSEQUENTIAL AMENDMENTS

*The Fines and Recoveries Act 1833 (c.74)*

30    1.—(1) The Fines and Recoveries Act 1833 shall be amended as follows.

(2) In section 33 for the words from "be incapable" to "is incapable" there shall be substituted "be without capacity (within the meaning of the Mental Incapacity Act 1995) to act as protector the Court of Protection shall be the protector of the settlement in his stead so long as he is without capacity".

35    (3) In sections 48 and 49 for the references to the judge having jurisdiction under Part VII of the Mental Health Act 1983 there shall be substituted references to the Court of Protection.

*The Improvement of Land Act 1864 (c.114)*

2. In section 68 of the Improvement of Land Act 1864—
40    (a) for "or receiver" there shall be substituted "manager with powers in relation to property and affairs";

    (b) for "or patient within the meaning of Part VII of the Mental Health Act 1983" there shall be substituted "or without capacity (within the meaning of the Mental Incapacity Act 1995) to receive the notice".

SCH. 8                                    *The Trustee Act 1925 (c.19)*

3.—(1) The Trustee Act 1925 shall be amended as follows.

(2) In section 36(9)—

   (a) for the words from "incapable" to "exercising" there shall be substituted "without capacity (within the meaning of the Mental  5 Incapacity Act 1995) to exercise";

   (b) for the words from "the authority" to the end there shall be substituted "the Court of Protection".

(3) In section 41(1) for the words from "incapable" to "exercising" there shall be substituted "without capacity (within the meaning of the Mental 10 Incapacity Act 1995) to exercise".

(4) In section 54(1)—

   (a) for "the authority having jurisdiction under Part VII of the Mental Health Act 1983" there shall be substituted "the Court of Protection";

   (b) for the words "a patient who is" there shall be substituted "a person 15 who is (within the meaning of the Mental Incapacity Act 1995) without capacity to exercise his functions as".

(5) In section 54(2)—

   (a) for the words from the beginning to "of a receiver" there shall be substituted "Where a person is without capacity (within the meaning of 20 the Mental Incapacity Act 1995) to exercise his functions as trustee and a manager appointed by the Court of Protection is acting for him or an application for the appointment of a manager";

   (b) for "the said authority" there shall be substituted "the Court of Protection";                                                                           25

   (c) for "the patient" in paragraphs (a), (c) and (d) there shall be substituted "the person concerned".

(6) For section 54(3) there shall be substituted—

   "(3) This section applies to a person in respect of whom the powers conferred by section 48 of the Mental Incapacity Act 1995 are exercisable 30 and have been exercised as it applies to a person without capacity within the meaning of that Act.".

(7) In section 55, except as it applies to existing orders made before the coming into force of this Act, for "Part VII of the Mental Health Act 1983" there shall be substituted "Chapter IV of Part I of the Mental Incapacity Act 35 1995".

*The Law of Property Act 1925 (c.20)*

4.—(1) The Law of Property Act 1925 shall be amended as follows.

(2) In section 22(1)—

   (a) for the words from "in a person suffering" to "no receiver" there shall be 40 substituted ", either solely or jointly with any other person or persons, in a person without capacity (within the meaning of the Mental Incapacity Act 1995) to convey or create a legal estate, his manager with powers in relation to property and affairs or (if no such manager";

   (b) for "the authority having jurisdiction under Part VII of the Mental 45 Health Act 1983" there shall be substituted "the Court of Protection".

(3) In section 22(2) for "incapable, by reason of mental disorder," there shall be substituted "without capacity (within the meaning of that Act)".

*The Land Registration Act 1925 (c.21)*

5.—(1) Section 111 of the Land Registration Act 1925 shall be amended as follows.

(2) In subsection (5)—

5    (a) for the words from "incapable" to "no receiver" there shall be substituted "without capacity (within the meaning of the Mental Incapacity Act 1995) to exercise any power as such a proprietor under this Act, his manager with powers in relation to property and affairs (or if no such manager";

10   (b) for "the authority having jurisdiction under Part VII of the Mental Health Act 1983" there shall be substituted "the Court of Protection";

(c) for "free from disability" there shall be substituted "not without capacity".

(3) In subsection (6) for "Part VII of the Mental Health Act 1983" there shall be
15   substituted "Chapter IV of Part I of the Mental Incapacity Act 1995".

*The Administration of Estates Act 1925 (c.23)*

6.—(1) The proviso to section 41(1) of the Administration of Estates Act 1925 shall be amended as follows.

(2) In paragraph (ii)—

20   (a) for the words from "incapable" to "affairs" there shall be substituted "without capacity (within the meaning of the Mental Incapacity Act 1995) to give the consent";

(b) for "or receiver" there shall be substituted "or his manager with powers in relation to property and affairs or any person authorised for that
25   purpose by the Court of Protection".

(3) In paragraph (iv) for "no receiver is acting for a person suffering from mental disorder" there shall be substituted "no manager with powers in relation to property and affairs is acting for a person without capacity to consent and no person has been authorised by the Court of Protection to consent on his behalf".

30   *The National Assistance Act 1948 (c.29)*

7.—(1) Section 49 of the National Assistance Act 1948 shall be amended as follows.

(2) For the words from "applies" to "affairs of a patient" there shall be substituted "applies for appointment as a manager under Chapter IV of Part I of the
35   Mental Incapacity Act 1995".

(3) For "such functions" there shall be substituted "his functions as manager".

*The U.S.A. Veterans' Pensions (Administration) Act 1949 (c.45)*

8. In section 1(4) of the U.S.A. Veterans' Pensions (Administration) Act
40   1949 for the words "or for whom a receiver has been appointed under section 105 of the Mental Health Act 1959 or section 99 of the Mental Health Act 1983" there shall be substituted "or as respects a person without capacity (within the meaning of the Mental Incapacity Act 1995) to manage and administer his property and affairs if a manager with powers in relation to property and affairs has
45   been appointed for him".

*The Variation of Trusts Act 1958 (c.53)*

9.—(1) Section 1 of the Variation of Trusts Act 1958 shall be amended as follows.

(2) In subsection (3) for the words from "shall be determined" to the end there shall be substituted "who is without capacity (within the meaning of the   5 Mental Incapacity Act 1995) to give his assent shall be determined by an order of the Court of Protection.".

(3) In subsection (6) for "the authority having jurisdiction under Part VII of the Mental Health Act 1983" there shall be substituted "the Court of Protection under Chapter IV of Part I of the Mental Incapacity Act 1995".   10

*The Administration of Justice Act 1960 (c.65)*

10. In section 12(1)(b) of the Administration of Justice Act 1960 for "under Part VIII of the Mental Health Act 1959 or under any provision of that Act" there shall be substituted "under the Mental Incapacity Act 1995 or under any provision of the Mental Health Act 1983".   15

*The Compulsory Purchase Act 1965 (c.56)*

11. For paragraph 1(2)(b) of Schedule 1 to the Compulsory Purchase Act 1965 there shall be substituted—

"(b) do not have effect in relation to a person without capacity as to whom powers have been exercised under Chapter IV of Part I of the   20 Mental Incapacity Act 1995 or a person as to whom powers are exercisable and have been exercised under section 48 of that Act."

*The Leasehold Reform Act 1967 (c.88)*

12.—(1) For subsection (2) of section 26 of the Leasehold Reform Act 1967   25 there shall be substituted—

"(2) Where a person is without capacity (within the meaning of the Mental Incapacity Act 1995) to manage and administer his property and affairs, his manager with powers in relation to property and affairs or, if there is no such manager, a person authorised in that behalf shall, under an   30 order of the Court of Protection, take his place as landlord for the purposes of this Part of this Act.".

(2) This amendment does not affect any proceedings pending at the coming into force of this Act in which a receiver or a person authorised under Part VII of the Mental Health Act 1983 is acting on behalf of the landlord.   35

*The Medicines Act 1968 (c.67)*

13.—(1) Section 72 of the Medicines Act 1968 shall be amended as follows.

(2) In subsection (1)(c) for "a receiver is appointed for him under Part VIII of the Mental Health Act 1959" there shall be substituted "a manager with power in relation to property and affairs is appointed for him under Chapter IV of Part I of the   40 Mental Incapacity Act 1995".

(3) In subsections (3)(d) and (4)(c) for "the receiver" there shall be substituted "the manager".

*The Family Law Reform Act 1969 (c.46)*

14. In section 21(4) of the Family Law Reform Act 1969 for the words from "suffering" to the end there shall be substituted "without capacity (within the meaning of the Mental Incapacity Act 1995) to give his consent, if consent is
5 given by the court giving the direction under section 20 of this Act or by a person authorised in that behalf by the Court of Protection.".

*The Local Government Act 1972 (c.70)*

15.—(1) Section 118 of the Local Government Act 1972 shall be amended as follows.

10 (2) In subsection (1)—

(a) for the words from "(hereafter" to "administering" there shall be substituted " is without capacity (within the meaning of the Mental Incapacity Act 1995) to manage and administer";

(b) for "the patient" in the next place where it occurs there shall be
15 substituted "the person concerned";

(c) for "the patient's", "the patient" and "mentally disordered" in paragraph (a) there shall be substituted "his", "he" and "without capacity" respectively;

(d) for "the patient's debts" and "the patient" in paragraph (b) there shall be
20 substituted "the debts of the person concerned" and "the person concerned" respectively.

(3) For subsections (4) and (5) there shall be substituted—

"(4) Before exercising their powers under this section in relation to any person a local authority shall give him notice in writing of their intention to do
25 so, specifying the amount and nature of the sums in respect of which the authority intend to exercise those powers.".

*The Matrimonial Causes Act 1973 (c.18)*

16. In section 40 of the Matrimonial Causes Act 1973—

(a) for the words from "incapable" to "administering" there shall be
30 substituted "without capacity (within the meaning of the Mental Incapacity Act 1995) to manage and administer";

(b) for "Part VIII of that Act" there shall be substituted "Chapter IV of Part I of that Act";

(c) the words "having charge of that person" shall be omitted.

35 *The Juries Act 1974 (c.24)*

17. In Group D in Schedule 1 to the Juries Act 1974 after "property and affairs" there shall be inserted "or for whom a manager has been appointed by the Court of Protection".

*The Consumer Credit Act 1974 (c.39)*

40 18. For section 37(1)(c) of the Consumer Credit Act 1974 there shall be substituted—

"(c) has any powers exercised in relation to him under Chapter IV of Part I of the Mental Incapacity Act 1995.".

*The Solicitors Act 1974 (c.47)*

19.—(1) The Solicitors Act 1974 shall be amended as follows.

(2) For section 12(1)(j) there shall be substituted—

"(j) while he is a person as to whom powers have been exercised
under Chapter IV of Part I or section 48 of the Mental          5
Incapacity Act 1995 as a person without capacity to act as a
solicitor;".

(3) For section 62(4)(c) and (d) there shall be substituted—

"(c) as his manager with powers in relation to property and affairs
appointed under Chapter IV of Part I of the Mental Incapacity  10
Act 1995; or

(d) as a person authorised to do so under that Chapter.".

(4) For paragraph 1(1)(f) of Schedule 1 there shall be substituted—

"(f) a manager with powers in relation to property and affairs has been
appointed under Chapter IV of Part I of the Mental Incapacity Act  15
1995, or powers under section 48 of that Act have been exercised, in
respect of a solicitor;".

*The Limitation Act 1980 (c.58)*

20. For section 38(3) of the Limitation Act 1980 there shall be substituted—

"(3) For the purposes of subsection (2) above a person is of unsound  20
mind if he is without capacity (within the meaning of the Mental
Incapacity Act 1995) to conduct legal proceedings.".

*The Public Passenger Vehicles Act 1981 (c.14)*

21. In section 57(1)(c) of the Public Passenger Vehicles Act 1981 for the
words from "becomes a patient" to "or" there shall be substituted "has any  25
powers exercised in relation to him under Chapter IV of Part I of the Mental
Incapacity Act 1995, or".

*The Mental Health Act 1983 (c.20)*

22.—(1) The Mental Health Act 1983 shall be amended as follows.

(2) In section 134(3) for paragraph (b) there shall be substituted—          30

"(b) any judge or officer of the Court of Protection, any of the Lord
Chancellor's Visitors or any person asked by that Court for a
report concerning the patient under section 52 of the Mental
Incapacity Act 1995;".

(3) After section 136(2) there shall be inserted—          35

"(3) In this section "place of safety" means protective accommodation as
defined in section 41(7) of the Mental Incapacity Act 1995 or a police
station."

*The Data Protection Act 1984 (c.35)*

23. In section 21(9) of the Data Protection Act 1984 for the words from  40
"incapable" to the end there shall be substituted "without capacity (within the
meaning of the Mental Incapacity Act 1995) to make a request".

*The Administration of Justice Act 1985 (c.61)*

24. For section 18(3) of the Administration of Justice Act 1985 there shall be substituted—

"(3) A licence held by a person under this Part shall terminate if
5 powers are exercised in relation to him under Chapter IV of Part I of this Act.".

*The Insolvency Act 1986 (c.45)*

25. In section 390(4) of the Insolvency Act 1986—

(a) in paragraph (c) the words "Part VII of the Mental Health Act 1983 or"
10 shall be omitted;

(b) after that paragraph there shall be inserted—

"(d) he is a person as to whom powers have been exercised under Chapter IV of Part I of the Mental Incapacity Act 1995.".

15 *The Public Trustee and Administration of Funds Act 1986 (c.57)*

26. In section 3 of the Public Trustee and Administration of Funds Act 1986 for subsections (2) to (5) there shall be substituted—

"(2) The Public Trustee—

(a) may act as a manager under Chapter IV of Part I of the Mental
20 Incapacity Act 1995;

(b) shall receive such reports and accounts as the court directs managers to submit to him under that Chapter;

(c) shall receive such security as the court requires a manager to give him under that Chapter; and

25 (d) may make such applications to the Court of Protection as are mentioned in section 47(3)(c) of that Act.".

*The Financial Services Act 1986 (c.60)*

27. In section 45(1) of the Financial Services Act 1986 for paragraph (f) there shall be substituted—

30 "(f) a judge of the Court of Protection when acting in the exercise of his functions under Part III of the Mental Incapacity Act 1995;".

*The Access to Health Records Act 1990 (c.23)*

28. In section 3(1) of the Access to Health Records Act 1990 for paragraph (e) there shall be substituted—

35 "(e) where the patient is without capacity (within the meaning of the Mental Incapacity Act 1995) to consent to the making of the application, his manager or any other person authorised under Chapter IV of Part I of that Act to make the application on his behalf.".

40 *The Child Support Act 1991 (c.48)*

29.—(1) Section 50 of the Child Support Act 1991 shall be amended as follows.

(2) In subsection (8) paragraphs (b) and (d) shall be omitted together with "or" at the end of paragraph (c), and for "receiver, custodian or appointee"
45 there shall be substituted "or custodian".

(3) After that subsection there shall be inserted—

"(9) Where the person to whom the information relates is without capacity (within the meaning of the Mental Incapacity Act 1995) to consent to its disclosure the "appropriate person" to consent shall be any manager appointed for him, or any other person authorised in that behalf, by     5
the Court of Protection.".

*The Social Security Administration Act 1992 (c.5)*

30.—(1) Section 123 of the Social Security Administration Act 1992 shall be amended as follows.

(2) In subsection (10)—     10
    (a) in paragraph (b) the words "a receiver appointed under section 99 of the Mental Health Act 1983 or" shall be omitted;
    (b) in paragraph (d) the words "sub-paragraph (a) of rule 41(1) of the Court of Protection Rules 1984 or" and "a receiver ad interim appointed under sub-paragraph (b) of the said rule 41(1) or" shall be     15
        omitted;
    (c) the word "receiver", where occurring after the paragraphs, shall be omitted.

(3) After that subsection there shall be inserted—

"(11) Where the person to whom the information relates is without     20
capacity (within the meaning of the Mental Incapacity Act 1995) to consent to its disclosure "the appropriate person" to consent shall be any manager appointed for him, or any other person authorised in that behalf, by the Court of Protection.".

*The Leasehold Reform, Housing and Urban Development Act 1993 (c.28)*     25

31.—(1) Paragraph 4 of Schedule 2 to the Leasehold Reform, Housing and Urban Development Act 1993 shall be amended as follows.

(2) For "incapable by reason of mental disorder (within the meaning of the Mental Health Act 1983) of managing and administering" there shall be substituted "without capacity (within the meaning of the Mental Incapacity Act     30
1995) to manage and administer".

(3) For the words from the beginning of sub-paragraph (a) to the end of the paragraph there shall be substituted "the place of the landlord shall be taken by his manager with powers in relation to property and affairs or, if there is no such manager, any person authorised in that behalf by the Court of Protection.".     35

(4) These amendments do not affect any proceedings pending at the coming into force of this Act in which a receiver or a person authorised under Part VII of the
Mental Health Act 1983 is acting on behalf of the landlord.

## SCHEDULE 9

REPEALS     40

| Chapter | Short title | Extent of repeal |
|---------|-------------|------------------|
| 15 & 16 Geo.5 c.5. | The Law of Property Act 1925. | Section 205(1)(xiii). |

| Chapter | Short title | Extent of repeal |
|---|---|---|
| 11 & 12 Geo.6 c.29. | The National Assistance Act 1948. | Section 47.<br>Section 48(1)(c).<br>In section 56(3) the words "other than offences under section 47(11)" and the words after "1970". |
| 14 & 15 Geo.6 c.57. | The National Assistance (Amendment) Act 1951. | The whole Act. |
| 7 & 8 Eliz.2 c.72. | The Mental Health Act 1959. | In Schedule 7, in Part I, the entry relating to section 205(1) of the Law of Property Act 1925. |
| 1965 c.12. | The Industrial and Provident Societies Act 1965. | In section 26, in subsection (1) the words "Subject to subsection (2) of this section" and subsection (2). |
| 1970 c.42. | The Local Authority Social Services Act 1970. | In Schedule 1, the entry relating to section 115 of the Mental Health Act 1983. |
| 1971 c.23. | The Courts Act 1971. | In Schedule 2, in Part IA the words "Master of the Court of Protection". |
| 1972 c.70. | The Local Government Act 1972. | In Schedule 29, paragraph 44(1). |
| 1973 c.32. | The National Health Service Reorganisation Act 1973. | In Schedule 4, paragraph 47. |
| 1979 c.54. | The Sale of Goods Act 1979. | In section 3(2) the words "mental incapacity or". |
| 1981 c.20. | The Judicial Pensions Act 1981. | In Schedule 1, in paragraph 1 the words "Master of the Court of Protection", except as respects a person holding that office immediately before the coming into force of this repeal or who had previously retired from that office or died. |
| 1981 c.54. | The Supreme Court Act 1981. | In Schedule 2, in Part II, paragraph 11. |
| 1983 c.20. | The Mental Health Act 1983. | Part VII.<br>Section 115.<br>In section 135, subsections (1), (3), (5) and (6) and in subsection (4) the words preceding "in the execution of a warrant issued under subsection (2) above".<br>In section 136(1) the words |

| Chapter | Short title | Extent of repeal |
|---|---|---|
| 1983 c.20.—<br>*cont.* | The Mental Health Act 1983.—*cont.* | "within the meaning of section 135 above".<br>In section 138(3) the words "135 or".⁵<br>In section 139(1) the words from "or in, or in pursuance" to "Part VII of this Act".<br>Section 142. 10<br>In section 145(1), in the definition of "patient" the words "(except in Part VII)".<br>In section 146 the words 15 "104(4), 110 (and so much of Part VII of this Act as is applied in relation to Scotland by that section)" and "142". 20<br>In section 147 the words "104(4), 110 (and so much of Part VII as is applied to Northern Ireland by that section)" and "142". 25<br>Schedule 3.<br>In Schedule 4, paragraphs 1(a), 4(a), (b) and (c)(ii), 5, 7, 14(a), 20, 22 and 25, in paragraph 27 the entry 30 relating to section 115, and paragraphs 32, 38 and 55.<br>In Schedule 5, paragraphs 26, 43, 44 and 45. 35 |
| 1985 c.29. | The Enduring Powers of Attorney Act 1985. | The whole Act. |
| 1986 c.57. | The Public Trustee and Administration of Funds Act 1986. | Section 2.<br>Section 3(7).<br>40 |
| 1990 c.41. | The Courts and Legal Services Act 1990. | In Schedule 11, the words "Master of the Court of Protection". |
| 1993 c.8. | The Judicial Pensions and Retirement Act 1993. | In Schedule 1, in Part II, the words "Master of the 45 Court of Protection", except as respects a person holding that office immediately before the coming into force of this 50 repeal or who had previously retired from that office or died.<br>In Schedule 5, the entries relating to the Master and 55 |

|  | Chapter | Short title | Extent of repeal |
|---|---|---|---|
|  | 1993 c.8.— *cont.* | The Judicial Pensions and Retirement Act 1993. —*cont.* | Deputy or temporary Master of the Court of Protection, except as respects a person holding any of those offices immediately before the coming into force of this repeal. |
|  |  |  | In Schedule 7, paragraph 5(5)(i)(g), except as respects a persons holding an office there mentioned immediately before the coming into force of this repeal. |

# APPENDIX B

## Participants of Working Party Meetings

**Organisations**
Age Concern
Alzheimer's Disease Society
Association of British Insurers
Association of County Councils
Association of Directors of Social Services
Association of Metropolitan Authorities
Benefits Agency
Barnardos
British Association of Social Workers
British Association of Social Workers (Special Interest Group on Ageing)
British Bankers' Association
British Medical Association
British Psychological Society
Building Societies' Association
CARE (Christian Action Research and Education)
Carers National Association
Citizen Advocacy Information and Training
Court of Protection
Department of Health
Department of Social Security
Help the Aged
Law Society Mental Health and Disability Sub-Committee
Law Society Group for the Welfare of People with a Mental Handicap
Liverpool Social Services Department
Lord Chancellor's Department
Medical Research Council
MENCAP
Mental Health Act Commission
MIND (National Association for Mental Health)
National Audit Office
National Development Team
National Schizophrenia Fellowship
Official Solicitor's Department
Public Trust Office
Royal College of General Practitioners
Royal College of Nursing
Royal College of Psychiatrists
RESCARE
SENSE
Terrence Higgins Trust

**Individuals**
Professor M Brazier (University of Manchester)
Mr R Brown
Mr D Carson (University of Southampton)
Dr S M Cretney, FBA, QC (All Souls College, Oxford)
Mr Gwyn Davis (University of Bristol)
Ms K Diesfeld (University of Canterbury, Kent)
Mr P Fennell (Cardiff Law School, University of Wales)

Mr J R S Guinness
Professor M Gunn (Westminster University)
Professor A Grubb (University of London, King's College)
Professor C Lyon (Keele University)
Mr D Lush
Ms A MacDonald (University of East Anglia)
Dr P Mason
Mr D Morgan (University of Glasgow)

# APPENDIX C

**Organisations who responded to our Consultation Papers**

Action for Dysphasic Adults
Action on Elder Abuse
Age Concern England
Alzheimer's Disease Society
Alzheimer's Disease Society (Oxfordshire Branch)
Association of British Insurers
Association of Chief Police Officers
Association of Community Health Councils for England and Wales
Association of County Councils
Association of Directors of Social Services
Association of Lawyers for Children
Association of Metropolitan Authorities
Association of the British Pharmaceutical Industry
Association of Women Solicitors
Barnardos
Bexley Community Health Council
Birth Control Trust
British Association of Social Workers
British Association of Social Workers (Special Interest Group on Ageing)
British Dental Association
British Geriatrics Society
British Medical Association
British Psychological Society
British Society of Dentistry for the Handicapped
Building Societies Association
Cardiff Workers with Elderly Mentally Infirm People
CARE (Christian Action Research and Education)
Carers National Association
Catholic Union of Great Britain and the Guild of Catholic Doctors
Cheshire Community Health Care Trust
Christian Medical Fellowship
Citizen Advocacy Information and Training
City of Coventry Social Services Department
Council of Her Majesty's Circuit Judges
Crown Prosecution Service
Department of Health
Department of Social Security
Doctors Who Respect Human Life
Edmund Plowden Trust
Elmbridge MENCAP
Family Law Bar Association
Family Rights Group
Feminists Against Eugenics
Friends of Brockwood Hospital
General Council of the Bar
Good Practices in Mental Health
Hampshire Social Services Department
Holborn Law Society
Home Office
Horizon NHS Trust
Independent Advocacy and Support Services Ltd
Independent Tribunal Service

Inner London Family Proceedings Court
Institute of Legal Executives
Intensive Care Society
Janssen Pharmaceutical Ltd
Justices' Clerks Society
Kent County Council
Leeds Advocacy
Linacre Centre for Health Care Ethics
Liverpool City Council
London Boroughs Children's Regional Planning Committee
London Borough of Richmond, Social Services Department
Lord Chancellor's Department
Magistrates' Association
Manchester NHS Community Support Team
Medical Defence Union Ltd
Medical Research Council
MENCAP
Mental Health Act Commission
Metropolitan Borough of Stockport Social Services
MIND (The National Association for Mental Health)
National Association for the Protection Sexual Abuse of Adults and Children with Learning Disabilities (NAPSAC)
National Development Team
National Schizophrenia Fellowship
Nationwide Building Society
North West Herts Community Health Council
North Western Mental Handicap Advisory Group
Official Solicitor's Department
People First of Lewisham
Phoenix NHS Trust
Police Federation of England and Wales
Pro-Choice Alliance
Registered Care Homes (Hampshire)
RESCARE
Royal College of Nursing
Royal College of Obstetricians and Gynaecologists
Royal College of Physicians
Royal College of Psychiatrists
Safe As Houses Alliance
SENSE
Service Development team, Royal Hamadryad Hospital
Social Care Association
Society for the Protection of Unborn Children
Solicitors' Family Law Association
Southampton and South West Hampshire Health Authority, Relatives Consultative Group
South Lewisham Community Team
Springfield Advice and Law Centre Ltd
Suffolk Carers Support Group
Surrey MENCAP
Terrence Higgins Trust
The Chartered Insurance Institute Society of Fellows
The College of Speech and Language Therapists
The Law Society, Mental Health and Disability Sub-Committee
The Law Society, Group for the Welfare of People with a Mental Handicap
The Medical Protection Society
The Methodist Church

The Newman Association
The National Autistic Society
The Patients' Association
United Kingdom Central Council for Nursing, Midwifery and Health Visiting
Voluntary Euthanasia Society (England)
Voluntary Euthanasia Society of Scotland
Watch Tower (Bible and Tract Society of Pensylvania)

## Individuals who responded to our Consultation Papers

Senior District Judge Angel
Professor T Arie
District Judge Ashton
Mr T Baber
Dr S Bailey
Mr M Baron
Mrs J I Baxter
Dr G C J Bennett and Mr J Ogg
Miss E H Blount
Miss I Boas
Mrs J Boniface
Mrs M Booth
Professor M Brazier
Ms J Bridgeman
Mr L Brooke
Mr R W S Brooks
Mr A Brown
Ms H Brown
Mr R Brown
Mr G J Calvert
Mr D Carson
Ms L Cohen
Mrs J Cole
Dr L B Cooke
Mr T Costello
Mr B Cox
Mrs Y Craig
Judge Peter Crane
Dr S M Cretney FBA, QC
Mrs A P Cull
Mr R Gwynn Davies
Ms K Diesfeld
Dr D Dickenson
Mr D H Dobson
Mr B M Edgington
Dr T A Evershed
Mr P J Farmer, Public Trustee
Mr P Fennell
Mr A Fergusson
Mr R Francis QC
Professor M Freeman
Mrs A Gardner
Mr E Gething
Mr R Goss
Mr L Gostin
Mrs A Grainger
Dr J A Muir Gray

Professor P Gray
Mr J R S Guinness
Professor M J Gunn
Mr T Hall and Ms M Taylor
Mr D J Hardwidge
Dr T Helme
Hempsons
Mr S E K Hewitt
Mr H F James
Professor B Jennett
Ms B Keane
Mr T Kelly
Dr G E Langley
Le Brasseurs
Mr M Linnett
Mr J Lugg
Mr D Lush
Mr R D Mackay
Mr W H McBryde
Mrs A B Macfarlane, Master of the Court of Protection
Mr D Mason
Mr H Medora
Ms J Murray
Mrs R Ogilvie
Dr G R Park
Payne Hicks Beach
Dr N Payne
Mr W K Prestwich
Mr Justice Rattee
Mrs P Riley
Dr G S Robertson
Professor H D C Roscam Abbing
Dr M Roy
Professor B I Sacks and colleagues
Mr P R Saunders
Ms J Seaman
Mrs V Sinason
Mr J F Skone
Dr P Smith
Dr S Spencer
Mr A Steer and colleagues
Ms K Stern
Miss J Sulek
Mr K Teasdale
Mr P J K Thompson
Mr M Took
Dr A Treloar and colleagues
Mrs S Turner
Dr T C Twining
Judge Peter Urquhart
Dr M Weller
Ms M Weber and Ms J Egan
Mrs S Whitfield
Mrs M E Winner
Mrs I Woodford
Mr C Yeadon